The French Economy

Westview Special Studies

The concept of Westview Special Studies is a response to the continuing crisis in academic and informational publishing. Library budgets for books have been severely curtailed. Ever larger portions of general library budgets are being diverted from the purchase of books and used for data banks, computers, micromedia, and other methods of information retrieval. Interlibrary loan structures further reduce the edition sizes required to satisfy the needs of the scholarly community. Economic pressures on university presses and the few private scholarly publishing companies have greatly limited the capacity of the industry to properly serve the academic and research communities. As a result, many manuscripts dealing with important subjects, often representing the highest level of scholarship, are no longer economically viable publishing projects—or, if accepted for publication, are typically subject to lead times ranging from one to three years.

Westview Special Studies are our practical solution to the problem. As always, the selection criteria include the importance of the subject, the work's contribution to scholarship, and its insight, orginality of thought, and excellence of exposition. We accept manuscripts in camera-ready form, typed, set, or word processed according to specifications laid out in our comprehensive manual, which contains straightforward instructions and sample pages. The responsibility for editing and proofreading lies with the author or sponsoring institution, but our editorial staff is always available to answer questions and provide guidance.

The end result is a book printed on acid-free paper and bound in sturdy, library-quality soft covers. We manufacture these books ourselves using equipment that does not require a lengthy make-ready process and that allows us to publish first editions of 300 to 1000 copies and to reprint even smaller quantities as needed. Thus, we can produce Special Studies quickly and can keep even very specialized books in print as long as there is a demand for them.

About the Book and Editors

This book brings together essays from several leading macroeconomists analyzing French economic performance in the recent past and examining such topics as unemployment, the tightening of exchange controls, the nationalization of banks, and the wage policies of the socialist government. It offers not only a wealth of well-ordered factual information on France, but also theoretical and empirical innovations ranging from exchange-rate econometrics to disequilibrium macroeconomics under rational expectations.

Jacques Melitz is a member of the research division of the French Institut National de la Statistique et des Economiques (INSEE) and professor of economics at the Institut des Etudes Politiques. **Charles Wyplosz** is associate professor of economics at the Institut Européen d'Administration des Affaires (INSEAD) at Fontainebleau.

The French Economy
Theory and Policy

edited by Jacques Melitz
and Charles Wyplosz

Westview Press / Boulder and London

A Westview Special Study

Copyright © 1985 by Westview Press, Inc.

Published in 1985 in the United States of America by Westview Press, Inc., 5500 Central Avenue, Boulder, Colorado 80301; Frederick A. Praeger, Publisher

Library of Congress Cataloging in Publication Data
Main entry under title:
The French economy.
    (A Westview special study)
mℝ· Issued also as Annales de l'INSEE, nos. 47–48, 1982.
    Proceedings at a conference held at INSEAD in
Fontainebleau on July 5–7, 1982.
        1. France—Economic conditions—1945-   —Congresses.
2. France—Economic policy—1945-   —Congresses.
I. Melitz, Jacques. II. Wyplosz, Charles. III. Annales de l'INSEE.
HC276.2.F698 1985   330.944'083   84-20828
ISBN 0-8133-7021-3

Printed and bound in the United States of America

10   9   8   7   6   5   4   3   2   1

Contents

PREFACE ● Page ix

Rudiger DORNBUSCH ● Page 1
INTRODUCTION

Gilles OUDIZ and Henri STERDYNIAK ● Page 9
**Inflation, employment and external constraints :
An overview of the French economy during the seventies**

COMMENTS by : William BRANSON (page 43)
Daniel LASKAR (page 49)

Paul KRUGMAN ● Page 51
The real wage gap and employment

COMMENTS by : Willem BUITER (page 71)
Edmond MALINVAUD (page 81)

Pentti KOURI, Jorge de MACEDO and Albert VISCIO ● Page 85
Profitability, employment and structural adjustment in France

COMMENTS by : Paul KRUGMAN (page 113)
Jacques MAIRESSE (page 114)

Olivier BLANCHARD and Jeffrey SACHS ● Page 117
**Anticipations, recessions and policy; an intertemporal disequi-
librium model**

COMMENTS by : Antoine d'AUTUME (page 145)
Pentti KOURI (page 147)

Mathieu FEROLDI and Jacques MELITZ ● Page 149

The Franc and the French financial sector

COMMENTS by : Barry EICHENGREEN (page 175)
Richard MARSTON (page 181)

Jeffrey FRANKEL ● Page 185

On the Franc

COMMENTS by : John BILSON (page 223)
Bruno SOLNIK (page 229)
Jacob FRENKEL (page 233)

Emil CLAASSEN and Charles WYPLOSZ ● Page 237.

Capital controls : some principles and the French experience

COMMENTS by : Paul De GRAUWE (page 269)
Maurice OBSTFELD (page 275)

Stanley BLACK ● Page 279

The effects of economic structure and policy choices on macro-economic outcomes in ten industrial countries

COMMENTS by : Giorgio BASEVI (page 301)
John MARTIN (page 303)

REPLY to BASEVI : Stanley BLACK (page 307)

Jean-Pierre LAFFARGUE ● Page 309

Fiscal and monetary policies under a flexible exchange-rate system

COMMENTS by : Patrick ARTUS (page 335)
Marcus MILLER (page 339)

ROUNDTABLE DISCUSSION ● Page 343

Contribution of : William BRANSON (page 343)
Jacob FRENKEL (page 347)
Edmond MALINVAUD (page 351)
Ronald McKINNON (page 355)

APPENDIX ● Page 359

Jacques MELITZ

The French financial system: mechanisms and questions of reform

NA

Preface

This volume brings together the proceedings of a conference held at the Institut Européen d'Administration des Affaires (INSEAD) at Fontainebleau on July 5, 6, and 7, 1982.

Summer conferences abound in the Paris region. That it was possible to attract an imposing international cast of economists within walking distance of the historic castle of Fontainebleau and one hour away from central Paris by car during the month of July is nothing especially surprising. But in this case there was a particular motivation for choosing the French site.

In the past, non-French economists have not often included contemporary France in their research agenda or watched with interest what French economists do and say when they work on their own economy. The purpose of the conference was to induce an exchange of views between French and foreign economists about the French economy, its problems and its prospects. Accordingly, not only do all of the papers deal with France but the division of the assignments between French and non-French participants is roughly half and half.

As in all cases of similar publications, we have a lot of debts to acknowledge. We owe particular thanks to the Délégation Générale à la Recherche Scientifique et Technique (DGRST) for financing the seminar out of which the conference sprung. We also owe many thanks to the Commissariat Général au Plan, the German Marshall Fund of the United States, the Cultural Services of the U.S. Embassy in Paris, the Banque de France, and the Centre National de la Recherche Scientifique (CNRS). Last but not least, we owe enormous thanks to Christine Laffargue, for translations, and to Françoise Dumontier, our editorial assistant.

Jacques Melitz and Charles Wyplosz

Introduction

by Rudiger Dornbusch

The Institut Européen d'Administration des Affaires (INSEAD) organized a conference in July 1982 on international aspects of the French macroeconomy. The conference brought together scholars from France, other parts of Europe, and the United States to present and discuss new approaches to problems of the French economy: the financial problem—inflation, budget deficits, public debt accumulation, and the weak franc—and the real problem—low profitability, insufficient capital formation, and rising unemployment. These are topics that seem perennial, certainly in regard to unsound finance and the weak franc. Kindleberger reminds us of the common belief that "the franc is weak whenever the Chamber of Deputies is sitting."[1] Although that may be true in a much broader perspective, the conference focused on the abrupt break in macroeconomic performance in the 1970s from sustained growth with reasonable stability to high and rising inflation and unemployment. This volume brings to a wider audience the papers and discussion of the conference and offers an opening of the French economy, at least in this limited sphere, to world trade. The organizers, Jacques Melitz and Charles Wyplosz, find the reward for their initiative in a fine collection of essays that will no doubt stimulate further work in France and perhaps a wider international interest in French macroeconomic research.

At the time of the conference, President Mitterand's one-year fling with isolated, Keynesian expansion had already crashed under the impact of a weakening franc. Many argued that in a short time two important lessons had been learned. The French experiment showed that a single country, taking an isolated initiative, could not break away from the crowd, which was trying to seek employment gains by Keynesian expansion. Moreover, the poor fate of the Bonn locomotives of 1978 had already shown that even coordinated Keynesian expansion can do no good. On the contrary, the very fact of coordination seemed to ensure highly inflationary consequences. The lesson for many observers seems obvious: Keynesian policies cannot solve classical problems stemming from excessively high real wages and a lack of sound finance. Indeed, the macroeconomic system seems ever less tolerant of such attempts, reacting quickly with accelerating inflation and barely any gains in employment.

That is, of course, not the whole story, as the US expansion under the impact of the Reagan tax cuts has amply demonstrated. For a while at least, super-easy fiscal policy, even isolated, is perfectly viable provided it is accompanied by tight money and conservative looks. Indeed, it is consistent with sharply cutting inflation under the impact of currency appreciation. Unfortunately, we do not know what really matters, the interest rates or the looks. But the US events notwithstanding, the failure of the Bonn summit policies and of Mitterand's expansion, beyond giving Keynesian policies a bad name, have had a fundamental influence on policy. These

1

experiments have reinforced the hand of fiscal conservatives in Europe and elsewhere, shifting the adjustment to wages and away from even contemplation of accompanying, transitory, fiscal-stabilization policy. The new mentality is summarized in the words of the IMF's managing director, J. de Larosiere:

> Over the past two decades several factors brought about an attitude of fiscal laxity on the part of the policy makers in many countries. For a variety of reasons the traditional stigma attached to fiscal deficits and growing public debt gave way to a certain nonchalance on the part of policy makers. Fiscal deficits no longer required justification, and they did not seem to have undesirable political repercussions, even when they occurred during nonrecessionary periods. . . . Traditional principles that had held that no deficit was justified if associated with unproductive investments, current expenditures, or permanent differences between expenditure or revenue were insidiously abandoned in favor of fiscal activism that made full employment and the expansion of welfare programs predominant objectives of economic policy. . . .[2]

But, of course, at best that view touches only part of Europe's macroeconomic problems. Debt issues in France, Germany and the UK have certainly come nowhere near levels signalling definite financial instability, and the problem of unemployment assuredly does have an aggregate demand component. Indeed, one must ask why the high and rising unemployment is thought to be sustainable while the low and rising public debt is unsustainable. Table 1 gives some of the French data for the past five years. The numbers make it difficult to give absolute priority to either the problem of low growth and high unemployment on one side or difficulties posed by large deficits (in good part cyclical) and high inflation.

Choosing macroeconomic priorities is not the only difficulty. A further difficulty, as the essays in this book so clearly show, is to identify precisely the macroeconomic problem. Is unemployment due to excessively high real wages or, at least in part, to a lack of aggregate demand? In the absence of precisely estimated production functions and exact data on technical progress and real costs, the broad facts do not give decisive guidance. But policy makers must answer that question at least implicitly as they set macroeconomic policies.

For those who accept a Keynesian unemployment diagnosis, there is still a question of how to move toward higher employment. Should one use real wage cuts, via nominal cuts or depreciation, or fiscal expansion? Those who favor real wage cuts would argue that they promote increased profitability and hence, increase investment, net exports, and thus, numbers of available jobs. Furthermore, a real wage-cutting strategy would avoid the risks associated with identifying the equilibrium as Keynesian or classical. Others would point out that reduced real wages might primarily cut aggregate demand, with little immediate offset through exports or investment.

Those who believe the economy is in fact in a high-real-wage, classical unemployment situation also face a choice of strategy. Should policy makers seek to validate the excessively high real wages by an investment strategy that raises productivity and creates jobs, by a reduction in nonwage labor costs, or by a cutback in the take-home real wage? Those who favor cutting real wages to move toward full employment, perhaps not surprisingly, favor nominal wage-freezes because they believe the real wage is sticky. Accordingly, they argue that there is a need for an explicit social consensus on real

Table 1. French Macroeconomic Conditions

	1979	1980	1981	1982	1983	1984*
Inflation	10.8	13.6	13.4	11.8	9.6	7.4
Unemployment Rate	5.9	6.3	7.3	8.0	8.1	8.7
Growth	3.3	1.1	0.3	1.8	0.6	0.6
Budget (% of GDP)	-0.7	0.2	-1.8	-2.6	-3.2	-3.5
Change in Budget:						
Discretionary	1.3	2.0	-1.0	-0.4	0	0.6
Cyclical	-0.1	-1.0	-1.0	-0.4	-0.6	-0.9
Current Account (% of GDP)	0	-1.4	-1.4	-2.3	-0.8	-0.0
Change in Competitiveness	-5.8	-4.3	+5.4	+3.4	+6.9	NA

Source: OECD and IMF, *Forecasts.

wage cuts rather than reliance on wage sluggishness to achieve, at best, transitory, inflationary gains in employment.

The real wage and profitability issue is behind some of the most interesting work in this volume. The introductory essay by Oudiz and Sterdyniak provides a general setting, and the papers by Krugman, Kouri/Macedo/Viscio, and Blanchard/Sachs provide different theoretical perspectives on the employment issue in the context of modern macroeconomics. As the discussion makes clear, there is little agreement on how precisely to see the issue. But it certainly is the case that some of these essays take us far in the direction of macroeconomic modeling, including business profitability and expectations, to seriously address problems of medium-term employment policy.

Anyone who looks for easy fiscal expansion will be disappointed by the budget data in Table 1. They tell a discouraging story. Even with a tightening of discretionary policies over the 1979–1984 period of almost 1.5 % of GDP, the cyclical deterioration of the budget leaves the economy with a large and seemingly persistent budget deficit. How can fiscal activism be defended in the face of persistent deficits? Some have argued that deficits may be undesirable, but that their relevance is altogether exaggerated compared to the difficulties posed for the economy, and for society, by continuing restraint on activity.[3] Should one not rather favor even larger short-run deficits to assure that the economy returns to growth and recovers enough dynamism to ultimately generate the tax revenues at high utilization rates that balance the budget? The very poor results after four years of an experiment to the contrary in the United Kingdom and Germany certainly do not make the case for fiscal orthodoxy. Even if one accepts the precarious fiscal situation in Belgium or Denmark and perhaps also Italy, there remains a strong case for a joint expansion by the United Kingdom and Germany with France in tow.

The issue of growth cannot be disregarded because, on current projections, Europe faces persistently high and perhaps even rising unemployment rates. Unfortunately there are few good stories of how this unemployment problem will ultimately be worked out. Two possible scenarios are these: 1) It would take a conservative government to get by with "unsound finance," and 2) The inevitable fall of the dollar, when and if it comes, will provide the room for noninflationary expansion. The latter in particular seems doubtful because a real depreciation of the dollar would cut into European external competitiveness. More likely , we would observe a falling dollar splitting the European Monetary System (EMS) between those countries that wish to take maximum advantage of the disinflationary effects and those that prefer to preserve some gain in competitiveness even at the expense of less reduction in inflation. Unfortunately the low inflation country, Germany, may be seeking further disinflation, thus potentially widening the European differentials in performance.

In pursuing further this sketch of macroeconomic issues and options, we find that two questions seem appropriate. First, why not monetary rather than fiscal expansion? Accepting for a moment that European deficits and debt accumulation are a problem, why should governments not seek a coordinated reduction in real interest rates by a once-and-for-all monetary expansion? The reduction in interest rates would stimulate activity and thus contribute not only to increased employment but also to some cyclical reduction in budget deficits. Moreover, the reduced interest rates would reinforce the budget improvement. It must be admitted that such a policy would be excellent if it could be achieved without exchange depreciation. If depreciation cannot be avoided then monetary expansion is inflationary, and potentially so in a dramatic way.

Because of the link that runs from reduced interest rates to depreciation and inflation, the question of decoupling via capital controls assumes a very special importance. The macroeconomic costs of capital mobility overshadow misallocation features of these controls. The open question is whether such controls can be administered in an effective way for anything but a short period. Half of the essays in this volume address the question of decoupling in one way or another. They deal with the monetary and financial determinants of the external value of the franc (Feroldi/Melitz and Frankel), with capital controls (Claassen/Wyplosz), and with the interaction between economic structure, policy effectiveness, and policy choices (Black and Laffargue). The papers do not come out with an unambiguous, uniform conclusion on monetary decoupling for an isolated country, but they certainly do not offer outright encouragement. Especially the careful analysis of capital controls in the Claassen/Wyplosz paper leaves doubts as to the tightness and persistence with which markets can be separated.

If isolated, expansionary monetary policy is ruled out we return once more to the fiscal issue. What is so perilous about deficit finance? One difficulty is obviously the large current-account deficit associated with isolated expansion, which of course could be solved by a joint move. The more basic worry is that deficit finance, by building up debt burdens, gives rise to growing financial difficulties and ultimately the risk of debt-liquidation via inflation. This view was prevalent in the interwar period, expressed particularly by Keynes, the 1927 UK Committee on National Debt and Taxation, Colin Clark, and more recently by Thomas Sargent. Keynes argued in 1926: "The level of the franc is going to be settled in the long run, not by speculation or the balance of trade, or even the outcome of the Ruhr adventure, but by the proportion of his earned income which the French taxpayer will permit to be taken from him to pay the claims of the French rentier."[4]

It is difficult to believe that the situation today justifies any such ideas. Keynes at the time addressed the choice of a post–World War I par for the franc, by fiat, and with it a determination of the real value of the French public debt. It is quite another thing to believe that a present-day French government should administer an unanticipated jump in the price level via exchange depreciation for the sole purpose of reducing the real value of debts. Figure 1 shows the ratio of central government debt to GDP in France. The debt:income ratio today is much lower than it was in the 1950s and 1960s. Even taking into account general government indebtedness, the debt:income ratio in no way has assumed alarming proportions although, of course, it shows a positive trend. But that is not how every policy maker sees the issue. To quote once more the IMF's managing director:

> One need not be an alarmist to visualize a situation where it becomes politically very difficult to introduce enough tax increases or enough cuts in noninterest expenditures to neutralize the growth of interest expenditure. When this happens the pressure on governments to inflate their way out of the problem may become irresistible. This, in the last analysis, is the main danger arising out of public debt accumulation.[5]

The overriding question seems to be whether, in the medium term, the current austerity strategy will not ultimately lead to larger debt accumulation than would a policy of deliberate, coordinated expansion that

Figure 1. The Ratio of Central Government Debt to GDP

restores jobs and prosperity. Real wage cuts and incomes policy, along with budget deficits and accommodating money, should all be part of such a package.[6]

Rudiger Dornbusch
Massachusetts Institute of Technology

● Notes

1. KINDLEBERGER, C. P., *International Short Term Capital Movements* (New York: Columbia University Press, 1983).

2. J. DE LAROSIERE, "The Growth of Public Debt and the Need for Fiscal Discipline." Remarks Before the 40th Congress of the Institute of Public Finance, Innsbruck, August 1984, reproduced in *IMF Survey*, 3 September 1984.

3. See R. LAYARD et al., "Europe: The Case for Unsustainable Growth." CEPS Papers, no. 8/9, Centre for European Policy Studies, Bruxelles, May 1984.

4. KEYNES, J. M. "The French Franc," in *Essays in Persuasion* (New York: W.W. Norton & Co., 1963), p. 105.

5. DE LAROSIERE, "The Growth of Public Debt." In the French tradition Jacques Rueff has gone further to say: "Tous ces enseignements m'ont conduit à une certitude: la liberté des personnes ne saurait survivre à un déficit prolongé. . . . Exigez l'ordre financier ou acceptez l'esclavage." JACQUES RUEFF, *Combat pour l'ordre financier*, Plan, 1982, p. 16.

6. LAYARD et al., "Europe: The Case for Unsustainable Growth."

Inflation, employment and external constraints:

An overview of the French economy during the seventies

Gilles OUDIZ *
and **Henri STERDYNIAK** **

* Centre d'Études Prospectives et d'Informations Internationales, Paris.
**Institut National de la Statistique et des Études Économiques, Paris.
The views expressed in this paper represent exclusively the positions of the authors and do not necessarily reflect those of the CEPII or INSEE.

The year 1974 saw a distinct break in the evolution of the French economy: before the first oil shock, it was characterized by a relatively high rate of growth of GDP which allowed a lower than average unemployment rate; since 1974, the growth of GDP has slowed down, the unemployment rate has increased continually and it has not proven possible to keep the inflation rate down. However, France did not experience huge public sector or foreign trade deficits, cumulative inflation, or exchange rate depreciation in the 1970's. In the coming years, the most crucial problem will be the steadily rising unemployment rate. Is it possible to grow faster without a deterioration of the current account of the balance of payments? Is it possible to create employment with rather slow growth of GDP?

9

Introduction

France, like its main European partners, has progressively become more open to foreign trade since the early days of the Common Market in 1958. The return to convertible currencies at this time has further increased the importance of international constraints on economic policies and goals within Europe. Although European economies have basically faced the same international environment, they have adapted themselves in very different ways and with unequal success.

In this paper we intend to discuss the major macroeconomic features of France in the last ten years in order to show first, what kind of growth took place before and after the first oil shock and, second, the nature of the problem with which the French government will have to deal over the next few years.

The first part of the paper will give a description of the basic macroeconomic evolutions and of the main aspects of economic policies. In the second part we shall analyse wage price dynamics and inflation mechanisms in France with the help of a description of the evolution of prices, wages, productivity and income shares and some estimates of wages and prices equations. In the third part we shall first present the evolution of French foreign trade and external balance. Then we shall discuss exchange rate movements, their influence on trade and the exchange rate policy pursued by the authorities.

We shall conclude by pointing to the main constraints that will interfere with growth and full employment in the coming years, and by trying to measure the possible alleviating effect of certain policy measures on these constraints.

1 The French economy during the seventies

Our first task is to draw a picture, necessarily brief, of the main macro-economic evolutions that took place during the seventies which will then allow us to point out the most important features of the French economy and to discuss the type of economic policy which was followed by the authorities.

1.1. Macroeconomic evolutions

a. Growth and employment

Until the first oil shock France was characterized by a GDP growth rate generally exceeding that of the main OECD countries (table 1) and rather consistently close to 6%. It is only after 1975 that the recession has led to a slower growth more akin to the OECD average. This allowed persistence of low unemployment rates during the first half of the seventies. Table 1 shows that in that period, unemployment in France was approximately one percentage point lower than for its main partners. The comparison with the United States in even more striking: an average of 2.6% unemployment in France as opposed to over 5% for the United States. In the second half of the seventies unemployment rose sharply in France as in most European countries. By the end of 1981 it had passed 7%, thus reaching a level comparable to American rates of unemployment.

The cumulative deterioration of employment growth in the last eight years resulted mainly from manufacturing. It appears that in all the leading OECD countries the slowdown in manufacturing growth has been rather sharp (table 3). In France the average growth rate of 6.2% observed during the years 1960-1973 fell to 2.2% from 1973 to 1981. This factor plus the moderate decline in the productivity of manufacturing industries are the basic sources of the rise of unemployement. From 1967 to 1973 employment rose by an average of 159,000 people a year, 76,000 of which came in manu-facturing, by contrast, from 1973 to 1980 total employment rose by only 54,000 per year while in manufacturing it decreased by 64,000 per year.

As is evident from table 3, the situation was quite different in the American economy where the importance of industrial employment had started decreasing in the late sixties. The moderate slowdown in overall growth and the huge decline in non-industrial productivity helped to maintain the growth of employment.

1 A.

TABLE 1

Inflation, growth, unemployment and capacity utilization rates 1970-1981

(Percent)

	France					Main OECD countries [1]		
	GDP Growth	CPI	GDP Deflator	Unemployment rate	Capacity under utilization rate	GDP growth	CPI	Unemployment rate
1970................	6.1	5.5	4.8	2.4	16.6	3.2	5.7	3.2
1971................	5.6	5.4	5.4	2.6	16.6	3.7	5.0	3.7
1972................	6.2	6.1	6.0	2.7	15.9	5.3	4.3	3.8
1973................	5.8	7.4	7.3	2.6	14.3	6.2	7.5	3.4
1974................	3.5	13.7	10.4	2.8	16.4	0.3	13.3	3.7
1975................	0.0	11.7	12.7	4.1	27.1	-0.5	11.0	5.4
1976................	5.1	9.6	9.6	4.4	20.9	5.2	8.0	5.4
1977................	3.2	9.5	8.5	4.7	19.9	4.1	8.1	5.1
1978................	3.9	9.3	9.2	5.2	19.5	4.0	7.0	5.1
1979................	3.6	10.6	10.2	5.9	17.9	3.5	9.3	4.9
1980................	1.2	13.5	11.5	6.3	18.4	1.2	12.2	5.6
1981................	0.2	13.3	11.3	7.6	22.1	n.a.	10.0	6.5

1. Canada, France, Germany, Italy, Japan, United Kingdom, USA.

Sources : INSEE and OECD.

b. The structure of demand and income

The fall in the annual growth rate of GDP from an average of 5.4% in 1969-1974 to 2.9% in 1975-1980 has resulted in a strong alteration of the structure of demand and income. The slowdown in growth should have implied a decrease of the rate of investment, which one can roughly evaluate. Under balanced growth the share of investment in GDP is proportional to the rate of growth plus the depreciation rate of capital. With an average depreciation rate of 7.5% over the seventies, the share of investment should have fallen by 19% whereas it was only reduced by 12%. Investment thus appears to have held up after 1974 even though, as table 2 shows, it did not make a leading contribution to overall growth (see the conclusions of P. DUBOIS [1980]). During the same period the share of firms in total income fell by 2%, an amount comparable to the decrease in the share of investment, which seems to imply that firms modify their profit targets in line with their investment plans.

TABLE 2

Growth and unemployment

(Percent)

Annual rate of growth	1970-1974	1975-1980	1981
GDP	5.4	2.9	0.2
Import	10.6	6.6	− 1.5
Export	12.8	5.7	4.6
Household spending	5.3	3.5	1.4
Firm spending	4.8	1.8	− 3.3
Government spending	2.5	3.0	1.9
Share in GDP			
Households :			
Income	77.5	81.7	84.4
Spending	73.5	76.9	80.3
Propensity to spend	0.948	0.941	0.950
Firms :			
Income	13.4	11.3	9.3
Spending	18.5	16.2	14.6
Income	8.7	6.3	5.6
Government :			
Spending	7.8	7.4	7.5
Trade balance	0.2	− 0.5	− 1.5

Source : INSEE.

The stable share of public expenditures in GDP shows that the bulk of growth clearly must be attributed to household spending. The rise of the share of household spending in GDP took place quite independently of any change in the average propensity to consume, which remained remarkably stable around 94.5 %. This evolution is basically linked to the favorable shift in the structure of income over the period. Starting from a level of 77.5 % during the years 1970-1974, the share of household income in GDP reached 81.1 % during the years 1975-1980, peaking at 84.4 % in 1981. This movement resulted mainly from the increase of net social transfers during all of the seventies, which has a counterpart in the fall in the share of profits. In 1981 it is clearly no longer feasible nor acceptable to let the rise of social transfers propel the growth of consumption : employers' social contributions have been a source of inflationary pressures and high labor costs on the one hand; while on the other hand the social security system faces an unprecedented deficit.

c. Inflation and unemployment

Figure 1 presents the combinations of unemployment and inflation observed in France and the main OECD countries during the last ten years.

FIGURE 1

Unemployment and inflation in France and in the group of seven major OECD countries 1970-1980

(Percent)

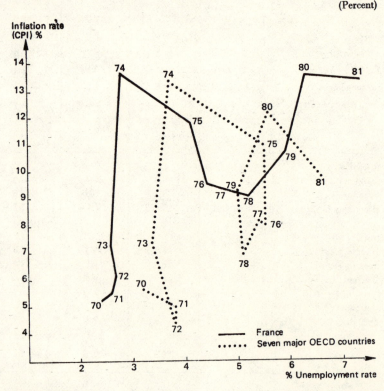

Source : OECD.

Paradoxically the French relative rate o{inflation increased during a period in which its relative growth diminished. Until the oil crisis, inflation in France was only moderately higher than the average, whereas after 1976 an acceleration of prices in France widened the gap.

The figure displays another disturbing evolution : a continuous rise of unemployment during the entire period independently of the fluctuations of inflation. Quite differently, the other main OECD countries experienced a slowdown in inflation and unemployment before the second oil shock. It should be noted however that these average figures reflect mostly American and German experience : most EEC countries faced an uninterrupted growth of unemployment.

d. Productivity and labor costs in manufacturing

As we have noted above, manufacturing productivity growth in France has been consistently rather high compared to the largest OECD countries (table 3). After 1973 the slowdown in productivity growth remained moderate in France, keeping the country, together with Germany, away from the lead among the main OECD countries.

These elements of good performance were largely dampened by the high rates of domestic inflation which took hold after 1973, as shown by the evolution of unit labor costs (table 3). In national currencies, French costs grew more than twice as fast as German ones and three times as fast as the Japanese. The depreciation of the franc significantly helped to reduce this gap and made the evolution of unit labor costs (measured in US dollars) comparable to German ones and much closer to those of Japan and the US.

e. The current account

The worsening of French competitive positions has deteriorated the trade balance, particularly in recent years. [1] However, it appears that France remained rather close to the average, if one refers to such a global indicator as the ratio of current account to GDP. Even the deficit of 1974 which was larger than the EEC or OECD averages, can be considered quite moderate if compared with the United Kingdom and Italy.

With reference to the 1970s as a whole one can only draw an ambiguous picture from the analysis of French basic macroeconomic evolutions. France has known neither the impressive successes of Japan or Germany nor the cumulative inflation of Italy or the United Kingdom. The outlook for the coming years, however, is much less reassuring. It appears that :

— The pattern of rapid economic growth with moderate inflation and high productivity that prevailed before the first oil shock is no longer possible

— The situation has considerably worsened in the last ten years in terms of growth, employment and inflation.

---

1. We shall discuss the structure of the trade balance more extensively in the third section of this paper. Detailed figures are presented in table 12.

TABLE 3

Manufacturing employment, output, and labor costs in the group of seven major OECD countries

(Average annual growth rates in percent)*

	Employment		Output per hour		Output		Unit labor costs in national currencies		Unit labor costs in US dollars	
	1960–1973	1973–1981	1960–1973	1973–1981	1960–1973	1973–1981	1960–1973	1973–1981	1960–1973	1973–1981
USA..............	1.5	0.7	3.0	1.7	4.7	2.3	1.9	7.7	1.9	7.7
Canada..........	1.9	0.6	4.5	1.6	6.3	2.0	1.8	9.4	1.9	6.4
Japan...........	3.0	— 0.4	10.7	6.8	13.0	6.5	3.5	2.7	4.7	7.2
Germany.........	0.5	1.6	5.5	4.8	5.3	1.8	3.7	4.7	6.1	9.2
Italy............	1.4	0.0	6.9	3.6	6.8	3.3	5.1	15.5	5.4	8.1
United Kingdom...	— 0.5	— 2.9	4.3	2.1	3.0	— 1.8	4.1	16.6	2.6	15.0
France...........	1.2	— 1.4	6.0	4.6	6.2	2.2	3.1	10.1	2.8	9.5

Source : US Department of Labor, BLS.

1.2. Economic policy

We shall limit ourselves to a discussion of the main macroeconomic indicators of French policies during the last ten or eleven years. It is clear that we thus omit some important aspects of structural policies such as industrial policies or income redistribution policies.

a. Fiscal policy

Up to 1974, budgetary policy in France was relatively neutral and sometimes restrictive. The goal of the authorities was mostly to achieve a balanced budget. After the first oil shock, on the contrary, the public sector borrowing requirement rose suddenly to nearly 3 % of GDP but remained near the equilibium of 1976-1980 except in 1978 (table 4).

It is necessary to look closer at public spending and income in order to distinguish between governmental policy choices and the results of the slowdown of growth. In a period of recession the budget tends to be automatically in deficit : fiscal income falls with activity and government spending follows its previous trend and is even enlarged by unemployment subsidies.

Table 4 shows that the ratio of government spending to GDP rose from 40 % in the early seventies to nearly 53 % in 1981. A more detailed analysis reveals that this is mostly due to the sharp rise of social transfers which various policies have been unable to prevent. If we compute this same ratio based on a regular growth [2] then we find a significant reduction, which is due mostly to lower unemployment subsidies. The « regular growth » deficit is of course much less fluctuating than the actual deficit. It shows that only in 1975 and 1978 did the French government have a truly expansionary policy and that the slowdown of growth has not led to a structural worsening of the public deficit.

b. Monetary policy

The French monetary system differs in many aspects from the American or English systems (see COUTIÈRE [1975], MELITZ [1976] or STERDYNIAK and VILLA [1977]). It is necessary to discuss these differences in order to explain the main characteristics of monetary policy in France.

The fact that commercial banks can get automatic refinancing from the Central Bank makes it irrelevant to consider money supply as exogenous and explains why the authorities have only limited control over monetary aggregates. Fundamentally, one may consider that the French monetary system has two regimes :

— One regime corresponds to the case when the authorities have an interest rate policy without any money growth rate target. The money market rate is fixed according to the exchange rate policy (see section 3

---

2. These computations differ from the more traditional "full employment" deficit. They take into account a hypothetical growth rate equal to an exponential weighted average of actual growth, on the basis of which government income and spending have been recomputed.

TABLE 4

Macroeconomic indicators of French economic policy 1970-1981

(Percent)

	Public sector borrowing requirement as percent of GDP		Public sector spending as percent of GDP		Social security and welfare spending as percent of GDP	Growth rate of M2 [1]	Credit interest rate	Long term interest rate [2]	Liquidity ratio of the economy [3]
	(a)	(b)	(a)	(b)					
1970	— 1.0	— 0.7	40.0	40.3	16.8	15.4	10.2	8.8	41.1
1971	— 0.9	— 0.6	40.1	40.4	16.9	17.9	8.9	8.7	43.5
1972	— 0.9	— 0.5	40.0	40.5	17.1	18.5	8.4	8.2	45.9
1973	— 1.1	— 0.6	40.1	40.6	17.4	14.5	10.5	9.1	46.3
1974	— 0.7	0.0	41.6	41.3	18.2	16.0	14.0	11.5	46.8
1975	+ 2.9	+ 1.0	46.1	43.9	20.6	16.5	12.1	11.0	48.0
1976	+ 0.5	— 1.1	46.7	45.0	20.9	17.3	11.1	11.0	48.7
1977	+ 0.9	— 0.8	46.9	45.0	21.7	12.3	11.5	11.4	48.7
1978	+ 2.1	+ 0.1	48.1	46.1	22.7	13.2	11.2	11.1	48.5
1979	+ 0.8	— 1.1	48.5	46.4	23.2	13.4	11.9	11.2	48.3
1980	+ 0.4	— 2.4	49.5	46.4	23.8	11.6	14.5	14.1	47.7
1981	+ 2.0	— 0.8	52.8	48.5	25.5	12.6	15.6	16.8	47.8

Column (a) represents the actual figure and column (b) the recalculated figure for a regular growth of GDP.

1. M2 consists of currency, commercial banks deposits and postal checking accounts.
2. Yield of 2nd category bonds.
3. Ratio of M2 to GDP.

Sources : INSEE and Banque de France.

below).   In this regime commercial banks, which do not face any refinancing constraints, fix their rates by taking into account the marginal cost of funds, i.e. the money market rate, and their liquidity ratio.   At the interest rate which commercial banks thus fix, credit supply is perfectly elastic in relation to demand.

— A second regime corresponds to the case in which the authorities wish to control monetary expansion.   Since 1973 the monetary authorities have decided to restrict bank credit by fixing quantitative ceilings for each bank (« encadrement du crédit »).   In fact, over these ten years, these ceilings have been unevenly binding and have really slowed down credit expansion only in 1974, 1977 and 1980 (see table 5).

TABLE 5

Indicator of credit restriction

	1973	1974	1975	1976	1977	1978	1979	1980
Credit users........	2,14	3,20	1,77	1,36	2,19	1,71	1,64	2,33
Banks.............	2,19	2,99	1,19	1,91	2,25	1,78	2,12	2,63

Note : This indicator measures the intensity of credit restrictions, and only its evolution should be taken into account.

Source : Banque de France.

These considerations will enable us to comment on the evolution of monetary variables appearing in table 4.

From 1971 to 1976, M_2 grew at an average rate of 17 %, as compared to a mere 10 % from 1964 to 1970.   The authorities started fixing a target growth of M_2 in Autumn of 1976 with the aim of bringing the rate eventually back to the levels observed at the beginning of the seventies.   Targets were progressively tightened from an annual growth rate of 12.5 % in 1977 to 10 % in 1981 (see table 6).   These goals were attained only in 1978 and 1980, but on the whole money growth fell by 4 to 5 percent.

TABLE 6

Money growth rates : targets and realization*

(Percent)

	1977	1978	1979	1980	1981
M_2 target growth rate..	12,5	12.0	11.0	11.0	10.0
M_2 actual growth rate.	13.9	12.2	14.4	9.7	11.4

* The figures represent the growth of M_2 from December to December.

Source : Conseil national du Crédit.

FIGURE 2

Growth rates of GDP deflator (P) and of M₂

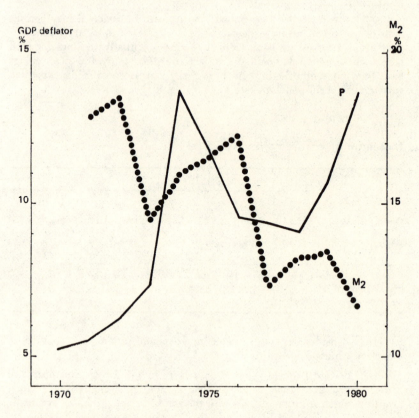

Sources : INSEE and Banque de France.

The causal link between money growth and inflation is, however, far from obvious. The comparison of the growth rates of M₂ and of the GDP deflator shows that inflation started slowing down in 1975, two years before a more restrictive monetary policy was applied. Furthermore, the acceleration of inflation after 1977 does not seem to have been dampened by the increasingly restrictive monetary targets (see figure 2).

As we shall see in section 3, interest rates have been fixed mostly according to exchange rates objectives. After correction for inflation (table 1), real interest rates on both credit and bonds remained positive, close to 3 %, until 1973. The acceleration of inflation in 1974-1975 brought real interest rates close to zero for credit and even made them negative for bonds. Subsequently and up to May 1981, real interest rates stabilized at a positive level around 1 or 2 %.

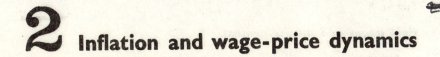

2 Inflation and wage-price dynamics

As noted earlier, the widening gap between inflation in France and its main partners is a fundamental problem for the French economy. Table 7 shows how a noticeable inflation differential with Germany emerged after 1968, when the rise in French inflation was aggravated by the wage increases of May, to which then was added the devaluation of the subsequent year. Both countries had of course to face the oil shock and its inflationary consequences. However, after 1975 the prices in Germany moved back more or less to the pre-1973 level whereas the anti-inflationary policies of the French authorities remained ineffective.

TABLE 7

Inflation rates in France and Germany

(Average annual growth rates in percent)

	1963/1967	1968/1972	1973/1975	1976/1980
France................	2.7	5.6	10.9	10.5
West Germany.........	2.7	3.8	6.6	4.1
Main OECD Countries...	2.6	4.8	10.5	8.9

Sources : OECD and INSEE.

In this section we shall present an empirical analysis of French inflation based on estimates of wage and price equations. We shall then try to explain the type of mechanism that prevented the slowdown of inflation in the last years.

2.1. Wage and price formation

Let us first discuss the joint evolution of real wages and unemployment ("augmented Phillips curve") since 1964 (figure 3).[3] The relationship between the two variables has clearly been modifed since 1970, perhaps as a result of the new wage-setting process which began in 1968. From 1970 onwards a marked effect of unemployment on real wages can be detected. Rising unemployment brought about a slow deceleration in growth of real wages over the next 10 years.

---

3. The exceptional wage increases of 1968 have been excluded from the curve.

FIGURE 3

Real wages and unemployment

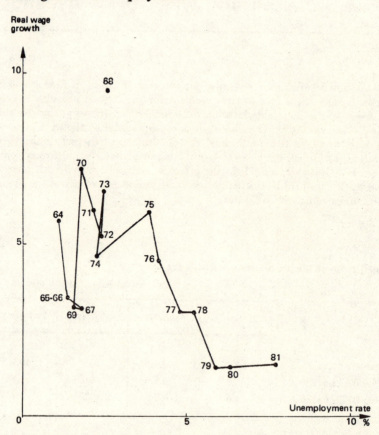

Source : INSEE.

The simultaneous estimation of a wage and a price equation presented in the appendix, part 1, does confirm the presence of a significant link between wages and unemployment. Moreover it appears that, with a lag of around one quarter, wages are totally indexed on consumer prices. [4] Short lags are also a characteristic of French price responses. The estimated price equation shows that the total amount of cost increases, resulting from either wages or import prices, is transferred into prices within less than two quarters.

Table 8 will allow us to discuss the evolution of the share of wages in relation to value added. In the way suggested by the Scandinavian model of inflation, one may compute the margin or scope for real wage increases which are compatible with stability of the share of profits and wages in value added (i.e. the warranted real wage growth):

$$\dot{W}RW = \dot{P}ROD + (\dot{P}Y - \dot{P}) - \frac{\Delta t}{1+t}$$

---

4. These results are consistent with most available empirical studies — see for example ARTUS *et Alii* [1981].

22

TABLE 8

Wages, unemployment and productivity

Années	Real wage[1]	Unemployment rate	Unemployment rate / Vacancies	Real minimum wage[1]	Real public wages[1]	Warranted real wage[1]	Labor productivity[1]	GDP deflator [CPI[1]	Social costs[2]	Share of wages in GDP
1964	5.6	1.1	5.0	0.2	6.3	6.2	5.2	1.4	0.4	67.3
1965	3.4	1.4	9.5	1.6	1.3	4.4	6.1	— 1.2	0.5	67.1
1966	3.4	1.4	7.3	1.6	2.2	4.4	3.7	— 1.0	0.3	66.8
1967	3.1	1.8	12.3	— 0.9	3.5	4.7	6.4	— 0.8	0.9	65.9
1968	9.5	2.1	10.8	33.8	13.2	8.4	7.7	— 0.4	0.1	67.5
1969	3.2	1.6	4.1	0.2	0.0	3.6	3.8	— 0.3	0.2	68.5
1970	7.2	1.8	3.9	1.8	6.6	7.0	6.9	— 0.1	0.3	68.3
1971	6.0	2.2	3.7	4.7	5.6	6.8	6.8	— 0.2	0.2	68.1
1972	5.2	2.4	2.9	7.8	6.6	6.8	7.3	— 0.3	— 0.2	66.8
1973	6.5	2.1	1.8	10.8	4.6	4.7	4.7	— 0.2	— 0.2	67.3
1974	4.6	2.3	2.6	7.4	5.6	—	3.2	— 3.2	— 0.4	69.6
1975	6.0	3.9	8.1	6.0	6.1	0.5	5.5	1.0	+ 1.3	72.0
1976	4.5	4.2	7.5	3.4	4.2	5.2	4.6	0.4	— 0.8	72.6
1977	3.0	4.8	10.4	3.3	2.1	4.2	2.8	— 1.1	+ 0.3	73.1
1978	3.0	5.2	13.9	3.0	2.5	1.3	6.0	0.2	0.5	71.0
1979	1.4	5.9	15.2	1.3	0.9	5.2	3.4	— 1.0	0.8	71.2
1980	1.4	6.3	16.9	1.1	0.4	1.5	0.2	— 1.9	0.0	74.0
1981	1.5	7.7	26.1	6.8	2.9	— 1.7	3.5	— 1.1	0.0	73.7

1. Twelve-month variation, in percentage terms.
2. Growth rate of $(1 + t)$ where t is rate of social costs per unit of money wage.

Source : INSEE.

where:

$\dot{\text{WRW}}$: Warranted real wage growth;

$\dot{\text{PROD}}$: Growth rate of labor productivity;

$\dot{\text{PY}}$: Growth rate of value added deflator;

$\dot{\text{P}}$: Growth rate of consumer price index;

t : rate of social costs per unit of money wage.

From 1966 to 1973 real wages grew at an average annual rate of 5.5%.

This was perfectly compatible with a 5.8 % value of $\dot{\text{WRW}}$, attribuable mostly to productivity gains. During the last eight years, $\dot{\text{WRW}}$ has fallen to an average of 2.3% because of the fall in labor productivity (3.6 % per year), the increase in the consumer price index relative to the value-added deflator (0.8% per year due to the rise in oil prices) and the rise in social security contributions (0.5% per year). During the same period, the annual increase of 3.2% in real wages led to an increase in the share of wages. Starting from a rather stable level of 67 to 68 percent up to 1974, this share grew to close to 74% of the total value added in 1981.

The three last years deserve special attention, for they indicate a significant change in the trend of real wages largely resulting from the fast rise of unemployment. This change did not, however, yield an improvement of profits because of the rise of social security contributions (1979), the rise in oil prices (1979 and 1980), and the following productivity slowdown (1980). On the whole it appears that these short term factors have delayed the reduction of inflation which is likely to begin now that real wages are growing only about a quarter as fast as before.

2.2. The wage-price system

Our wage and price equations can be rewritten in the following simplified way:

$$\dot{\text{W}} = a_0 \dot{\text{P}} + (1 - a_0)\, \dot{\text{P}}_{-1} - a_1 \text{U} + a_2$$

$$\dot{\text{P}} = b_0 [b_1 \dot{\text{P}}_m + (1 - b_1)\, (\dot{\text{W}} - \dot{\text{PROD}})] + (1 - b_0)\, \dot{\text{P}}_{-1} + b_2$$

This yields:

$$\dot{\text{P}} = c_0 \dot{\text{P}}_m + c_1 \dot{\text{P}}_{-1} + c_2 (a_2 - a_1 \text{U} - \dot{\text{PROD}}) + c_3$$

where:

$$c_0 = b_1 b_0 \Delta^{-1}$$
$$c_1 = [1 - b_0 (a_0 + b_1 - b_1 a_0)] \Delta^{-1}$$
$$c_2 = b_0 (1 - b_1) \Delta^{-1}$$
$$c_3 = b_2 \Delta^{-1}$$
$$\Delta = 1 - (1 - b_1) b_0 a_0$$

and $\dot{\text{P}}_m$ is the growth rate of import prices, U, the unemployment rate.

This relation is equivalent to an open economy long-run Phillips curve, as can be explained in two steps. First, a variation in import prices is eventually totally reflected in consumption prices. As we have seen above, both the mean lags of indexation of prices based on wage costs, and wages based on consumption prices, are around one quarter. If one incorporates these results in our equations, the mean lag of indexation of consumption prices on import prices can be seen to rise to 11.5 quarters, as shown by the reduced price equation:

$$\dot{P} = 0.92\,\dot{P}_{-1} + 0.08\,\dot{P}_m + 0.13\,(U_o - U)$$

where $U_0 = 5.7 - 2.5\,\dot{PROD}$.

An increase of 10% in import prices, stemming for example from a devaluation of the franc, will thus lead to an increase in domestic inflation of 2.8% within a year. This result tends to support the idea that the authorities can possibly modify the real exchange rate through nominal depreciation of the franc. However such an effect will disappear in the medium term.

But, in the medium term, b_2, which is a function of capacity utilization rates, is equal to zero and the equation determines a level of unemployment, U_o, compatible with the equality of foreign and domestic inflation.

This "natural rate" of unemployment is a decreasing function of productivity growth. It amounts to 2% if labor productivity grows at 6% per year and reaches 5.7% if there is no productivity gain. The reduced-form equation shows that in order to slow down inflation by 0.5% in one year, the authorities would have to accept a rate of unemployment one percent above the "natural" rate.

On the whole two factors would thus tend to change the rate of inflation favorably. First, the computations indicate that the unemployment rate in France has grown so high as to lead in the medium run to a structurally lower rate of inflation, that is, unless this phenomenon is concealed by short term shocks, as was the case in 1979, 1980 and 1981. Second, social costs, which have grown markedly since 1975, thereby increasing inflation by around 0.5% (see FEROLDI, RAOUL and STERDYNIAK [1982]), will not grow in the near future. This optimistic view is of course largely dependent on the future of the franc. If the French currency enters into a vicious circle of cumulative depreciation the situation is likely to worsen in the near future.

3 The current account and the exchange rate policy

The purpose of this section is to point out the main features of the external constraints which weighed on the French economy during the 1970s and to discuss the way the authorities tried to deal with these constraints through an active exchange rate policy. We shall first briefly describe the structure of the current account and the competitiveness of the French economy.

3.1. The current account in the 1970s

a. Structure of the current account

The trend current-account was positive for most of the 1960's with the major exception of 1969, when the growth of GDP reached 7%. The French experience of the 1970's, on the whole, has been far less happy (table 9). Figure 4 allows a closer look at the structure of the balance of goods and services. France has been able to meet increasing oil deficits basically because of gains in trade of manufactured goods and services. The balance in services improved markedly during the last ten years and has attained practically the same level as the balance of manufactured goods. It should be noted that these services consist mostly of engineering, technical cooperation and tourism.

The positive balance in manufactured goods is very unevenly distributed among various sectors. France has mainly developed exports of automobiles and equipment goods but has lost important ground at home as well as abroad in other areas such as household equipment goods and intermediary goods. This specialization in professional equipment goods has involved a strong rise of exports to socialist countries and developing countries, which has been promoted partly by very advantageous credit terms. Under such conditions it is not surprising that the elasticity of these exports has appeared to be quite low with respect to prices. These exports have also accounted for most of the growth of the terms of trade in manufacturing since 1971. They have thus been crucial in limiting the impact of the oil shock on the total terms of trade.

b. The openness of the French economy

Like all of its European partners France has opened itself widely to foreign trade in the past twenty years. Table 10 shows that this opening up has not slowed down in recent years, as the ratio of exports to home production increased from around 20% in 1970 to 36% in 1981. A more detailed analysis confirms the same sectoral differences we noted above. Two sectors, professional equipment goods and automobiles, have expanded their ratio of exports to output to a very important level : 50.4% in the former case, 42.9 % in the latter. The high import penetration ratio for equipment goods, on the other hand, reveals a crucial weakness of the French economy. Despite export development in this area, the country must import a large share of its own equipment. Further, the imbalance of trade in household equipment goods shows that any increase in consumption is bound to have a negative effect on the current account.

TABLE 9

The current account

(billions of francs)

	1973	1974	1975	1976	1977	1978	1979	1980	1981
Goods.................	+ 1.5	— 20.9	+ 5.6	— 22.6	— 11.9	+ 7	— 6.1	— 50.8	— 48.6
Services................	+ 3.1	+ 2.7	+ 5.3	+ 5.9	+ 11.1	+ 24.7	+ 28	+ 35.3	+ 30.3
Unilateral transfers....	— 7.7	— 10.9	— 11.2	— 11.7	— 13.9	— 14.8	— 17.1	— 17.6	— 22.6
Current account........	— 3.1	— 29.1	— 0.3	— 28.4	— 14.7	+ 16.9	+ 4.8	— 33.1	— 41.1
Current account/GDP (%).............	— 0.2	— 2.3	0	— 1.5	— 0.7	0.6	— 0.1	— 1.3	— 1.5
Current account/GDP OECD average....	0.3	— 0.7	0.1	— 0.4	— 0.4	0.2	— 0.5	— 0.8	n.a.

Sources : INSEE and OECD.

FIGURE 4

Trade balances

(Values per quarter in billions of Francs)

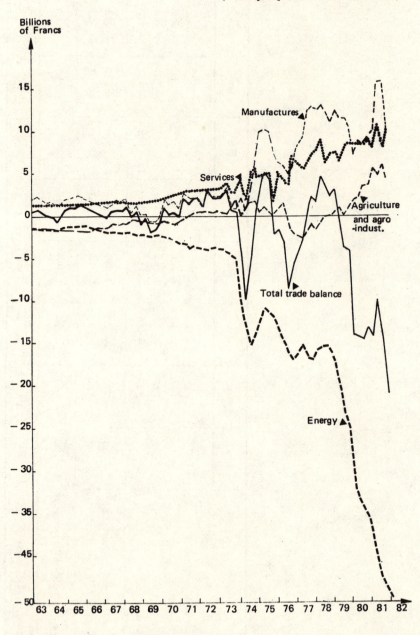

Source: INSEE, Tendances de la conjoncture.

TABLE 10

Home and export performance of French manufacturing*

Year	Manufactured goods		Professional equipment		Vehicles		Household equipment goods	
	(1)	(2)	(1)	(2)	(1)	(2)	(1)	(2)
1970	19.4	20.4	25.4	25.7	17.6	31.5	28.5	17.5
1971	20.1	21.2	26.0	27.0	18.8	32.1	30.7	17.5
1972	22.3	22.7	29.6	29.2	19.8	34.6	32.7	18.9
1973	24.4	24.3	33.4	31.8	21.0	34.1	34.1	21.6
1974	25.9	26.4	36.5	35.6	20.8	36.8	34.6	21.8
1975	25.5	28.2	33.6	38.4	23.2	42.6	37.2	24.6
1976	28.7	28.8	38.7	42.4	26.1	37.2	36.8	20.7
1977	29.0	30.7	38.6	43.6	25.7	38.8	37.9	23.0
1978	30.0	31.8	38.9	45.0	25.2	38.6	38.1	23.6
1979	32.5	32.9	43.0	46.7	26.9	39.8	42.2	25.9
1980	34.6	33.5	47.6	47.0	28.9	41.0	44.5	26.4
1981	35.7	36.8	48.1	50.4	31.7	42.9	46.1	27.0

Source : INSEE.

* Column 1 represents the ratio of imports to home demand and column 2 the ratio of exports to manufacturers' production (1970 francs).

TABLE 11

Geographical pattern of French foreign trade in manufactures

(Percent)

	1970		1979	
	Imports	Exports	Imports	Exports
EEC [1].............	70.6	51.2	68.7	49.7
USA................	9.8	5.9	6.2	5.2
Japan..............	0.9	0.9	1.8	1.0
OI [2].............	10.4	17.6	12.3	16.1
OPEC..............	0.8	5.6	2.0	8.5
DC [3].............	5.5	15.2	5.8	14.9
EAST [4]...........	2.0	4.6	2.8	4.6

1. Excluding Denmark.
2. OI: Other industrialized countries.
3. DC: Developing countries.
4. EAST: Eastern Europe Socialist countries.

Source : CEPII (CHELEM).

c. Trade patterns

It is well-known that France trades mostly with its European partners (table 11). Trade within the EEC accounts for around 50% of exports of manufactures, of which nearly 20% consists of trade with Germany. After 1974, Opec's share in French exports of manufactures rose by around 3%, mostly because of the rapid increase of trade with Middle Eastern countries. The figures in table 11 show the distribution of French imports from foreign countries after the oil shock. The share of imports from the USA, and to a lesser extent from the EEC, fell noticeably between 1970 and 1979.

d. Competitivity

As we have seen in the first section, the gains in productivity in French manufacturing industries have not prevented a deterioration in relative unit labor costs, especially as compared with Germany. The depreciation of the franc helped to moderate the decline in competitivity over the 1970's. (table 12) Computations of relative unit labor costs of French manufacturing, unadjusted for exchange rate changes, confirm that the higher inflation in France relative to its partners led to regularly declining competitivity.

TABLE 12

Measures of French competitivity in manufacturing

Year	Relative unit labor costs in national curencies [1]	Relative unit labor costs in France [1]	Internal competi- tivity [2]	External competi- tivity [3]	Export profita- bility [4]	Effective exchange rate [5]
1970..........	100	100	100	100	100	100
1971..........	98.5	100.5	97.2	102.8	99	102
1972..........	98.4	97.9	91.4	104	95	99.4
1973..........	97.1	92.1	87.4	103.7	93	94.8
1974..........	97.5	97.8	92.4	110.3	94	100.3
1975..........	93.3	84.5	85.4	103.2	92	90.5
1976..........	91.5	86.2	84	107.6	91	94.2
1977..........	91.9	91.9	85.1	112.5	92	100
1978..........	90.5	91.6	83	112.1	91	101.2
1979..........	88.2	88.4	81.1	110.5	91	100.3
1980..........	84.5	84.9	78.3	110	89	100.5
1981..........	80.9	91	79.4	117.5	90	112.4

1. Ratio of unit labor costs of competitors to unit labor costs of French manufacturing.
2. Internal competitivity is measured by the ratio of import prices to home production prices in manufactures.
3. External competitivity is measured by the ratio of an index of competitors prices to export prices.
4. Export profitability is measured by the ratio of export prices to home production prices.
5. Index of the number of units of Francs per unit of foreign currency.

Source : INSEE.

The influence of exchange rate depreciation, especially in 1971, 1974, 1977 and 1981 is clearly seen in the second column of table 12. During these years, relative unit labor costs of French industry improved in exchange-rate-adjusted terms whereas the corresponding figures in national currencies show a deterioration. It is clear, however, that such improvements are short-lived. They disappear as soon as the franc stabilizes, as for example in 1973 and 1975.

The fluctuations of competitivity, as measured by relative export prices, show the same importance of exchange rates movements. But, contrary to relative unit labor costs, relative export prices have had a tendency to fall over the last ten years. This trend can be attributed partly to the very strong competition that French firms have faced on external markets as reflected in the declining ratio of export prices to prices of production in manufacturing. Finally, the index of internal competitivity fell from 100 in 1970 to under 80 in 1981. This strong deterioration has not been altered by the depreciation of the franc, especially not in 1981. The deterioration is the basic factor underlying the present disequilibrium of the French current account.

e. Econometric analysis of French trade in manufactures

The econometric analysis of foreign trade in manufacturing allows us to comfort some of the conclusions of the above discussion (detailed estimates follow in the Appendix, part 2).

Export and import prices adjust very quickly, though not fully, to exchange rate movements. On the other hand, the reaction of trade flows to any change in relative prices takes about a year.

A modification of the exchange rate thus leads to the traditional J curve with an adverse terms-of-trade effect lasting over one year. This result is confirmed by large macroeconomic models (see DEBONNEUIL, STERDYNIAK [1982], AGLIETTA and *alii* [1979]) which take into account both trade in non-manufactured goods (i.e. raw materials, oil, agricultural products and services) and domestic retroactions.

The sectoral differences in export performance and import penetration are also reflected in significant differences in prices elasticities (table 13). It is clear that exports of equipment goods are markedly less sensitive to competitive pressures than exports of other manufactures such as intermediary goods. Import flows appear largely insensitive to relative prices except in the case of consumption goods. It would then seem that import penetration is more the result of structural causes than adverse competitive positions, at least as regards intermediary and equipment goods.

TABLE 13

Price elasticities of exports and imports of manufacturing

	Exports	Imports
Equipment goods [1]	0.85	0.36
Intermediary goods [1]	1.80	0.26
Consumption goods [1]	1.56	1.32
Manufactured goods [2]	1.60	0.89

Sources :
1. See CATINAT [1982];
2. See Appendix to this paper.

3.2. The exchange rate policy

a. The franc during the seventies

The devaluation of 1969 put an end to ten years of stability of the French currency. During most of the 1970s, the authorities have had to let the franc depreciate in order to maintain trade equilibrium whenever restrictive domestic policies proved either unsuccessful or infeasible. We shall briefly comment here on the evolution of the franc during these years.

December 1971 to December 1973

In December 1971, the Smithsonian Institute agreement led to an appreciation of 8.6% of the franc dollar exchange rate. Shortly after (April 1972), the franc joined the « snake » linking the major European currencies relative to the dollar and it managed to stay in the arrangement until January 1974. During this period the franc/dollar rate rose by 24% whereas the franc/deutschemark rate fell by 10%. By the end of 1973 the increase of inflation, further aggravated by the oil shock and the deterioration of the trade balance, resulted in very strong pressures on exchange markets and the withdrawal of the franc from the "snake".

January 1974 to March 1976

The slowdown in growth led to a progressive improvement of the trade balance and a short-lived return to equilibrium. From the second quarter of 1974 to the second quarter of 1975 the franc gained 15% relative to the dollar and 10% relative to the deutschemark.

In the light of these improvements the authorities decided to reenter the "snake" a second time in July 1975. However the expansionary fiscal policy of J. Chirac soon led to an important trade deficit and forced the authorities to leave the "snake" once again in March 1976.

March 1976 to March 1979

The March 1976 experience proved quite costly in terms of official reserves and the exchange rate. Within six months the effective exchange rate of the franc fell by around 10%. The following restrictive policy (« Plan Barre ») allowed a progressive improvement of the current account which reached equilibrium at the end of 1977 and was positive in 1978 and 1979. During these years the franc rose in terms of dollars while tending to depreciate in terms of deutschemarks, a favorable evolution both in regard to the terms of trade and competitivity.

March 1979 to December 1981

Finally in March 1979, France and the main European countries, except the United Kingdom, founded the EMS. Due to the weakness of the deutschemark and to the relative stability of the exchange markets, the franc managed to remain in the system without any change until October 1981, when it was devaluated by 8%.

b. Exchange rate policy and the European currencies

As we have seen, the French authorities have faced strong pressures on the exchange markets on many occasions. They have, in most cases, tried to "lean against the wind" by pegging the franc as much as they could in order to stabilize its exchange rate. Two instruments have served for this exchange rate policy: official reserves and the interest rate. [5] This of course has limited the autonomy of domestic monetary policy.

---

5. See Artus et Alii [1981] for a modelisation of the authorities' reaction functions.

It seems quite clear that since 1971 the French monetary authorities have often tried to stabilize the parity of the franc against the other European currencies, while allowing the franc/dollar rate to move according to the fluctuations of the dollar against the European currencies as a whole (or more specifically against the deutschemark). We have tried to provide empirical support for this view by estimating various equations of exchange rate and interest rate determination (see Appendix, part 3).

A simple estimate of the relationship between the franc/dollar and the exchange rate of a basket of European currencies against the dollar shows that the latter accounts for over 80% of the fluctuations of the franc. This would suggest that most of the variance of the franc/dollar rate derives from factors that do not specifically pertain to the French economy.

Estimation of an official reaction function for the interest rate indicates that if we separate the average European interest rate from the eurodollar interest rate, the two yield significantly different coefficients. French interest rates appear to be mostly influenced by the former; indeed the coefficient of the eurodollar rate is not significantly different from zero.

It is well known that during the seventies the effective exchange rate of the dollar depreciated both in nominal and real terms (see BRANSON [1980]). A basic consequence, of course, is that the Purchasing Power Parity relation does not hold between the dollar and most of the main world currencies. The franc is no exception in that respect. Econometric tests of PPP using quarterly data for exchange rates and industrial production prices for the period 1971-1980 yield insignificant coefficients in the case of the dollar/franc exchange rate. On the contrary, however, the same relation proves quite satisfactory in the medium run when it is estimated for the franc relative to a basket of European currencies. This is shown in figure 5. At least prior to the EMS, however, the franc faced very large fluctuations which can be interpreted as an exchange rate cycle.

At the beginning of the cycle the franc is bound to European currencies by a stability agreement. A higher inflation rate progressively leads to a decline in the French competitivity and to a slowdown in growth. Then the authorities attempt to maintain activity through expansionary policies, thus leading to a trade deficit, a fall of the franc amplified by unfavorable expectations and eventual withdrawal from the exchange rate system. The authorities finally adopt a restrictive policy which brings back the trade balance into equilibrium and allows the franc to go back into the European exchange rate system.

Before 1977, this cycle functioned in a very destabilizing way, the exchange rate tending to overshoot its PPP equilibrium value. For example the franc joined the snake for the second time in 1975 at a level far too high to be sustainable over a long period. On the contrary, before the beginning of the EMS, the authorities allowed the franc to depreciate well under its equilibrium value thus keeping a comfortable margin which proved very useful in stabilizing the system.

FIGURE 5

The exchange rate of the franc relative to the European currencies*

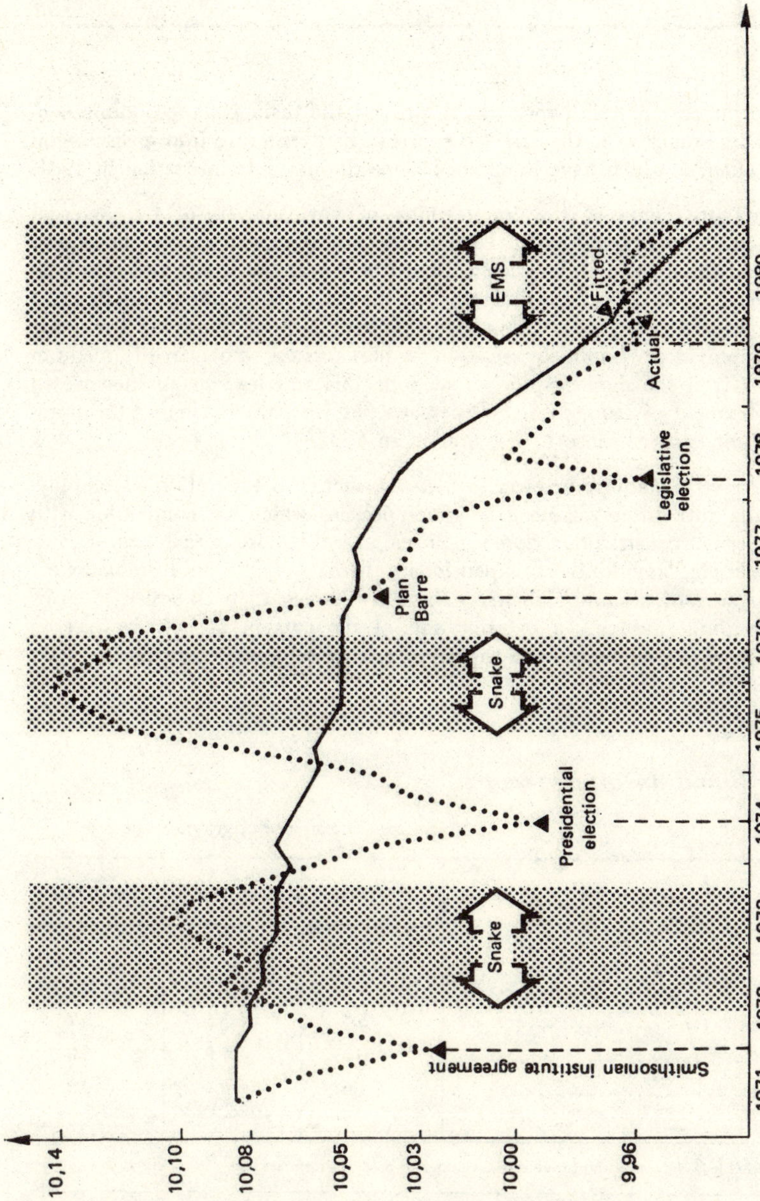

* Number of units of "European currency" per unit of franc, the dotted line represents the actual values of the exchange rate and the continuous line the value of the exchange rate as estimated by the following equation:

$$\log s = 10.14 + 0.0015\,T + 1 \sum_{i=0}^{-5} \alpha_i \left(\frac{P_e}{P_f}\right)_{-i}$$

where T is a time trend, P_f is an index of manufacturing production prices in France and P_e an index of manufacturing production prices in the main European countries.

Conclusion

The purpose of this paper was to present the main macroeconomic evolutions in France over the last ten years without entering into a discussion of the changes which have intervened since the new administration in 1981.

What are some of the implications of our analysis of the external constraints weighing on France? During the coming years the most crucial problem that the French authorities will need to face is the steady rise of unemployment. A very crude estimate of the main trends, as appearing in table 14, shows that, even if we admit a regular reduction of the hours worked, [6] total employment should decrease, or at best remain stable, in the medium term. Given the demographic projections this will lead to an increase in unemployment of around 130,000 persons per year, thus bringing the number of unemployed close to 2.7 million in 1987.

In order to stabilize or even slow down such a deterioration of employment the authorities will need to adopt policies which are compatible with the external constraints. Some policies are therefore clearly ruled out. For example, any kind of expansionary fiscal policy would immediately lead to current account deficits. The only choice then is either to grow faster without inducing a deterioration of the current account or else to create more employment with the same rate of economic growth.

TABLE 14

Growth and unemployment

(Average annual rate of growth in percent)

	1973/1967	1980/1973	1987/1981*
GDP..................................	6.1	2.7	2.5
Productivity............................	5.4	3.3	3.7
Hours.................................	− 0.8	− 1.0	− 1.0
Employment..........................	1.6	0.4	− 0.2

* 1987/1981 figures are approximate estimates of medium term trends.

Source : INSEE.

---

6. The projection of the average decline of 1% of hours over the next five years would lead weekly hours to decrease from 40.7 in 1981 to 38.3 in 1987.

The first type of policy can only be achieved through real exchange rate depreciation. The real exchange rate elasticity of the potential growth which is compatible with trade equilibrium can be evaluated as 0.7, based on our estimates of exports and imports functions. This shows that the impact of real exchange rate depreciation, however essential it may be, is limited. [7]

The discussion of wage-price adjustments also shows any nominal devaluation of the franc to have no long term effect on the real exchange rate. The EMS agreement has further prevented the French authorities from devaluing thus far as much as the widening inflation differentials of the last few years would even allow. Under such conditions real depreciation of the franc implies a reduction in unit labor costs of French manufacturing industries. [8] We have seen that the rise of unemployment has markedly reduced the growth of real wages. A further reduction in this growth, however, would lead to a decline in household purchasing power which would neither be socially acceptable nor beneficial for growth or employment. But it should be noted that the ratio of social costs to total labor costs went from 31% in 1970 to 38% in 1982. It seems necessary therefore first to stop this evolution and then to take steps to reverse it, thereby improving the competitivity of French products. This would allow for some increase in the potential growth of the French economy.

Such a policy of course requires expansionary fiscal policy (to reach potential growth), and additionally implies social spending, both of which would need to be financed through public deficits.

Policies of a different nature will then need to be adopted in order to face rising unemployment. In the long term the decisive influences on unemployment will obviously be the structural changes in French industry and in the socio-economic system. However in the short run more jobs can be created through policy actions not necessarily aiming to promote growth but to modify the demand for labor. Two examples can be given.

One of them would consist of fiscal policy measures increasing the relative cost of capital in order to induce substitution of labor for capital. In a relevant study, ARTUS, STERDYNIAK and VILLA [1980] conclude that a diminution of 5% of employers' social contributions, with compensation in the form of an 18% increase of value-added taxes on investment, would eventually lead to a rise of 10% in employment (*i.e.* 600,000 jobs in 10 years). The desirability of this type of measure of course raises many questions because of the implications for technological progress. But past evolutions (table 15) suggest some scope for the measure since the relative cost of labor has risen steadily until 1976 and was much lower in 1968.

---

7. In order to reduce unemployment by 1 million, an increase of 10% of the GDP would be needed, *i.e.* a fall of 14% of the real exchange rate.

8. The very low present level of mark-up rates does not allow a sustained reduction in production prices without a reduction in costs (see section 2).

TABLE 15

Relative cost of labor to capital in France

(Average annual growth rates in percent)

1964–1967	1968–1973	1974–1976	1977–1980
— 0.7 %	13.8 %	5.8 %	— 2.1 %

Source : INSEE.

The second measure is a continuation of the basic trend of reductions in the number of hours worked per week since 1968. This tendency had noticeably weakened in recent years because of the legal limitation of 40 hours per week. But policy decisions in the begining of 1982 have lifted this barrier and permitted further reductions to be scheduled which would lead to a 35-hour week by 1985. However attractive this next policy may be as a means of reducing unemployment, it has several serious drawbacks (see OUDIZ, RAOUL, STERDYNIAK [1979]). First, it implies an anticipated reduction in productive capacity which may induce a major reorganization of production and therefore could lead in the short run to a worsening of the current account. Second, it will need to be associated with a reduction in monthly wages unless productivity gains resulting from work reorganization prove high.

APPENDIX

All the estimates in this appendix rest on data from the quarterly national accounts, INSEE.

1. Wage and price formation

The following equations were estimated simultaneously using a Full Information Maximum Likelihood procedure :

$$\dot{W} = 1.86 + 0.066\ M\dot{W} + 0.213\ \dot{PW} - 0.451\ \log\frac{U}{V} + 0.976\ \dot{P}$$
$$\phantom{\dot{W} = }(11.9)\ (1.3)\phantom{M\dot{W}}\ (4.0)\phantom{\dot{PW}}\ (7.9)\phantom{\log\frac{U}{V}}\ (21.9)$$

$$\dot{P} = -0.163\ (MAC - MAC_{-1}) + 0.80\ \dot{TF} + 1.11\ b_1.\dot{P}_m$$
$$\phantom{\dot{P} = }(2.2)\phantom{-0.163\ (MAC - MAC_{-1})}\ (1.3)\phantom{\dot{TF}}\ (4.4)$$

$$+ 0.96\ (1 - b_1)\left(\dot{W} - \dot{PROD} + \frac{\Delta t}{1+t}\right)$$
$$(14.9)$$

Sample period: 1965-I to 1981-IV (the observations corresponding to the second and third quarters of 1968 were excluded); t-ratios in parentheses.

Lags were introduced for $\log\frac{U}{V}$ and $\dot{P}$ in the wage equation and for $\dot{TF}$, $\dot{P}_m$, $\left(\dot{W} - \dot{PROD} + \frac{\Delta t}{1+t}\right)$ in the price equation·

Mean lag of $\dot{P}$ in the $\dot{W}$ equation.................... 0.93 quarters
(1.8)

Mean lag of $\dot{P}m$ in the $\dot{P}$ equation.................. 1.15 quarters
(2.4)

Mean lag of $\left(\dot{W} - \dot{PROD} + \frac{\Delta t}{1+t}\right)$ in the $\dot{P}$ equation... 1.62 quarters
(3.7)

$\dot{W}$: Growth rate of hourly wages;

$\dot{PW}$: Growth rate of real hourly wages in public firms;

$M\dot{W}$: Growth rate of real hourly minimum wage;

$\dot{P}$: Growth rate of consumer prices;

U   : Ratio of unemployment to total labor force;

V   : Ratio of vacancies to total labor force;

MAC : Productive capacity underutilization rate;

TF   : Taxes and interest payments per unit of value added;

PRO : Growth rate of labor productivity;

$\dot{P}_m$: Growth rate of import prices;

b_1 : Average share of imports in total supply;

t : Rate of social contribution per unit of money wage.

2. Econometric analysis of trade in manufacturing

1. *Import prices*

$$\text{Log } P_m = 0.11 - 0.004 \text{ T} + 0.15 \log P_d + 0.54 \log P_c$$
$$\phantom{\text{Log } P_m = } (8.0) \quad (9.1) \qquad (1.8) \qquad\quad (8.7)$$
$$+ (1 - 0.15 - 0.54) \log (P_m)_{-1}$$

Sample period: 1970-I to 1981-IV, *t*-ratios in parentheses:

$$\text{SEE} = 1.5\%; \quad \text{D.W.} = 1.75$$

P_m : Import price of manufactured goods;
T   : Time;
P_d : Domestic production prices of manufactured goods;
P_c : Price of competitors on home markets.

2. *Export prices*

$$\text{Log } P_x = 0.45 - 0.0007 \text{ T} + 0.45 \log P_d + 0.26 \log P_{xc}$$
$$\phantom{\text{Log } P_x = } (0.5) \quad (6.7) \qquad\quad (5.3) \qquad\quad (4.7)$$
$$+ (1 - 0.45 - 0.26) \log (P_x)_{-1}$$

Sample period: 1970-I to 1981-IV, *t*-ratios in parentheses:

$$\text{SEE} = 1.3\%; \quad \text{D.W.} = 1.67$$

P_x : Export price of manufactured goods;
P_{xc} : Price of competitors on export markets.

3. *Imports*

$$\text{Log } \frac{M}{M+Q} = -1.26 - 72.44 \frac{1}{T+50} + 1.5 \text{ INV} + 0.67 \frac{1}{\text{MAC}} - 0.89 \log \frac{P_m}{P_d}$$
$$\phantom{\text{Log } \frac{M}{M+Q} = } (21.1) \quad (16.1) \qquad\quad (6.0) \qquad (1.5) \qquad\quad (8.15)$$

Sample period: 1966-I to 1981-IV:

$$\text{SEE} = 1.8\%; \quad \text{D.W.} = 1.38$$

M   : Import volume of manufactured goods;
Q   : Domestic production of manufactured goods;
INV : Share of investment plus inventory formation in total supply;
T   : Time trend.

Lags were introduced for $\frac{P_m}{P_d}$ (average lag: 2.3 quarters), and for MAC (average lag 0.7 quarters);

4. Exports

$$\text{Log } X = 5.46 + 0.96 \text{ Log DM} + 0.69 \ 10^{-4} \text{ MACA} + 1.60 \text{ Log } \frac{P_{zc}}{P_z}$$
$$\quad (65.4) \ (61.2) \qquad\qquad (1.0) \qquad\qquad\qquad (6.2)$$

Sample period: 1968-I to 1981-IV:

$$\text{SEE} = 2.7\%; \quad \text{D.W.} = 1.48$$

X : Export volume of manufactured goods;
DM : World demand of manufactured goods;
MACA : MAC — 0.0002 MAC^2.

Lags were introduced for $\frac{P_{zc}}{P_z}$ (average lag : 7.1 quarters).

3. The franc and the European currencies

1. *Short-term fluctuations of the franc:*

The following equation relates the franc/dollar rate to the franc exchange rate against a basket of European currencies (deutschemark: 40%, florin: 10%, Belgian franc: 20%, lira: 20%, pound: 10%) to the exchange rate of this same basket against the dollar :

$$\text{Log F/\$} = -9.92 - 0.0038 \text{ T} + 0.89 \text{ Log EUR/\$} + 0.32 \frac{X}{M}$$
$$\qquad\quad (48.1) \ (1.7) \qquad (8.6) \qquad\qquad (2.1)$$

Sample period: 1971-III to 1981-IV:

$$\text{SEE} = 2.3\%; \quad R^2 = 0.93; \quad \text{D.W.} = 1.7$$
$$\text{CORC Procedure: RHO} = 0.84$$
$$(9.7)$$

F/\$: Exchange rate of the franc against the dollar;
EUR/\$: Exchange rate of the European currencies basket against the dollar.

2. *Money market interest rate:*

$$\text{FR} = 9.54 + 0.15 \text{ (EUR} - \text{FR)} - 7.7 \frac{X}{M} + 0.83 \text{ ER} + 0.04 \text{ USR}$$
$$\quad (1.5) \quad (1.9) \qquad\qquad (1.3) \qquad (4.5) \qquad (0.3)$$

Sample period: 1971-III to 1980-IV

$$\text{SEE} = 0.77; \quad \text{Mean of dependent variable} = 8.82; \quad R^2 = 0.92; \quad \text{D.W.} = 1.6$$
$$\text{CORC procedure: Rho} = 0.67$$
$$(5.5)$$

FR : French money market rate;
EUR : Eurofranc interest rate; [1]
ER : Weighted European interest rate;
USR : Eurodollar rate;

---

1. The imperfect mobility between eurofranc and franc markets accounts for interest rate differentials reflecting expectations of future exchange rates.

● References

AGLIETTA M., ORLEAN A. and OUDIZ G. — (1980) "L'industrie française face aux contraintes de change", *Économie et statistique,* no. 119, February, p. 35-63.

ARTUS P., BOURNAY J., MORIN P., PACAUD A., PEYROUX C., STERDYNIAK H. and TEYSSIER R. — (1981) *METRIC, une modélisation de l'économie française,* INSEE.

ARTUS P., STERDYNIAK H. and VILLA P. — (1980) "Investissement, emploi et fiscalité", *Économie et statistique,* no. 127, November, p. 115-127.

BRANSON W. — (1980) " United States International Trade and Investment since World War II ", *in The American Economy in Transition,* ed. by FELDSTEIN M., University of Chicago Press, p. 183-257.

CATINAT M. — (1982) " Disequilibrium foundations for exports and imports ", note INSEE, service des "Programmes", August.

COUTIÈRE A. — (1979) "Le système monétaire français", *Statistique et études financières,* no. 17, p. 33-80.

DEBONNEUIL M. and STERDYNIAK H. — (1982) "Apprécier une dévaluation", *Économie et statistique,* no. 142, March, p. 41-61.

DUBOIS P. — (1980) "La rupture de 1974", *Économie et statistique,* no. 124, August, p. 3-20.

FEROLDI M., RAOUL E. and STERDYNIAK H. — (1982) "Sécurité sociale et évolution macro-économique", *Économie et statistique,* no. 143, April, p. 59-78.

MELITZ J. — (1976) "Un modèle pour la détermination du stock de monnaie et son application à la France", *Annales de l'INSEE,* no. 24 p. 41-76 et no. 25, p. 63-101.

OUDIZ G., RAOUL E. and STERDYNIAK H. — (1979) "Réduire la durée du travail, quelles conséquences?", *Économie et statistique,* no. 111, May, p. 3-17.

STERDYNIAK H. and VILLA P. — (1977) "Du côté de l'offre de monnaie", *Annales de l'INSEE,* no. 25, January-March, p. 3-62.

VILLA P., COHEN D. and ROCCA M. — (1980) "Structure de bilan et comportements des agents, le modèle DEFI", note INSEE, Service des Programmes, November.

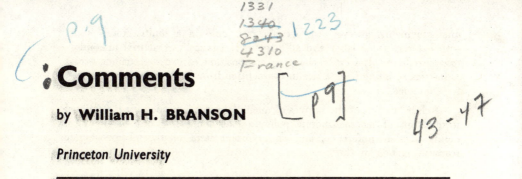

Comments

by William H. BRANSON

Princeton University

This is an excellent paper for the beginning of a conference on international aspects of macroeconomics in France, and it was a pleasure to read. The paper presents an analytical survey of economic developments in France since the early 1970s, setting the empirical framework for a discussion of the current situation, policy prospects, and directions for research. In my discussion of the paper, I would like to focus on points that might serve as themes for the conference. To some extent, in my remarks here, I will be establishing the empirical background for my later discussion of "Macroeconomic Policy in France" during the concluding round-table. There are five points that I would like to pick up in the OUDIZ and STERDYNIAK paper: (1) the steady rise in unemployment in the 1970s; (2) the neutral demand policy stance; (3) the connection between the productivity slowdown and stagflation; (4) the asymmetry between export and import price behavior; and (5) exchange rate policy. I will discuss these points in turn.

1. Unemployment since 1970

The first point to notice is the steady rise in unemployment in France since the early 1970s. In table 8 of the paper, we see that the unemployment rate has risen every year since 1969, with the single exception of a drop from 2.4 % in 1972 to 2.1 % in 1973. In 1970 the unemployment rate was 1.8 %; in 1981 it was 7.7 % and in 1982 it is undoubtedly above 8 %. This steady rise in unemployment contrasts strongly with U.S. data. To be sure, there also has been a positive trend in unemployment in the US, from under 5 % in 1969 to over 10 % in 1982. But US unemployment is sensitive to aggregate demand, and fluctuates around that trend with the business cycle, while unemployment in France seems to rise almost independently of demand conditions.

This suggests that there are different causes of unemployment in France and the US. We should expect to see a larger weight for "Keynesian" unemployment in the U.S., but a larger weight for "classical" or "structural" unemployment in France. To the extent that the French experience is typical of Europe, this would be true for Europe also.

The distinction between classical and structural unemployment is useful. Classical unemployment generally is analyzed in a one-good model with a homogeneous labor force and a rigid real wage. The basic idea is that the average economy-wide real wage is stuck above equilibrium. Structural unemployment, however, can be analyzed only in a multisectoral model with heterogeneous labor and adjustment resistance. Structural unemployment would result from a changing composition of excess demands across industries resulting from a rise in competition from the developing countries, for example.

A clear analysis of the sources of unemployment is needed for the rational formulation of macroeconomic policy. This should be one of the focal points of the conference, and an important item on the macroeconomic research agenda in Europe.

2. Demand policy in the 1970s

In any analysis of the causes of stagnation and rising unemployment, we will have at some point to ask whether demand policy has been particularly tight. This appears not to have been the case in France in the 1970s.

Consider first the stance of fiscal policy. In their table 4, Oudiz and Sterdyniak show data for public sector spending and the public sector borrowing requirement, as fractions of GDP. From 1970 to 1981, public sector spending rose from about 40 % of trend GDP to 48 %. All of this rise can be attributed to the rise of transfer payments (social security and welfare spending) from about 17 to 26 % of trend GDP. Much of this increase was matched by increasing tax revenue, however. The public sector borrowing requirement was around 0.6 % of trend GDP in the early 1970s; in 1981 it was 1.5 %. Thus the rise in transfer payments has been slightly expansionary.

Monetary policy apparently has attempted to hit targets both for interest rates and money growth, a difficult if not inconsistent policy. Oudiz and Sterdyniak argue convincingly in section III, backed up by the last section of equations in the Appendix, that the Bank of France has attempted to keep the interest rate high enough to prevent depreciation of the franc, or at least slow it down, in the face of a differential rate of inflation against Germany. Curiously, this policy has resulted in rather rapid rates of money growth, as shown in table 4. Money growth was sufficiently rapid to require application of credit restrictions to restrain it. These are indicated in table 5.

The rates of monetary growth seem high as compared with the US, the UK, or Germany. It would be interesting to have the cause-and-effect relationships between these growth rates and inflation sorted out, and the coexistence of rapid money growth and the authorities' attempts to keep interest rates relatively high remains a puzzle.

However, it is clear that monetary policy was not contractionary on the 1970s. Comparison of the data for inflation in table 2 and money growth in table 4 shows that in every year in the 1970s the M2 money stock grew faster than the GNP deflator. The CPI grew faster than the money stock only in 1980 and 1981. Thus over the decade, real balances increased substantially; by my calculation using the GNP deflator real balances increased by 92 % from 1970 to 1981. This is hardly restrictive monetary policy.

So monetary and fiscal policy, taken together, have been generally expansionary in France in the period since 1970. This would make it very difficult to argue that aggregate demand policy has caused the rise in unemployment. It also makes Keynesian unemployment before 1981 seem unlikely as a major source of the problem, and strengthens the case for classical or structural unemployment.

3. The productivity slowdow and stagflation

In their discussion of wage and price equations for France, OUDIZ and STERDYNIAK show how the productivity slowdown of the mid-1970s can explain much of the stagflation — rising unemployment and inflation — since then. The equations are discussed at the end of section II and in the first section of the Appendix.

A schematic version of these equations that brings out the major point is the following, using the paper's notation :

(1) $\dot{W} = -aU + \dot{P}$;   (2) $\dot{P} = \dot{W} - (\dot{PROD})$.

In the Appendix, the estimated value of the coefficient of $\dot{P}$ in the $\dot{W}$ equation (1) is. 0.916, close enough to unity for the example here. The solution of (1) and (2) for the « natural » rate of unemployment U* as a function of the rate of growth of productivity $(\dot{PROD})$ is

(3) $U^* = -\frac{1}{a} (\dot{PROD})$.

OUDIZ and STERDYNIAK estimated the coefficient of $(\dot{PROD})$ in equation (3) to be -2.5 (they could have made the readers' calculations easier by noting that productivity growth is measured at a quarterly rate.)

From the period 1966-1974 to 1974-1981 the growth rate of productivity fell by 3.6 percentage points, annual rate, according to the paper's data. This is a decrease of nearly 0.9 percentage points on a quarterly basis, giving a rise in the estimated " natural " rate of 2.25 percentage points. If we add this to the average 1974-1975 unemployment rate of 3.1, we get an increase to around 5.3 %, close to the numbers for 1978-1979.

Thus the productivity slowdown way have increased the " natural " rate of unemployment, shifting the short-run Phillips curve of the mid-1970s sharply to the right. This confronted macroeconomic policy-makers with a suddenly worsened trade-off, and a choice between tightening demand policy to slow the inflation or easing to fight the upward trend in unemployment. The productivity slowdown can explain 2 to 3 percentage points of the rise in French unemployment since the early 1970s.

4. Export and import price behavior

The " small-country " assumption is probably the most widely-used in trade theory. It assumes that world prices are unaffected by the country in question. In particular, this means an infinitely elastic world demand for the country's exports and world supply of its imports at exogenously-determined world prices. In this case a change in the exchange rate has no effect on the terms of trade, and the normal effect on the trade balance. It is clear from the evidence presented by OUDIZ and STERDYNIAK that France is not such a small country. The price elasticity of supply of imports to France is high, but the price elasticity of her export demand is much lower. This is a pattern that is increasingly becoming a standard model for countries whose exports are fairly concentrated but imports are more diverse. It is consistent with conventional trade theory which predicts that countries will concentrate production in their area of comparative advantage, and export these products in exchange for an entire range of world goods. We might call these countries « semi-small », with market power on the export side, but not the import side.

The easiest way to see the asymmetry in the behavior of France's trade prices is to consider a devaluation that raises competitors' prices in francs, P_c and P_{xc} in the price equations of section II of the Appendix, proportionately. The estimates say that after two quarters the import price P_m will have risen by 71 % of the devaluation, but the export price P_x will have risen by only 34 %.

The estimated equations for trade prices can be combined with the export and import demand equations to obtain implicit supply elasticities, using the log-linear formulation in BRANSON [1972] and BRANSON and KATSELI [1982]. Let e present the exchange rate, and d and s represent the price elasticities of demand and supply, respectively. Then the ratio of the changes in export and import prices to the percentage devaluation are given by

$$\dot{P}_x/e = d_x/(d_x - s_x); \quad \dot{P}_m/e = s_m/(d_m - s_m)$$

The long-run estimate of $\dot{P}_x/e$ from the Appendix is 0.37 and the estimate of d_x is — 1.6; these imply $s_x = 1.7$ for manufactured goods, a reasonable number. The long-run estimate of $\dot{P}_m/e$ is 0.78 and the estimate of d_m is — 0.89, implying that $s_m = 3.13$. Consistent with the semi-small country model, the price elasticity of supply of imports is greater than the price elasticity of demand for exports in France.

The asymmetry between the short-run adjustment of export and import prices to changes in exchange rate implies that in the short run, exchange rate fluctuations cause significant and potentially costly fluctuations in the terms of trade. For example, a 10 % devaluation yields a 3.5 % (0.071 — 0.034) deterioration in the terms of trade in two quarters. These fluctuations in the terms of trade must either be passed on to retail prices or absorbed in profit margins, generating either price or profit variance. This is one reason for the general policy objective of smoothing out exchange rate fluctuations.

5. Exchange-rate policy

OUDIZ and STERDYNIAK come out quite clearly against the use of fluctuations in the nominal exchange rate to stabilize the current account. The Appendix equations for export and import prices give only the direct effects of exchange-rate changes. The price-wage equations show that domestic prices are essentially a mark-up on wages and wages are effectively indexed ex post to the CPI. Thus exchange-rate changes pass through fairly quickly to wages and domestic prices. This means the real exchange rate is not very sensitive to changes in the nominal exchange rate.

In addition, the trade equations show fairly long lags for export quantities behind price changes (mean lag of 7 quarters) and a pronounced J-curve. Thus exchange rate fluctuations do not seem to be effective for current account stabilization, but they do tend to destabilize domestic prices.

OUDIZ and STERDYNIAK stop short of support for a policy that effectively stabilizes the real exchange rate, with a slight trend toward depreciation due to low world income elasticity for French goods (0.96). But an outside discussant need not exercise such caution. This seems to me to be the best prescription for French exchange-rate policy.

● References

BRANSON W. H. — (1972) " The Trade Effects of the 1971 Exchange Rate Realignments ", *Brookings Papers on Economic Activity*, 1972.

BRANSON W. H. and L. T. KATSELI. — (1982) " Currency Baskets and Real Effective Exchange Rates ", in M. Gersovitz *et al.* (eds), *The Theory and Experience of Economic Development*, London, George Allen and Unwin, pp. 194-214.

Comments [p.9]

by **Daniel LASKAR**

CEPREMAP

Gilles OUDIZ and Henri STERDYNIAK have written an excellent and useful overview of the French Economy during the 70's. It seems to me, however, that, in their analysis, they underestimate the role of monetary policy as a determinant of the internal situation of the country, and especially of inflation. From the examination of figure 2 which compares the evolution of the money supply growth rate and the inflation rate, they conclude that there is no obvious link between these two magnitudes. Consequently their analysis of the French inflation does not rely upon the study of the course of monetary policy but refers to the wage-price dynamics. It is actually difficult to draw definite conclusions from the examination of a graph like figure 2. We should indeed at least take into account lags which, depending on the shocks for example, may vary. However, if we look at the first part of the period under study, and then also compare France and Germany, we can bring some elements to the issue.

For in the beginning of the 70's we already observed a rise of inflation in Europe. One of the causes was the increase of the money supply in these countries. This increase was made easier by the dollar reserves inflows, which were themselves linked to the US balance of payments deficit. Monetary growth was greater than nominal income growth, and, therefore, we could qualify it as « autonomous ». In the case of France this clearly appears in table 4 (last column) of the paper, where we see a big rise of the liquidity ratio of the economy during the first years of the 70's.

While at the beginning of 1973 some countries like Germany switched to a more restrictive monetary policy, this was not the case for other countries, including France. Thus, in annual rates, money supply growth rates (M1) were very similar in these two countries in 1971 and 1972 (around 13 %), but the German rate fell to 5.3 % and 5.9 % in 1973 and 1974, while the French rate stayed at 9.9 % in 1973 and 12.6 % in 1974 (data from IFS). So, as the authors point out, whereas after 1975 the inflation rate in Germany moves back to levels close to the ones before the first oil shock, in France the inflation rate stayed at a higher level. Thus, it seems that monetary policies in these two countries allow us to understand better this difference.

This aspect is actually underlined by Stanley BLACK's paper which is also presented at this seminar. According to this paper we could say that two explanatory elements enter. The first has to do with the level of the trade-off between inflation and unemployment, which is mainly determined by the state of "labor relations". The second is related to the strength with which monetary policy, used as a stabilization tool, reacts to inflation.

While the authors of the present paper analyze the first aspect in detail, the second point does not appear. Actually they refer to existing studies which show that interest rate policy has been mostly directed at an exchange rate target. We can make two comments on that. First, the money stock does not seem to have been influenced to such an extent by external targets. Such a possible disconnection between the interest rate which is manipulated and the money stock, may probably be explained by the segmentation of French financial markets. Second, imperfect substitutability between domestic and foreign financial assets, and capital controls, should give some autonomy to domestic interest rates, which may allow them to then be partly directed at internal targets. This is consistent with the results found by BLACK, where estimated reaction functions of the monetary authorities show that the interest rate depends not only on foreign variables as the international market interest rate, but also on internal variables, as unemployment and inflation. On the other hand, the results which OUDIZ and STERDYNIAK refer to emphasize the dependence on foreign variables. More work on this point, therefore, seems to be needed.

The real wage gap and employment

Paul KRUGMAN *

* P. KRUGMAN : Professor,
Massachusetts Institut
of Technology, Cambridge,
USA. I would like to thank
Jeffrey SACHS and Charles
WYPLOSZ for helpful
comments.

The 1970's were marked by stagnant employment and steadily rising unemployment in
France and in Europe as a whole. The best
available explanation of this problem is the
emergence of a " real wage gap " — i.e., a rise
in labor costs relative to their market-clearing
levels. There are, however, some empirical
problems with this view : it fails to account
for the rise in labor's share, and it seems to
predict a much larger fall in employment than
has actually occurred. This paper suggests
that these facts can be explained if we argue
that firms have been constrained in their ability to reduce their workforce If this view
is adopted, it implies that the secular upward
trend in unemployment will continue for some
time.

Introduction

It is by now widely accepted that the problem of unemployment in Europe is not a simple matter of inadequate aggregate demand. In the United States, where Keynesian concepts still seem to work fairly well, the experience of the last nine years has been one of recession, recovery, and recession once more. In Europe, the experience has been more one of secular stagnation, a sort of slow-motion slump in which for some countries —France among them—the economy's cyclical position has seemed to grow steadily worse. In the EEC countries as a whole, the unemployment rate rose in every year from 1975 to 1980. France did even worse than others: its unemployment rate was a little below the EEC average in 1973, a little above it by 1980.

A number of authors have recently converged on the same explanation of the "European disease". In the work of BRUNO and SACHS [1981], BRANSON and ROTEMBERG [1979], MODIGLIANI and PADOA-SCHIOPPA [1978], MALINVAUD [1982], and others, the argument is that "eec-itis" is essentially classical unemployment. That is, it is the result of real wages set too high by trade union or government action. This view has gained considerable acceptance, to the point that the OECD now regularly calculates measures of the "real wage gap". The main appeal of this view is that by attributing unemployment to a real rigidity rather than a nominal one, it makes the persistence of the unemployment problem easier to understand. Keynesian unemployment depends on money illusion or misperceptions about the aggregate price level, both of which seem unlikely to have persisted this long. If the problem is instead one which arises from market power aimed at real targets, there is no necessary reason why unemployment should be self-correcting. Furthermore, the emphasis on real wage claims as the proximate cause of economic stagnation suggests a political root to the problem, one which seems plausible and in any case allows economists to pass the buck to political scientists.

The view that unemployment is the result of a real wage gap is, then, a persuasive one. If one attempts to apply simple models of classical unemployment to the data, however, several problems arise. The first problem is one of timing. By the most commonly used measure, the share of labor compensation in value added, the big push in wages in Europe was during the first half of the 1970's, with little change in the wage gap since. Yet unemployment has continued to rise. A second problem is one of magnitudes. As we will show below, simple models suggest that the effects of excessive real wages on employment should actually be substantially larger than what we have seen.

The final problem is a rather odd one. Somewhat surprisingly, the way that " real wage gaps " have usually been computed in practice—by the change in the labor share in value added—is not in fact justifiable in terms of the existing theoretical models of classical unemployment. In these models, in fact, an increase in the real wage can cause labor's share to move either way. What is more surprising, then, is that in fact the real wage increases of the early 1970s did increase labor's share so dramatically. There seems to be something wrong with both the method and the model.

The purpose of this paper is to confront these difficulties with the "real wage gap view" of unemployment, and to suggest a possible explanation. The paper is in four sections. Section 1 presents some evidence on the relationship between real wages and employment in Europe, with special emphasis on France. Section 2 presents a simple model of classical unemployment. It shows that such a model seems seriously inconsistent with the evidence presented in the previous section. In Section 3 a modified model is developed in which it is assumed that firms cannot immediately reduce their labor forces when real wages rise. I argue that this model, while still a drastically oversimplified depiction of the situation, may serve as a useful first cut at understanding the upward trend in unemployment in France and elsewhere. Finally, Section 4 discusses some important remaining puzzles.

To preview the conclusions, the analysis in this paper suggests two important modifications to the new familiar idea of attributing unemployment to a real wage gap. First, the way the real wage gap is usually calculated tends systematically to understate the actual amount real wages would have to fall to restore full employment. This understatement has been increasing over time, so that the apparent levelling off of the wage gap in Europe may be largely illusory. Second, a once-for-all increase in the wage gap tends to produce a sustained process of rising unemployment. It seems likely that for France this process is still far from completion—in other words, unless either the real wage gap is closed or something else is done, the secular rise in the unemployment rate will continue.

1 Wages and employment: A look at the data

The peculiarity of European, and especially French, macroeconomic performance in the 1970s may perhaps best be brought out by a comparison with the United States. The US has hardly been a paragon of macroeconomic success. The point is, however, that US experience still seems to make sense in a Keynesian framework modified to allow for inflationary expectations. As figure 1 shows, the US unemployment rate gyrated substantially during the 1970s. By contrast, European unemployment simply crawled upward steadily. A slightly different perspective emerges when we look at employment. Figure 2 shows rates of growth of total employment in the US, the EEC, and France: in the US employment increased substantially in almost all years; in Europe it stagnated. Once again France looks similar to the EEC average, but slightly better in this case.

A useful way to look at these figures is to ask how they fit the textbook view of macroeconomic fluctuations. Students are usually taught to view macroeconomics in terms of trend and cycles—that is, the economy has a potential output determined by productivity and the size of the labor force, around which it fluctuates in booms and slumps. On average, employment should grow at the same rate as the labor force. In a rough way the US experience in the 70's fits this view. In Europe, on the other hand, the situation looks less like trend and cycle than like trend and trend—the upward trend of the labor force and the flat or declining trend of employment.

The remarkable stability of total employment in Europe already looks like more than a coincidence. Looking at these figures, there is a compelling impression of a situation in which existing jobs are protected, but firms are unwilling to add new employees. That there is some truth to this view is confirmed by sharply rising rates of youth unemployment in Europe, and by widespread anecdotal evidence that entry into employment or young people has become very difficult. The stylized fact is that employment is frozen: no mass firings, but no large-scale hirings. Later in the paper we will present a simple theoretical model which predicts this result.

Before proceeding to models, however, we should look at what remains the best available explanation of Europes's unemployment problem: the emergence of a "real wage gap". As SACHS [1979] has documented and as is now familiar, in the period 1969-1975 there was a real wage explosion in Europe. Real wages grew at well above their earlier rates in many countries, even though declining productivity growth and worsening terms of trade made "warranted" increases less than they had been. Real compensation grew even more, because of increased social insurance charges. The obvious implication is that these increases reduced the demand for labor, accounting for the stagnation of the 1970's.

FIGURE 1

Standardized unemployment rates

(From OECD, *Economic Outlook*)

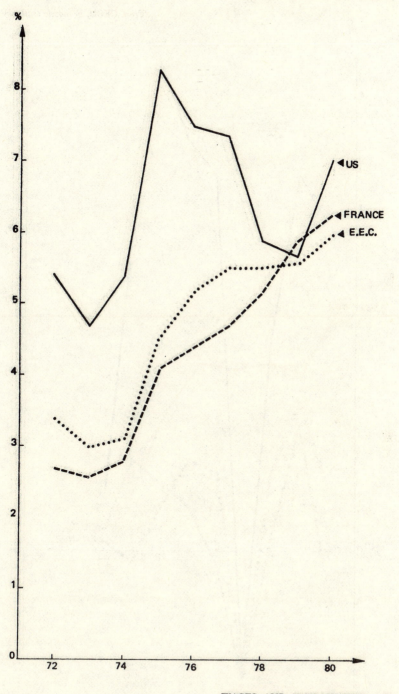

WAGES AND EMPLOYMENT   55

FIGURE 2

Rates of growth of total employment

(From OECD, *Economic Outlook*)

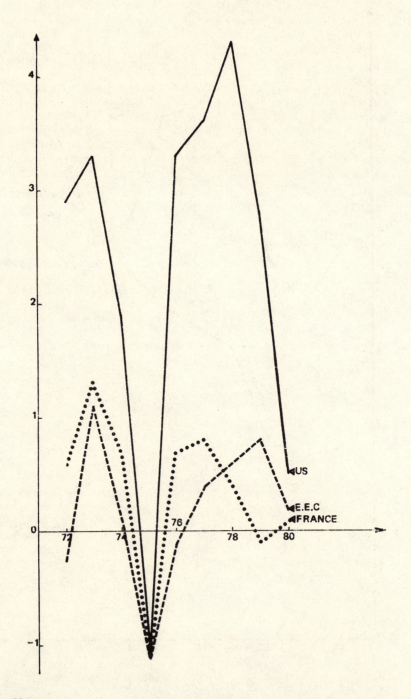

FIGURE 3

Shares of compensation in factor income

(From OECD, *National Account Statistics*)

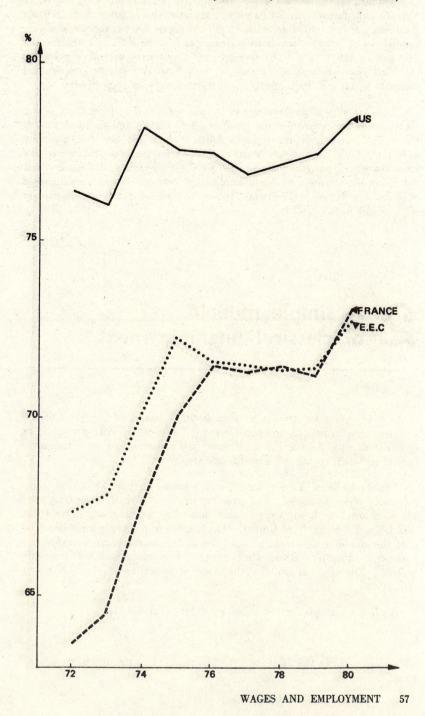

The force of this view can be illustrated by looking at figure 3. This figure shows the share of labor compensation in factor incomes in the US, France, and the EEC. This might seem a plausible way of measuring changes in the real wage relative to its market-clearing level; the OECD *Economic Outlook* measure of the "warranted" real wage is precisely that wage consistent with constant factor shares. As we will see later, this is not in fact a reliable measure; but it is still informative. As the figure shows, there was a substantial rise in labor's share both in France and in the EEC as a whole in the first half of the 1970's. The increase was about five percentage points in the EEC as a whole, about eight points in France, implying proportional increases in labor's share of eight and thirteen percent respectively.

These are very large numbers; as we will see, the surprising thing is that the surge in real wages did not produce much more unemployment than it has. Also puzzling is the timing. Labor's share did not rise gradually over the 1970's, as unemployment did. The bulk of the increase in the labor share took place in the years 1973-1976. Why, then, did employment not fall in these years, and did unemployment continue to rise after the wage push had levelled off? To attempt to answer these questions we will explore some simple formal models.

2 A simple model of classical unemployment

In this section we develop a "rock bottom" model of the effect of real wages on employment in an open economy. The model will turn out to be inconsistent with the data in some important respects, and we will need to modify it; but it constitutes a useful first step.

The model is of a "semi-large" open economy, one which has some monopoly power in trade. The economy produces a single composite good which is used both for exports and domestic consumption. Production uses labor and other, fixed factors. The balance of payments must be balanced; the size of the current account deficit is introduced as an exogenous parameter. Finally, real wages in terms of consumption goods are exogenously fixed. The model is similar to the model of protection developed in KRUGMAN [1982].

We begin with production. The production function is

(1) $$Q = Q (K, L)$$

where K is fixed in the short run; the function Q ( ) has the usual properties.

The demand for exports is decreasing in the price of domestic goods relative to foreign:

$$(2) \qquad\qquad X = X(p)$$

Real domestic expenditure, A, which we measure in terms of domestic goods, is divided between domestic goods and imports in proportions which depend on the relative price of domestic goods:

$$(3) \qquad\qquad H = 1 - \mu(p) A$$

$$(4) \qquad\qquad M/p = \mu(p) A$$

Let w_h be the real wage in terms of domestic goods, i.e., the "real product wage"; and let w_a be the wage in terms of absorption, which we will identify with consumption. Then w_a is proportional to w_h and also increasing in the relative price of domestic goods:

$$(5) \qquad\qquad w_a = w_h \cdot g(p)$$

where $\partial \log w_a / \partial \log p = \mu$.

Finally, the balance of payments must balance. Letting D be the current account deficit in terms of foreign goods, we must have

$$(6) \qquad\qquad pX + D - M = 0$$

Our model consists of six equations in eight variables: Q, X, H, M, w_a, w_h, p, D. We will treat two variables as exogenous: the level of the consumption real wage w_a and the size of the current account deficit D. The reason for taking w_a as given exogenously is, of course, because the whole point of our exercise is to analyze the impact of the creation of a "real wage gap". We treat D as exogenous partly because we want to examine the short run tradeoff between the current account and employment, partly because any adequate theory of current account determination requires an examination of intertemporal issues which lie far outside the scope of this paper.

Consider, then, the effects in our model of changes in the real wage. The first point to note is that employment is decreasing in the real *product* wage. Specifically, the proportional change in employment for a given proportional change in w_h is

$$(7) \qquad\qquad \widehat{L} = -\frac{\sigma}{1-\alpha} \widehat{w}_h$$

where σ is the elasticity of substitution between capital and labor, and α is the initial labor share. The change in output is

$$(8) \qquad\qquad \widehat{Q} = -\frac{\alpha\sigma}{1-\alpha} \widehat{w}_h \equiv -\gamma \widehat{w}_h$$

The change in the real product wage is itself in turn a function of the desired change in the real consumption wage and the change in the relative price of domestic goods:

$$(9) \qquad\qquad \widehat{w}_h = \widehat{w}_a - \mu \widehat{p}$$

To determine the change in p, we use the balance of payments condition. Assume $D = 0$ throughout; then absorption equals domestic income or

$$(10) \qquad \hat{A} = \hat{Q}$$

By (4), the change in imports is

$$(11) \qquad \hat{M} = \hat{Q} + \varepsilon_M \hat{p}$$

where ε_M is the price elasticity of import demand. The change in exports is

$$(12) \qquad \hat{X} = - \varepsilon_x \hat{p}$$

where ε_x is the elasticity of export demand.

So the balance of payments condition is

$$(13) \qquad \hat{Q} + (\varepsilon_x + \varepsilon_m - 1)\hat{p} = 0$$

Substituting back, we get the following:

$$(14) \qquad \hat{p} = \frac{\gamma}{\Delta}\, \hat{w}_a$$

$$(15) \qquad \hat{w}_h = \frac{\varepsilon_x + \varepsilon_m - 1}{\Delta}\, \hat{w}_a$$

$$(16) \qquad \hat{L} = \frac{-\sigma}{1-\alpha} \cdot \frac{\varepsilon_x + \varepsilon_M - 1}{\Delta}\, \hat{w}_a$$

$$(17) \qquad \hat{Q} = -\frac{\alpha\sigma}{1-\alpha} \frac{\varepsilon_x + \varepsilon_M - 1}{\Delta}\, \hat{w}_a$$

where $\Delta = \varepsilon_x + \varepsilon_M - 1 + \mu\gamma$.

These equations trace out the impact of an increase in the real wage in terms of consumption goods. In part such an increase is reflected in the real product wage (15); but the rising real product wage means reduced output and hence reduced demand for imports, so the relative price of domestic goods rises (14). The fact that part of the real wage increase comes via terms-of-trade improvement means that the fall in employment and output in (16) and (17) is less than it would be if we were considering a closed economy.

These are simple expressions, and we will put plausible numbers to them in a moment. First, however, let us also examine the tradeoff between output, employment, and the current account. Suppose we increase the allowed current account deficit from zero to a small quantity d (measured in foreign goods). The first effect to notice is that expenditure rises relative to output:

$$(18) \qquad \hat{A} = \hat{Q} + d/pQ$$

Imports are therefore determined by

$$(19) \qquad \hat{M} = \hat{Q} + d/pQ - \varepsilon_M \hat{p}$$

Substituting, we find the tradeoffs between the current account deficit as a proportion of GDP and the terms of trade, real product wage, employment, and output:

$$(20) \qquad \hat{p} = \frac{1 - \mu^2}{\mu \Delta} \cdot \frac{d}{pQ}$$

$$(21) \qquad \hat{w}_h = -\frac{1 - \mu^2}{\Delta} \frac{d}{pQ}$$

$$(22) \qquad \hat{L} = \frac{(1 - \mu^2)\gamma}{\alpha \Delta} \cdot \frac{d}{pQ}$$

$$(23) \qquad \hat{Q} = \frac{(1 - \mu^2)\gamma}{\Delta} \cdot \frac{d}{pQ}$$

The mechanism here is the following: by allowing an increased current account deficit, we allow an increased relative price of domestic goods. This in turn means that the product wage can fall for any given consumption wage. So the demand for labor and hence output rise.

These expressions are in terms of a few parameters, all of which have been the subject of extensive empirical investigation. "Typical" values for the elasticities would be $\sigma = 1$, $\varepsilon_z = 2$, $\varepsilon_M = 1$. The only other parameters are the labor share and the share of imports in income. Suppose we consider a "round number France" with $\alpha = 2/3$, $\mu = .25$. Then the magnitude of the "multipliers" on real wages and the current account deficit are as shown in Table 1. The left column shows the elasticities of the terms of trade, the real product wage, employment, and output with respect to the real consumption wage; the right column the semi-elasticities of the same variables with respect to the current account deficit as a share of GDP.

TABLE 1

Real wage and current account multipliers

	w_a	d/pQ
p	0.8	1.5
w_h	0.8	− 0.375
L	− 2.4	1.125
Q	− 1.6	0.75

The current account effects, while far from insignificant, do not seem especially large. France's current account balance in the 1970's ranged between − 2.3 and + 0.6 percent of GDP; in terms of these numbers, this would suggest variations of little more than three percent in employment, two percent in output.

The multipliers on the real wage are, however, very large considering the size of the real wage gap estimates of Section 1. A real wage increase of thirteen percent – the number we found for France – should produce a fall in employment of more than twenty-five percent. If one takes this model literally, the question is not why unemployment rose so much, it is why it rose so little.

But in any case, can we use the rise in labor's share to measure the real wage gap? Or to put it another way, would an increase in the real wage in this model be reflected in an equal increase in labor's share of factor incomes? The answer, which is obvious on reflection, is no. Labor's share should always rise proportionately less than the real wage, because firms will lay off workers and raise the capital-labor ratio. In fact, labor's share need not rise at all; if $\sigma = 1$, which is the most commonly cited estimate and the number we used in Table 1, the distribution of factor incomes will not change. If $\sigma > 1$ labor's share will actually fall.

Our model, then, which we created to explain unemployment, turns out to create two new problems. First, why did real wage increases get reflected in such a dramatic increase in the labor share; second, why did employment and output fall so *little*? To try to explain these, we will have to modify the model.

3 A modified model: Labor as a quasi-fixed factor

The stylized facts in France and Europe as a whole are that real labor costs increased sharply relative to their warranted level in the first half of the 1970's; but that firms did not by and large respond by firing large numbers of workers. Instead, employment remained roughly constant and the increase in labor compensation came out of profits. How can we modify the model of classical unemployment to explain this? The hypothesis which we will pursue in this section is a simple one: *firms are not free to fire workers.*

Even in pure *laissez-faire* economies, firms may be reluctant to lay off workers whenever the wage exceeds the marginal product. Issues of goodwill, the advantage of an experienced labor force, or implicit contracts may make total employment somewhat sticky. In modern Europe, however, these factors, are reinforced by legal and political constraints. A discussion of European labor market institution is beyond the scope of this paper and the competence of its author; we will simply follow out here the implications of the assumption that firms cannot fire workers.

The difference between a model with free adjustment of labor and one without is illustrated at the micro level by Figure 4.

The figure shows the determination of output, employment, and the factoral distribution of income for a representative firm with a given capital stock. On the horizontal axis is the firm's employment; on the vertical

FIGURE 4

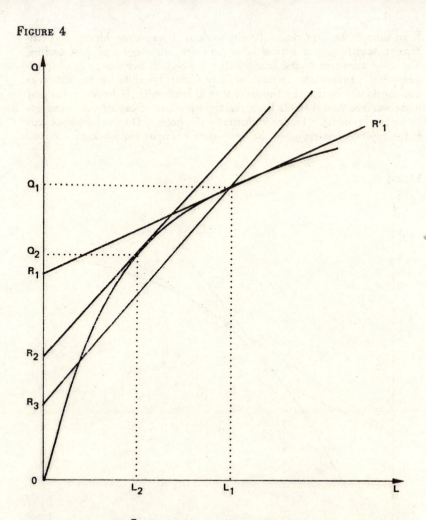

axis its output. Q $(\bar{K}, L)$ is the production function. We assume that the firm is initially in full equilibrium, facing a real product wage equal to the slope of R_1R_1'; thus employment is L_1, output is Q_1; total labor compensation is R_1Q_1 and the operating surplus is OR_1.

Now suppose the real product wage rises. If the firm were free to reduce its employment, employment and output would fall, say to L_2 and Q_2 respectively. Operating surplus would fall to OR_2, but since output has fallen as well, the capital share in income need not have fallen.

If the firm is *unable* to lay off workers, however, employment is frozen at L_1. Since the labor is there, there is no point in not using it; output remains at Q_1. Total wage payments rise to R_3Q_1, while the operating surplus falls to OR_3. In contrast to the previous case, labor's share unambiguously goes up, by the full amount of the real wage increase.

At this point the firm is out of equilibrium; the marginal cost of a worker is more than she is worth. How can the firm adjust? Over time there are two answers. One is to let the labor force shrink through attrition.

Even though the firm cannot fire its workers, it can cease hiring, and retirement, mortality, and normal labor turnover will cause a gradual decline. The other answer is capital accumulation. The firm can engage in « capital-deepening » investment to raise labor productivity while leaving the wage bill constant. Notice, by the way, that a firm which is forced to employ more workers than it wants has a marginal product of capital which exceeds its average product. Figure 5 illustrates the point. On the horizontal axis is the capital-labor ratio, on the vertical axis output per worker.

FIGURE 5

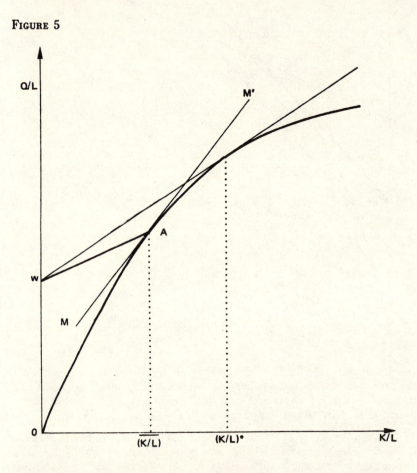

The firm pays the wage OW, but is unable to reduce its labor force to achieve the profit maximizing capital-labor ratio $(K/L)^*$. Instead, it is stuck with $(\bar{K}/L)$. The *average* return to capital is then equal to the slope of WA. But the marginal return, the return relevant for investment decisions, is the slope of the tangent line MM'. The point is that in an economy where firms are not free to change their labor forces —where labor is a "quasi-fixed" factor— average profitability will not be a very good indicator of the incentive to invest.

Let us turn next from micro to macro. Suppose the economy consists of many firms like the representative firm just described. Then the economy-

wide behavior of employment after a real wage increase will be similar to
that of a single firm with excess labor. There will be some blurring of
the results, if only because different firms will have different experiences :
some firms will face such favorable conditions that they want to add to their
employment in spite of its cost. On the other hand, a situation where most
firms would like to reduce their labor forces tends to reduce even this flexibility. Firms will be reluctant to hire workers if they cannot fire them if
conditions change. Also, workers will be reluctant to leave jobs if there
is little hiring elsewhere, so that turnover and the ability of firms to adjust
employment through attrition will decline.

The end result should be a path of employment something like that
illustrated in Figure 6. On the vertical axis are logarithms of total labor
force and employment; on the horizontal axis time. At time t_0, we suppose,
there is a once-for-all increase in real wages relative to their previous long-run
trend. The initial result is to put firms in the disequilibrium situation of
Figure 4. Over time, firms reduce the gap between wage and marginal
product through a combination of attrition and capital-deepening; employment slowly declines. At some point, say t_1, firms are no longer stuck
with surplus labor, and employment growth resumes; it does so, however,
at a slower rate than before the initial wage push, because firms have substituted into more capital-intensive methods of production.

FIGURE 6

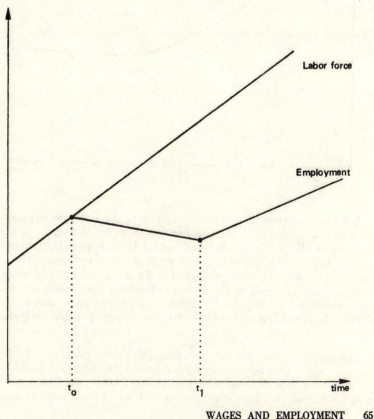

The unemployment rate may be measured by the vertical distance between the labor force path and the employment path; it rises steadily during the initial adjustment period, and indeed continues to rise, although more slowly, even after employment growth resumes.

What about the distribution of income? Consider Figure 4 again. The initial effect of the real wage push is a rise in labor's share. As firms raise the capital labor ratio by increasing the numerator and reducing the denominator, the share will fall again—probably (if $\sigma \approx 1$) to close to its original level. The path is illustrated in Figure 7.

FIGURE 7

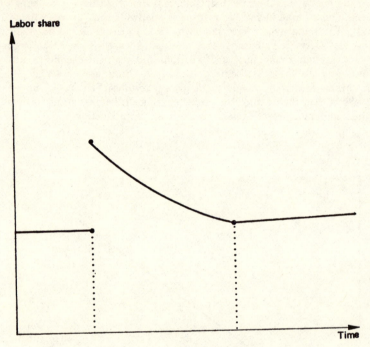

If we now attempt to relate this analysis to the European experience, two main points stand out. First, as discussed in the last section, the potential employment effects of real wage increases of the size actually experienced are very large; the implication is that such countries as France have only partially adjusted. In terms of Figure 6, France is only part of the way between t_0 and t_1. Second, the decline in the labor share which the model predicts has not yet happened. An obvious explanation is that the gap between the actual real wage and the wage consistent with full employment has continued to rise.

The models we have laid out allow us in principle to calculate this "true" real wage gap. That is, we can calculate how much real wages would have to fall to eliminate the disequilibrium between firms' actual and desired labor forces, and then how much further they would have to fall to induce firms to absorb the unemployed. Table 2 presents an example of such a calculation. It is a "hypothetical" calculation for France —"hypothetical" because it is based on a number of *ad hoc* assumptions. First, 1972 is taken as a base, both for the labor share and for the "full-employment unemployment rate". Second, it is assumed that increased employment would mean a simple movement of equivalent workers from the pool of unemployed to the employed— *i.e.*, no differences in quality, and no changes in the labor from "additional worker": or "discouraged worker" effects. Finally, the calculation is based on the assumed parameters used in Table 1, above.

Given these "ad hockeries", the numbers should not be taken too seriously. The general suggestion of a large and growing real wage gap, however, is probably right. Again, real wage gaps of the size indicated can produce much larger falls in employment than France has seen; so the table suggests that the secular rise in the unemployment rate has far from ended.

TABLE 2 :

The real wage gap in France : a hypothetical calculation

	% excess in labor share	% additional wage cut to restore full employment	Total real wage gap
1972...............................			
1973...............................	1.3	0	1.2
1974...............................	6	0	6
1975...............................	10	0.6	10.7
1976...............................	12.2	0.7	13.1
1977...............................	11.9	0.8	12.9
1978...............................	12.2	1.1	13.5
1979...............................	11.9	1.4	13.5
1980...............................	14.6	1.6	16.4

4 Some caveats

The model of European employment problems presented here could hardly be simpler. Real wages were exogenously raised above their market-clearing level; firms were not free to lay off workers. The result was, I have argued, a secular upward trend in unemployment, with the burden disproportionately falling on those just entering the labor force.

A model this simple must be oversimplified; and it is. There are three objections which are immediately apparent. One is not serious; one is serious and raises an important puzzle; one is serious and touches on a deep mystery.

The first objection is the assumption in our analysis of marginal cost pricing. The manufacturing sector in Europe, as everywhere, is typically inhabited by oligopolists rather than pure competitors. Some sort of markup pricing might, therefore, be more realistic than what we have used. In qualitative terms, however, this would not change the results—for example, MODIGLIANI and PADOA-SCHIOPPA (1980) use a markup pricing equation, yet get results similar to ours.

A much more serious question is how to reconcile a model of classical unemployment and excess labor with the very short-run behavior of prices and output in Europe. European business cycles and the inertia of inflation have been much less apparent than in the U.S., but they have been there; why should firms vary their output at all if labor is a quasi-fixed factor? It seems that, in spite of our emphasis on real factors, there is still some kind of nominal rigidity present. Until this rigidity is convincingly modelled, the classical unemployment view of Europe's problems will rest on a shaky foundation.

Finally, and most disturbingly, this model —like most analyses— does not explain why the real wage push and the rise in unemployment were accompanied by a slowdown in productivity growth. If anything, productivity growth should have accelerated, as firms switched their investment from capital widening to capital deepening. The approach taken in this paper amounts to implicitly assuming that the rate of growth of total factor productivity just exogenously slowed down—the moral equivalent of an oil price increase. This is unsatisfactory; the coincidence is too strong. A personal guess is that the productivity slowdown and the real wage surge were both symptoms of an underlying sea change in attitudes: a politicization of economic relations. But this is pure speculation, reaching beyond what economists —or anybody— know how to model.

In spite of the objections, one hopes that the analysis here provides a useful way of interpreting Europe's employment problem. The main message of this paper is that this problem is even worse than it appears at first sight; that unless something fundamental is changed, we can expect the upward trend in unemployment to continue.

• References

Branson W. and J. Rotemberg. — [1980] "International Adjustment with Rigid Wages", *European Economic Review*, Dec.

Bruno M. and J. Sachs, — [1981] "Supply versus Demand Approaches to the Problem of Stagflation", *Weltwirtschaftliches Archiv*.

Krugman P. — [1980] "The Macroeconomics of Protection with a Floating Exchange Rate", in K. Brunner and L. Meltzer, eds., *Monetary Regimes and Protectionism*, North-Holland.

Malinvaud E. — "Wages and Unemployment", *Economic Journal*, March.

Modigliani F. and T. Padoa-Schioppa. — [1978] "The Management of an Open Economy with '100 % plus' Indexation", *Princeton Essays in International Finance*, n° 130.

Sachs J. — [1979] "Wages, Profits, and Macroeconomic Adjustment: a Comparative Study", (1979/2) *Brookings Papers on Economic Activity*.

Comments [p51]

by **Willem H. BUITER**

London School of Economics and NBER

My comments can be divided into comments on KRUGMAN's paper and comments inspired by KRUGMAN's paper. The former category contains a brief diagrammatic summary of KRUGMAN's analysis, some comments on «irreversible» employment and labour's share and a refutation of the proposition that in KRUGMAN's model firms would accumulate capital in response to an increase in the wage rate. The second category contains a discussion of the highly unfortunate real wage gap measures published by the OECD and the EEC and some thoughts on the need to « socialize » investment in a socialist economy.

1. A diagrammatic summary of Krugman's paper

The formal model of KRUGMAN can be represented in the simple diagram drawn below (fig. 1).

FIGURE 1

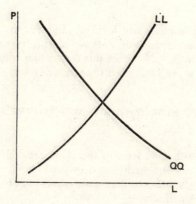

In the case where employment is determined as the (notional) demand for labour by competitive firms, equations (1) and (2) summarize the analysis. K is the capital stock, L employment, w_a the real consumption wage, Q (K, L) the production function, $w_h \equiv \dfrac{w_a}{g\,(p)}$ the real product wage; p the terms of trade, X exports, μ the share of imports in domestic absorption and D the exogenous current account deficit.

$$(1) \qquad Q_L(K, L) = \frac{w_a}{g\,(p)} \qquad\qquad\qquad (LL)$$

$$(2) \qquad Q\,(K, L) = \frac{X(p)}{\mu\,(p)} + (1 - \mu\,(p)) \frac{D}{p\mu\,(p)} \qquad (QQ)$$

Equation (1) is the labour market «equilibrium» schedule. Equation (2) represents equilibrium in the market for domestic output, given an exogenous trade balance disequilibrium.

Equations (1) and (2) can each be solved for L as follows:

$$(1') \qquad L = f\,(K, w_a, p) \qquad\qquad\qquad (LL)$$

$$f_k = \frac{-Q_{LK}}{Q_{LL}} > 0\,; \quad f_{w_a} = \frac{1}{g\,Q_{LL}} < 0\,; \quad f_p = \frac{-w_h}{Q_{LL}}\frac{\mu}{p} > 0.$$

$$(2') \qquad L = g\,(K, p, D) \qquad\qquad\qquad (QQ)$$

$$g_K = \frac{-Q_K}{Q_L} < 0\,; \quad g_p = \frac{X'}{\mu} - \left(\frac{pX+D}{p\mu^2}\right) - \frac{(1-\mu)\,D}{p^2\,\mu} < 0 \text{ if } D \simeq 0\,;$$

$$g_D = \frac{1 - \mu\,(p)}{p\,\mu\,(p)\,Q_L} > 0.$$

KRUGMAN's comparative statics are easily verified from figure 2. An increase in the workers' real reservation wage reduces employment and improves the terms of trade. An increase in the exogenous deficit permits a higher level of employment and improved terms of trade. A larger capital stock worsens the terms of trade and has an ambiguous effect on employment.

The case where labour can't be fired is represented by replacing (1) by:

$$(3) \qquad\qquad\qquad L \geqq L$$

L is the historically predetermined level of employment. If this constraint is binding, LL becomes vertical and does not shift in response to an increase in w_a or a reduction in K. Note that this means that when labour is a fixed factor, an increase in w_a will not affect the terms of trade.

2. "Irreversible" employment and labour's share in national income

KRUGMAN assumes that, at least in the short run, labour can't be fired. ׃labour on the payroll is actually used in production, neither output nor employment will fall when the workers' reservation wage w_a rises and labour's share will increase dramatically.

In Western Europe it is clearly inappropriate to treat labour as a costlessly variable input. The case analysed by KRUGMAN is the simplest and most extreme form of costs-of-employment adjustment. More satisfactory dynamic models of internal adjustment costs of capital and indeed of labour (ARROW [1960], LUCAS [1967], GOULD [1968], SARGENT [1978]) are available, that would permit KRUGMAN's short-run analysis to be embedded in a longer-run adjustment process.

FIGURE 2

Effect of an increase in w_a

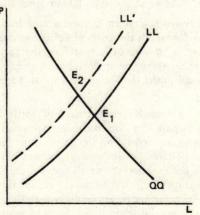

Effect of an increase in D

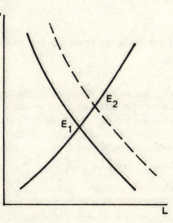

Effect of an increase in K

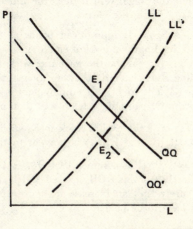

Even if employment cannot be reduced in the short run, hours per man can be reduced, causing output and output per worker to decline. Another form of « adjustment » is through firms going out of business altogether, something that becomes more likely when labour shedding is difficult.

Finally, there is, even in Western European countries, a sizeable sector of mainly small firms for which the costs of firing are much lower than for the larger firms. Even in the short run therefore, the aggregate economy is likely to experience some reduction in man-hours, employment and output in response to real wage push; the thrust of KRUGMAN'S model is, however, likely to be correct.

In the presence of irreversible employment or costly lay-offs, the firm's employment decision is part of a non-trivial intertemporal optimization programme. Current decisions depend on the entire future path of output and input prices. The « notional » competitive demand for labour given by Q_L (K, L) $= w_h$ does not describe the firm's optimal employment rule even when the « no-layoffs » constraint is not binding. If capital stock adjustment is costly too, this provides a further reason (additional to those considered in the next section) why it will not be optimal for firms to respond to an increase in the real wage by investing in additional capital in order to raise the marginal product of labour.

3. Capital deepening as a response to excess labour after a wage increase

I have great difficulty following KRUGMAN'S demonstration that firms may wish to accumulate capital after an increase in the real wage renders binding the constraint that labour can't be fired. First there is the technical problem of determining the scale of firms. If the production function Q (K, L) is linear homogeneous in K and L the (unconstrained) optimal size of the firm is indeterminate. Only the optimal $\frac{L}{K}$ is determinate. In the early part of the analysis KRUGMAN takes K as fixed. This allows a determinate (unconstrained) optimal choice of L. In the wage push exercise, L is treated as fixed and K becomes the choice variable. This convenient switch does not really solve the scale indeterminancy problem, however. If K is a choice variable and the wage were to fall, the indeterminancy of firm size re-emerges.

Consider KRUGMAN'S figure 1, reproduced below as figure 3. With K given at $\bar{K}$ the unconstrained optimal level of employment when the wage rate is represented by $R_1R'_1$ is L_1. When the wage increases, as indicated by the steeper slope of the line $R_3R'_3$ and $R_2R'_2$, the unconstrained optimal level of employment (given $\bar{K}$) falls to L_2. If employment is constrained to stay at L_1, profits decline from OR_1 to OR_3. KRUGMAN then proposes that firms, treating L as fixed at L_1, raise the capital stock to $\bar{\bar{K}}$, such that $R_4R'_4$ (which has the same slope as $R_2R'_2$ and $R_3R'_3$) is tangent to the new production function Q $(\bar{\bar{K}}, L)$ at L = L_1. (It is assumed that $Q_{KL} > O$; constant returns ensures $Q_{KL} \geqslant 0$). Clearly «profits» OR_4 exceed OR_3. But the increase in «profits» $OR_4 - OR_3$ surely isn't an increase in «pure» profits. The additional capital services have to be paid for.

The source of KRUGMAN's error is his failure to consider the cost of capital. To avoid the scale indeterminancy problem I shall assume in what follows that the production function has decreasing returns to K and L.

FIGURE 3

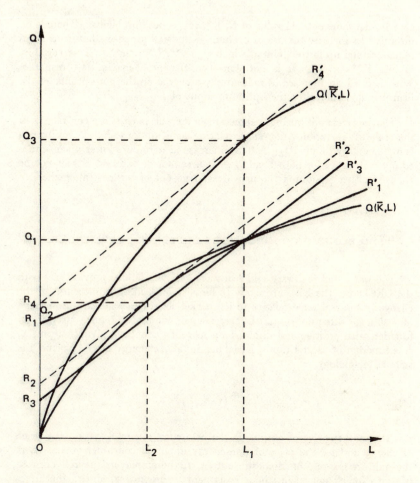

Consider a competitive firm which rents capital at a real rental rate ρ^* and hires labour at a real wage w^*. The first-order conditions are:

$$Q_K (K, L) = \rho^*$$

$$Q_L (K, L) < w^*$$

Let the solution with ρ^* and w^* be K* and L*. Now consider an increase in the wage to w^{**} with ρ constant at ρ^*. The «normal» response is a new equilibrium solution (K**, L**) with K** < K* and L** < L*. If labour can't be fired, the new solution is:

$$Q_K (K^*, L^*) = \rho^*$$

$$Q_L (K^*, L^*) < w^{**}$$

Clearly, the same optimal value of K, K*, solves both problems. There is no incentive to increase the use of capital. KRUGMAN proposes that firms accumulate capital up to the point at which $Q_L (K^{**}, L^*) = w^{**}$. This certainly implies K** > K*. It is not, however, the profit-maximizing response. With L fixed an increase in w is simply a charge on the pure profits of the firm. It does not alter the optimum input of K.

The «normal» optimizing response to an increase in costs is a contraction in the scale of operations, not an expansion as KRUGMAN argues. With two complementary inputs ($Q_{LK} > 0$) an increase in w implies lower unconstrained optimal values for both K and L. If L cannot be reduced K will not be changed either (assuming the firm doesn't go out of business altogether).

4. "The economic foundations of real wage gap measures"

The warranted real wage and real wage gap calculations provided by both the OECD and the EEC are likely to be very misleading as measures of the change in the real wage relative to its market-clearing level, *i.e.* as a measure of real wage disequilibrium. Consider a non-increasing returns production function with positive and diminishing marginal products, giving output, Y, as a function of capital input, K, labour input, L, energy input, E, and the state of technology, τ.

(4) $$Y = F (\tau, K, L, E)$$

p is the market price of output, w the before-tax money wage, p_E the price of energy and p_m the price of non-energy imported consumer goods. t_i is the indirect tax rate on domestic output, t_e the employers' payroll tax rate (a proxy for all non-wage labour costs paid by employers) and t_w the direct tax rate on labour income.

The first-order conditions for the competitive, profit-maximizing demands for labour and energy, given K, are :

(5*a*) $$F_L (\tau, K, L, E) = \frac{w (1 + t_e)}{p (1 - t_i)}$$

(5*b*) $$F_E (\tau, K, L, E) = \frac{p_E}{p (1 - t_i)}$$

Solving (5b) for E as a function of τ, K, L and $\dfrac{p_E}{p\,(1-t_i)}$ and substituting the resulting expression into (5a) yields

(6)
$$F_L\left(\tau, K, L, \Psi\left(\tau, K, L, \frac{p_E}{p\,(1-t_i)}\right)\right) = \frac{w\,(1+t_e)}{p\,(1-t_i)}$$

$$\text{where } \Psi_1 = -\frac{F_{E\tau}}{F_{EE}}$$

$$\Psi_2 = -\frac{F_{EK}}{F_{EE}}$$

$$\Psi_3 = -\frac{F_{EL}}{F_{EE}}$$

$$\Psi_4 = \frac{1}{F_{EE}}$$

So the proportional rate of change of money wages consistent with a constant demand for labour is (approximately) given by :

(7)
$$\widehat{w} = \widehat{p} - (dt_e + dt_i) + \left(\varepsilon_{L\tau} - \frac{\varepsilon_{LE}\,\varepsilon_{E\tau}}{\varepsilon_{EE}}\right)\widehat{\tau} + \left(\varepsilon_{LK} - \frac{\varepsilon_{LE}\,\varepsilon_{LK}}{\varepsilon_{EE}}\right)\widehat{K}$$

$$+ \frac{\varepsilon_{LE}}{\varepsilon_{EE}}\left(\widehat{\frac{p_E}{p\,(1-t_i)}}\right)$$

where $\varepsilon_{\ell'_m} \equiv \dfrac{mF_{\ell'_m}}{F_{\ell'}}$, the elasticity of the marginal productivity of ℓ with respect to m. $\widehat{w}$ may be called the (competitive) constant-employment warranted rate of growth of money wages.

The expression

$$\left(\varepsilon_{L\tau} - \frac{\varepsilon_{LE}\,\varepsilon_{E\tau}}{\varepsilon_{EE}}\right)\widehat{\tau} + \left(\varepsilon_{LK} - \frac{\varepsilon_{LE}\,\varepsilon_{LK}}{\varepsilon_{EE}}\right)\widehat{K}$$

measures the proportional change in the *marginal productivity* of labour due to technical change and capital accumulation at a *given* level employment. This may well be a far cry from the proportional change in the *average* productivity of labour measured at *actual* (and in general distinct) levels of employment, which is the input into the real wage gap calculations. As KRUGMAN points out, in a two-factor capital-labour production function with a unit elasticity of substitution, average productivity rises when employment falls in such a way that with marginal productivity pricing of factors labour's share will always be constant. A less than unitary elasticity of substitution is required for an increase in the real wage to result in an increased real wage gap, as measured by the EEC and the OECD.

Unless the production function is "separable" in energy such that $F_{LE} = 0$ and $\varepsilon_{LE} = 0$, changes in the « real » price of energy will affect $\widehat{w}$ in (7). If, as seems plausible, $\varepsilon_{LE} > 0$ then an increase in the real price of energy lowers the constant-employment warranted rate of growth of money wages. Let w_h be the real product wage (at market prices) and w_a the real consumption wage (before income tax).

(8a)
$$w_h \equiv \frac{w}{p}$$

(8b)
$$w_a = \frac{w}{p^\alpha\, p_E^\beta\, Pm^{1-\alpha-\beta}} \qquad 0 < \alpha, \beta, \quad 1 - \alpha - \beta \leqslant 1$$

α is the share of domestic output in consumption, β the share of energy and $1 - \alpha - \beta$ the share of non-energy imports. If energy is produced domestically, output Y refers just to non-energy output and L and K to non-energy sector employment and capital stock respectively. It follows immediately that the (competitive) constant-employment warranted rate of growth of the real product wage, $\hat{w}_h$, and the (competitive) constant-employment warranted rate of growth of the real consumption wage, $\hat{w}_a$, are [1]:

$$(9a) \quad \hat{w}_h \equiv \hat{w} - \hat{p} = -(dt_e + dt_i) + \left(\varepsilon_{L\tau} - \frac{\varepsilon_{LE}\,\varepsilon_{E\tau}}{\varepsilon_{EE}}\right)\hat{\tau} + \left(\varepsilon_{LK} - \frac{\varepsilon_{LE}\,\varepsilon_{EK}}{\varepsilon_{EE}}\right)\hat{K}$$

$$+ \frac{\varepsilon_{LE}}{\varepsilon_{EE}}\left(\frac{\hat{p}_E}{p\,(1 - t_i)}\right)$$

$$(9b) \quad \hat{w}_a = \hat{w} - \alpha\hat{p} - \beta\hat{p}_E - (1 - \alpha - \beta)\,\hat{p}_m = (1 - \alpha)\,(\hat{p} - \hat{p}_m) + \beta(\hat{p}_m - \hat{p}_E)$$

$$- (dt_e + dt_i)$$

$$+ \left(\varepsilon_{L\tau} - \frac{\varepsilon_{LE}\varepsilon\,\varepsilon_{E\tau}}{\varepsilon_{EE}}\right)\hat{\tau} + \left(\varepsilon_{LK} - \frac{\varepsilon_{LE}\,\varepsilon_{EK}}{\varepsilon_{EE}}\right)\hat{K} + \frac{\varepsilon_{LE}}{\varepsilon_{EE}}\left(\frac{\hat{p}_E}{p\,(1 - t_i)}\right)$$

The constant-employment warranted rate of growth of wages only considers labour demand. To obtain the (competitive) full employment warranted rate of growth of wages both demand and supply (including labour force growth) must be considered.

Let labour supply be a non-decreasing function of the after-tax real consumption wage, *i.e.* :

$$(10a) \qquad \frac{w\,(1 - t_w)}{p^\alpha\,p_E^\beta\,p_m^{1 - \alpha - \beta}} = h\,(Le^{-nt}) \quad h' \geqslant 0$$

Note that this implies :

$$(10b) \qquad \hat{L} = n \qquad \text{when } h' = + \infty$$

Labour force growth is assumed to occur at a proportional rate n. Competitive equilibrium in the labour market is characterized by

$$(11) \qquad w = \frac{p\,(1 - t_i)}{(1 + t_e)}\,F_L\left(\tau, K, L, \Psi\left(\tau, K, L, \frac{p_E}{p\,(1 - t_i)}\right)\right)$$

$$= \frac{p^\alpha\,p_E^\beta\,p_M^{(1 - \alpha - \beta)}}{1 - t_w}\,h\,(Le^{-nt})$$

When L is variable, equation (7) becomes :

$$(7') \qquad \hat{w} = \hat{p} - (dt_e + dt_i) + \left[\varepsilon_{L\tau} - \frac{\varepsilon_{LE}\,\varepsilon_{E\tau}}{\varepsilon_{EE}}\right]\hat{\tau} + \left[\varepsilon_{LK} - \frac{\varepsilon_{LE}\,\varepsilon_{EK}}{\varepsilon_{EE}}\right]\hat{K}$$

$$+ \frac{\varepsilon_{LE}}{\varepsilon_{EE}}\left[\frac{\hat{p}_E}{p\,(1 - t_i)}\right] + \left[\varepsilon_{LL} - \frac{\varepsilon_{LE}\varepsilon\,\varepsilon_{EL}}{\varepsilon_{EE}}\right]\hat{L}$$

78

The equilibrium proportional change in employment is (for $h' < +\infty$) :

$$(12) \quad \hat{L} = -\Omega(1-\alpha)(\hat{p}-\hat{p}_m) - \Omega\beta(\hat{p}_m-\hat{p}_E) + \Omega(dt_i + dt_w + dt_e)$$

$$-\Omega\left[\varepsilon_{L\tau} - \frac{\varepsilon_{LE}\,\varepsilon_{E\tau}}{\varepsilon_{EE}}\right]\hat{\tau} - \Omega\left[\varepsilon_{LK} - \frac{\varepsilon_{LE}\,\varepsilon_{EK}}{\varepsilon_{EE}}\right]\hat{K} - \Omega\frac{\varepsilon_{LE}}{\varepsilon_{EE}}\left[\frac{\hat{p}_E}{p\,(1-t_i)}\right]$$

$$-\Omega\frac{h'Le^{-nt}}{h}\,n$$

where :

$$\Omega = \left[\varepsilon_{LL} - \frac{\varepsilon_{LE}\,\varepsilon_{EL}}{\varepsilon_{EE}} - \frac{Le^{-nt}\,h'}{h}\right]^{-1}$$

If we are willing to make the usual assumption that $\varepsilon_{LL} - \frac{\varepsilon_{LE}\,\varepsilon_{EL}}{\varepsilon_{EE}} < 0$, then $\Omega < 0$. Substituting (13) into (7') we obtain the competitive full employment warranted rate of growth of the money wage rate. Two special cases are of some interest.

a. « Real wage resistance ». This is the case where $h' = 0$ (a horizontal labour supply schedule whose position is unaffected by labour force growth). For this case we have

$$(14\,a) \qquad \hat{w} = \hat{p} + dt_w - (1-\alpha)(\hat{p}-\hat{p}_m) - \beta(\hat{p}_m-\hat{p}_E)$$

$$(14\,b) \qquad \hat{w}_h = dt_w - (1-\alpha)(\hat{p}-\hat{p}_m) - \beta(\hat{p}_m-\hat{p}_E)$$

$$(14\,c) \qquad \hat{w}_a = dt_w$$

b. Perfectly inelastic labour supply; $\hat{L} = n$. In this case

$$(15) \qquad \hat{w} = \hat{p} - (dt_e + dt_i) + \left(\varepsilon_{L\tau} - \frac{\varepsilon_{LE}\,\varepsilon_{E\tau}}{\varepsilon_{EE}}\right)\hat{\tau} + \left(\varepsilon_{LK} - \frac{\varepsilon_{LE}\,\varepsilon_{EK}}{\varepsilon_{EE}}\right)\hat{K}$$

$$+ \frac{\varepsilon_{LE}}{\varepsilon_{EE}}\left(\frac{\hat{p}_E}{p\,(1-t_i)}\right) + \left(\varepsilon_{LL} - \frac{\varepsilon_{LE}\,\varepsilon_{EL}}{\varepsilon_{EE}}\right)n$$

5. The socialisation of investment

Socialism, in most of its incarnations, is inimical to private profit. Buoyant private capital formation presupposes that the private owners of the means of production be capable of appropriating a satisfactory share of value added in the production process. The rational private response to policies

---

1. The constant-employment warranted rate of growth of the value added wage — the money wage deflated by the price of value added (or GDP deflator) — is given by
$$\hat{w} - [(1+\eta)\hat{p} - \eta\,\hat{p}_E] \text{ where } \eta = \frac{Ep_E}{pY - Ep_E}.$$

aimed at reducing the private returns to investment is a « private investment strike ». The rational government response to a private investment strike is for the public sector to take over the task of accumulating real capital. Very high marginal tax rates on « unearned » income and other charges on private profit will eliminate the inequalities associated with private ownership of the means of production only by reducing the rate of capital formation. Animal spirits must be fed. The necessity to plan and control both the size and composition of a nation's investment programme places a serious burden on socialist governments. The temptation to go for « redistributional » socialism alone, before an alternative intertemporal allocation mechanism has been put into place is strong, because the incentive, information and administrative problems involved in a socialized investment strategy are so formidable. The consequence of giving in is economic decline in a matter of years.

It will be interesting to watch how the various socialist experiments in Western Europe attempt to solve the accumulation problem.

● References

Arrow K. J. — (1960) "Optimal Capital Policy with Irreversible Investment", in *Value, Capital and Growth*, J.N. Wolfe ed., p. 1-19.

Gould J. P. — (1968) "Adjustment Costs in the Theory of Investment of the Firm", *Review of Economic Studies*, 35, p. 47-55.

Lucas R. E. — (1967) "Adjustment Costs and the Theory of Supply", *Journal of Political Econony*, 75, p. 321-334.

Sargent T. J. — (1978) "Estimation of Dynamic Labour Demand Schedules under Rational Expectations", *Journal of Political Economy*, 86, p. 1009-1044.

p.51

Comments [p57]

by **Edmond MALINVAUD**

INSEE, Paris

Paul KRUGMAN makes a good point in the second part of his paper. But I find it difficult to accept the first part and, on the whole, I have a different perception of the French real wage gap problem from his.

It is true that in France firms may not feel free to lay off workers, although such an action is not forbidden, often occurs and was more quickly adopted after the second than after the first oil shock. In the case of an autonomous increase of real wages, forced unwillingness to fire workers will have two consequences that are well established in section 3 of the paper : the labor's share of income will rise more than it would otherwise do, some firms will be induced to engage in « capital-deepening » investment.

I should say, however, that KRUGMAN's analysis of this phenomenon is not complete, or rather that his analysis makes two implicit assumptions that are not realistic. The first one, on which I shall come back later, requires that firms perceive no constraint on their sales; the second one concerns the reaction of the real cost of capital.

The argument for figures 3 and 4 assumes that, at least by time t_1 if not before, this cost has been adapted to the new real wage, so that a point on the price frontier of the production function occurs. If it is more realistic to consider that the cost of capital remains too high with respect to the new level of the labor cost, then the type of analysis developed in the paper would lead to the conclusion that firms ought to progressively go out of business at the speed imposed by labor turnover, at least if returns to scale are constant.

But I must probably concentrate my comments on the consequences drawn from the model of section 2. Let me first assume, as is done in this section, that a pure situation of classical unemployment prevails.

I am quite astonished by the application made by Paul KRUGMAN of his formulas : as a quick look at equations (16) and (22) immediately shows that the desired change in employment is almost proportional to the elasticity of substitution of the production function ; the value 1 is taken as typical for this elasticity, thus explaining the figures in table 1, from which the conclusion is drawn that the « employment gap » has been much smaller in France than it should have been. But equations (7) and (8) assume that the volume of capital is being held constant. Moreover, as I shall argue later, one can hardly speak of a French real wage gap before 1974; hence, for the comparison made in the paper, one should refer to a short-term elasticity of substitution, which is probably closer to zero than to one, so that it is understandable that real wage increases got reflected in a labor share increase. (It would be interesting to make computations for a putty-clay technology and to study under which conditions a one-shot increase in real wage induces a progressive increase in unemployment).

The main question raised by the paper is, however, to know whether one can properly deal with the actual relation between real wage and employment while sticking to the assumption that firms perceive no constraint on their sales. Common observation suggests rather the contrary. Insufficient demand for their output remains today the main reason why firms do not expand production, so that it seems, at first sight, that Keynesian unemployment (plus a limitation on labor lay-off) prevails rather than classical unemployment. If such is the case, high wages ought not to be taken as responsible for unemployment.

I have argued elsewhere that we do not seem to be in a situation of pure Keynesian unemployment : on the one hand, excess demand for goods occurs in some sectors; on the other hand, and this is probably much more important, a lack of profitability may be responsible for an insufficient growth of productive capacities, which would in the long run react on employment even while excess capacity could permanently prevail (MALINVAUD [1982]). It would then be true that a decrease of real wages would improve employment, but according to formulas that are quite different from those found in the paper.

A related argument, taking the balance of payment deficit as a constraint on demand management policy, has been developed recently by J. DRÈZE and F. MODIGLIANI [1981]. An application to Belgium leads to the conclusion that the short-term elasticity of employment with respect to the real wage rate should be low, while a quite significant impact could appear in the long run through the effect on productive capacities.

But are real wages too high in France today, and if so, by how much? The answers to these questions have, I am afraid, to be based on other evidence than the one used in the paper.

Should we take the pre-1974 period as being the benchmark against which we ought to judge the present situation ? So far as I understand it, the implicit argument would be that, on the one hand, before 1974 relative prices were in equilibrium, the real wage and real interest rate defining a point on the price frontier of the production function, and that, on the other hand, changes in the terms of trade, technical progress and capital accumulation have on the whole been neutral since then, so that the relative prices associated with an equilibrium ought to lead today to the same labor share as was observed before 1974.

If I do not consider the above argument as fully convincing, it is not only because of the assumptions on what occurred between 1973 and today, nor because of the difficulty of defining what an equilibrium ought now to be (would it imply only a satisfactory degree of utilization of equipments or full employment ?). It is also because the pre-1974 relative price structure implied a substantial excess of the net profit rate earned by productive operations over the real interest rate (I evaluate this excess as having been roughly of 7 per cent). Such a large pure profit rate was probably compatible with the then-felt needs of fast growth. Should it be taken as required today?

All things considered, I come to the conclusion that we should directly discuss the present situation without much reference to the past if we want to face the challenge of an objective determination of what real wages ought to be in France now. (I admit, however, that subjective evaluations, mine in particular, give some weight to the recent evolution of the labor share.) This is indeed a difficult challenge. Paul KRUGMAN has given us some elements that will have to find their place in the discussion; but the problem seems to be much more complex than a quick reader of his paper could think.

● References

DRÈZE J. and MODIGLIANI F. — (1981) "The trade-off between wages and employment in an open economy (Belgium)", *European Economic Review*, January·

MALINVAUD E. — (1982) "Wages and unemployment", *The Economic Journal*, March.

85 - 112

Profitability, employment and structural adjustment in France

Pentti J. K. KOURI,
Jorge Braga de MACEDO
Albert J. VISCIO *

In this paper, we present a dynamic model which explains output, employment and energy consumption in the French manufacturing sector in terms of the expected and actual path of wage rates and energy prices in units of output. The model has two distinguishing features. First, the rate of capacity utilization is determined explicitly from profit-maximizing behavior and it is viewed as the crucial adjusting variable in the short run. Second, we assume complete lack of substitutability between capital, labor and energy inputs ex post. Aggregating over vintages, the model generates the observed decline in profitability and utilization of existing capacity. The results of the simulation are very encouraging, and a simultaneous estimation of the model under static expectations is rejected by the data.

* Pentti J. K. KOURI: New York University, Helsinky University and NBER; Jorge Braga DE MACEDO: Princeton University and NBER; Albert J. VISCIO: New York University.

Introduction

In this paper, we present a dynamic model which explains output, employment and energy consumption in the French manufacturing sector in terms of the expected and actual path of wage rates and energy prices in units of output. The model has two distinguishing features: First, the rate of capacity utilization is determined explicitly from profit-maximizing behavior and it is viewed as the crucial adjusting variable in the short run. Second, we assume complete lack of substitutability between capital, labor and energy inputs ex post.

Accordingly, adjustment to changes in relative factor prices occurs only slowly over time, as the existing capital stock is replaced by new capital and by production techniques consistent with the new pattern of relative factor prices. The putty-clay structure of production implies that profitability of new capital, as measured, for example, by Tobin's q, can behave quite differently from the profitability of old capital, a point often emphasized in recent discussions about investment behavior. A further important implication of the putty-clay assumption is that an abrupt increase in production costs may cause a discrete reduction in the productive capacity, because old capacity can no longer be profitably operated.

The paper is organized as follows. Section 1 motivates the model by a brief discussion of French growth, focusing on the decline of profitability and employment in manufacturing. The basic model is developed in Section 2 and compared with the standard putty-putty model. We show that only in the stationary equilibrium can we represent the relationship between output and factor inputs in terms of a standard production function. We contrast this solution with the one obtained when relative factor prices are not expected to change as well as with the general case where factor prices are expected to change at different rates.

Assuming a fixed planned lifetime of each vintage, industry — wide output, employment and energy demand are derived. The model, modified to allow for overhead labor, is estimated and simulated using data on French manufacturing from 1950 to 1979 in Section 3. The *effects of changes in expected real factor prices on the factor proportions of new plants are quantified as well as the optimal rate of utilization and the profitability of each vintage. When utilization and profitability are aggregated across vintages, their recent decline is consistent with the decline in profitability and employment emphasized in Section 1. Extensions of the analysis are pointed out in the conclusion.*

1 Stylized facts

1.1. The international scene

The decade of the 1970's was a watershed in the economic development of the old industrial countries. The erosion of monetary stability from the late 1960's, the collapse of the Bretton Woods system of fixed exchange rates, the first oil shock, and the unprecedented increase in the prices of other raw materials in 1973/1974 brought an end to a quarter of a century of high and stable growth at full employment. The past ten years have been characterized by slow growth, high unemployment, monetary instability, and inflation that is only now showing signs of deceleration. Most importantly, the past decade has also brought to the surface underlying long term tendencies of structural change in the world economy, caused by demographic and technological changes, the competitive challenge of Japan and of the newly industrialized countries, and the increase in the real cost of energy.

These developments in the global economy have affected Europe with particular severity. Indeed, it had not really recovered from the global recession of 1974/1975 when the second oil shock and the "dollar shock" of 1981/ 1982 brought about the recession in the midst of which we still are. The average rate of growth of the European countries from 1973 to 1980 was only 1.6 per cent in comparison with an average growth rate of 4.6 per cent in the previous decade. The performance of the European countries after the 1974/ 1975 recession contrasts with that of the United States. The 1974/1975 recession was more severe in the United States than it was in Europe, but from the second half of 1975 the United States experienced a strong and sustained boom supported by expansionary fiscal and monetary policies. Although Europe, too, recovered from the recession in 1976 supported by fiscal stimulus and inventory build-up, the recovery was halted and growth remained slow through the 1970's, as macroeconomic policies, particularly in Germany and France, continued to emphasize disinflation.

The differences in strategies of economic policy adopted by the United States on the one hand and Germany on the other, contributed to the depreciation of the US dollar, culminating in the "dollar crisis" of October 1978. The depreciation of the dollar, viewed with alarm by the European governments, helped the slowing down of inflation in Europe while it also led to a deterioration in the price and cost competitiveness and a decline in the profitability of European manufacturing.

As the boom of 1975/1978 came to an end in the United States and macroeconomic policies became more concerned with inflation, the dollar stabilized and in 1979 Europe showed clear signs of recovery while inflation was still decelerating. [1] The incipient recovery was, however, soon brought to an end first by the second oil shock and then by the impact of the restrictive monetary policy adopted by the United States. As a result of slow growth and structural changes, unemployment has become a serious problem in all European countries. Indeed, the average unemployment rate of the EEC countries has increased every year since 1973, from 3 per cent in 1973 to 8 per cent in 1981, and it is still increasing.

1.2. The French experience

Until the Mitterrand government, whose policies we do not plan to discuss in this paper, the performance of the French economy has followed the general pattern of the European countries, particularly that of Germany. From 1973 to 1981, the rate of growth of GDP was only 2.6 per cent, whereas it had been 5.4 per cent in the period 1949-1973. Like Germany and other European countries, France experienced an aborted recovery in 1976. Decline of growth in manufacturing has been even more abrupt: from 5.8 per cent in the post war period to only 1.7 per cent from 1973 to 1981. Behind this average decline are significant changes in the composition of industrial production. Thus, from, 1975 to 1980, the motor vehicle and transportation industry increased at an annual rate close to 19% p. a. and machinery and equipment goods increased at 14% p.a. while consumer goods, intermediate goods and consumer durables increased only at about 10% p.a. at current prices. [2]

FIGURE 1

Profitability of manufacturing

(% p. a.)*

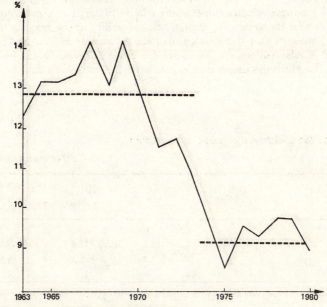

* *Source :* Column (2) of table 1 and 1980 estimate.

1. A «European perspective» on this period can be found in GIERSCH (1981). Further details in KOURI, MACEDO and VISCIO (1982).

2. A detailed study of the changing structure of output in France during the fifties and sixties, as well as of the changes within manufacturing can be found in DUBOIS (1974). More recent accounts are in DELESTRÉ (1979) and COLLET *et al.* (1980). Using principal components analysis, RIGAL (1982) identifies three turning points during the period 1965-1979, namely 1969, 1972, and 1978.

Because of slow growth and demographic developments that caused a substantial increase in labor supply, especially of women and young people, unemployment became a particularly serious problem in France in the 1970's. The rate of unemployment increased from 2.6 per cent in 1973 to close to 8 per cent in 1981.

High and increasing unemployment has however contributed little to the moderation of inflation. In terms of consumer prices, inflation has remained stubbornly above 9 per cent, averaging 10 per cent for the 1973-1981 period. Unlike in many other countries during this period, consumer prices rose faster than wholesale prices, which averaged 7.9 per cent for the same period.

Although French inflation has been higher than that of her major trading partners, there has been little change in the price and cost competitiveness of French industry from the early 1970's to 1981, because of the depreciation of the French franc, and higher than average productivity increase. [3]

As in all European countries, there has however been a substantial erosion of profitability in the manufacturing sector. According to table 1, the share of the operating surplus in total manufacting output declined from an average of 13 per cent in period 1963-1973 to an average of 9 per cent in the period 1974-1979. This decline was largely the result of an increase in the share of total labor compensation from 33 per cent to 36 per cent. Despite the sharp increase in the cost of energy, its share in gross output remained around 6 per cent because of a substantial reduction in the energy intensity of manufacturing production. The same occurred with other intermediate inputs, whose price did not however change substantially relative to the price of gross output. Figure 1 further illustrates the erosion of profitability in the manufacturing sector and suggests that this development started already before the first oil shock. A similar pattern can be found for other European countries, and it reflects the much discussed wage explosion of the late 1960's and the early 1970's. [4]

TABLE 1

French manufacturing: cost structure

(% of gross output)*

Period	Labor [1]	Energy [2]	Operating surplus [3]	Other intermediate inputs [4]
1963-1973...............	33.2	5.5	12.8	48.5
1974-1979...............	35.7	5.7	9.3	49.3

* Gross output (Q) and value added (X) in industrial subsectors (U4 + U5 + U6) from the DMS databank.

Sources:
1. Total labor costs (TLC) obtained by adding the wage bill (SALVS$_1$), social security contributions by employers (SCOCS$_1$) and fringe benefits (PSOCS$_1$) for the subsectors i = U4, U5, U6 from the DMS databank.
2. Energy costs (EC) obtained by multiplying energy consumed (including refinery losses) by category by its price in francs, from UN, *World Energy Supplies 1950-1974*, and IEA, *Energy Balance of OECD Countries 1974-1978*.
3. = (X − TLC)/Q.
4. = 1 − (X + EC)/Q.

TABLE 2

French manufacturing: price and quantities

(% p.a.) *

A	Total Labor Costs [1]	Wholesale Price of Energy [2]	Price of Output [3]	Product Wage [1,3] (w)	Real price of Energy [2,3] (s)
1959-1973..........	9.1	3.1	3.4	5.6	— 0.2
1974-1979..........	16.6	16.9	10.4	5.8	5.6

B	Output [1] (X)	Labor [2] (N)	Energy [3] (E)	Capital [4] (K)	Average Utilization rate (%) [5]
1959-1973..........	6.6	0.5	3.4	7.	73.9
1974-1979..........	2.5	— 1.6	0.4	3.7	71.7

* The notation used for the series is the same as in the text and in the Data Appendix.

Source A :

1. In mechanical and electrical industries. Includes required social security contributions, from *SLM*, p. 225.
2. Fuel and energy for industries wage, value-added tax excluded, from *SLM*, p. 219.
3. Price of industrial goods, tax included, from *IFS*, line 63.

Source B :

1. Gross output in industrial subsectors (U4 + U5 + U6), 1970 francs from *SLM*, p. 78.
2. Employment in industrial subsectors times average weekly hours worked from *SLM*, p. 30, 33.
3. Same as Table 1, column 2.
5. Same as Table 4, column 1.

Table 2 summarizes the evolution of the basic prices and quantities relevant to the manufacturing sector. Panel A, column (3) shows that the average rate of increase of the product wage was close to 6% throughout the period, while the real price of energy, which was constant from 1959 to 1973, increased to about 6% in the following period. This was substantially in excess of the "warranted" rates of increase implied by measured factor productivity growth, obtained from Panel B as 4% p.a. and 2% p.a. respectively. The converse

3. GRILICHES and MAIRESSE [(1982), p. 6] mention a « push » type explanation for the faster productivity growth in France relative to the US. They present evidence against explanations of the productivity slowdown, based on the investment shortfall and on the increase in the price of raw materials, as hypothesised by BRUNO (1981). They also find some effect of R & D on productivity at the firm level but not at the industry level.

4. Comparative perspectives are provided by NORDHAUS (1972), GORDON (1977) and SACHS (1979). Due to data availability, we could not present figures before 1963 in table 1. The ratios usually reported refer to all non-financial enterprices, of which only half are manufacturing firms. There are also no series on the price of non-energy intermediate inputs and the series on the wholesale price of energy is the index used in table 2.

was true—particularly for energy—in the period 1959-1973. Column (1) of Panel B shows that the rate of growth of output declined from 6.6% to 2.5%, while labor input, which had been constant in the period 1959-1973, declined at a rate of 1.6% p.a. in 1974-1979. While this is one of the crucial facts behind the French unemployment problem, it was in part due to the reduction in the length of the work week. [5] As mentioned, the increase in the real price of energy kept its use by the manufacturing sector constant in 1974-1979, after an increase of over 3% p.a. in 1959-1973 (column 2 of Panel B).

Using consistent figures on gross (net) capital stock and gross investment in manufacturing from *SLM*[6], we obtain annual growth rates of 5.5% (6.6%) and 8% per annum respectively over 1959-1973 and a drop to 4.7 (3.9) and — 2.2% in 1974-1979. Similarily, survey data on capacity utilization show a drop from 84.3% for 1959-1973 to 83% in 1974-1979. Using variables constructed in Section 3 below, and reported in column (4) and (5), we see that corresponding to a drop in the rate of growth of net capital from 7% to 4%, our measure of average optimal capital utilization would have dropped from 74% to 72%. This is consistent with the excess of observed over warranted factor price growth and is, of course, the counterpart of the decline in profitability discussed above.

2 The model

We view the manufacturing sector as a collection of plants of differing characteristics in terms of their production capacity, and labor and energy requirements. These three crucial features are chosen at the time a plant is built and define its vintage. We do not allow any flexibility in the choice of the production technique *ex post* nor do we allow any retrofitting of old plants, although such possibilities are obviously a relevant consideration. A crucial aspect of the actual behavior of firms is, in our view, the adjusting role of the utilization of capacity. In other putty-clay models, changes in utilization are, if anything, an afterthought. [7]

Our emphasis in this section is on the specification of a plant of a given vintage. Unlike standard vintage models of growth, this turns out to be the crucial building block of the model. [8] Because we take investment as exogenous and focus on the utilization of different vintages, the analysis of aggregation over plants is left until we deal with the problem of estimating an industry-wide model in the next section.

2.1. The basic setup

When a plant is built, say in period $t = i$, the firm decides on initial investment, I_i, on the capacity of the plant and on the (effective) labor and energy requirements per unit of capacity, which remain fixed for the lifetime of the plant. A plant is closed down when the present discounted value of profits is equal to zero.

The capacity of the plant declines over its lifetime because of physical depreciation, which we assume for convenience to take place at a constant rate, δ. Then, in period t, the maximum capacity of a plant built in period i, $\bar{Z}_i^t$, is given by:

$$(1) \qquad \bar{Z}_i^t = y_i \, \bar{u} \, I_i \, (1 - \delta)^{t-i} = y_i \, \bar{u} \, K_i^t$$

where y_i and $\bar{u}$ are defined subsequently.

Note that the maximum capacity of the plant is determined at the time it is constructed and cannot be changed thereafter. However, in each period, maximum capacity can be utilized more or less intensively, so that utilized capacity is given by:

$$(2) \qquad Z_i^t = y_i \, u_i^t \, K_i^t$$

where $u_t^i/\bar{u} = Z_t^i/\bar{Z}_t^i$ is the rate of utilization of capacity of plant i on period t, relative to maximum capacity.

We assume that labor and energy inputs vary with the rate of capacity utilization:

$$(3) \qquad N_i^t = a_i \, u_i^t \, K_i^t$$

$$(4) \qquad E_i^t = b_i \, u_i^t \, K_i^t$$

---

5. Taking also into account the length of paid vacation and the incidence of strikes on the annual average of hours worked, as in MAIRESSE and SAGLIO (1971, p. 114) would lower the estimate of N, table 2 in 1956, 1963 and above all, 1968 and 1969.

6. We are grateful to Mr. P. ARTUS for this precious reference.

7. While this is true of the exhaustive work on putty-clay of JOHANSEN (1972, esp. p. 35), mention should be made of a sizable literature on capital utilization which concentrates on shift-work and « rhythmic input prices » e.g. WINSTON (1974) and (1977) and BETANCOURT and CLAGUE (1981). Also, a model of utilization focusing on investment demand is in ABEL (1981).

8. See in particular JOHANSEN (1959), SOLOW (1962), SOLOW et al. (1966) and CASS and STIGLITZ (1970). Empirical implementations in a growth context are in BLISS (1965) for England, BENASSY et al. (1975), FOUQUET et al. (1978) and VILARES (1980) for France, SANDEE (1976) for Holland and BENTZEL (1979) for Sweden. Other useful references are SALTER (1966), ATTIYEH (1967), JOHANSEN (1972), ISARD (1973), FUSS (1977), ANDERSON (1981) and BEAN (1981).

The output of the plant, X_t^i, increases with capacity utilization, but at a diminishing rate. This reflects the fact that, as we approach maximum capacity utilization, input productivity declines. Capturing this feature by a very simple parametrization, Φ, we write our output function as :

$$(5) \qquad X_t^i = y_i\, \Phi\,(u_i^i)\, K_t^i$$

where $\Phi\,(u_i^i) = u_i^i\left(\bar{u} - \frac{1}{2}u_t^i\right)$.

Note that maximum output is defined by $u_t^i = \bar{u}$.

When the plant is constructed, the firm has to decide on how to allocate its investment between capacity creation, labor saving and energy saving. For a given level of investment, the firm can increase labor or energy productivity but at the cost of a lower level of capacity. This fundamental trade-off is parametrized as:

$$(6) \qquad y_i = a_i^\alpha\, b_i^\beta$$

where $\alpha + \beta < 1$.

Substituting from (1) through (5) into (6) we can write output as a function of factor inputs and the utilization rate:

$$(7) \qquad X_t^i = \psi\,(u_i^i)\, N_t^{i\,\alpha}\, E_t^{i\,\beta}\, K_t^{i\,\sigma}$$

where $\sigma = 1 - \alpha - \beta$

and $\quad \psi\,(u_i^i) = u_t^{i\,1+\sigma}\left(\bar{u} - \frac{1}{2}u_t^i\right)$.

Note that, although (6) appears to be very similar to the standard production function specification, our model imposes strong restrictions on the choice of N_t^i, E_t^i and u_t^i, which eliminate the apparent substitutability between labor, energy and capital inputs *ex post*. Note further that it is the variation of capacity utilization which allows one to discriminate between our specification and standard putty-models. The difference between our specification and the standard putty-clay models, where variable inputs are proportional to output, is also apparent from equation (7).

2.2. The maximization problem

Given total investment, I_i, the technology of the plant is chosen so as to maximize the present discounted value of expected profits. The time horizon of this optimization problem, T_i, is endogenously determined. We assume that the firm is competitive and takes both input and output prices as exogenously given. We measure factor prices in units of output and denote the product wage prevailing at time t by w_t and its expectation by $\tilde{w}_t$, where it is understood that expectations are formed at $t = i$, when the investment decision is made. Similarly, we denote the actual and expected real price of energy by s_t and $\tilde{s}_t$ respectively. A further simplification is that expected profits are discounted at a constant rate, r.

We now maximize the present discounted value of profits per initial investment, denoted by $\tilde{\pi}_i^i$, subject to the technology constraint in (5).

The Lagrangian is written as:

$$(8) \qquad \mathcal{L}_i^i = \tilde{\Pi}_i^i - \gamma^i (y_i - a_i^\alpha b_i^\beta)$$

where $\displaystyle \tilde{\Pi}_i^i = \sum_{t=i}^{T_i} [y_i \, \Phi(u_i) - a_i u_i \tilde{w}_t - b_i u_i^i \tilde{s}_t] \; [(1-\delta)/(1+r)]^{t-i}$

γ^i is a Lagrange multiplier,

and $\tilde{w}_i = w_i, \tilde{s}_i = s_i$.

The cut-off point is determined by:

$$(8') \qquad \tilde{\Pi}_{T_{i+1}}^i = \sum_{T_{i+1}}^{\infty} [y_i \, \Phi(u_i) - a_i u_i \tilde{w}_t - b_i u_i^i \tilde{s}_t] \; [(1-\delta)/(1+r)]^{t-i} \leqslant 0$$

The optimal rate of utilization is chosen each period according to realized real factor prices, given a_i, b_i, y_i and $\bar{u}$. Thus, in any period t, we have:

$$(9) \qquad \frac{\partial \tilde{\Pi}_t}{\partial u_i^i} = y_i \, \Phi'(u_i) - a_i w_t - b_i s_t = 0$$

According to (9), the marginal benefit in increased output from an increase is utilization equals unit variable costs. Solving for the rate of utilization, we obtain:

$$(10) \qquad u_t^i = \bar{u} \, (1 - \tilde{a}_i w_t - \tilde{b}_i s_t)$$

where $\tilde{a}_i = a_i / y_i \bar{u}$

$\qquad \tilde{b}_i = b_i / y_i \bar{u}$

Thus, given the labor and energy output ratios, $\bar{a}_i$ and $\bar{b}_i$, u_t^i varies with contemporaneous (realized) real factor prices since a_i, b_i and y_i are chosen at the time the plant is built and remain fixed as long as the plant operates. Given the lifetime of the plant, they are determined from the following first-order conditions:

$$(11) \qquad \frac{\partial \Phi_i^i}{\partial y_i} = \sum_{t=i}^{T_i} \Phi(u_t^i)\, g^{t-i} - \gamma^i = 0$$

$$(12) \qquad \frac{\partial \Phi_i^i}{\partial a_i} = - \sum_{t=i}^{T_i} u_t^i\, \tilde{w}_t\, g^{t-i} + \gamma^i \alpha\,(y_i/a_i) = 0$$

$$(13) \qquad \frac{\partial \Phi_i^i}{\partial b_i} = - \sum_{t=i}^{T_i} u_t^i\, \tilde{s}_t\, g^{t-i} + \gamma^i \beta\,(y_i/b_i) = 0$$

where $g = (1-\delta)/(1+r)$.

From (11) we see that the shadow cost of capital productivity is always equal to the present discounted value of additional output. Substituting from (11) into (12) and (13), we get:

$$(12') \qquad \alpha \sum_{t=i}^{T_i} \Phi(u_t^i)\, g^{t-i} = \sum_{t=i}^{T_i} u_t^i\,(a_i/y_i)\, \tilde{w}_t\, g^{t-i}$$

$$(13') \qquad \beta \sum_{t=i}^{T_i} \Phi(u_t^i)\, g^{t-i} = \sum_{t=i}^{T_i} u_t^i\,(b_i/y_i)\, \tilde{s}_t\, g^{t-i}$$

2.3. The choice of technology

Using (10) to substitute for u_t^i and rearranging, we express (12') and (13') as two quadratic equations in $a_i\, w_i$ and $b_i\, s_i$, with coefficients that are functions of real factor prices relative to the ones prevailing in period i :

$$(14) \quad \bar{a}_i^2\, w_i^2\,(2-\alpha)\,\mu_2 + 2\bar{a}_i\,\bar{b}_i\, w_i\, s_i\,(1-\alpha) - \bar{b}_i^2\, s_i^2\,\alpha\nu_2 - 2\bar{a}_i\, w_i\,\mu_1 + \alpha\rho = 0$$

$$(15) \quad -\bar{a}_i^2\, w_i^2\,\beta\mu_2 + 2\bar{a}_i\,\bar{b}_i\, w_i\, s_i\,(1-\beta) + \bar{b}_i^2\, s_i^2\,(2-\beta)\,\nu_2 - 2\bar{b}_i\, s_i\,\nu_1 + \beta\rho = 0$$

$$\mu_2 = \sum_{t=i}^{T_i} (\tilde{w}_t/w_i)^2\, g^{t-i} \Big/ \sum_{t=i}^{T_i} (\tilde{w}_t/w_i)\,(\tilde{s}_t/s_i)\, g^{t-i}$$

$$\mu_1 = \sum_{t=i}^{T_i} (\tilde{w}_t/w_i)\, g^{t-i} \Big/ \sum_{t=i}^{T_i} (\tilde{w}_t/w_i)\,(\tilde{s}_t/s_i)\, g^{t-i}$$

$$\rho = \sum_{t=i}^{T_i} g^{t-i} \Big/ \sum_{t=i}^{T_i} (\tilde{w}_t/w_i)\,(\tilde{s}_t/s_i)\, g^{t-i}$$

ν_2 and ν_1 having expressions in $\tilde{s}_t/s_i$ equivalent to μ_2 and μ_1 in the numerator and the same denominator.

Equations (14) and (15) define two hyperbolas in $\bar{a}_i\, w_i$, $\bar{b}_i\, s_i$.[9] There will always be one intersection in the positive quadrant associated with the optimum solution. There is, however, no analytical solution in general. In some special cases, an explicit solution can be obtained. One such case is when the relative price of the two factors is not expected to change. Then we can aggregate labor and energy inputs into a single factor. In (14) and (15), $\mu_2 = \nu_2 = 1$ and $\mu_1 = \nu_1$, so that by adding we obtain:

$$(16) \qquad (\tilde{a}_i w_i + \tilde{b}_i s_i)^2 (1 + \sigma) - 2 \mu_1 (\tilde{a}_i w_i + \tilde{b}_i s_i) + \rho (1 - \sigma) = 0$$

The negative root of (16) gives minimum variable costs: [10]

$$(17) \qquad \tilde{a}_i w_i + \tilde{b}_i s_i = \frac{1}{1 + \sigma} \left(\mu_1 - \sqrt{\mu_1{}^2 - (1 - \sigma^2) \rho} \right)$$

The expression on the right-hand side of (1) captures the effect of factor price variablity on the choice of technology. Using (17) to substitute for $\tilde{b}_i s_i$ in (14) and for $\tilde{a}_i w_i$ in (15) and solving for $\tilde{a}_i$ and $\tilde{b}_i$, we get:

$$(18) \qquad \tilde{a}_i = \frac{H_i \, \alpha/w_i}{1 + \sigma}$$

$$(19) \qquad \tilde{b}_i = \frac{H_i \, \beta/s_i}{1 + \sigma}$$

where $H_i = \dfrac{\mu_1^2 - \rho (1 + \sigma) - \mu_1 \sqrt{\mu_1^2 - \rho (1 - \sigma^2)}}{-\mu_1 \sigma - \sqrt{\mu_1^2 - \rho (1 - \sigma^2)}}$

When factor prices are expected to remain constant, $\mu_1 = \rho = 1$, the square root term reduces to σ, and $H_i = 1$, so that variable costs are fixed:

$$(20) \qquad \tilde{a}_i w_i + \tilde{b}_i s_i = \frac{1 - \sigma}{1 + \sigma}$$

In this case, the planned rate of capacity utilization is also constant, and independent of factor prices. In fact, using (20) in (10), we obtain:

$$(21) \qquad u_t^i = \frac{\tilde{a}}{1 + \sigma} 2\sigma$$

Recalling equation (7) above, we see that in this special case the standard production function representation applies to our specification. We can then interpret α, β and σ as the shares of labor, energy and capital costs in output.

When factor prices vary over the lifetime of the plant, the rate of utilization also varies. When the relative price of the two factors is constant, we

---

9. The equation for these hyperbolas can be derived by rotating the axes by one half of an angle whose contangent is given by $(2 - \alpha) \nu_2 + \beta \alpha \mu_2/2 \, (1 - \alpha)$ for (14) and minus $(2 - \beta)\nu_2 + \beta \mu_2/2 \, (1 - \beta)$ for (15) and defining a new origin. Details are available upon request.

10. The positive root is $\tilde{a}_t w_i + \tilde{b}_i s_i = 1$ for both equations. It implies from (10) that $u_i = 0$ and is associated with an indefinite form for H_i.

can use (18) and (19) to substitute for $\tilde{a}_i$ and $\tilde{b}_i$ in (10) and we obtain the planned rate of utilization in period t as:

(22)
$$u_t^i = \frac{\hat{u}}{1+\sigma}\,(1+\sigma - H_t\,v_t^i)$$

where $v_t^i = \alpha\dfrac{w_t}{w_i} + \beta\dfrac{s_t}{s_i}$

In this case, there is no production function representation of technology which is independent of factor prices. The term in utilization in (7) now becomes:

(23)
$$\psi(u_t^i) = \frac{1}{2}\left(\frac{\hat{u}}{1+\sigma}\right)^{2+\sigma}(1+\sigma - H_t\,v_t^i)^{1+\sigma}\,(1+\sigma + H_t\,v_t^i)$$

2.4. The life span of the plant

As we have noted, the planned lifetime of the plant depends on the expected time path of factor prices. The actual lifetime of the plant may of course be different to the extent that there are expectational errors. In general, the lifetime of a plant is a decreasing function of the rate of increase of factor prices. This can be seen clearly in the spread case when both factor prices increase at a constant rate, say μ. In this case, the planned shut-off date of the plant is given by setting u_t^i equal to zero in equation (22) above:

(24)
$$H_i(1+\mu)^{T_i} = \frac{1+\sigma}{1-\sigma}$$

where H_i depends on μ as shown in equation (19) above.

In general, the cut-off point is determined jointly with the technology coefficients from (8'), (14) and (15).

2.5. Solution for the plant

Our model of the plant is completely specified by equations (3), (4), (5), (6), (8'), (14) and (15). When relative factor prices are not expected to change, we can use (18) and (19) in (5) to obtain:

(25)
$$y_i = (UH_i)^{(1-\sigma)/\sigma}\,(\alpha/w_i)^{\alpha/\sigma}\,(\beta/s_i)^{\beta/\sigma}$$

where $U = \dfrac{\hat{u}}{1+\sigma}$

Substituting for y_i in (18) and (19), we have:

(26)
$$a_i = (UH_i)^{1/\sigma}\,(\alpha/w_i)^{(1-\beta)/\sigma}\,(\beta/s_i)^{\beta/\sigma}$$

(27)
$$b_i = (UH_i)^{1/\sigma}\,(\alpha/w_i)^{\alpha/\sigma}\,(\beta/s_i)^{(1-\alpha)/\sigma}$$

Note from (26) and (27) that the choice of technology at time i depends not only on factor prices prevailing at time i but also on the time profile of factor prices relative to their initial level. This latter effect, captured by H_i, is symmetric because relative factor prices are expected to remain constant.

When factor prices are expected to be constant, the first effect is ruled out and factor proportions are determined by a weighted average of prices prevailing at time i.

When a constant (common) growth rate for factor prices, μ, is expected, then an increase in μ lowers H_i and therefore increases labor and energy productivity.

We now write the solution under static expectations ($H_i = 1$) by substituting a_i, b_i and y_i in (3), (4) and (6), to yield:

$$(28) \qquad X_i^i = \frac{1}{2} U^{1+\sigma/\sigma} (\alpha/w_i)^{\alpha/\sigma} (\beta/s_i)^{\beta/\sigma} [(1+\sigma)^2 - v_i^{i2}] K_i^i$$

$$(29) \qquad N_i^i = U^{1/\sigma} (\alpha/w_i)^{1-\beta/\sigma} (\beta/s_i)^{\beta/\sigma} (1+\sigma - v_i^i) K_i^i$$

$$(30) \qquad E_i^i = U^{1/\sigma} (\alpha/w_i)^{\alpha/\sigma} (\beta/s_i)^{1-\alpha/\sigma} (1+\sigma - v_i^i) K_i^i$$

In general, equation (7) above holds and it indicates the relationship between our model and the standard production function for a plant. Before proceeding with the estimations, we discuss the aggregation of plants.

2.6. Aggregation

In any given period the manufacturing sector consists of a collection of plants with different labor and energy requirements. Those differences exist because the plants have been built in different periods, with old technologies influenced by past as well as expected current and future factor prices. It is important to note that, even with perfect foresight, different vintages would embody different technologies except in the special case when factor prices are constant. Errors in expectations add another consideration. If variable costs turn out to be higher than anticipated, labor and energy productivities of older vintages are smaller than would have been optimal with perfect foresight, and old plants will be shut-off sooner than anticipated. This is obviously an important consideration in view of the unanticipated increase in energy cost in the 1970's.

Because of differences between vintages, there is no aggregate production function in our model. An aggregate production function exists only in the stationary case of constant expected and actual factor prices.

A further important cause of differences between vintages is embodied technological progress. We can easily capture it by adding shift parameters A_i and B_i in equations (3) and (4). We also assume a fixed planned lifetime of T years for all vintages, after which the plant is scrapped. [11] We can then write the aggregate functions as:

$$(31) \qquad X_t = \sum_{i=t-T}^{t} y_i \, \varphi \, (u_i^i) \, K_t^i$$

$$(32) \qquad N_t = \sum_i a_i \, A_i \, u_t^i \, K_t^i$$

$$(33) \qquad E_t = \sum_i b_i \, B_i \, u_t^i \, K_t^i$$

---

11. A justification of the fixed life assumption in French manufacturing appears in ATKINSON and MAIRESSE (1978).

3 Simulation

3.1. General procedure and results

To implement empirically the aggregate system in (31) through (33), we make the following simplifying assumptions. We neglect embodied technological progress (i.e. set $A_i = B_i = 1$ above) but allow for labor-augmenting technological progress. We assume that the manufacturing sector faces the same product wage and real prices of energy, the same α and β coefficients and the same maximum utilization rate $\bar{u}$. In fact, we have no way of identifying $\bar{u}$, so that it would be appropriate to interpret the parameter U defined in (28) through (30) as a scale parameter. But U involves $\bar{u}$ raised to $(1 + \sigma)/\sigma$ and therefore, when estimating α and β, we have to set $\bar{u} = 1$. Since actual real factor prices are not subject to choice and affect all vintages identically, we also treat them as scale parameters and reinterpret (26) and (27) in terms of a measure of expectational errors defined as the ratio of actual to expected real factor prices, to yield, under stationary expectations:

$$(34) \qquad a_t = (1 + \sigma)^{-1/\sigma} \, (\alpha \omega_t^i)^{(1 - \beta)/\sigma} \, (\beta \pi_t^i)^{\beta/\sigma} \, w_t^{-(1 - \beta)/\sigma} \, s_t^{-\beta/\sigma}$$

$$(35) \qquad b_t = (1 + \sigma)^{-1/\sigma} \, (\alpha \omega_t^i)^{\alpha/\sigma} \, (\beta \pi_t^i)^{(1 - \alpha)/\sigma} \, w_t^{-\alpha/\sigma} \, s_t^{-(1 - \alpha)/\sigma}$$

where $\omega_t^i = w_t/w_i$

$\pi_t^i = s_t/s_i$

Note that (34) and (35) are applicable when real factor prices are expected to change at the same rate because H_t does not depend on ω_t^i or π_t^i. Then, according to (18) and (19), w_t and s_t would have to be divided by H_t. When relative factor prices are expected to vary, however, we have to solve (14) and (15), given α and β, and then simulate the model.

In this Section, we introduce a feature excluded from the model in Section 2 for expositional convenience. This is the existence of overhead labor, which we assume to be proportional to capacity.

To equate the variables in (31) through (33) with observed gross output [12] employment and energy demand, we define a scale parameter C_i for each of the three equations, which (since $\bar{u} = 1$) reflects the particular units in which the observed variables are measured as well as embodied technical progress. In the employment equation, another scale parameter is implicity included in the coefficient for overhead labor, n:

$$(36) \qquad X_t^0 = C_X X_t + \varepsilon_t^X$$

(37)
$$N_t^o = C_N N_t + n K_t + \varepsilon_t^N$$

(38)
$$E_t^o = C_E E_t + \varepsilon_t^E$$

where $K_t = \sum_i K_t^i.$

To determine α, β, n and the C's in the system (36) through (38) we use a full-information maximum likelihood procedure based on K_t^i, ω_t^i and π_t^i for each vintage, then we aggregate over vintages. The estimation is carried out subject to the inequality constraints:

i. $\;0 < \alpha < 1;$

ii. $\;0 < \beta < 1;$

iii. $0 < \sigma < 1.$

The model is estimated over the period 1950 through 1979 with annual data. We use a reported (net) capital stock estimate for K_t^i, $i = 1950$, assume that all vintages prior to 1950 are identical and form K_t^i using gross investment in year $t > i$, under the assumptions that $\delta = .10$ and $T = 30$ years. [13] Expectations are discounted at a rate of 10% p.a., so that $g = .82$.

The model is estimated under static expectations, that is to say the case when a_t and b_t are related by linear equations (18) and (19) rather than by the quadratic equation (14) and (15). The model is also simulated for the general case of equations (14) and (15) but conditional on postulated values for α and β which we take to be close to the ones reported in Table 1 above. [14] The latter simulation also includes the assumption of a constant growth of the product wage of 3% p.a. over the whole period, reflecting in part labor-augmenting technical change, and a constant expected real price of energy. [15] The shocks of the seventies are then simulated on variants of the dynamic base case.

---

12. Strictly speaking, we should have netted out non-energy intermediate inputs, and thus adjust α and β measured relative to gross output as in Table 1. Because of the nearly fixed relative price, however, this adjustment would only affect the scale parameter. Also α only reflects the share of production labor.

13. See CARRÉ, DUBOIS and MALINVAUD (1972) and MAIRESSE (1972) for detailed studies of the French capital stock. See also DELESTRÉ (1979 b) and *SLM*. Note that a lifetime of 30 years is substantially higher than the one chosen in other estimates — see MAIRESSE [(1972), p. 59] — even without allowing for the distinction between equipment and buildings. The present combination probably allows for too little disembodied capital augmenting technical progress, which was found by MAIRESSE (1977) and (1978) to be important in the French case. A 5 % rate of depreciation would come closer to the mark but then the series on net capital would be almost double of the corresponding series reported in *SLM*, whereas with a 10 % depreciation the two series are very close.

14. Expected computing costs prevented a simultaneous estimation of α, β, n and the C's in the dynamic case but we obviously intend to perform it. The details of the estimation procedure are available upon request.

15. See Table 2. Alternative estimates of disembodied technical progress are 4.3 % in MAIRESSE and SAGLIO [(1971), p. 107], 2.6 % for labor and — 0.9 % for capital in BENASSY, FOUQUET and MALGRANGE [(1975), p. 35] and 2 % in MAIRESSE (1978).

TABLE 3

Estimation and simulation results

(*t*-values in parentheses)

	(1) Static Expectations	(2) Dynamic Simulation
$\tilde{w}_t$..........................	w_t	$w_i (1.03)^t$
$\tilde{s}_t$..........................	s_t	s_i
Parameters		
α...............................	0.060	0.30*
β...............................	0.010	0.05*
C_X...............................	0.006 (15.607)	0.022 (2.850)
C_N...............................	6 655.4 (32.5)	3 441.2 (5.9)
n...............................	— 8.34 (— 4.21)	12.76 (2.21)
C_E...............................	0.003 (3.335)	0.002 (12.856)
Goodness of fit		
$R^2{}_X$...............................	0.996	0.980
$R^2{}_N$...............................	0.999	0.998
$R^2{}_E$...............................	0.977	0.993
χ^2...............................	6.044	232
Serial correlation		
ρ_X...............................	0.818 (4.405)	0.948 (5.106)
ρ_N...............................	0.675 (3.633)	0.893 (4.810)
ρ_E...............................	0.912 (4.910)	0.778 (4.192)

* Assumed values.

Estimation results for the two cases are reported in Table 3. Because of the different values of α and β, the estimates are not directly comparable. Also, for the period 1950-1958 the results are less reliable because of the greater weight of the arbitrary base value of the capital stock and of changes in the system of national accounts, which implied a different definition of the manufacturing sector. [16] As shown in the third panel, the first-order serial correlation of the residuals is generally very high. Nevertheless, the likely misspecification of the process of capital accumulation, due to the effect of variations in depreciation rates and in scrappage as a function of changes in expected profitability, might well introduce higher-order auto-regressive errors, which are not corrected for. The existence of inequality constraints precludes explicit significance tests on the parameters α and β reported in the first panel of Table 3. Because of the constraints, there is no guarantee that the error terms be orthogonal to the dependent variable. Therefore, the summary statistic R^2 reported in Table 3, second panel, is actually the square of the correlation coefficient between fitted and actual values. This is a good indicator of the explanatory capabilities of the model.

The scale parameters (and the coefficients of auto-correlation) have an asymptotically normal distribution: significance tests based thereon are reported in parentheses below the coefficients in the first panel of table 3 which, again, are not directly comparable. The overall significance test of the regression has a χ^2 distribution, whose value is reported in the second panel.

FIGURE 2

Actual and fitted values in the dynamic case:
employment equation

(Billion Man-Hours) *

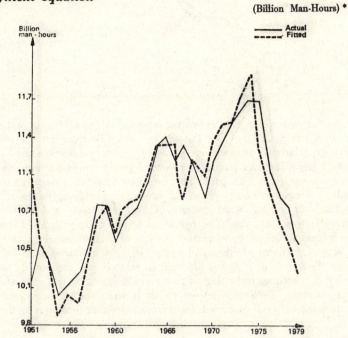

* *Source:* 1959-1979. 1971 base employment linked to 1950-1959. 1956 base employment times average workweek in hours, all from *SLM* times 52.

16. From 1959 to 1979, data is based on the 1971 "enlarged system of national accounts" (SECN) and includes investment by private firms in three subsectors or "branches", intermediate goods (code U 04), machines (U 05) and consumption goods (U 06). From 1950 to 1959, however, it is based on the 1962 system, which divides manufacturing into seven branches (denoted U 06 to U 12). These changes affected the series on employment (1956 classification over 1971 classification is 1.042 in 1959) and production (similar ratio is 0.903 in 1959). Further details in INSEE (1978).

FIGURE 3

Actual and fitted values in the dynamic case: energy equation

(10ᵇˢ British thermal units)*

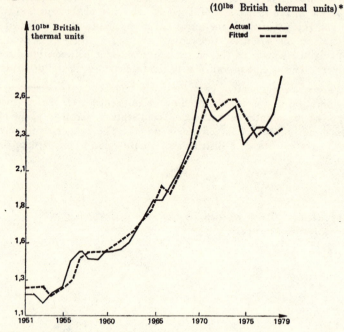

* *Source:* Column (2) of table 1.

In the case of static expectations, reported in the first column, the coefficient on overhead labor has the wrong sign. To interpret the result that large expectational errors cause ω_t^i and π_t^i to vary considerably. If α and β were large, large variations in v_t^i would result, the utilization rate will be driven toward zero and could become negative. Since negative utilization leads to scrappage of the plant, the maximum likelihood values of α and β are likely to be small when the environment is characterized by large expectational errors. On the other hand, under static expectations, the standard production function representation applies so that we expect α and β to be close to the shares of labor and energy in gross output shown in table 1. Since the values of α and β reported in table 3 are implausibly low, even taking into account technological change, (which would justify the assumption of a constant effective wage) we conclude that static expectations do not capture the behavior of French manufacturing sector firms during the sample period.

The second column reports maximum-likelihood estimates of the scale parameters conditional upon the choice of α and β. Figures 2 and 3 plot the actual and fitted values for the employment and energy equations respectively over the whole sample period (the fit of the first equation is comparable). It is clear that the model can explain a substantial portion of the variation in output, employment and energy consumption in changes inutilization rates across vintages and suggests the usefulness of this approach. The fit is worse in the fifties, no doubt due to the greater weight of the base period capital stock. Accordingly, figure 4 plots index values of a_i and b_i

from 1959 to 1979, with base 1973 = 100. There is a continuous decline in a_t whereas b is almost flat until the late sixties. Conversely, during most of the 1974-1979 period, b_t declines more than a_t. A similar pattern would obtain under static expectations, in part because we took a fairly high rate of depreciation and discount. Nevertheless, because of the expectation of a 3% increase in wages in the dynamic simulation, the values of a_t and b_t are uniformly lower than under static expectations.

FIGURE 4

Factor proportions by vintage

(Index 1973 = 100)

a_i ——
b_i -----

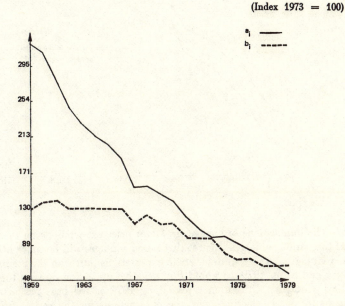

3.2. Changes in factor price expectations

In general, when there are changes in expected factor prices, there will be offsetting changes in the factor proportions of new vintages and in the utilization rate of old vintages. Specifically, differences in a_t, b_t and u_t across vintages derive from differences in α, β and σ, as well as in ω_t and π_t. To reflect the shocks of the seventies documented in tables 1 and 2, suppose that in 1974 expectations of factor prices change. If product wages are expected to grow at a rate $\mu = 5\%$ rather than at 3% p.a., there will be a decline of 12.5% in a_t and a decline of 4% in b_t relative to the base dynamic case we have been discussing. Conversely if the real price of energy is expected to increase at a rate $\nu = 3\%$ p.a., so that the two rates are the same, there will be an immediate decline of 14% in b_t and a decline of 1% in a_t. Suppose now that both factor price expectations change, so that wages are expected to grow at 5% and energy prices are expected to grow at 3% p.a. Then the decline for a_t is 13% and for b_t it is 17%. In all these examples, we observe negative cross-effects.

FIGURE 5

Utilization of old vintages in 1979 (= 10)

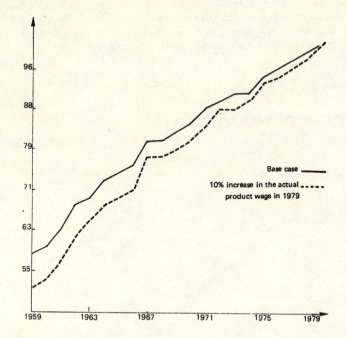

The implications of changes in factor price expectations on the utilization of the various vintages suggest that newer vintages will be more utilized than old vintages. Indeed, under static expectations (but with the assumed values of α and β), in 1979 we would find negative utilization rates of the 1950 and 1951 vintages. Utilization rates taking 1979 as the base period are shown in figure 5. Neglecting again the observations for the early fifties, we see that the utilization of the 1959 vintage in 1979 is 58 % and that an increase in expectational errors brought about by a 10% increase in the 1979 product wage leads to a drop in utilization of the 1959 vintage to 51%. For comparison, the utilization rate would have been 44 % under static expectations.

3.3. The average utilization rate

A measure of average utilization of the capital stock in each year can be obtained by aggregating the utilization rate of each vintage in operation in that year. This measure, denoted by u^*, is reported in figure 6 for the base dynamic case. It shows a decline, from 76 % in 1959 to 71 % in 1979. The evolution mirrors the one of measures based on the output gap or survey data from the late sixties but the increase in the early sixties is not reflected in our measure, possibly because of the weight of the base period capital stock.

FIGURE 6

Average utilization rate (u*)

(%)

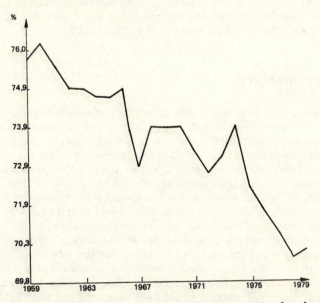

In table 4, we simulate again the shocks of the seventies by showing the effects of changes in expected factor prices on u^* as a proportion of the dynamic base case of column 2 of table 3. As before, we have set the expected rate of growth of wages at $\mu = 5\%$ in column 1, the expected rate of growth of energy prices at $\nu = 3\%$ in column 2 and combine both shocks in column 3.

TABLE 4

Average utilization rates (%)

	Base case [1]	Expected wage increase [2]	Expected energy price increase [3]	Combination [4]
1973..................	73	0	0	0
1974..................	73.9	0.1	0	0.2
1975..................	72.2	0.7	0.4	0.9
1976..................	71.6	2.7	2.3	2.8
1977..................	71.1	3.1	2.7	3.3
1978..................	70.5	3.5	2.9	3.7
1979..................	70.6	3.5	2.8	3.7

1. Series reported in figure 8 ($\mu = 0.03$, $\nu = 0$).
2. $\mu = 0.05$, $\nu = 0$ in 1973, percent over base case.
3. $\mu = 0.03$, $\nu = 0.03$ in 1973, percent over base case.
4. $\mu = 0.05$, $\nu = 0.03$ in 1973, percent over base case.

While the year-to-year changes in a_i and b_i were negligible relative to the change in the year of the shock, the opposite holds for u^*, where the impact effect is very small compared to the effect in 1979. Comparing the effect of the wage and oil shocks in table 4, we see that the response of average utilization is much more significant in columns 1 and 3 than it is in column 2, as suggested above in the discussion of tables 1 and 2.

3.4. Profitability

Finally, to present data on the profitability of manufacturing, we have to correct our measure of output for non-energy raw materials. Taking their share in output as constant over the period (as suggested by table 1), we can compute profits for each vintage as a percentage of net output. In the dynamic base case, we see that, if the share is one half of gross output, then profitability declined from about 24% in 1953 to 14.5% in 1958, increased to 19.3% in 1961 and slowly declined to about 14% in the mid sixties. After a drop to .10% in 1969-1970, this measure falls rapidly to 2.3% in 1975 and zero thereafter. If the share of raw materials were 40 %, as shown in colum (2) of table 5, profitability would also decline substantially in the seventies, as suggested by figure 1 above, but the rate of profit in 1979 would still be about 5%. Note further that, measuring profits by vintage, we see that in 1979 no vintage before 1956 would be in operation and similarily that 1950 vintages would have been scrapped after 1975.

TABLE 5

*Profitability of manufacturing**

(as a percent of net output)

1970	(1) $\zeta = 0.5$	(2) $\zeta = 0.6$
1...............................	9.8	20.7
2...............................	8	19.2
3...............................	5.6	15.7
4...............................	5.8	16.6
5...............................	2.3	12.2
6...............................	0	9.1
7...............................	0	7.1
8...............................	0	6.1
9...............................	0	4.7

* Measured as a weighted average (using gross outputs weights) of profitability by vintage defined as $\left(\zeta y_i \, \Phi \left(u_t^i \right) - a_i \, u_t^i \, w_i - n w_i - b_i \, u_t^i \, s_t \right) / \zeta y_i \, \Phi \left(u_t^i \right)$.

Conclusion

The results reported in Section 3 have to be regarded as indicative of the usefulness of the approach defended in this paper rather than precise estimates. Our interpretation of the decline of profitability in Section 1 emphasized the importance of the wage explosion of the late sixties, continued into the seventies, as well as the effect of the oil shock. Since our model recognizes that it takes time to adjust factor proportions to factor price shocks and that it takes longer the lower the rate of capital formation, we were able to compare the effects of a sudden change in the price of energy to the effects of an increase in the expected rate of growth of real wages. We found that, as suggested by Figure 1, the decline in profitability started before the oil crisis, but that the energy shock was responsible for making older vintages unprofitable sooner than anticipated. The greater share of the wage bill in gross output was one reason for the stronger effect of wage growth in factor proportions but the effect of expectational errors was also found to be important in contrasting results under static expectations to the dynamic simulation of the model.

This being said, the limitations of the analysis should be borne in mind. The most serious ones are certainly the omission of investment and of the international aspects, which only appear here indirectly through the energy shock or some constraint on the price of output. These items (as well as a refinement of the estimation procedure in the present set-up) are in the authors' research agenda.

Data Appendix

	w	*s*	X	N	E	K
1950	34.5	93,5	120.7	10.2	1.07	68.1
1951	31.6	80.7	130.6	10.5	1.22	70.3
1952	37.3	90.6	131.9	10.4	1.20	72.5
1953	40.6	92.5	135.3	10.1	1.14	74.3
1954	43.6	94.9	141.7	10.2	1.21	75.1
1955	46.0	93.1	150.0	10.3	1.27	76.7
1956	50.9	96.4	163.9	10.5	1.44	79.2
1957	52.7	102.5	177.9	10.8	1.51	83.2
1958	54.4	105.1	183.8	10.8	1.47	87.3
1959	54.8	109.5	188.3	10.5	14.5	91.2
1960	56.2	105.3	210.5	10.7	1.51	96.4
1961	60.4	103.6	222.4	10.8	1.53	104.1
1962	65.8	103.7	238.1	11.0	1.57	113.0
1963	69.1	100.9	256.1	11.3	1.65	121.3
1964	72.7	98.7	273.1	11.4	1.76	129.4
1965	76.2	97.0	279.4	11.2	1.85	136.7
1966	79.0	96.3	303.6	11.3	1.89	145.3
1967	89.6	103.7	311.0	11.2	1.96	154.0
1968	90.7	96.9	324.3	10.9	2.09	162.1
1969	95.1	98.1	366.9	11.2	2.30	175.2
1970	100.0	100.0	390.7	11.4	2.65	190.1
1971	108.2	106.8	413.4	11.5	2.48	206.5
1972	116.9	105.2	442.1	11.6	2.43	222.8
1973	122.7	100.9	476.1	11.7	2.47	240.4
1974	120.8	121.1	494.2	11.7	2.55	254.8
1975	134.8	126.1	465.6	11.1	2.28	263.2
1976	144.9	127.9	505.0	10.9	2.41	273.7
1977	153.9	131.5	518.3	10.8	2.40	283.2
1978	165.3	133.4	529.7	10.5	2.47	291.7
1979	171.3	138.4	549.4	10.2	2.74	297.5

● References

ABEL, A. — (1981) "A Dynamic Model of Investment and Capacity Utilization", *Quarterly Journal of Economics*, August, pp. 379-403.

ANDERSON, G. J. — (1981) "A New Approach to the Empirical Investigation of Investment Expenditures", *The Economic Journal* (91), March, pp. 88-103.

ATKINSON, M. and J. MAIRESSE. — (1978) "Length of Life of Equipment in French Manufacturing Industries", *Annales de l'INSEE* (30-31), pp. 23-48.

ATTIYEH, R. — (1967) "Estimations of a Fixed Coefficients Model of Production", *Yale Economic Essays* (7), Spring, pp. 1-40.

BEAN, C. R. — (1981) "An Econometric Model of Manufacturing Investment in the U.K.", *The Economic Journal* (91), March, pp. 106-121.

BENASSY, J. P., D. FOUQUET and P. MALGRANGE. — (1975) "Estimation d'une fonction de production aux générations de capital", *Annales de l'INSEE* (19), pp. 3-52.

BENTZEL, R. — (1979) "A Vintage Model of Swedish Economic Growth from 1870 to 1975", *in* B. CARLSSON, G. ELIASSON and I. NADIRI, eds.. — *The importance of the technology and the permanence of structure in industry growth*, New York: IUI Conference Report.

BETANCOURT, R. and C. CLAGUE. — (1981) *Capital Utilization, A Theoretical and Empirical Analysis*, Cambridge: University Press.

BLISS, C. J. — (1965) *Problems of Fitting a Vintage Capital Model to U.K. Manufacturing Time Series*, paper presented to the World Congress of the Economic Society, Rome.

BRUNO, M. — (1981) *Raw Materials, Profits and the Productivity Slowdown*, NBER Working Paper no. 660 R, April.

CARRÉ, J. J., P. DUBOIS and E. MALINVAUD. — (1972) *La croissance française. Un essai d'analyse économique causale de l'après-guerre*. Paris, Seuil. 1972 (New Edition 1976).

CASS, D. and J. STIGLITZ. — (1969) "The Implications of Alternative Saving and Expectations Hypotheses for Choice of Technique and Patterns of Growth", *Journal of Political Economy* (77), July-August, pp. 586-627.

COLLET, J. Y., H. DELESTRÉ and P. TEILLET. — (1980) « Travail et capital dans les Comptes nationaux », *Économie et statistique*, no. 127, November, pp. 7-19.

DELESTRÉ, J. — (1979a) "Les facteurs de production dans la crise", *Les Collections de l'INSEE*, Series E, no. 67, August.

DELESTRÉ, J. — (1979b) "L'accumulation du capital fixe", *Économie et statistique*, no. 114, September, special issue « Le patrimoine national ».

DUBOIS, P. — (1974) « Fresque historique du système productif », *Les Collections de l'INSEE*, Series E, no. 27, October.

FOUQUET, D., J. M. CHARPIN, H. GUILLAUME, P.-A. MUET, D. VALLET. — (1978) " DMS Modèle dynamique multisectorel ", *Les Collections de l'INSEE*, Series C, no. 64-65, September.

FUSS, M. A. — (1977) "The Structure of Technology over Time: a Model for Testing the Putty-clay Hypothesis", *Econometrica* (45), November, pp. 1797-1821.

GIERSCH, H., editor. — (1981) *Macroeconomic Policies for Growth and Stability, A European Perspective*, Tubigen; J.C.B. Mohr.

GORDON, R. — (1977) "World inflation and monetary accomodation in eight countries," *Brookings Papers on Economic Activity*, (8), pp. 409-477.

GRILICHES, A. and J. MAIRESSE. — (1982) *Comparing Productivity Growth: An Exploration of French and U.S. Industrial and Firm Data*, NBER Working Paper no. 961, April.

INSEE. — (1978) « L'ancien et le nouveau système de Comptabilité nationale », *Les Collections de l'INSEE*, Series C, no. 160, April.

ISARD, P. — (1973) "Employment Impacts of Textile Imports and Investment: A Vintage Capital Model, *American Economic Review* (63), pp. 402-416.

JOHANSEN, L. — (1959) "Substitution vs. Fixed Production Coefficients in the Theory of Economic Growth: A Synthesis ", *Econometrica*, April, pp. 157-176.

—— (1972) *Production Functions, An Integration of Micro and Macro, Short Run and Long Run Aspects*, Amsterdam: North Holland, 1972.

KOURI, P., J. de MACEDO and A. VISCIO. — (1982) *Profitability, Employment and Structural Adjustment in France*, NBER Working Paper no. 1005, October.

MAIRESSE, J. — (1972) "L'évaluation du capital fixe productif", *Les Collections de l'INSEE*, Series C, no. 18-19.

—— (1977) " Deux essais d'estimation du taux moyen de progrès technique incorporé au capital », *Annales de l'INSEE* (28), pp. 39-76.

—— (1978) " New Estimates of Embodied and Disembodied Technical Progress ", *Annales de l'INSEE* (30-31), pp. 681-720.

MAIRESSE, J. and A. SAGLIO. — (1971) "Estimation d'une fonction de production pour l'industrie française", *Annales de l'INSEE* (6), pp. 77-117.

NORDHAUS, W. — (1972) "The Worldwide Wage Explosion ", *Brookings Papers on Economic Activity* (3), pp. 431-464.

PHELPS, E. — (1963) " Substitution, Fixed Proportions, Growth and Distribution ", *International Economic Review* (4), pp. 265-268.

SACHS, J. — (1979) " Wages, Profits and Macroeconomic Adjustment ", *Brookings Papers on Economic Activity* (20), pp. 269-319.

SALTER, W. — (1960) *Productivity and Technical Change,* Cambridge: University Press.

SANDEE, J. — (1976) *A Putty-Clay Model for the Netherlands,* paper presented at the European Meeting of the Econometric Society.

SLM. — (1981) *Le Mouvement économique en France 1949-1979, Séries Longues Macroéconomiques,* INSEE, May.

SOLOW, R. — (1962) "Substitution and Fixed Proportions in the Theory of Capital ", *Review of Economic Studies* (29), pp. 207-218.

SOLOW, R., J. TOBIN, Ch. v. WEIZSÄCKER and M. YAARI. — (1966) " Neoclassical Growth with Fixed Factor Proportions ", *Review of Economic Studies* (33), April, pp. 79-115.

VILARÈS, M. J. — (1980) « Fonctions de production aux générations de capital : théorie et estimation », *Annales de l'INSEE* (38-39), pp. 17-41.

WINSTON, G. — (1974) " The Theory of Capital Utilization and Idleness ", *Journal of Economic Literature* (12), December, pp. 1301-1320.

—— (1977) " Capacity, an Integrated Micro and Macro Analysis ", *American Economic Review* (67), February, pp. 418-422.

Comments [p85]

113

by Paul KRUGMAN

Massachussetts Institute of Technology, Cambridge, USA

When the putty-clay hypothesis was first proposed it was of little practical relevance. The period between the Korean War and the Yom Kippur War was characterized by steady growth and smoothly changing factor prices; and for steady-state growth it makes little difference whether changes in the capital-labor ratio are possible only *ex-post* or also *ex-ante*. The 70's, however, have been punctuated by large, unexpected changes in energy prices, and to a lesser extent in real labor costs. These changes have made the dynamics of factor substitution a problem of crucial importance.

What KOURI, de MACEDO and VISCIO have done is to develop an empirically workable version of the putty-clay model. The key element in their formulation is the idea of variable utilization rates, with a cost to excessively high utilization which prevents the extreme results characteristic of more usual putty-clay set-ups, in which plants are used either at 100 or at zero percent of capacity. This has two advantages. First, it is arguably more realistic (although if the putty-clay hypothesis is applied to machines rather than to entire plants I am not sure that it may not hold up better than a casual look at utilization rates suggests). Second, variable utilization rates «smooth» the model. Instead of the discrete on-off decisions between different vintages which would occur in a standard model, we get continuous movements in relative utilization which make both analysis and estimation far easier.

Given the immense difficulty of the task, the authors should be congratulated on the success they have achieved. It seems unfair to carp at particular simplifications. I do, however, worry about one of the simplifying assumptions made in the estimation. This is the assumption that the only technical change is disembodied growth in the efficiency of labor. The motivation for this assumption is, of course, clear: it immensely simplifies the estimation problem. On the other hand, it seems to remove one of the main empirically appealing features of putty-clay models, the idea that vintages of recent date are more efficient than older ones, and that a basic point of investment is to modernize — not merely deepen — the capital stock.

That said, the model is still a very nice one. One wishes for more. For example, it would be interesting to have seen the dynamics of energy demand after an energy price shock. To do this would, of course, have required an investment path; but even with a very crude or *ad hoc* investment formulation the results would have been worth seeing. For it is precisely this dynamic aspect, the fact that the adjustment to changes in factor prices takes time, which is the distinguishing feature of the whole approach.

Comments [85] 114 - 116

by Jacques MAIRESSE

INSEE and Ecole des Hautes Etudes en Sciences Sociales, Paris, France

---

The study by P. KOURI, J. DE MACEDO, and A. VISCIO is a fine example of an econometric work that balances the attention given to the theoretical derivation and the empirical implementation of the model. It is also an original and innovative attempt in a very difficult field of investigation. The authors should be particularly praised for their great care in gathering and using data from France, a land that is foreign to them. Of course, even in the best of econometric works, it is possible to quarrel or worry about some simplifying features and some of the compromises made. I shall merely indicate several problems of this sort that I encountered. Some of the difficulties I raise concern the limitations of the capital vintage approach in general.

1.a. The first of my main queries is about the form of the $\phi(u_i^t)$ function and the interpretation of u_i^t. Clearly, the quadratic form adopted is required to make explicit computation possible. But I have no good intuition about the sensible nature of this assumption, or whether using another functional form would make much difference. The interpretation of u_i^t in terms of a rate of utilization seems also somewhat ambiguous and raises at least a semantic question. As stated in the model, u_i^t varies uniquely in response to changes in factor prices and thus appears to be independent of fluctuations in demand. Accordingly, it would seem preferable to simply consider u_i^t as a price-dependent efficiency parameter. This is in fact the interpretation adopted by E. BERNDT and D. WOOD in a recent study, which contains a vintage production model and offers many interesting points of comparison with the present one.[1]

b. My second remark is more closely related to the fact that demand considerations play no explicit role in the model: that is, given investment, employment, and energy consumption are explained only in terms of actual and expected factor prices. There is also no explicit allowance for lag effects or partial adjustment behavior. Thus, there is nothing in the model that could account for labor hoarding and the productivity cycle. This may

---

1. E. BERNDT and D. WOOD, "Energy Price Changes And The Induced Reevaluation Of Durable Capital In US Manufacturing During The OPEC Decade," Massachusetts Institute of Technology Working Paper, March 1984.

be one of the reasons why the serial correlation of the errors in the estimated equations is so high.

c. Given that factor prices and investment are the only explanatory variables, there is very limited flexibility in the model (in terms of number of parameters). Hence, I am rather surprised by the goodness of fit. I could not, however, find anything spurious going on in the background. This might add even greater weight to the authors' conclusion regarding the usefulness of their approach.

d. My last particular query is about the treatment of technical progress and also relates to the question of the interpretation of u_i^t. It is obviously difficult to identify separately the u_i^t, the vintage technical parameters a_i and b_i, and the embodied technical progress terms A_i and B_i. This has led the authors to simplify by assuming the absence of embodied technical progress ($A_i = B_i = 1$). But surely this is unrealistic and should be considered only as a first approximation. (In this connection, however, I am also puzzled by the choice of a 10 % rate of depreciation.)

2. There has been in recent years a renewed interest in vintage production models of the clay-clay or putty-clay types. But although I think this is indeed a very interesting and worthwhile line of research, I have mixed feelings about the econometric work done in this area for two general, and partly contradictory, sorts of reasons.

a. Although vintage production models are an important step toward realism, they are still very unrealistic. Indeed, it is not even clear that we are not guilty, once more, of the fallacy of misplaced concreteness in believing that vintage models are more appropriate than the more traditional aggregate-production-function type models. We think that at the shop or plant levels, techniques are very rigid and best characterized in terms of fixed coefficients activities. Even at the most down-to-earth level, however, there is usually some nonnegligible room for substitution between factor requirements. Most important, however, it is a long way from the application of fixed coefficients to the firm to their application to the industry and then to manufacturing as a whole. As we move to more highly aggregate levels, the scope for flexibility widens. Varying service lives of investment are the usual source of flexibility in clay-clay specifications, and varying utilization rates play a similar role in the present study. But these are only two of many possibilities. Even for a well-defined product in a given industry, a wide variety of well-identified production techniques may exist that cannot be distinguished simply according to vintage. In addition, different firms can produce different product mixes, use more or less qualified or experienced workers, or combine different sorts of energy. Further, firms in different locations or on slightly different markets (through product-differentiation) may face different price conditions. For example, there is a very large dispersion of real wages (per unit of production) even within four-digit industries in French manufacturing. All these different possibilities are ignored in a strict vintage production model. The traditional putty type production function may be better after all.

b. Though much too simple to do justice to the complexity of the real economy, vintage production models are nonetheless too complicated to be estimated confidently with the usual available data. As we do not have direct information on the distributions of output, employment, and energy consumption according to different investment vintages, these distributions must in fact be derived from the estimates of the model. This, of course, is achieved only at the cost of various simplifying assumptions that cannot be truly tested. Thus, the necessary balance in econometrics between data and a priori hypotheses is seriously compromised. Despite the theoretical appeal of the capital vintage approach, one must recognize that it involves some severe empirical drawbacks.

In closing, I would like to go back to my introductory praise of the quality, interest, and originality of the work of our three authors. Detailed critiques and general reservations can always be made about any econometric study; but they should not hide the merits of a good one. As the saying goes: "La critique est aisée, el l'art est difficile."

117 - 144

Anticipations, recessions and policy; an intertemporal disequilibrium model

Olivier J. BLANCHARD
and Jeffrey SACHS *

* Harvard University, Cambridge, Mass., USA. We thank DRI for letting us use their computer, and the NSF for financial assistance.

This paper presents an intertemporal disequilibrium model with rational expectations, i.e. a model in which prices and wages may not adjust fast enough to maintain continuous market clearing. Therefore, optimizing firms and households base their intertemporal plans on anticipations of both future quantity constraints and future prices. Such a model shows clearly that the effect of a policy depends not only on its current values but its anticipated path. After a presentation of the model and its basic dynamics, we therefore consider the effects of various paths of fiscal policy on the economy.

Introduction

Both France and the United States have recently experienced major political changes. As a result, current economic policy is different from what it was, and even larger changes are anticipated in the coming years. Although the goal of those policies is to accomplish structural changes, stronger defense and less government intervention in the US, more equal income distribution and industrial reorganization in France, they will have and already are having macroeconomic effects on investment, consumption and employment. High anticipated deficits are blamed for the high long-term real interest rates in the US, anticipations of a higher fiscal burden on firms are blamed for the sluggishness of private investment in France.

The purpose of this paper is to present a model in which effects of anticipated as well as current changes in policy can be analyzed. Technically the model is an intertemporal disequilibrium model with rational expectations, i.e. a model in which agents take the anticipated future into consideration as rationally as they can, but where prices and wages may not adjust fast enough to maintain full employment. The paper therefore builds on two recent strands of research in macroeconomic fluctuations : rational intertemporal choice and disequilibrium analysis.

The first approach has emphasized that most decisions are intertemporal and thus depend as much on anticipated as on current prices. It has focused in particular on intertemporal substitution of consumption or leisure by households, on the optimal employment-investment decisions by firms (see for example, books by BARRO [3,] LUCAS [18], SARGENT [24]). This approach has led to a better understanding of the dynamic effects of either policies or real disturbances (in our own work for example, fiscal policy [2], oil price shocks [22]). Almost all of the work in this area has, however, maintained the assumption of market clearing, at least in the goods market (HALL [12] and SACHS [22] allow for a non-labor-market-clearing real wage).

The second approach, disequilibrium theory, has emphasized that, if prices are not fully flexible, most decisions must take into account not only prices but quantity constraints. It has focused in particular on the implications for consumption and labor supply decisions by households, and for employment decisions of firms, giving a better foundation to many standard macroeconomic relations. It has shown how equilibria correspond to different regimes, each with distinct implications for policy. Although most of the work in this area has recognized the potential importance of anticipated future constraints (most notably MALINVAUD [20]), it has usually not modeled behavior explicitly as intertemporal or considered the implications of rational expectations (an exception is NEARY and STIGLITZ [21]).

Can both approaches be combined? We believe that they can, in that agents attempt to make rational choices and to anticipate the future, even when some prices are not fully flexible. We realize that the assumption of rational expectations is overly strong and the lack of explicit foundations of price inertia is unsettling. Rational expectations appear however to be the most neutral way of allowing agents' decisions to depend on the future. We also believe that a model with more firmly grounded price inertia (possibly from desynchronization, such as in [25] and [8]) would lead to similar results, although we have not in this model attempted such an undertaking [1].

The model we derive is slightly beyond analytical tractability. An analytical treatment can only be offered by taking shortcuts, something we have explored in [6], [9]. The choice here has been to solve the complete model by numerical simulations. Given that the model is derived from maximizing behavior and that its size is small enough, results can easily be traced to specific assumptions about parameters and policy.

The paper is organized as follows : Section 1 characterizes households' and firms' behavior, as well as the intertemporal equilibrium. In particular, it clarifies the role of short and long interest rates in investment and consumption decisions, and the relation between market value, profit, profitability, the real wage and investment. It shows how the expectation of future constraints may lead to anticipatory buying by consumers and firms. Section 2 displays the basic dynamic mechanisms of the model, through a focus on the following questions: What is the role of investment, both through demand and supply, in the transmission of shocks, a question stressed by MALINVAUD [20])? Can sharp deflations in response to lower money growth be destabilizing, as suggested by KEYNES and *more recently by* TOBIN [26]? *Is the responsiveness of real wages to unemployment stabilizing or destabilizing, a question raised throughout the research on disequilibrium (starting with* BARRO-GROSSMAN [4])? *Section 3 returns to one of the policy issues relevant in France today : What happens if firms anticipate an increase in their fiscal burden in the future? No attempt is made to fit specific facts and magnitudes, our intention being to clarify the various economic forces set in play by such anticipations. More generally, our focus in most of the paper is as much on methodology as on substantive economic issues. Carefully calibrated simulation models will be necessary to reach firm answers to many of the issues raised in the paper.*

---

1. We believe that models of price inertia will lead to price structures in which relative prices, except for the real wage, are approximately correct, but in which their average level, the price level, does not adjust quickly. As this paper relies on price level and real wage inertia only (and so implicitly assumes all other relative prices to be flexible), we feel that results would not be drastically changed by a more explicit derivation of price behavior.

1 The model

1.1. General description

Our choice has been to build the simplest model in which households and firms have nontrivial intertemporal choices. Thus, we assume that the economy is closed and that there is one produced good, used either for consumption or investment. There are three tradable assets, money, debt and equities.

Households and firms take as given both current and anticipated prices and quantity constraints. Although the future may be uncertain, they act as if they know it with certainty[2]. Households are all identical and maximize the discounted sum of utility; their problem is intertemporal as they have to choose between consumption now and consumption later. Firms are identical and maximize their value, which is the discounted sum of anticipated cash flows. Labor is a variable factor but capital is quasi-fixed: changes in capital are costly, so that the investment decision presents also an intertemporal problem.

The solutions to the maximization problems of households and firms give a set of *actual demands* (or supplies) which satisfy both the budget constraint and (current and anticipated) quantity constraints. (These are, in the disequilibrium terminology, "Dreze" demands [11]). We can also, for both maximization problems, find for each constraint the lowest value of this constraint such that it is not binding. We shall refer to this set of values as the set of *shadow demands* (these correspond to "Benassy" demands). It follows that each actual demand can be expressed as the minimum of the constraint and the shadow demand.

Each market has rationing rules governing the allocation of goods to the constrained side; we allow these rules to depend on shadow demands. Market clearing requires that two conditions be satisfied: the first is that at most one side of the market be constrained, the second that actual demand and actual supply be equal. We follow others in this field by allowing asset prices to adjust and thus asset markets to clear. We do not however follow standard usage in our treatment of the labor market: we assume that households supply all the labor demanded by firms and that firms are therefore never constrained in the labor market. By doing so, we eliminate the regime of "repressed inflation" (following Malinvaud's terminology [19]) and are left with only two regimes, a "Keynesian regime" when suppliers of goods

---

2. This strong assumption allows us to formalize agents and firms as solving certainty problems. While convenient, and probably necessary at this stage, it does not allow us to look at the effects of uncertainty per se on behavior.

are constrained and a "classical regime" when buyers of goods are constrained. We feel that little is lost by this simplification, at least for the experiments we consider, and that the benefit in increased simplicity is substantial.

Prices adjust over time as functions, not of excess actual demands which are, by construction, identically zero, but of excess shadow demands.

At any time t, an intertemporal equilibrium is a sequence of shadow demands, a sequence of actual demands and a sequence of prices, consistent with maximizing behavior and the rationing rules, such that both current and future markets are anticipated to clear. If exogenous variables take over time their anticipated values, the intertemporal equilibrium is actually realized over time. If at some time $t+\tau$, there are unanticipated changes in current or anticipated exogenous variables, a new intertemporal equilibrium for period $t+\tau$ and future periods must be recomputed.

We now describe the model in detail.

1.2. The behavior of firms

All firms are identical and we shall not distinguish between individual and aggregate values. The time index t will also be deleted, whenever convenient.

The technology of the firm is characterized by:

a) A *production function*, with constant returns to scale:

$$Q = F(K, L)$$

b) An *installation function*, giving the number of goods used up in installation of I units of investment:[3]

$$I \Phi (I/K) \; ; \quad \Phi (0) = 0 , \quad \Phi' (.) > 0$$

The total number of goods needed to invest at rate I is therefore:

$$J = I + I \Phi (I/K) = I (1 + \Phi (I/K))$$

c) An *accumulation equation*, with exponential depreciation at rate μ:

$$\dot{K} = I - \mu K$$

The firm takes as given the sequence of real wages and real interest rates $\{W/P, r\}_{t=0,\ldots,\infty}$ and the sequence of constraints on the amount of goods it can can sell and the amount of goods in can invest, $\{\bar{Q}, \bar{I}\}_{t=0,\ldots\infty}$. By assumption, there are no constraints on the amount of labor it can buy. The firm maximizes its value, which is the present value of cash flows:

$$V = \int_0^\infty (Q - (W/P) L - J) \, e^{- \int_0^t r_s \, ds} \, dt$$

Let $e^{-\int_0^t r_s\,ds} q_t$ be the costate variable associated with the accumulation equation, and λ_Q, λ_I the Lagrange multipliers associated with the quantity constraints; the Hamiltonian is therefore:

$$H = e^{-\int_0^t r_s\,ds} [F(K, L) - (W/P)L - I(1 + \Phi(I/K)) + q(I - \mu K)$$
$$+ \lambda_Q(\bar{Q} - F(K, L)) + \lambda_I(\bar{I} - I)]$$

Necessary conditions for maximization are:

$$F_L(K, L)(1 - \lambda_Q) = W/P \quad ; \quad \lambda_Q(\bar{Q} - Q) = 0 \quad ; \quad \lambda_Q \geqslant 0$$
$$1 + (I/K)\Phi'(I/K) + \Phi(I/K) = q - \lambda_I \quad ; \quad \lambda_I(\bar{I} - I) = 0 \quad ; \quad \lambda_I \geqslant 0$$
$$\dot{q} = (r + \mu)q - (1 - \lambda_Q)F_K(K, L) - (I/K)^2 \Phi'(I/K)$$

$$\lim_{t \to \infty} e^{-\int_0^t r_s\,ds} q_t K_t = 0$$

They can be rewritten more intuitively as follows;

Define shadow labor demand and quantity supply L^d, Q^s s.t. :

(1) $\qquad\qquad L^d, Q^s \,|\, F_L(L^d, K) = W/P \quad ; \quad Q^s = F(K, L^d)$

(2) Then $\qquad\qquad Q = \min(Q^s, \bar{Q}) \quad ; \quad L \,|\, F(K, L) = Q$

Define shadow investment and investment spending, I^d, J^d s.t. :

(3) $I^d, J^d \,|\, 1 + \Phi(I^d/K) + (I^d/K)\Phi'(I^d/K) = q \quad ; \quad J^d = I^d(1 + \Phi(I^d/K))$

(4) Then $I = \min(I^d, \bar{I}) \quad ; \quad J = \min(J^d, \bar{J}) \quad , \quad J \equiv I(1 + \Phi(\bar{I}/K))$ and :

(5) $\dot{q} = (r + \mu)q - (W/P)(F_K(K, L)/F_L(K, L)) - (I/K)^2 \Phi'(I/K)$

(6) $\lim e^{-\int_0^t r_s\,ds} q_t K_t = 0$

Given the capital stock, the real wage and the possibly binding output constraint, the employment and output decisions of the firm are straightforward. The investment decision is of more interest and is characterized by equations (3) through (6) : To see what they imply, we can rewrite them further. Inverting (3), and integrating (5) forward subject to the transversality condition (6) gives :

(7) $I = \min(I^d, \bar{I}) \quad ; \quad I^d/K = H(q) \quad ; \quad H(1) = 0 \quad ; \quad H'(.) > 0$

(8) $q = \int_0^\infty [(W/P)(F_K(K, L)/F_L(K, L)) + (I/K)^2 \Phi'(I/K)] e^{-\int_0^t (r_s + \mu)\,ds}\,dt$

---

3. Costs of adjustment are a simple way of deriving a well-behaved flow investment demand. The specific functional form is a special case of Lucas [17] which preserves CRTS of technology with respect to K, L, I. This subsection builds heavily on ABEL [1], HAYASHI [13] and BLANCHARD [9].

Investment is the minimum of shadow investment and the constraint. Shadow investment in turn depends on q, the present value of marginal profits, usually called Tobin's q. Marginal profit is the sum of two terms; the second is the reduction in the cost of installation made possible by an additional unit of capital and is a minor factor in profits. The first is more interesting and depends very much on the regime.

In the classical regime, i.e. if the firm is not output constrained, the marginal product of labor equals the wage and this first term is simply the marginal product of capital. Furthermore, if the firm does not anticipate to be ever output constrained in the future, a particularly nice result arises: the shadow price q is equal to the observable average value of capital V/K (HAYASHI [13]). In the absence of constraints on investment spending, there is then a direct relation between the firm's value and its investment behavior. An increase in the real wage for example decreases employment, the marginal product of capital, and thus investment and the value of the firm.

In the Keynesian regime, the firm is output constrained. The first term then is the marginal wage savings, i.e. the real wage times the marginal rate of substitution. There is no longer a close relation between q and V/K, between investment and the value of the firm. The effect of an increase in the real wage is now to increase the marginal wage savings and to increase q and investment as capital becomes more attractive than labor to produce the same level of output. Although it now increases investment, the increase in the wage still decreases profit and thus the value of the firm. An increase in output increases both marginal and average profit and thus both q and V/K.[4] The effect on marginal profit however depends on the elasticity of substitution [5] while the effect on average profit does not.

Finally, the effects of a constraint on investment demand are easily characterized. Anticipated constraints on investment demand lead, *ceteris paribus*, to an anticipated lower capital accumulation, thus to higher marginal profits, to a higher q and higher investment demand today. It therefore generates anticipatory buying of investment goods. The effect is represented graphically in figure 1.

Since asset markets are assumed to clear and the financial structure of firms is thus irrelevant for firms' or agents' decisions, the following structure is convenient: Firms have real debt B outstanding, paying the real interest rate. They finance all investment from retained earnings and do not issue new debt or new equity. The assumption that there is real debt outstanding implies that there is an observable interest rate but is otherwise irrelevant. (The assumption that all investment is internally financed implies that in equilibrium personal savings are zero.) The amount of profits paid to equity owners is as a result:

(9) $$\pi = (Q - (W/P)\, L - J - rB)$$

FIGURE 1

Anticipatory purchases of investment goods

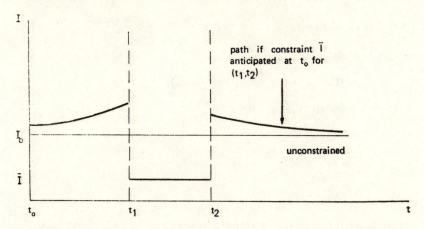

1.3. The behavior of consumers-workers

All consumers are identical and we shall not distinguish between individual and aggregate values.

Consumers derive utility from consumption and real money balances. Leisure does not explicitly enter the utility function; desired labor supply is L^*. Households take as given the sequence of prices, real wages, real interest rates and profits paid to equity owners, as well as the sequence of labor they supply and the amount of goods they can buy $\{L, \bar{C}\}_{t=0,\ldots,\infty}$. They maximize the present value of utility:

$$U = \int_0^\infty u\,(C, M/P)\, e^{-\delta t}\, dt$$

Defining $A \equiv B + M/P$, the budget constraint can be written as:

$$\dot{A} = rA + (W/P)\,L + \pi - [(r + \dot{P}/P)\,(M/P) - C]$$

---

4. Considering the effects of a change in output only makes sense for an output constrained firm. The « neoclassical » approach is slightly confusing in this respect when it treats output as given, but maintains the assumption that the wage equals the marginal product of labor.

5. Around $W/P = F_L\,(K, L)$ and for L given by $Q = F\,(K, L)$ the effect of a change in output on marginal profit is given by :

$$\frac{d}{dQ}\left[(W/P)\,(F_K\,(K, L)/F_L\,(K, L))\right] = (F_K\,(K, L)/F_L\,(K, L))\,\sigma_{KL}^{-1}$$

where σ_{KL} is the elasticity of substitution between K and L. Thus, the smaller σ_{KL}, the larger the effects of a decrease in output on marginal profit.

Define the costate variable associated with the budget constraint as $e^{-\delta t} x_t$, and the Lagrange multiplier associated with the quantity constraint on consumption as λ_C. The Hamiltonian is then:

$$H = e^{-\delta t} \left[u\left(C, M/P\right) + \lambda_C \left(\bar{C} - C\right) + x\left(rA + (W/P)\,L + \pi - (r + \dot{P}/P)\,M/P - C\right)\right]$$

Necessary conditions for maximization are:

$$u_C\left(C, M/P\right) = x + \lambda_C \quad ; \quad \lambda_C\left(\bar{C} - C\right) = 0 \quad ; \quad \lambda_C \geqslant 0$$

$$u_m\left(C, M/P\right) = x\left(r + \dot{P}/P\right)$$

$$\dot{x} = (\delta - r)\,x$$

$$\lim_{t \to \infty} e^{-\delta t}\,x_t = 0$$

They can be rewritten more intuitively as follows:

Define shadow consumption demand C^d such that;

(10) $C^d \mid u_C\left(C^d, M/P\right) = x$

(11)   Then $C = \min\left(C^d, \bar{C}\right)$

(12) $u_m\left(C, M/P\right) = x\left(r + \dot{P}/P\right)$

(13) $\dot{x} = (\delta - r)\,x \quad ; \quad \lim_{t \to \infty} e^{-\delta t}\,x_t = 0$

In the absence of constraints on consumption, consumers equalize the marginal rate of substitution between money balances and consumption to the nominal interest rate. The path of consumption is determined by (13) which gives the behavior of marginal utility, and the budget constraint. Approximately, (13) gives the shape of the path and the budget constraint the highest feasible level of this path.

Current constraints on consumption lead to forced savings and more consumption later. Anticipated constraints have the same effect on consumption as on investment. They lead to anticipated forced savings, thus to a higher feasible level of consumption today. The effect is represented graphically in figure 2 when $\delta = r$ and M/P is constant, so that agents choose the highest feasible constant level of consumption.

We shall introduce the government later.

1.4. Equilibrium given prices and wages

Equilibrium in the goods market, requires that actual supply equals actual demand. It also requires that at most one side be constrained. From (2), actual aggregate supply is

$$Q = \min\left(Q^s, \bar{Q}\right)$$

FIGURE 2

Anticipatory consumption spending

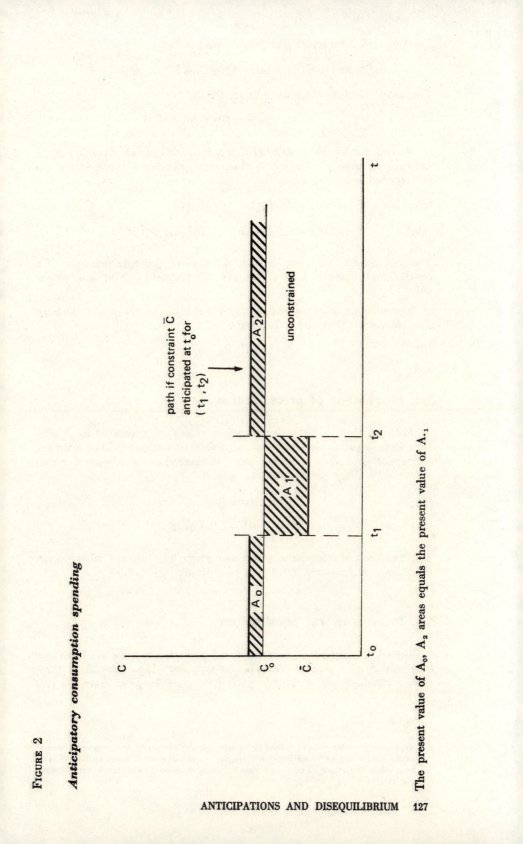

The present value of A_0, A_2 areas equals the present value of $A_{\cdot 1}$

From (4) and (11), actual aggregate demand is

$$Q = \min(Q^d, \bar{Q}) \quad \text{where} \quad Q^d \equiv C^d + J^d \quad , \quad \bar{Q} \equiv \bar{C} + J$$

The above conditions for equilibrium imply:

$$(14) \qquad\qquad \bar{Q} = \min(Q^s, Q^d)$$

Rationing rules are as follows : If supply is constrained, there is uniform rationing of firms. If demand is constrained, consumption and investment are rationed according to:

$$(15) \qquad \bar{C} = C^d - a(Q^d - \bar{Q}) \quad ; \quad a \in [0, 1]$$

$$(16) \qquad J = J^d - (1 - a)(Q^d - \bar{Q}) \quad ; \quad I \mid I(1 + \Phi(I/K)) = J$$

Thus, in general, rationing depends on shadow aggregate demand. If a equals 0 or 1, however, there is rationing of investment only or consumption only.

In the labor market, we have assumed that firms can always hire the labor they demand. Thus, labor is given by:

$$(17) \qquad\qquad \bar{L} \mid F(\bar{L}, K) = \bar{Q}$$

1.5. Movement of prices and wages

Although there is by construction zero excess actual demand in all markets, shadow excess demands may be different from zero. Thus a natural assumption is to allow prices and wages to respond to these excess demands over time.[6] They are assumed to follow:

$$(18) \qquad\qquad \dot{P}/P = \beta(Q^d - Q^s)$$

$$(19) \qquad\qquad \dot{W}/W = \theta(\bar{L} - L^*) + \sigma\dot{P}/P$$

β, θ measure the response of prices and wages to goods and labor market conditions. σ measures the degree of indexing of wages.

1.6. Intertemporal equilibrium

The set of equations is reorganized and presented in table 1. Equations (1.1) to (1.6) give shadow demands and supplies. These depend on three sets of variables, policy variables (M), state variables given from the past

---

6. An alternative formalization would be to solve for flexible prices and wages and assume partial adjustment of actual prices and wages. In the absence of more explicit assumptions about the source of price and wage inertia, it it difficult to decide which formalization is better.

(P, W, K) and costate variables which depend on the anticipated future (q, x). Equations (1.7) to (1.11) show how actual demands and supplies follow from shadow demands and supplies.

Equation (1.12) determines the real interest rate from equality of money demand and money supply. Equations (1.13) and (1.14) give the equations of motion of the costate variables (q, x), equations (1.16) to (1.18) the equations of motion of the state variables (P, W, K). Finally, equation (1.19) gives the behavior of V, which does not affect any other variable in the model.

TABLE 1

The complete model: equations of motion

(1.1) $L^d \mid F_L(L^d, K) = W/P$

(1.2) $Q^s \mid Q^s = F(K, L^d)$

(1.3) $I^d \mid 1 + \Phi(I^d/K) + (I^d/K)\Phi'(I^d/K) = q$

(1.4) $J^d \mid J^d = I^d(1 + \Phi(I^d/K))$

(1.5) $C^d \mid u_C(C^d, M/P) = x$

(1.6) $Q^d \mid Q^d = C^d + J^d$

(1.7) $\bar{Q} = \min(Q^d, Q^s)$

(1.8) $L \mid F(K, L) = \bar{Q}$

(1.9) $\bar{C} \mid \bar{C} = C^d - a(Q^d - \bar{Q})$

(1.10) $J \mid J = J^d - (1-a)(Q^d - \bar{Q})$

(1.11) $I \mid J = I(1 + \Phi(I/K))$

(1.12) $u_m(\bar{C}, M/P) = x(r + \dot{P}/P)$

(1.13) $\dot{q} = (r + \mu)q - (W/P)(F_K(K, L)/F_L(K, L)) - (I/K)^2 \Phi'(I/K)$

(1.14) $\dot{x} = (\delta - r)x$

(1.15) $\lim\limits_{t \to \infty} x_t e^{-\delta t} = 0 \quad ; \quad \lim\limits_{t \to \infty} K_t q_t e^{-\int_0^t r_s ds} = 0$

(1.16) $\dot{P}/P = \beta(Q^d - Q^s)$

(1.17) $\dot{W}/W = \theta(L - L^*) + \sigma \dot{P}/P$

(1.18) $\dot{K} = I - \mu K$

(1.19) $\dot{V} = rV - [(\bar{Q} - (W/P)L) - J]$

At any point of time, an intertemporal equilibrium is a sequence of quantities $(L^d, Q^s, I^d, J^d, C^d, Q^d, L, \bar{Q}, I, J, \bar{C}, K)$ and a sequence of prices (r, q, x, P, W, V) which, given the sequence of policy (M) and initial conditions (P_o, W_o, K_o) satisfy equations (1.1) to (1.9) for the current and all future periods.

1.7. Steady state

Before we turn to the dynamics, we briefly characterize the steady state of the model, when $\dot{P} = \dot{W} = \dot{K} = \dot{x} = \dot{q} = 0$. We denote steady state values by stars. Intertemporal utility maximization implies, from (1.14), that $r^* = \delta$. The interest rate is always equal to the subjective discount rate in steady state; equivalently the long-run elasticity of savings at δ is infinite. From (1.3) and (1.8), as $I = I^d$, q must be sufficient to generate gross investment equal to depreciation;

$$q^* = 1 + \Phi(\mu) + \mu\,\Phi'(\mu) > 1$$

In turn, (1.13) determines the marginal product of capital and thus the steady state level of capital stock:

$$K^* \mid F_K(K^*, L^*) + \mu^2\,\Phi'(\mu) = (\delta + \mu)\,q^*$$

If $\mu = \dot{0}$, so that $q = 1$, this condition reduces to the familiar condition:

$$F_K(K^*, L^*) = \delta$$

Consumption is determined by:

$$C^* = F(K^*, L^*) - \mu K^*(1 + \Phi(\mu))$$

Finally, the level of real money balances is given by:

$$u_m(C^*, M/P^*)/u_C(C^*, M/P^*) = \delta$$

Money is clearly neutral in the long run in this model.

2 Comparative dynamics

To show the basic dynamics of the model, this section concentrates on the dual role of investment as a determinant of demand and later of supply through capital accumulation, and on the stabilizing or destabilizing role of prices and wages.

2.1. Functional forms and parametrization

To simulate the model, specific functional forms must be chosen for utility and technology, and numerical values must be chosen for the parameters. These assumptions are summarized in Table 2.

TABLE 2

Functional forms, parameters and steady state values

Consumers

$$u = (\xi C^{-\rho_1} + (1 - \xi) (M/P)^{-\rho_1})^{-1/\rho_1}$$

$$U = \int_0^\infty (\ell n \, u_t) \, e^{-\delta t} \, dt$$

$$\xi = 0.95 \quad ; \quad \rho_1 = 6 \Rightarrow \sigma_{Cm} = 1/(1 + \rho_1) = 0.14$$

$$\delta = 0.03$$

Firms

$$Q = \gamma (\alpha K^{-\rho_2} + (1 - \alpha) L^{-\rho_2})^{-1/\rho_2}$$

$$\varphi (I/K) = b . (I/K) \quad ; \quad \dot{K} = I - \mu K$$

$$\gamma = 0.25 \quad ; \quad \alpha = 0.25 \quad ; \quad \rho_2 = 1 \Rightarrow \sigma_{KL} = 1/(1 + \rho_2) = 0.5$$

$$b = 4 \quad ; \quad \mu = 0.025$$

Rationing rules and price adjustment

$$\beta = 0.03 \quad ; \quad \theta = 0.015 \quad ; \quad \sigma = 1$$

$$a = 0.9$$

Exogenous variables

$$L^* = 8 \quad ; \quad M = 4$$

Implied steady state values

$Q^* = 2$	$(W/P)^* L^* = 1.50$	$r^* K^* = 0.25$
$C^* = 1.78$	$J^* = 0.22$	$I^* = 0.20$
$r^* = 0.03$	$P^* = 2$	$W^* = 0.375$
$q^* = 1.2$	$V^* = 9.60$	$K^* = 8$

Instantaneous utility is CES in consumption and money balances. The elasticity of substitution between utility in different periods is assumed to be unity, so that cardinal utility is logarithmic. (Under uncertainty, this last assumption implies unit constant relative risk aversion.)

The production function is also CES in capital and labor. The installation function $\varphi (I/K)$ is linear in I/K, so that total cost of installation is quadratic in I.

The unit period is a quarter. Thus all flow variables and parameters with a time dimension are at quarterly rates. There is no attempt to calibrate the model to fit a particular economy; parameter values are chosen to either be reasonable, or to fit existing empirical evidence or to have reasonable implications. Implied steady state values for the main variables are given also in Table 2. A few parameters require justification.

The elasticity of substitution between consumption and real money balances is also the interest elasticity of money demand. It is chosen to be 0.14, which corresponds to empirical estimates of this long-run elasticity. [7] The subjective discount rate δ implies a steady-state annual interest rate of 12 %, which is roughly in line with the average profit rate on corporate capital in the U.S.

The convexity coefficient for installation costs, b, implies that a ratio of annual investment to capital of 10% leads to average installation costs equal to 10% of the purchase price of capital, and marginal installation costs equal to 20 % of purchase price. [8] The elasticity of substitution σ_{KL} has been chosen to be relatively low, 0.5, to reduce the scope for substitution of capital and labor in response to short-run changes in factor prices.

The price and wage adjustement parameters will be discussed later; they clearly do not affect the steady state. The proportion of rationing allocated to consumption, a, is chosen to equal approximately its share in aggregate demand, 0.9.

2.2. Method of solution

Dynamic simulations present two problems usually not encountered in macroeconomic simulations.

The first is standard in rational expectations models. The initial values of q, x and V are not given from the past but determined from the requirement that the transversality conditions be satisfied. A dynamic simulation is thus a two-point boundary value problem, with initial conditions for K, P, W and terminal conditions for q, x and V, (i. e. the transversality conditions). The technical method of solution is that of multiple shooting (see [16] for details).

The second is specific to disequilibrium models and comes from the presence of minimum functions. We replace the minimum function ([1.7] in Table 1) by a CES function with low elasticity. In practice, an elasticity of 0.005 is enough to replicate the minimum rule.

We now turn to the simulations. [9] The first two focus on the behavior of quantities, and to do so, assume fixed prices and wages ($\beta = \theta = 0$).

2.3. Simulation 1. Demand shocks and Keynesian unemployment

Suppose agents decide to save more in order to consume more later, i.e. that there is a temporary decrease in the subjective discount rate. More precisely, assume that δ decreases unanticipatedly at time 0 and thereafter follows :

$$\delta = 0.03 + 0.9\,(\delta_{-1} - 0.03) \quad ; \quad \delta_0 = 0.025$$

The effects are summarized in Table 3, for three different sets of values of σ_{Cm} and σ_{KL}.

TABLE 3

A temporary decrease in the discount rate; P, W fixed

	Reference case ($\sigma_{Cm}=0.14$; $\sigma_{KL}=0.5$)			High σ_{Cm} (Flat LM) ($\sigma_{Cm}=2$; $\sigma_{KL}=0.5$)			Low σ_{KL} (Steep IS) ($\sigma_{Cm}=2$; $\sigma_{KL}=0.1$)		
	1	2	3	4	5	6	7	8	9
Quarter.....	0	4	12	0	4	12	0	4	12
Variable									
C..........	−2.6	−1.6	−0.7	−6.8	−4.3	−1	−2.5	−1.6	−0.7
q..........	1	0.2	−0.1	−3.3	−0.7	0.5	−3	0.4	0.2
QD........	−1.9	−1.6	−1	−8.7	−4.8	−1.5	−4.7	−1.4	−0.6
QS........	0.0	0.3	0.3	0.0	−0.8	−0.7	0.0	−0.8	−0.3
r..........	−2	−1.2	−0.4	−0.4	−0.4	−0.0	−2	−1.2	−0.8
V/K.......	3.6	2.2	0.7	2.3	2	1.6	3.5	2.3	1.1
u..........	2	1.7	0.9	11	5.5	1.2	5.4	1.4	0.5

All variables are in % deviation from steady state except.
 u : unemployment rate, measured in %.
 r : absolute deviation from steady state, measured in % at annual rate.

The central role is played by investment. Lower aggregate demand lowers output and this in turn has two effects : it lowers the demand for money and thus the sequence of anticipated interest rates; it lowers the sequence of anticipated marginal profits. Which of the two lower sequences dominates and whether q and investment go up or down depends crucially on σ_{Cm} and σ_{KL}.

---

7. The time-separable utility function we use implies the same short- and long-run elasticities of money demand both with respect to consumption and interest rates.

8. Actual estimates of this installation cost coefficient, b, derived from regressions of investment on market value, are much higher. They are however implausibly high and likely to be biased upwards (see [7]).

9. Checking global stability before proceeding with simulations would be desirable but is impossible. Checking local stability if feasible. Stability conditions would combine the results of BLANCHARD and KAHN [10] for linear systems with rational expectations and the results of ITO [14] for systems with regimes and possibly discontinuous derivatives. We have not checked them but have not encountered problems of convergence in simulation.

If σ_{Cm} is large, the demand for money is very interest elastic, interest rates decrease little and q goes down. If σ_{KL} is very small, the decrease in output and employment reduces strongly marginal profit [10] and q also goes down. These two cases are shown in columns 4 to 6 and 7 to 9 respectively.

The response of investment in turn, through a multiplier effect, decreases consumption. The larger and more prolonged the decrease in investment, the larger the initial decline in consumption and thus the overall recession. The similarity of our results to the simple ISLM is striking : the impact effect is larger, the flatter the LM (the larger σ_{Cm}), the steeper the IS (the smaller σ_{KL}). As the recession slowly ends, net investment becomes positive again. In none of the three cases does the economy experience a supply constraint; it always remains in Keynesian unemployment.

Table 3 also shows clearly the different behavior of marginal q which affects investment and is unobservable, and average q which might be observable through the stock market valuation of firms. Although q may go down, V/K goes up in all three cases : the effect of lower real rates dominates the effect of lower average profit. Thus, the stock market goes up while output and possibly investment go down.

2.4. Simulation 2. Supply shocks and classical unemployment

Suppose that the economy is affected by an adverse, unanticipated technological shock which disappears over time. More precisely, assume that γ follows after t_o :

$$(\gamma - 0.25) = 0.9\,(\gamma_{-1} - 0.25) \quad ; \quad \gamma_0 = 0.2375$$

This decrease of productivity of 5 % initially is in the spirit of a temporary increase of the price of oil (see [22] for a specific treatment of such an increase with a more adequate treatment of technology). The effects are summarized in Table 4, again for three sets of values of σ_{Cm} and σ_{KL}.

The central role is again played by investment, this time not as a component of demand but as a determinant of supply through capital accumulation. The impact effect on production however depends only on the technology : after the decrease in productivity, employment must decrease until the marginal product of labor is again equal to the unchanged real wage. The size of the adjustment depends on σ_{KL}. If σ_{KL} is low, the required decrease in employment is small; if σ_{KL} is larger, the decrease is larger. The impact effect on the marginal product is independent of σ_{KL} to the first order and proportional to the share of capital in output.

The adjustment process and the length of the period of classical unemployment depends however very much on investment. Two effects are again present: the first is a lower sequence of real interest rates, the second is a lower sequence of marginal products. Whether the first or the second dominates depends again on the interest elasticity of money demand.

TABLE 4

A temporary decrease in productivity; P, W fixed

	Reference case ($\sigma_{Cm}=0.14$; $\sigma_{KL}=0.5$)			High σ_{Cm} ($\sigma_{Cm}=2$; $\sigma_{KL}=0.5$)			Low σ_{KL} ($\sigma_{Cm}=0.14$; $\sigma_{KL}=0.1$)		
	1	2	3	4	5	6	7	8	9
Quarter.....	0	4	12	0	4	12	0	4	12
Variable									
C..........	− 14.2	− 7.6	− 1.7	− 7.4	− 7.4	− 7.0	− 6.9	− 3.9	− 0.7
q..........	5.9	2.7	0.0	− 5.5	− 3.1	− 0.5	2.7	1.5	0.0
QD........	15.2	8.2	1.6	− 5.5	− 4.0	− 2.0	7.6	3.9	0.5
QS........	− 10.7	− 6.4	− 0.2	− 10.7	− 9.4	− 7.4	− 5.8	− 3.3	− 0.9
K..........	0.0	1.0	1.1	0.0	− 2.8	− 4.9	0.0	0.5	0.7
r...........	− 7.7	− 5.0	− 1.4	0.0	0.0	0.0	− 4.6	− 2.8	− 0.5
u..........	8.2	4.5	1.0	8.1	7.4	6.2	1.3	0.2	− 0.6

See Table 3 for definitions.

Columns 4 to 6 show how, if interest rates do not adjust, investment falls and the recession is subtantially deeper and longer.

What happens to shadow aggregate demand in the process of adjustment is ambiguous. Although both q and wealth may go down, the anticipation of constraints on both consumption and investment spending may lead both consumers and firms to attempt anticipatory buying. The anticipatory buying effect dominates in the first and third cases in Table 4, the lower wealth and q effect dominates in the second case. In all cases, however, shadow aggregate demand is less than supply and both firms and consumers are rationed in their purchases. Thus investment is less than the value implied by q.

We now turn to the effects of price-wage dynamics on the process of adjustment. For this, we shall consider the effects of an unanticipated decrease in nominal money by 5 % which is assumed by agents to be permanent. The reference values of β, σ, θ are 0.03, 1, 0.015 respectively. The value of β implies that an excess shadow demand of 10 % increases prices by 2.4 % over a period of a year[11]. The value of σ implies complete indexing of

10. Around $W/P = F_L(K, L)$ and for L given by $Q = F(K, L)$ the effect of a change in output on marginal profit is given by :

$$\frac{d}{dQ}[(W/P)(F_K(K, L)/F_L(K, L))] = (F_K(K, L)/F_L(K, L))\,\sigma_{KL}^{-1}$$

where σ_{KL} is the elasticity of substitution between K and L. Thus, the smaller σ_{KL}, the larger the effects of a decrease in output on marginal profit.

11. There is inflation therefore only if there is excess demand for goods. This assumption is acceptable only because we have assumed a zero rate of growth of money. If this rate of growth were positive, the price equations would have to be modified.

wages and the value of θ implies that 5 % unemployment in excess of the natural rate (zero in our model) decreases real wages by 2.4 % over a period of a year.

2.5. Simulation 3. The adjustment of prices and the stabilizing Mundell effect

TOBIN [26] recently formalized an argument of KEYNES that a fast adjustment of prices may lead to a larger recession in response to a decrease in money growth: jif prices adjust fast, there will be a large decrease in inflation and expected inflation. Thus real rates will increase both because of higher nominal rates and because of lower expected inflation; this second channel is usually referred to as the Mundell effect. Thus the faster the prices adjust, the larger the Mundell effect, the higher the real rate and the larger, TOBIN suggests, the effect on aggregate demand. [12]

We now check in our model the effects of the speed of adjustment of prices on the impact of the decrease in money and the length of the recession. The results are given in Table 5 for three values of β, 0.01, 0.03, 0.05.

TABLE 5.

The adjustment of prices and the Mundell effect
The effects of a decrease in money

	Reference case $(\beta = 0.03)$			Slow ajustement $(\beta = 0.01)$			Fast adjustment $(\beta = 0.05)$		
	1	2	3	4	5	6	7	8	9
Quarter.....	0	4	12	0	4	12	0	4	12
Variable									
C.........	−5.0	−2.9	−0.2	−4.9	−4.2	−2.5	−5.0	−1.9	1.1
q..........	−6.6	−1.8	1.7	−7.9	−3.9	0.1	−6.1	−0.6	1.7
QD.......	−9.3	−4.5	0.7	−10.2	−7.1	−3.1	−9.0	−2.7	1.7
QS........	0.0	3.3	4.8	0.0	3.6	7.5	0.0	0.3	2.8
r..........	2.4	2.0	1.2	0.8	0.8	0.8	3.6	2.4	0.4
u..........	11.6	4.6	−2.4	12.7	7.8	1.7	11.2	2.4	−3.1
P..........	0.0	−2.1	−4.9	0.0	−0.8	−2.5	0.0	−3.0	−5.7
W/P.......	0.0	−4.2	−5.0	0.0	−5.1	−9.3	0.0	−3.6	−2.7

See Table 3 for definitions.

The Mundell effect is present: the faster the adjustment of prices, the larger the increase in the initial interest rate. The impact effect of the decrease in money is however smaller, the faster prices adjust. The reason for both results in this model is clear: faster price adjustment indeed means higher real rates initially, but lower nominal and real rates later as real money balances increase faster; the faster the price adjustment, the lower the increase in long real rates. Consumption, through wealth, and investment, through q, depend mostly on long real rates. The short-term rate has only one direct effect, given wealth and q, the effect of bending the path of consumption (equation [1.14]) thus inducing consumers to postpone consumption temporarily. The simulations suggest that this effect, although present, is not very strong. Thus, in our model, faster price adjustment leads to a smaller and shorter recession, contrary to TOBIN's analysis [13].

Note that the long period of high unemployment leads to lower real wages. In all three cases, these lower real wages require a period of overemployment: after the initial recession, the economy experiences a temporary boom, starting in quarter 8 in the first case, in quarter 16 in the second, and quarter 6 in the third. The boom is a Keynesian boom, with aggregate demand below supply. The economy thereafter returns to equilibrium. We now turn to the speed of real wage adjustment.

2.6. Simulation 4. Responsiveness of real wages and Keynesian unemployment

As emphasized by many authors, a decrease in the real wage is likely to improve the economy in a classical regime but may well have perverse effects in a Keynesian regime. We now consider the effects of real wage responsiveness in such a case. Table 6 reports the effects of the decrease in money, for three different values of θ, 0.005, 0.015 and 0.045.

Because of our formalization of consumers and our assumption of no liquidity constraints, the distribution of output between profits and real wages has no income distribution effect on consumption. Real wages however have an effect on investment : for an output constrained firm, if real wages are anticipated to be lower for a sufficiently long period of time, the firm will aim at a lower capital/labor ratio and thus further decrease investment. The result will therefore be a further decrease in aggregate demand.

This impact effect is there in table 6. Large responsiveness of real wages leads to a larger decrease in investment and aggregate demand; the difference is however small across values of θ.

---

12. The Mundell effect is currently felt in the U.S. where as the result of lower money growth, high nominal rates and lower inflation have led to short-term real rates around 8 %.

13. To reverse these results and obtain the Tobin result, the short-term rate must have a strong impact on economic activity. This may be the case if, for example, there are institutional restrictions in financial markets, leading to rationing of specific sectors such as housing, when short rates increase.

Of more interest is the process of adjustment which is not monotonic but cyclical, due to the interaction of investment, output and real wages. The initial period of recession and low investment is followed by a period of expansion and higher investment. This is particularly clear when real wages are very responsive. During this adjustment, aggregate demand is sometimes larger than aggregate supply, as in column 6 and the economy oscillates between Keynesian and classical regimes.

TABLE 6

Real wage responsiveness and Keynesian unemployment

	Reference case ($\theta = 0.015$)			Large responsiveness ($\theta = 0.045$)			Small responsiveness ($\theta = 0.005$)		
	1	2	3	4	5	6	7	8	9
Quarter.....	0	4	12	0	4	12	0	4	12
Variable									
C..........	−5	−2.9	−0.2	−4.6	−1.0	−1	−5	−3.4	−1.9
q..........	−6.6	−1.8	1.7	−7.6	−0.8	2.1	−5.9	−1.8	0.4
QD........	−9.3	−4.5	0.7	−9.7	−2.1	4	−8.9	−4.9	−2.1
QS........	0	3.3	4.8	0	14.3	0.3	0	−0.6	0.3
r..........	2.4	2	1.2	2.8	4.8	−2.4	2	1.2	0.4
u..........	11.6	4.6	2.4	12.1	1.3	−1	11.1	5.2	1.3
P..........	0	−2.1	−4.9	0	−3.3	−6.3	0	−1.6	−3.1
W/P......	0	−4.2	−5	0	−11.7	−0.4	0	−1.4	−2.3

See table 3 for definitions.

We now turn to the effects of an anticipated profit tax.

3 Anticipations of a profit tax

The accession of a socialist governement obviously creates large changes in anticipations. Among those changes, two are likely to complicate the task of economic policy initially. The first is the anticipation of large budget deficits in the future, partially monetized and leading to higher inflation. The second is the anticipation of lower profits by firms, either because of higher real wages and compensation, or higher taxation of firms (see KOLM [15]). Although these anticipations may, in the case of France, not be warranted, real and financial decisions based on them will affect interest rates, the stock market, exchange rates as well as investment, consumption and so on. An understanding of these anticipation effects is important for the conduct of economic policy. In this section, we focus on the effects of the anticipations of lower profits, summarizing the anticipations of various changes in the tax structure by an anticipation of a higher tax rate on profits.

3.1. Taxes and the government budget constraint

For our purpose, we need to introduce only two taxes. The first is a tax at rate τ on profit $Q - (W/P)L$. The second is a lump-sum tax or subsidy on income. The government budget constraint is:

$$\tau \left(Q - (W/P)\, L \right) + T = 0$$

An increase in τ implies a corresponding decrease in T; thus a higher profit tax does not, *ceteris paribus*, affect the income of consumers but only its composition.

The presence of a profit tax modifies two of the equations of Table 1 in Section I. The terms (W/P) $(F_K (K, L)/F_L (K, L))$ in equation (1.13) and $(Q - (W/P)L)$ in equation (1.19) are now premultiplied by $(1 - \tau)$.

3.2. The effects of an actual profit tax

We first consider the effects of the actual implementation of an increase in τ, from 0 to 0.2, unanticipated and permanent. The effects are summarized in Table 7.

Two elements explain the results of Table 7. The first is the long-run elasticity of savings with respect to interest rates; the second, the degree of wage responsiveness to unemployment.

The first is readily understood by looking at the steady state effects of the profit tax. In steady state, the interest rate has to remain equal to the subjective discount rate. As q^* is also unchanged, the after-tax marginal product of capital is invariant to changes in the tax rate. In steady state, therefore, the tax is entirely shifted from capital to labor. [14] The decrease in the capital stock depends on the elasticity of substitution between capital and labor. For the assumed value of 0.5 for σ_{KL}, the capital stock decreases by 14 % and so does the capital labor ratio. The real wage is then lower by 8 % and output lower by 4 %.

The degree of wage response to unemployment determines the dynamics of adjustment, particularly the speed at which the tax is shifted from capital to labor. With flexible wages, as the capital decreases and full employment is maintained, wages decrease, the after-tax marginal product increases and q returns to its steady state value. If real wages do not adjust, however, as the capital decreases employment too decreases. The after-tax marginal product remains the same and q remains below its steady state value. In the extreme case of permanently fixed real wages, this conflict about income distribution leads to complete capital decumulation over time, and zero employment. If real wages respond to unemployment, the economy goes through a protracted period of unemployment and capital decumulation.

---

14. The result that the interest rate remains unchanged and that the tax is ultimately shifted to labor follows from the assumption that agents are—or act as if they were—infinitely long lived. If agents have finite horizons, the tax would only be partially shifted to labor. If, however, the economy is small and open and there are no restrictions on capital movements, the steady-state interest rate would again equal the foreign interest rate and the tax would be fully shifted to labor.

Table 7 shows that the adjustment takes the economy through two regimes. The imposition of the tax leads to a decrease in investment demand and a period of Keynesian unemployment (there are two conflicting effects on consumption: the first is the anticipation of lower income, the second the anticipation of constraints on future consumption spending. In the two cases considered, the anticipatory buying effect dominates). As capital decu-

TABLE 7

Profit tax and real wage responsiveness

	Reference case ($\theta = 0.015$)				Small responsiveness of wages ($\theta = 0.005$)			
	1	2	3	4	5	6	7	8
Quarter.....	0	4	12	40	0	4	12	40
Variable.								
C..........	1.4	2.2	−1.2	−2.6	3.2	0.1	−4.5	−5.4
q..........	−11.1	−5.1	−2.4	−0.4	−10.9	−5.1	−2.8	−0.8
QD........	−6.7	−1.1	−1.3	−3.8	−4.9	0.4	−3.7	−7
QS........	0	−2.3	−3.9	−4.2	0	−4.2	−6.7	−7.2
K..........	0	−5.1	−9.1	−13.5	0	−5	−9.5	−16.4
r..........	2.8	0.8	−1.3	−0.2	4	−1.1	−1.4	0.0
u..........	8.3	0.9	1.6	0	6	3.5	5.4	3.5
W/P.......	0	−2	−3.7	−7	0	−0.5	−2	−7.2

See Table 3 for definitions.

FIGURE 3

Effects of an unanticiped profit tax

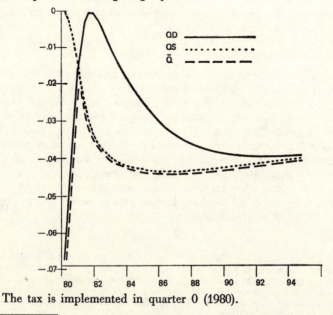

The tax is implemented in quarter 0 (1980).

mulates, the economy enters a phase of classical unemployment (after 4 quarters in the first case, 2 quarters in the second), which lasts for more than 30 quarters in the first case, more than 50 in the second case. If the responsiveness of real wages to unemployment is small, capital decumulates below its new steady state level during the adjustment process.

3.3. The effects of an anticipated profit tax

Suppose now that the tax, instead of being currently implemented, is anticipated for some time in the future. Table 8 reports the effects of such anticipations. For both simulations, quarter 0 is the quarter in which firms start anticipating the profit tax; this quarter may be the quarter of the elections, or a prior quarter if the outcome of the elections was anticipated. In the first simulation, the profit tax is anticipated for 8 quarters ahead and in the second simulation for 12 quarters ahead. [15,16]

TABLE 8

Effects of an anticipated profit tax

	Profit tax anticipated for quarter 8				Profit tax anticipated for quarter 12			
	1	2	3	4	5	6	7	8
Quarter.....	0	4	8	12	0	4	8	12
Variable								
C..........	0.9	2.1	1.3	−0.9	0.7	1.4	1	0.8
q..........	−5.8	−4.3	−5	−3.2	−4.1	−3	−3.4	−4.4
QD........	−3.6	−1.6	−1.5	−1.6	−2.6	−1.2	−1.2	−1.8
QS........	0	−1.2	−3.1	−4.1	0	−0.9	−2.2	−3.1
K..........	0	−3.1	−5.7	−8	0	−2.2	−4	−5.6
r..........	1.6	1.4	0.3	−1.3	1.2	0.9	0.3	0.3
u..........	4.3	0.9	1.8	2.3	3	0.7	1.2	1.8
W/P.......	0.0	−1.3	−1.8	−2.8	0	−0.9	−1.3	−1.8

See table 3 for definitions.

---

15. Firms are unlikely to have such precise anticipations. They are more likely to think that the profit tax rate may be increased with some probability which is an increasing function of time. We could formalize this by considering the sequence of expected values of their subjective distribution of tax rates. We could not however characterize the effects of uncertainty *per se* on their behavior.

16. If the government does not actually intend to increase the profit tax, these simulations give only the anticipated future as of quarter 0. If in quarter 8 in the first case (or 12 in the second), there is no increase in the profit tax and agents revise their anticipations, the outcome in quarters 8 and following will be different from table 8.

The effects are simple. The change in anticipation leads to a substantial decline in investment (and a decrease in the stock market of 7 % in the first case, 5 % in the second). This decline in investment demand leads to a Keynesian recession. As capacity decreases, the economy goes into classical unemployment even before the profit tax is implemented. The process of adjustment after the implementation is similar to the one described above.[17]

FIGURE 4

Effects of an Anticiped Profit Tax

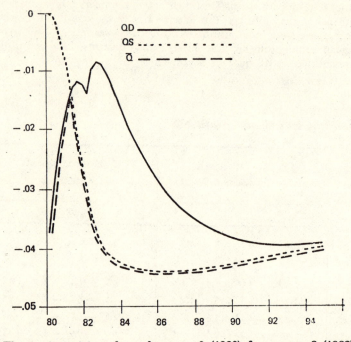

The tax is anticipated as of quarter 0 (1980) for quarter 8 (1982).

Thus anticipations of a profit tax lead first to Keynesian unemployment, then, later on, to classical unemployment. If faced with such anticipations, what should be the response of the government? The answer to this question is difficult but the following remarks can be made.

The most obvious strategy, if the government does not plan any increase in profit taxes, is to attempt to modify anticipations by the presentation of a credible set of fiscal policies for the short and medium terms.

17. In this case, excess shadow demand for goods is never very large and thus there is no substantial inflation. It is however quite possible to generate as a result of an adverse supply shock (profit tax, increased price of some input or technological shock), a period of classical unemployment, a decrease in capital accumulation due to the conflict in income distribution and substantial inflation as chronic excess demand remains. Such an outcome may have some explanatory power for what happened in the second half of the 70's.

The second is to use a short-term expansionary policy to avoid the initial recession, while anticipations of a profit tax disappear. This may be done by measures to help either consumption or investment. Helping consumption may not be successful if the economy is already close to classical unemployment. Helping investment may increase both demand and supply. Thus, the best policy may be, ironically, a temporary reduction in the profit tax, which has effects both directly and as a signal of the government's intentions.

Conclusion

The effect of a policy on the economy depends very much on whether it has been anticipated or not, on how long it is expected to last and so on. The model developed in this paper, which allows for rational firms and households, as well as for imperfectly flexible prices, is well adapted to characterize the effects of policy in such cases.

It is obviously too preliminary to be a reliable guide to policy: The lack of foundations of price inertia, the infinite life assumption which implies no income distribution effects, the closed economy assumption all need to be relaxed. We believe however that, such as it is, it can shed light on the effects of policy.

● References

[1] ABEL A. B. — *Investment and the Value of Capital*, Ph. D. thesis, Massachusetts Institute of Technology, 1978.

[2] ABEL A. B. and BLANCHARD O. J. — « An Intertemporal Model of Saving and Investment », forthcoming *Econometrica*, May 1983.

[3] BARRO J. — *Macroeconomic Analysis*, mimeo, 1981.

[4] BARRO R. J. and GROSSMAN, HERSCHEL I. — *Money, Employment and Inflation*, Cambridge, Cambridge University Press, 1976.

[5] BENASSY J. P. — « Neo-Keynesian Disequilibrium in a Monetary Economy », *Review of Economic Studies*, 42, 1975, p. 503-523.

[6] BLANCHARD O. J. — «Output, the Stock Market and Interest Rates», *American Economic Review*, 71, March 1981, p. 132-143.

[7] —— « What is Left of the Multiplier-Accelerator? », *American Economic Review*, 71, May 1981, p. 150-155.

[8] —— « Price Desynchronization and Price Level Inertia », *Indexation, Contracting and Debt in an Inflationary World*, Cambridge, MIT Press, R. Dornbusch and M. Simonsen (eds.) forthcoming, 1983.

[9] —— « Dynamic Effects a Shift in Savings; the Role of Firms », forthcoming *Econometrica.*, July 1983.

[10] BLANCHARD O. J. and KAHN C. — « The Solution to Linear Difference Models under Rational Expectations », *Econometrica*, 48, July 1980, p. 1305-1313.

[11] DRÈZE J. H. — « Existence of an Exchange Equilibrium under Price Rigidities », *International Economic Review*, 16, June 1975, p. 301-320.

[12] HALL R. E. — « The Macroeconomic Impact of Changes in Income Taxes in the Short and the Medium Runs », *Journal of Political Economy*, 86, April 1978, S 71-85.

[13] HAYASHI F. — « Tobin's Marginal *q* and Average *q* : A Neoclassical Interpretation », *Econometrica*, 50, January 1982, p. 213-224.

[14] ITO T. — « Filippov Solutions of Systems of Differential Equations with Discontinuous Right Hand Sides », *Economic Letters*, 4-1979, p. 349-354.

[15] KOLM S. C. — *La Transition socialiste*, Paris. CERF, 1977.

[16] LIPTON D., POTERBA J., SACH J., and SUMMERS, L. — « Multiple Shooting in Rational Expectations Models », *Econometrica*, 50, September 1982, p. 1329-1334.

[17] LUCAS R. E. — « Adjustment Costs and the Theory of Supply », *Journal of Political Economy*, 75, August 1967, p. 321-334.

[18] —— *Studies in Business Cycle Theory*, Cambridge, MIT Press, 1981.

[19] MALINVAUD E. — *The Theory of Unemployment Reconsidered*, Oxford, Basil Blackwell, 1977.

[20] —— *Profitability and Unemployment*, Cambridge, Cambridge University Press, 1980.

[21] NEARY P. J. and STIGLITZ J. E. — « Expectations and Constrained Equilibria », forthcoming *Q.J.E.*, 1983.

[22] SACHS J. — « Energy and Growth under Flexible Exchange Rates », *The International Transmission of Economic Disturbances*, Cambridge, MIT Press, J. Bhandari and B. Putnam (eds.), forthcoming.

[23] —— « Wages, Profits and Macroeconomic Adjustment : A Comparative Study », *Brookings Papers on Economic Activity*, 2, 1979, p. 269-319.

[24] SARGENT T. J. — *Macroeconomic Theory*, New York, Academic Press, 1979.

[25] TAYLOR J. — « Staggered Wage Setting in a Macro-Model », *American Economic Review*, 69, May 1979, p. 108-113.

[26] TOBIN J. — « Keynesian Models of Recession and Depression », *American Economic Review*, 65, May 1975, p. 195-202.

Comments [p. 117]

by Antoine d'AUTUME

Lille I University

The BLANCHARD and SACHS article is an important theoretical contribution to the non-market-clearing approach to macroeconomics. Some people dismiss this approach on the a priori ground that it does not supply any theoretical foundations for the assumption of imperfect price flexibility. What the authors do however is to follow this approach without too many apologies and to show that it is a fruitful one.

In my opinion we are not far away with this paper from what may be a canonical model of intertemporal disequilibrium, playing roughly the same role as the one played in a more static framework by the famous three-regime model notably analysed by BARRO-GROSSMAN, BENASSY and MALINVAUD. The crucial features here are the use of TOBIN's q to derive a genuine investment behavior and the perfect foresight assumption. This leads to a tractable model providing many insights and allowing for various applications and developments. The theoretical progress is unmistakable. To achieve full success, I think however that the analytical treatment should be carried a little further. Simulation would probably then also remain necessary, but at least the working of the model should be more thoroughly explored.

I will thus limit my comment to a few formal points. These concern mainly the role of the transversality conditions. I think that these conditions *must not* be considered merely as a technical issue, or as an auxiliary device to make sure that the model will not explode. The role of these transversality conditions is to determine the initial values of the costate variables q and x, and these are important from an economic point of view since it is through them that future conditions, and especially the expected future constraints, affect the present situation. This is particularly clear in the consumer problem : the differential equation governing x is very simple and the important phenomenon − the wealth effect −− passes through x_0.

Thus I regret in the first place that the transversality condition in the consumer problem clearly has not been written correctly : the condition in the paper does not imply any restriction on the value of x_0. Moreover the a priori condition on the evolution of A, which is necessary for the problem to be meaningful, is missing. Of course the formulation of transversality conditions in infinite time is still a somewhat open question but there seems to be no doubt, in the present case, that the traditional condition

$$\lim_{t \to +\infty} x e^{-\delta t} A = 0$$

holds.

Let us turn now to the interpretation of figures 1 and 2. I found the related discussion interesting and important but still somewhat frustrating because the method of analysis is not very explicit. This method seems to me related to the following conditions, based on HAYASHI, which state an expression for the initial values q_0 and x_0 deriving from the transversality conditions :

$$q_0 \, k_0 = V_0 - \int_{\{I=\bar{I}\}} \lambda_I \, I \exp \left(-\int_0^t r_s \, ds \right) dt - \int_{\{Q=\bar{Q}\}} \lambda_Q \, \bar{Q} \exp \left(-\int_0^t r_s \, ds \right) dt$$

$$x_0 \, (A_0 + W_0) = \frac{1}{\delta} - \int_{\{c=\bar{c}\}} \lambda_c \, \bar{C} \, e^{-\delta t} \, dt$$

V_0 stands for the value of the firm and W_0 for the discounted sum of wages and profits. The integrals are calculated over the domain where the constraint effectively applies. The second relationship is derived on the basis of a CES utility function (see table 2) and using the corrected transversality condition.

The path described in figure 2 derives from the second preceding formula. When going from an unconstrained situation to a constrained one x_0 decreases and thus desired consumption increases. This conforms to intuition; since the consumer's wealth is given, if he must consume less from t_1 to t_2 he will consume more for the rest to his life.

If the producer expects not to be constrained we have $q_0 K_0 = V_0$. This is HAYASHI's result : marginal q = average q. If the producer expects to be constrained, we have to take into account the deadweight loss of future constraints. I must admit that the previous formula does not seem to me to imply the behavior described on figure 1 and I must express my perplexity before this figure (I do not even see in which case the unconstrained producer would choose to maintain a given absolute level of investment...).

Lastly I would have been happy if the paper had dealt with the possible occurrence of an infinity of solutions in a dynamic model with rational expectation. To this end it would be necessary to distinguish clearly between the relationships describing individual behavior and the ones describing market equilibrium. Once again the transversality conditions would play a crucial role.

Comments [p. 117]

147-48

by Pentti KOURI

New York University, Helsinky University, and NBER

BLANCHARD and SACHS develop an elegant model of an economy that alternates between states of Keynesian and classical unemployment. In a Keynesian state the real money stock is "too low" and firms are constrained by lack of effective demand. In a classical state, the real wage rate is "too high" and buyers are constrained in the output market. BLANCHARD and SACHS assume away a third state of disequilibrium, that of repressed inflation, to simplify their dynamic analysis. One justification for assuming away excess demand in the labor market might be that real wages adjust immediately upwards while they adjust only slowly downwards. BLANCHARD and SACHS, however, simply postulate that labor supply adjusts passively to labor demand.

The novelty of the BLANCHARD and SACHS model is the explicit specification of household and firm behavior in terms of continuous-time intertemporal optimization subject to exogeneously given prices *and* quantity constraints which may or may not be binding. It is assumed further that households and firms have perfect foresight with respect to the time path of prices and quantity constraints, and that the economy is always in expectational equilibrium although markets fail to clear. One might, of course, ask why economic agents do not incorporate any of the information concerning future excess demand in their pricing decisions. As it is, BLANCHARD and SACHS assume "as if" prices and wages were determined by an outside "price and wage control board" that follows mechanical rules of price adjustment. In particular it adjusts prices in response to *realized* excess demand in *real time* rather than in response to conjectural excess demand. Accordingly excess supply or demand can persist for a long time, which is, of course, a feature that BLANCHARD and SACHS want to have in their model.

I would like to note one feature of the price adjustment rule that BLANCHARD and SACHS assume. As it is specified, prices respond to changes in production costs only gradually through changes in excess demand. This contrasts with the standard mark-up price equation and is obviously responsible for some of the dynamic properties of the BLANCHARD-SACHS model. For example, a reduction of nominal wages is not immediately passed on to prices in their model and accordingly may lead to a reduction rather than an increase in investment and aggregate demand.

A central and novel feature of the BLANCHARD-SACHS model is the modelling of capital formation in a way that explicitly incorporates quantity constraints (MALINVAUD has, of course, emphasized capital accumulation from a somewhat different point of view). As BLANCHARD and SACHS demonstrate, the effects of changes in real wages or in the cost of capital are quite different depending on the current and expected future state of the economy. If firms are constrained by effective demand and expect to be so constrained also in the future, an increase in nominal wages leads to an increase in investment because of capital-labor substitution. It will also lead to an increase in effective demand in the BLANCHARD-SACHS model because the wage increase is not passed on to prices. Thus paradoxically an increase in wages may increase employment in the short run. The model would seem to imply that labor will benefit also in the medium term because the supply of capital relative to labor will increase. Since BLANCHARD and SACHS do not distinguish between capacity-increasing and labor-saving capital, investment is always good for labor. Even if firms invest today to save labor, they can convert the additional capital to higher capacity with higher employment and lower productivity in the future. This is obviously not possible if one takes a richer, vintage view of capital.

BLANCHARD's and SACHS' discussion of the Mundell effect is interesting and relevant : is it possible as TOBIN has suggested that rapid price adjustment makes recessions more severe because of the effect of anticipated price deflation on relative asset yields? Simulation of the BLANCHARD-SACHS model suggests that this is not the case : the faster prices adjust, the less is the effect of monetary contraction on unemployment. This result might not hold, however, if one introduced liquidity trap considerations or the possibility of bankruptcies and shifts in liquidity preference in the process of severe price deflation.

The simulation exercises that BLANCHARD and SACHS carry out in the last few pages of their paper concerning actual and anticipated profits taxes illuminate the usefulness of their model in tracing out the dynamic effects of policy changes. In their model a profits tax is completely shifted to wages in the long run because the supply of capital is assumed to be infinitely elastic at the subjective rate of time preference. In the short run, the effect of a profit tax depends crucially on the state of the economy as well as on future expectations.

A profits tax increases the cost of capital and therefore causes firms to substitute labour for capital. In the simulations that are reported this positive effect on employment is, however, more than offset by the depressing effect of lower investment on aggregate demand. The economy enters a period of Keynesian unemployment. As the supply of capital is reduced the economy moves on to a state of classical unemployment. If the real wage rate does not adjust, capital decumulation proceeds without limit. In the long run, technology and the cost of capital determine the equilibrium real wage rate. In other words, long run demand for labor is infinitely elastic. This is a strong implication of the model, and it obviously depends on the rather special assumptions that the authors make about saving behavior and technology.

In summary, BLANCHARD and SACHS have provided us with a useful tool for analysing dynamic adjustment of the economy to changes in policy. This issue is of great importance, for the feasibility of policies that are desirable from the long run point of view often depends on their short term and medium term effects.

149-74

The Franc and the French financial sector

Mathieu FEROLDI
and Jacques MELITZ*

* We wish to thank Françoise
DUMONTIER for computer assistance. We have also benefited from the comments of
Barry EICHENGREEN, Richard
MARSTON, Charles WYPLOSZ,
and innumerable colleagues
at INSEE.

This paper provides a test of the asset-market
approach to the franc in a four-asset model
with central bank intervention on all markets,
an exogenously given dollar-deutschemark, and
the use of full information maximum likelihood. Foreign assets are considered as substitutes for each of the different home assets.
Therefore no independent structural equation
for capital movements is possible, and all four
asset markets interact in the determination of
the franc.

Introduction

We shall present a model of the French franc which will appear too complicated to many eyes, but whose basic complication is precisely the element that we wish to defend. The source of the complication is not the franc. However, French circumstances will necessarily enter into the picture since our argument is that exchange rate analysis requires a basic modelisation of the national financial sector.

The underlying sources of the complexity are three : exchange rate uncertainty; the distinction between money and securities; and the endogeneity of the ratio of money to securities. Market uncertainty makes it impossible to explain international differences in interest rates strictly on the basis of expected movements of the exchange rate. Attitudes toward risk matter too. The distinction between money and securities implies that the exchange rate is not necessarily in equilibrium because any single home-debt market is so. Excess supplies or demands of foreign assets are then still possible. The endogenous ratio of money to other debt assets means that the risk premium on home securities (positive or negative) relative to foreign securities cannot be attributed strictly to uncertainty. This premium can change without any movement in exchange rate uncertainty (or no change in subjective probability distributions about future exchange rates), simply because of a movement in the relative scarcity of home securities to money. One reason for the endogeneity of the ratio of money to securities is essential in all exchange rate analysis : namely, the presence of a managed float. It follows, in this view, that the exchange rate, the home interest rate, and the ratio of money to securities must be determined jointly. That is, the exchange rate can only be explained within the context of general financial analysis.

One important feature of our particular treatment is an attempt fully to incorporate the budget constraint in every relevant sector. The balance-of-payments identity is consequently present in the analysis. But nevertheless there is no independent structural equation for capital movements. Such an equation has no place since we consider a number of different home assets as alternatives to foreign ones, and capital movements in our model therefore depend on a basic admixture of structural elements from different markets, and can only be properly determined residually from the balance-of-payments identity. In general, enough attention has not yet been given to the fact that only under highly restrictive conditions does an independent structural equation for capital movements make sense. [1]

---

1. One of us has tried to develop this view more fully elsewhere recently : see MELITZ [1983].

The model: formal aspects

Table 1 provides the accounting framework for our model. There are four asset markets: money (M), bank credit (C), interest-bearing securities (S), and foreign assets (F). Securities comprise bonds and equities, public and private — everything but money and bank credit. In addition, there are four sectors: government (g), commercial banks (b), nonbank firms and households (fh, f for firms, h for households), and the foreign (n). The first four rows of the table relate to the identities in the four asset markets. For example, row 1 says: [2]

$$(1) \qquad\qquad M_{fh} + M_n = \underline{M_g} + D$$

The columns relate to the wealth or budget restraint for each individual sector. For example, column (5) (by necessity broken up in two parts) says:

$$(5) \qquad M_{fh} + S_h + eF_{fh} = C_f + C_h^{st} + C_h^{lt} + S_f + \Sigma\,(SAV_{fh})^*$$

Thus the table forms eight identities. The variable underlined once in each row is the one which is determined by the relevant market identity. The variable underlined twice in each column is the one which is determined by the relevant budget constraint. One of the accounting identities in the model, as in any complete macroeconomic system, cannot determine a variable independently of the values of the variables that are determined by all of the other accounting identities in it. There is therefore one column, (6), where no variable has been underlined twice. The variable underlined three times in this column is supposed to be determined by the balance sheet condition of the Treasury, as distinct from the central bank. This condition is :

$$(9) \qquad\qquad \Sigma\,(G - TX)^* = \underline{\underline{S_g}} + T^*$$

Thus, the Treasury's need to finance its deficits supposedly determines S_g. Note that the sum of (6), (7), and (9) would produce the monetary-sector balance sheet :

$$M_g + D = C_g^* + C_b + T^* + F_g$$

---

2. M_g in eq. (1), or the government money issue, is not limited to currency, but includes postal checking accounts, and the large deposits at the French savings banks. It should also be noted that D includes the deposits at the nationally owned commercial banks as well as the private commercial banks. Students of the French monetary system agree, though, that there is little to distinguish between the behavior of these two sets of commercial banks. Whether this will continue to be so in the future, following the nationalization measures of 1981-1982 is something that we cannot say. However, based upon the long French experience in managing public commercial banks as if they were private, we do not expect commercial banks to break with their previous behavior pattern.

TABLE 1. — *The accounting framework*

	USES				SOURCES			
	(5) f h	(6) g	(7) b	(8) n	(5) f h	(6) g	(7) b	(8) n
Money [M] (1)........	M_{fh}			M_n		M_g	D	
Bank credit [C] (2)...		C^*_g	C_b		C_f C^{st}_h C^{lt}_h			C_n^*
Securities [S] (3)	S_h			S_n	S_f	S_g		
Foreign assets [F] (4).	eF_{fh}	F_g						eF_n
Items which cancel out in defining the four asset markets.....		REFI T^*	BR^*			BR^* T^*	REFI	
Accumulated net savings.........		$\Sigma(G-TX)^*$		$\Sigma(X-IM)^*$	$\Sigma(SAV_{fh})^*$			

M_{fh} = money held by firms plus households;
M_n = money held by foreigners;
M_g = money issued by government
D = commercial bank deposits
C^{st}_h, C^{lt}_h = short-term and long-term borrowing of households from banks, respectively;
e = price of the dollar in terms of francs (FF/$);

BR = commercial bank reserves;
REFI = commercial bank refinancing;
T = direct lending of the central bank to the Treasury;
$G - TX$ = current government deficit;
$X - IM$ = current account surplus;
SAV_{fh} = current saving by firms and households.

Closing the system will be one extra definition and twelve empirical equations. The definition is :

$$(10) \qquad\qquad M = M_g + D$$

The twelve empirical equations consist of eleven structural equations and an expression for the anticipated rate of depreciation of the franc $(\dot{e}_a)$. We shall state these 12 equations momentarily as follows :

(11)	$C_b(\ \ )$	(17)	$S_n(\ \ )$
(12)	$C_h^{st}(\ \ )$	(18)	$S_h(\ \ )$
(13)	$C_h^{lt}(\ \ )$	(19)	$\dfrac{D}{M}(\ \ )$
(14)	$(C_f + S_f)(\ \ )$	(20)	$RM(\ \ )$
(15)	$M_{fh}(\ \ )$	(21)	$e(\ \ )$
(16)	$M_n(\ \ )$	(22)	$\dot{e}_a \equiv \ \dots$

RM is the rate of intervention of the Bank of France on the "money market", and corresponds to the discount rate of the theoretical literature.

The starred variables in table 1 are exogenous. As can be seen, we treat all commodity flows as exogenous, and will similarly later view all commodity prices as exogenous. Thus, as a major limitation of our analysis, we only consider financial interdependencies in exchange-rate determination.

If we count up all the variables in table 1 that are neither underlined nor starred, we find eight of them: M_{fh}, M_n, D, C_h^{st}, C_h^{lt}, C_f, S_h and S_n. These endogenous variables are then determined by the empirical equations. Which eight of these equations determines which of these eight endogenous variables is obvious in each case. The four endogenous variables corresponding to the four extra equations are the exchange rate, e [essentially determined by eq. (21)], the anticipated rate of depreciation of the franc, $\dot{e}_a$ [eq. (22)], the rate of central bank intervention on the "money market", RM [eq. (20)], and the price of commercial bank credit, R (eq. (11) since eq. (2) already determines C_b). All told we have then a system of 22 equations in 21 unknowns (since, as explained, one of the equations, which we take as (6), is not independent). The unknowns are the 9 underlined variables in table 1, plus the 8 additional ones in the table, plus M, e, $\dot{e}_a$, RM, and R. [3]

The satisfaction of Walras' law is implicit since all of the budget restraints are satisfied. Upon examination, the law may be said to eliminate the market for foreign assets F, since everything in row (4) is solved through the identities. But it should also be noted that the market for F is intimately involved in the system, partly because of the role that we will subsequently assign to the foreign interest rate, e, and $\dot{e}_a$ in the structural equations, partly because F_g, or official reserves, will enter as an argument in the official reaction function $e(\ \ )$, eq. (21), and in the supply of commercial bank credit $C_b(\ \ )$, eq. (11).

F_g should have been written eF_g in conformity with the notation eF_{fh} and eF_n since it refers to official foreign reserves *in francs*. But our notation simplifies matters at little cost since exchange gains and losses by the government do not affect our measure of official reserves. These gains and losses are part of an omitted (exogenous) residual in the budget restraint for government, eq. (6). Changes in the exchange rate, e, hence, do not have any capital-value effects on official reserves, F_g, and will not do so throughout the analysis. In the same way, we value home securities, S, at issue prices. Therefore, movements in the bond rate also will have no valuational effects on S, that is, S_h, S_f, S_n or S_g.

Before leaving these purely formal aspects a word may be added about capital movements. If we convert the budget restraint on foreigners, eq. (8), in first-difference form, and we substitute $eF_{fh} + F_g$ for eF_n, we obtain the balance-of-payments identity :

(8.1) $$\Delta F_g + e\Delta F_{fh} + \Delta C_n = \Delta S_n + \Delta M_n + (X - IM)$$

The expression for capital movements (CM) in our system is therefore :

(8.2) $$CM = e\Delta F_{fh} + \Delta C_n - \Delta S_n - \Delta M_n$$

After various substitutions for the endogenous terms, this equation resolves down to :

$$CM = (X - IM)^* - \Delta M_{fh}(\ \ ) - \Delta M_n(\ \ ) + \Delta C_b(\ \ ) + \Delta C_g^* + \Delta T^*$$

Thus, as we have already stressed, capital movements have no independent existence in the system.

---

3. An important point of comparison in the literature are the two works of Ray FAIR [1979a, b].

2 The model: empirical aspects

2.1. Even this skeletal description already reflects in important ways some empirical conditions in France. The balance sheet identity for the banks, eq. (7), reflects the fact that the banks are always indebted to the government rather than the reverse. This debt, REFI, consists of credit that the commercial banks refinance with the central bank. The only sort of quantitative restrictions on them are the "encadrements du crédit" or official ceilings on credit expansion. These ceilings became increasingly important in the 1970's. But the ceilings are subject to major exemptions, based on various credit priorities. As a result, it remains correct, now as ever, to regard bank refinancing, REFI, as the residual element in the banks' balance sheet identity [eq. (7)]. In fact, the commercial banks are so secure in the current arrangements that they do not hold any capital-market assets at all for their protection. Official regulations further do not permit them to hold any open position in foreign currency. Since they abide by these regulations (certainly on a quarterly-average basis), we neglect the matching foreign-currency items on both sides of their balance sheet. Another omission, which could prove more troublesome for the future, however, is the banks' issues of securities. Since 1979 and especially 1980 banks have turned significantly to the securities market for funds, as this has been one of their routes of escape from the "encadrement du crédit". It may become necessary to model banks' supply of securities in the future.

The bond rate is exogenous in our system. The French authorities set this rate below the market-clearing level. This then creates a queue, in which the government always has first place. But since the tail of the queue is never served, the private corporate sector is permanently rationed on the bond market. [4] Thus starved for long-term bond issues, this sector substitutes equities to some extent, but mostly increases borrowing from the banks. As a result, a higher bond rate *reduces* the firms' demand for bank credit by allowing firms to sell more bonds to households. Further, an increase in the government issue of bonds at any bond rate increases firms' demand for bank credit. A number of features of the model are then easily understood.

---

4. There have been times in recent years, especially during René Monory's tenure as Minister of the Economy in 1978-1981, when the bond rate was set close to the equilibrium market level. On these occasions, the private corporate sector was less rationed. There have also been occasional days and sequences of days throughout the 1970's when the high-priority bond issue failed to sell at the officially desired prices. But this situation never lasted; thus it makes little difference. As a permanent condition, the private corporation cannot sell more bonds in France by simply dropping its price. For further institutional detail covering all of the empirical issues in this section, see MELITZ [1982*b*]. A couple of less summary, still compact treatments, are Antoine COUTIÈRE [1977]; and Raymond PENAUD [1978].

First, it makes sense to view government securities, S_g, as the residual element in the government accounting identity, eq. (6), since the government is always able to finance itself through bond issue. Second, S_f can be logically regarded as the residual of eq. (3) since private corporations simply float as much as they can on the securities market. Accordingly, our aggregation of private and public issues in a single securities market is well grounded. Finally, it is reasonable also to lump together desired issues of debts by firms, $C_f + S_f$, as we do in eq. (14). Since S_f always makes up a lower proportion of total debt than the firms would wish, the price of bank credit, R, really defines the marginal cost of the total debt, and the bond rate, R_b, only fixes a certain rent. Firms then decide their total borrowing, $C_f + S_f$, on the basis of R (cf. also Patrick ARTUS *et al.*, *METRIC* [1981]).

2.2. Let us now state the twelve empirical equations, (11) – (22), more explicitly.

TABLE 2

The Empirical Equations

---

(11) $\qquad C_b = C_b\,(\overset{+}{\beta},\ \overset{+}{Y_p}\overset{+}{P_a},\ \overset{+}{B_u},\ \overset{-}{CC})$

$\qquad$ where $\quad \beta = R - (RM + RC)\left(1 - \dfrac{D\,(1-r)}{M}\right)$

$\qquad$ and $\quad B_u = F_g + T + C_g$

(12) $\qquad \dfrac{C_h^{st}}{P} = \dfrac{C_h^{st}}{P}\left(\overset{+}{Y_p},\ \overset{?}{Y_t},\ \overset{-}{R},\ \overset{+}{\dot{P}_a},\ \overset{-}{\dfrac{P_{dur}}{P}},\ \overset{-}{CC}\right)$

(13) $\qquad \dfrac{C_h^{lt}}{P} = \dfrac{C_h^{lt}}{P}\left(\overset{+}{Y_p},\ \overset{-}{R},\ \overset{+}{\dot{P}_a},\ \overset{-}{\dfrac{P_{cons}}{P}},\ \overset{+}{TERM},\ \overset{-}{CC}\right)$

(14) $\qquad \dfrac{C_f + S_f}{P} = \dfrac{C_f + S_f}{P}\,(\overset{+}{Y_p},\ \overset{-}{Y_t},\ \overset{-}{R},\ \overset{+}{\dot{P}_a},\ R^{us} \overset{+}{+\dot{e}_a},\ \overset{+}{e},\ \overset{+}{R_c},\ \overset{-}{CC})$

(15) $\qquad \dfrac{M_{fh}}{P} = \dfrac{M_{fh}}{P}\,(\overset{+}{Y_p},\ \overset{?}{Y_t},\ \overset{-}{R_b},\ \overset{-}{\dot{P}_a},\ R^{us} \overset{-}{+\dot{e}_a},\ \overset{+}{e})$

(16) $\qquad \dfrac{M_n}{eP^{us}} = \dfrac{M_n}{eP^{us}}\,(\overset{+}{R_d},\ \Sigma\,\overset{+}{(IM - X)},\ R^{us} \overset{-\ \cdot}{+\,e_a})$

(17) $\qquad \dfrac{S_n}{eP^{us}} = \dfrac{S_n}{eP^{us}}\,(\overset{+}{R_b},\ \Sigma\,\overset{+}{(IM - X)},\ R^{us} \overset{-\ \cdot}{+\,e_a})$

(18) $\qquad \dfrac{S_h}{P} = \dfrac{S_h}{P}\,(\overset{+}{Y_p},\ \overset{?}{Y_t},\ \overset{+}{R_b},\ R^{us} \overset{-\ \cdot}{+\,e_a},\ \overset{+}{e})$

TABLE 2 *(suite)*

(19) $\quad \dfrac{D}{M} = \dfrac{D}{M}\left(\overset{+}{R},\ RM \overset{-}{+} RC,\ \dfrac{\overline{CEIL}}{P},\ \overline{R}_d,\ \overset{?}{Y_p},\ \overset{?}{Y_t},\ \overset{?}{\dot{P}_a}\right)$

(20) $\quad RM = RM\left(\overset{+}{e},\ \dfrac{\overline{DM}}{\$},\ \overset{+}{R^{us}},\ \overset{+}{R^{ger}},\ \dfrac{X}{IM}\right)$

(21) $\quad e = e\left(\overline{F}_g,\ \dfrac{\overset{+}{DM}}{\$},\ \overset{+}{RM}\right)$

(22) $\quad \dot{e}_{a,t} = \dot{e}_{t-1} + 0.3\,(\dot{P}_{a,t} - \dot{P}^{us}_{a,t} - \dot{e}_{t-1}) - 0.1\,(R - R^{us} - \dot{e}_{t-1})$

(22.1) $\quad = 0.8\,\dot{e}_{t-1} + 0.3\,(\dot{P}_{a,t} - \dot{P}^{us}_{a,t}) - 0.1\,(R - R^{us})$

β : marginal net rate of return to commercial banks on their credit;

B_u : unborrowed monetary base;

r : legal reserve requirement;

CC   : credit controls; published index of the tightness of the "encadrement" based on yes-no replies of a sample of firms to the question: do you have difficulties obtaining bank credit?

F_g : official foreign reserves. In the case of B_u in the supply of bank credit, F_g corresponds exactly to official foreign reserves. But in the official reaction function [eq. (21)], F_g is net of the induced foreign borrowing in foreign currencies of the nationalized firms, like the Électricité de France or the National Railways (SNCF). This induced borrowing is then treated as exogenous;

Y_p : permanent income (real):

$$Y_{p,t} = \left[\sum_{i=0}^{7}\left(\dfrac{a}{1+g}\right)^i\right]^{-1} \sum_{i=0}^{7} a^i Y_{t-i}$$

where $a = 0.9$, $g = $ growth rate of Y, Y = real GDP;

Y_t : transitory income (real):

P   : price level of GDP;

$\dot{P}_a$: anticipated inflation:

$$\dot{P}_{a,t} = \left(\sum_{i=0}^{7} a^i\right)^{-1} \sum_{i=0}^{7} a^i \dot{P}_{t-1}$$

P_a : anticipated price level;

P_{dur} : price of consumer durables (official index):

P_{cons} : price of residential construction (official index);

P^{us} : price level of GDP in US;

$\dot{P}^{us}_a$: anticipated rate of US inflation (same formula as for $\dot{P}_a$);

TABLE 2 *(suite et fin)*

R : rate of interest on commercial bank overdrafts. Unpublished series available from the Bank of France which generally serves in econometric work to measure the marginal rate of return on commercial bank credit;

RC : interbank rate for expanding credit within the credit ceilings. Unpublished series available from the Bank of France;

R^{us} : one-month interest rate on eurodollar deposits;

R^{ger} : daily rate on Lombard credit;

R_c : return on business capital; gross profits divided by the value-added of firms;

R_b : interest rate on private bonds (first-category);

R_d : legal rate of interest on deposits at the savings banks;

TERM : maximum term on mortgage credit;

CEIL : ceiling on deposits at the savings banks which yield non-taxable income;

DM/\$: price of US dollar in terms of deutschemarks.

The marginal franc of credit that the commercial banks supply yields a gross return of R. For every such franc, the banks lose a fraction of deposits, $1 - D(1 - r)/M$, for which they must pay RM. We then consider that they must pay the additional price RC on this fraction of deposits, where RC is the cost of buying the facility of issuing credit within the ceilings from the banks who have unused capacities to expand credit. To the extent of $1 - D(1 - r)/M$, RC dissuades bank credit expansion in the same way as RM. (With respect to $D(1 - r)/M$, or the commercial banks' own share of the market, RC is not a dissuasive factor for banks as a whole since it is a return to some banks as well as a cost to others).[5] B_u or the unborrowed monetary base promotes credit expansion by offering the commercial banks the capacity to finance reserve losses without paying RM. This variable therefore relates to a separate aspect of bank profitability. For any pair of values of β and B_u, the amount of credit that the banks are willing to supply reflects their evaluation of customer credit risk. This explains why we include $Y_p P_a$, or a measure of nominal activity, as an argument in the equation. CC is an index of the weight of the credit ceilings, and rests on survey evidence. Of course, the interest rate RC also reflects these ceilings, but does so to a lesser extent, since the cost of issuing credit becomes very steeply progressive at the ceilings. Our treatment of CC obviously reflects the view that though credit controls limit the influence of bank profitability, they do not drown out this influence entirely (for institutional material supporting this view, see MELITZ [1982b]).

---

5. We treat RC as exogenous, though this is not exactly right. But it is acceptable as a simplification. The Bank of France watches this rate closely and essentially controls it through the administration of the « encadrement ».

There are no foreign variables in eqs. (12) and (13). This assumes, quite reasonably, that households do not borrow from abroad. On the other hand, foreign variables are very much present in eqs. (14) through (18). The presence of the exchange rate in these equations rests on familiar portfolio considerations. Ordinary portfolio analysis suggests that a rise in e means too many dollars relative to francs both on the asset and the liability sides (see William BRANSON [1977] and Clas WIHLBORG [1978]). An application of the logic of transactions-demand to importers similarly implies that a rise in e means too little money in francs in these people's hands (see MELITZ [1982a]). We incorporate these factors in the two foreign demand equations by assuming that foreigners value their franc assets at dollar prices converted back into francs, thus by treating the dependent variables of eqs. (16) and (17) as M_n/eP^{us} and S_n/eP^{us}. As regards Frenchmen, however, we handle the issue by including e as a separate argument in the equations. [6]

The total wealth available for distribution between home and foreign assets is a further, necessary argument in eqs. (15) through (18). For foreigners then, we need a measure of world wealth. But following a suggestion by BRANSON [1977], we simply use the cumulative value of the deficit in the French current account as a proxy for this wealth (cf. BRANSON, Hannu HALTTUNEN, and Paul MASSON [1979]).

Obviously this proxy has its weaknesses since foreigners are perfectly able to bid for francs on the basis of their non-franc wealth. Yet it is reasonable to assume that the desired investment of foreigners in franc assets will be largely proportional to the franc claims that are available to them in the aggregate.

The demand for franc assets by Frenchmen, on the other hand, is clearly proportional to their total wealth, and not simply their cumulative claims on foreigners. Permanent income then is a proxy for such wealth in eqs. (15) and (18). As regards eqs. (12) and (13), relating to household debt, Y_p may be interpreted similarly, since desired borrowing of households is clearly limited by their ability to repay out of future income. In the case of eq. (14), concerning desired borrowing by firms, Y_p should probably be understood differently, as referring to the permanent level of sales.

The D/M equation, (19), is a quasi-reduced form, since R and RM + RC enter strictly as influences on the yield on commercial bank deposits. To explain, R and RM + RC affect bank profitability, thereby the services that banks are willing to pay on their deposits, and through this channel their share of the market for money issues. The variables Y_p, Y_t, and $\dot{P}_a$ enter in this equation because of possibly different elasticities of influence on D and government money, M − D.

The two official reaction functions, (20) and (21), involve the assumption that the French authorities devote their instruments, F_g and RM, exclusively to external objectives. These equations also imply that the French authorities are concerned with the deutschemark as well as the dollar.

Eq. (22) says that individuals base their expectations of the exchange rate partly on theory. More specifically, the market believes in the importance of purchasing power parity in the commodities market and interest rate parity in the assets market. Consequently, in so far as there are deviations from these two principles, people expect corrections. We set the extent of these corrections *a priori* on the basis of an examination of the profiles of anticipated depreciation resulting from different response coefficients. We simply chose the coefficients that gave us the most reasonable profiles. In particular, we looked for an anticipated depreciation of the franc in the first three quarters of 1976, when France left the snake, and an expected stabilization soon thereafter, with the announcement of the Barre Plan. Of course, nothing we did assures the convergence of the expected depreciation of the currency by the market with the predicted depreciation of the currency by the model. Because of market uncertainty, however, the importance of this criticism is not clear in our eyes. In any event, it was necessary to estimate the model with our simplified view of market expectations before we could even tackle the issue of consistent expectations, which is now a possible extension of our work [7].

3 The fitted form

We have estimated eqs. (11) though (19) on the basis of quarterly data for 1970.3-1978.4. The reason for starting in 1970 is that some recent revisions in the financial series have not yet been retrapolated prior to this year. We ended in 1978 in order to leave at least eight quarters for post-sample simulations (which we have not yet had any success in performing). The two official reaction functions are estimated only for a smaller interval, or 1971.3-1978.4, the period of flexible exchange rates. Our procedure was first to engage in one-stage-least-squares (OLS) experiments with all of the equations, paying attention to the lag structure and the Durbin-Watsons as well as all the rest. Next, we settled on exact forms for all of the equations. Then finally we tried to get full-information-maximum-likelihood estimates (FIML) for the entire system of 22 equations. We did so without entertaining high hopes because our system is highly nonlinear. The non-linearities stem from two factors : first, the loglinear nature of some of our structural equations together with our linear balance sheet constraints and definitions; and second, the occurrence of endogenous variables as numerators or denominators of ratios (for example, C_f/P, D/M, *etc.*) or as elements of more complex terms

---

6. Note that the positive sign of e in the demand for credit by firms, or eq. (14), is destabilizing. There are now a number of analyses of this problem : see Dale HENDERSON and Kenneth ROGOFF [1981]; John MARTIN and Paul MASSON [1979]; and MELITZ [1982a].

7. Our specification takes no account of French controls on foreign capital movements. But these capital controls hardly changed during our sample period, 1970-1978. See Jean MATHIS [1981] and the companion article in this volume by Emil CLAASSEN and Charles WYPLOSZ [1982]. Since the Socialists came to power in 1981, such controls have been tightened, however, and therefore the issue may arise.

(*e.g.*, RM in the formula for β). But thanks to Bronwyn and Robert HALL's program Time Series Processor (TSP), we did get FIML estimates for the system as a whole. This then assures us of estimates that are consistent, or subject to all of the theoretical constraints in the system, which is important in the case of a model like ours where, by construction, the determination of the exchange rate cannot be associated with any single market. For example, any OLS estimate of the exchange rate based on the official reaction function for the exchange rate would only be of limited interest.

Our OLS experiments also necessitated a number of departures from our proposed theoretical structure of the model. The big problem turned out to be the equation for the household demand for securities, in which we persistently got highly significant, but wrong signs for the interest rate variables. No reasonable action we would take would resolve the problem. The series for S_h/P is striking in one respect : it declines significantly over the sample period. Why should French households have reduced their real holdings of financial titles to property over 8 1/2 years of economic expansion averaging around 4 % annually? The probable answer lies in the fact that they also invested heavily in construction.[8] The series for the sum of securities and mortgages, $(S_h + C_h^{lt})/P$, is indeed a growing one. It is then possible that household investment in securities and demand for mortgages cannot be analysed separately. A further indication of this is that we also had a lot of difficulty with the equation for household mortgages.[9] Of course, if our basic hypothesis is correct, then we might have been expected to get good results by introducing construction variables in the household demand for securities and similarly introducing security-market variables in the demand for mortgages. We tried and failed. What did work was to treat household demand for securities and mortgages as a single decision, and to consider the proportion of securities to the total as simply a function of the desired stock of housing. In place of eqs. (13) and (18), therefore, we have substituted :

$$(23) \quad \frac{C_h^{lt}+S_h}{P} = \frac{C_h^{lt}+S_h}{P}\left(\overset{+}{Y}_p, \overset{?}{Y}_t, \overset{-}{R}, \overset{+}{P}_a, \overset{+}{R}_b, \frac{\overset{-}{P_{cons}}}{P}, \overset{-}{R^{us}} + \overset{.}{e}_a, e, \text{TERM}, \overset{-}{\text{CC}}\right)$$

and

$$(24) \quad \frac{S_h}{C_h^{lt}+S_h} = \frac{h}{C_h^{lt}+S_h}\, (\Sigma \; \overline{\text{HCONS}})$$

where HCONS is household investment in construction.

We were also generally unable to enter both e and $\dot{e}_a$ in any of the equations except the two demands by foreigners, (16) and (17), where e is present by construction. (Incidentally, the OLS estimates of these two equations with M_n/P and S_n/P present as the dependent variables instead of M_n/eP_{us} and S_n/eP_{us} are quite similar.) With regard to the other equations where e and $\dot{e}_a$ are both supposed to appear, we essentially faced a choice between one or the other which we always tried to settle in favor of $\dot{e}_a$. However, $\dot{e}_a$ does not always work, and this led us to use the anticipated exchange rate, e_a, or $e_{t-1} + \dot{e}_a$, in eqs. (14) and (23) . e_a does not have the same properties as $\dot{e}_a$: it reflects the lagged value of the exchange rate as well as the anticipated movement, and hence pertains to the level as well as the anticipated change of the exchange rate. This is not necessarily a disadvantage in the case of eq. (14), or the demand for credit of firms, where $\dot{e}_a$ and e both have the same theoretical sign. However, it is a weakness in eq. (23), where the two signs are opposite, and therefore the negative sign of e_a depends, in theory, on a predominant influence of $\dot{e}_a$ as opposed to e_{t-1}.

Our other deviations from the preferred structural forms of our equations can be dealt with summarily. French interest rates were insignificant in the two demand equations for foreigners. Nevertheless we retained R_d in the foreign demand for money on theoretical grounds because it had the right sign (and t values around 1 to 1.6). Similarly, R^{us} would not enter in the demand for credit by French firms. Also, we dropped anticipated inflation in the demand for money because it interfered with the bond rate. The institutional variables CEIL, TERM, and R_d generally gave us difficulty. CEIL notably would not enter in real terms in the D/M equation, but only in nominal ones. Finally, the credit control variable, CC, entered on the supply side, but not the demand one, of the market for bank credit.

Since we have turned to the FIML estimates, we have not revised the structural forms of our OLS estimates, not for any reason of principle, but simply because we have not yet advanced to that stage of analysis.

4 The estimates

Table 3 presents the FIML estimates for 1970.3-1978.4 (in Part A); the standard errors of the estimates (s.e.e), the mean value of the absolute errors ($|\bar{u}|$), and the coefficient of autocorrelation in the residuals (ρ) (Part B);

---

8. To elaborate, France emerged from the second world war, like a number of continental European countries, with a serious housing problem. But this problem was aggravated in France by a substantially higher rate of urbanization than her neighbors. This urbanization meant a significant gap between the geographical distribution of the population and the distribution of construction. An important stock of secondary residences in the countryside resulted from this gap, but did little to attenuate the demand for construction. Indeed, it may even have contributed to the demand because of desired maintenance and modernization of the secondary homes. Rapid urbanization has persisted in France in the 1970's. This helps to see why French households wished to invest enough in housing as to want to disinvest in securities (in real terms).

9. Compare the specification and the estimates of these two equations in the French quarterly model METRIC (Patrick ARTUS et al. [1981, p. 386-387]). In general, the most striking difference between our modelisation of the financial sector and that in METRIC (ibid., Part VII) concerns exchange rate determination, with respect to which the authors of METRIC follow Jacques ARTUS [1976]. In regard to exchange-rate determination in METRIC, see also Patrick ARTUS, Pierre MORIN, and Henri STERDYNIAK [1979].

Table 3

The FIML Estimates

A. *The structural equations.*

(11)
$$C_b = -503\,100 + 899\,414\,\frac{\beta_t + \beta_{t-1}}{2} + 3.09\,\frac{5\,(Y_p\,P_a)_t + (Y_p\,P_a)_{t-1}}{6}$$
$$(15.1)\qquad(7.3)\qquad\qquad(15.7)$$

$$+\,2.80\sum_{i=t}^{t-3} a_i B_u - 216\,CC - 25\,580\,Z_1$$
$$(35.7)\qquad\quad(14.8)\qquad(6.26)$$

$$a_t = 0.16 \qquad a_{t-1} = 0.30 \qquad a_{t-2} = 0.32 \qquad a_{t-3} = 0.22$$
$$Z_1 = 1978.1 - 1978.2$$

(12)
$$ln\,\frac{C_h^{st}}{P} = -9.7 + 0.75\,ln\left(\frac{C_h^{st}}{P}\right)_{t-1} + 0.91\,ln\,Y - 0.22\,\frac{Y_t}{Y}$$
$$\phantom{ln\,\frac{C_h^{st}}{P} =}(1.93)\quad(9.5)\qquad\qquad\quad(2.07)\qquad\quad(0.45)$$

$$-\,7.08\,R + 2.63\,\dot{P}_a - 0.17\,\frac{P_{dur}}{P}$$
$$(11.1)\qquad(6.8)\qquad(1.53)$$

(23)
$$ln\,\frac{C_h^{lt} + S_h}{P} = 0.44 + 0.33\,ln\,Y_p - 1.36\sum_{i=t-2}^{t-9} b_i(R - \dot{P}_a)$$
$$\phantom{ln\,\frac{C_h^{lt} + S_h}{P} =}(0.98)\quad(5.6)\qquad\quad(2.68)$$

$$+\,1.58\sum_{i=t-2}^{t-9} b_i R_b - 0.71\sum_{i=t}^{t-7} d_i\,\frac{P_{cons}}{P} - 1.27\sum_{i=t}^{t-7} d_i R^{us} - 0.21\,ln\,e_a$$
$$(5.2)\qquad\quad(5)\qquad\qquad(8)\qquad\qquad(8.3)$$

$$
\begin{array}{llll}
b_{t-2} = 0.07 & b_{t-3} = 0.12 & b_{t-4} = 0.15 & b_{t-5} = 0.16 \\
b_{t-6} = 0.16 & b_{t-7} = 0.15 & b_{t-8} = 0.12 & b_{t-9} = 0.07 \\
d_t = 0.07 & d_{t-1} = 0.12 & d_{t-2} = 0.15 & d_{t-3} = 0.16 \\
d_{t-4} = 0.16 & d_{t-5} = 0.15 & d_{t-6} = 0.12 & d_{t-7} = 0.07 \\
\end{array}
$$

(14)
$$ln\,\frac{C_f + S_f}{P} = -0.81 + 3.17\,ln\,Y_p - 1.44\,\frac{Y_t}{Y} + 0.02\,TENS$$
$$\phantom{ln\,\frac{C_f + S_f}{P} =}(0.63)\quad(12.4)\qquad\quad(6.35)\qquad(2.42)$$

$$-\,5.51\sum_{i=t}^{t-7} f_i R + 4.46\sum_{i=t-1}^{t-7} g_i\,\dot{P}_a$$
$$(13.6)\qquad\quad(11.2)$$

$$+\,4.24\sum_{i=t}^{t-7} j_i\,R_c + 0.42\sum_{i=t-1}^{t-7} h_i\,ln\,e_a$$
$$(6.29)\qquad\quad(7.7)$$

TABLE 3 *(suite)*

$f_t = 0.24$ $f_{t-1} = 0.21$ $f_{t-2} = 0.17$ $f_{t-3} = 0.14$
$f_{t-4} = 0.10$ $f_{t-5} = 0.07$ $f_{t-6} = 0.05$ $f_{t-7} = 0.02$
$g_t = 0.20$ $g_{t-1} = 0.18$ $g_{t-2} = 0.16$ $g_{t-3} = 0.14$
$g_{t-4} = 0.12$ $g_{t-5} = 0.09$ $g_{t-6} = 0.07$ $g_{t-7} = 0.04$
$h_{t-1} = 0.02$ $h_{t-2} = 0.03$ $h_{t-3} = 0.11$ $h_{t-4} = 0.19$
$h_{t-5} = 0.25$ $h_{t-6} = 0.26$ $h_{t-7} = 0.18$
$j_t = 0.01$ $j_{t-1} = 0.03$ $j_{t-2} = 0.09$ $j_{t-3} = 0.14$
$j_{t-4} = 0.19$ $j_{t-5} = 0.21$ $j_{t-6} = 0.20$ $j_{t-7} = 0.13$

TENS: indicator of tension in the labor market; the logarithm of the ratio: unemployment divided by unsatisfied demand for labor.

(15)
$$ln \frac{M_{fh}}{P} = -\ \underset{(1.86)}{2.61} + \underset{(8.4)}{0.78}\ ln\left(\frac{M_{fh}}{P}\right)_{t-1} + \underset{(2.05)}{0.34}\ ln\,Y - \underset{(2.57)}{0.37}\ \frac{Y_t}{Y}$$
$$-\ \underset{(2.39)}{0.63}\ R_b - \underset{(6.25)}{0.43}\ R^{us} - 0.0237\ \dot{e}_a$$

(16)
$$ln \frac{M_n}{eP^{us}} = -\ \underset{(9.54)}{8.37} + \underset{(0.91)}{0.96}\ R_d + \underset{(16.8)}{0.48}\ ln\,\Sigma\,(IM-X) - \underset{(3.76)}{1.08}\ R^{us}$$
$$-\ \underset{(17.6)}{1.62}\ ln\,e_a$$

(17)
$$ln \frac{S_n}{eP^{us}} = \underset{(6.9)}{8.05} + \underset{(17.3)}{0.62}\ ln\left(\frac{S_n}{eP^{us}}\right)_{t-1} + \underset{(6.15)}{0.61}\ ln\,\Sigma\,(IM-X)$$
$$-\ \underset{(2.94)}{2.83}\ R^{us} - \underset{(2.32)}{0.29}\ \dot{e}_a$$

(24)
$$\frac{S_h}{C_h^{lt}+S_h} = \underset{(4.78)}{1.49} + \underset{(8.23)}{0.62}\left(\frac{S_h}{C_h^{lt}+S_h}\right)_{t-1} - \underset{(4.77)}{0.12}\ ln\,\Sigma\,HCONS$$

(19)
$$\frac{D}{M} = -\ \underset{(16.1)}{4.28} + \underset{(3.1)}{0.42} \sum_{i=t-2}^{t-7} k_i R - \underset{(5)}{0.25} \sum_{i=t}^{t-5} l_i\,(RM+RC)$$
$$-\ \underset{(4.07)}{2.99} \sum_{i=t}^{t-7} m_i\,CEIL\,(1+R_d) + \underset{(18.4)}{0.40}\ ln\,Y_p - \underset{(0.21)}{0.02}\ \frac{Y_t}{Y}$$
$$+\ \underset{(0.67)}{0.74} \sum_{i=t}^{t-7} n_i\,\dot{P}_a$$

TABLE 3 *(suite)*

$$k_{t-2} = 0.30 \quad k_{t-3} = 0.24 \quad k_{t-4} = 0.19 \quad k_{t-5} = 0.14$$
$$k_{t-6} = 0.09 \quad k_{t-7} = 0.04$$
$$l_t = 0.11 \quad l_{t-1} = 0.18 \quad l_{t-2} = 0.21 \quad l_{t-3} = 0.21$$
$$l_{t-4} = 0.18 \quad l_{t-5} = 0.11$$
$$m_t = 0.07 \quad m_{t-1} = 0.12 \quad m_{t-2} = 0.15 \quad m_{t-3} = 0.16$$
$$m_{t-4} = 0.16 \quad m_{t-5} = 0.15 \quad m_{t-6} = 0.12 \quad m_{t-7} = 0.07$$
$$n_t = 0.18 \quad n_{t-1} = 0.26 \quad n_{t-2} = 0.26 \quad n_{t-3} = 0.21$$
$$n_{t-4} = 0.13 \quad n_{t-5} = 0.04 \quad n_{t-6} = -0.03 \quad n_{t-7} = -0.05$$

(20)
$$\begin{aligned}
RM = {} & 0.20 + 0.56\ RM_{t-i} + 0.27\ e - 0.08\ \frac{DM}{\$} \\
& (6.48) \quad (8.7) \qquad\qquad (2.92) \quad (2.73) \\[4pt]
& + 0.25\ \frac{3R^{ger} + R^{us}}{4} - 0.15\ \frac{X}{IM} \\
& \ \ (4.5) \qquad\qquad\quad\ (5.4)
\end{aligned}$$

(21)
$$\begin{aligned}
e = {} & 3\,217 - 0.098\ F_g + 0.43\ \frac{DM}{\$} + 0.18\ RM - 913\ Z_2 \\
& \quad\ (4.7) \quad (19.5) \qquad (27) \qquad\ (6.5) \qquad (4.8)
\end{aligned}$$

$$Z_2 = 1976.1 - 1976.2$$

B. *The standard errors of estimates (s.e.e.), the mean errors* $(\bar{u})$, *and the coefficients of autocorrelation* (ρ).

	s.e.e. (%)	$|\bar{u}|$	ρ
C_b	0.1	~ 0	0.06
C_h^{st}	3.2	0.1	0.10
C_h^{lt}	0.9	0.1	0.27
C_f	0.6	0.1	0.54
$C_f + S_f$	0.1	~ 0	-0.12
$C_h^{lt} + S_h$	1.5	0.1	0.02
S_h	1	0.1	0.63
S_f	1.6	0.1	0.57
S_n	6.9	0.9	0.06
M_{fh}	0.1	~ 0	0.28
M_n	1.4	0.2	-0.11
D	1	~ 0	0.38
F_g	1.7	1.1	0.29
eF_{fh}	11.4	3.6	0.09
RM	6.9	2.5	0.22
R	7	0.3	0.17
e	1.8	0.4	0.10

TABLE 3   *(suite et fin)*

C. *The implicit demand for foreign assets by French firms and households.*

a. long run.

(5)
$$\frac{eF_{fh}}{P}(10^{-3}) = \text{constant} - 4\,200\,R + 2\,400\,R_b + 1\,800\,R^{us} + 2\,700\,R_c$$
$$+ 3\,060\,\dot{P}_a + 285\,ln\,e_{t-1} + 381\,\dot{e}_a + 764\,ln\,Y$$
$$- 1\,510\,\frac{Y_t}{Y} - 176\,\frac{P_{dur}}{P} + 466\,\frac{P_{cons}}{P} + 129\,\text{TENS}$$

b. current-quarter.

(5)
$$\frac{eF_{fh}}{P}(10^{-3}) = \text{constant} - 1\,040\,R + 550\,R_b + 380\,R^{us} + 30\,R_c$$
$$+ 640\,\dot{P}_a + 14\,ln\,e_{t-1} + 110\,\dot{e}_a + 74\,ln\,Y$$
$$- 1\,490\,\frac{Y_t}{Y} - 44\,\frac{P_{dur}}{P} + 3.3\,\frac{P_{cons}}{P} + 129\,\text{TENS}$$

and the implicit private French demand for foreign assets (Part C). [10]   In these estimates, we have constrained the value of the coefficient of anticipated depreciation in the home demand for money.   Otherwise the sign of this coefficient changes and the demand for money deteriorates ($\dot{e}_a$ in the demand for securities also becomes insignificant).   However, no general inference should be drawn from this, since by and large, quite the opposite, the FIML estimates permitted us to remove constraints that the OLS ones had necessitated.

The FIML estimates are not dramatically different from the OLS ones on the whole.   Only two equations are largely affected: the household demand for short term bank credit and the desired ratio of commercial bank deposits to money.   The interest rate elasticities of the supply and demand of bank credit are also substantially higher in the FIML estimates.

---

10. In order to perform the FIML estimates for this sample period as a whole, we set RM and e equal to their observed values in both reaction functions during the four early quarters of fixed exchange rates (or 1970.3-1971.2), using the same technique as in MELITZ and STERDYNIAK [1979].   Correspondingly, our s.e.e., $\bar{u}$, and ρ statistics for these two variables in the table relate strictly to 1971.3-1978.4.   The lack of distributed-lag influence of e_a in equation (23) stems strictly from the fact that our computer program limited us to the estimate of four distributed-lag influences per equation.

There are six omitted endogenous variables in Part B: S_g, M, M_g, eF_n, $\dot{e}_a$, and REFI.

S_g, M_g, and REFI are of no interest.   The s.e.e., $\bar{u}$, and ρ statistics for e_a would only be misleading.   Those for M are approximately the same as for M_{fh} (M = M_{fh} + M_n), and those for eF_n are somewhere between the ones for F_g and eF_{fh} (though closer to those for eF_{fh}; $eF_n = F_g + eF_{fh}$).

We may first examine the s.e.e., $\bar{u}$, and ρ statistics in the table. There are three very high coefficients of autocorrelation: for S_h, S_f, and C_f. Upon analysis, all three can be attributed to the equation for the ratio of S_h to $S_h + C_h^{lt}$ [eq. (24)], since the ρ values of the estimates of $S_h + C_h^{lt}$ and $S_f + C_f$ are, respectively, nil and moderately negative. (S_f of course, follows mainly from S_h via the definition of S or eq. (3)). The FIML estimates thus reveal a problem in eq. (24) that the OLS estimates had given us no reason to suspect since the Durbin-Watson of the OLS equation is 1.71. The only other ρ values that are somewhat high are those for M_{fh}, D, C_h^{lt}, F_g and RM, but they are less worrisome. [11]

There is only one high mean error and only one high standard error of estimate in the table, both of which apply to eF_{fh}, which is determined residually, and therefore may involve a cumulation of errors in other variables. In the other cases the $\bar{u}$'s and s.e.e.'s are mostly quite low. Those for commercial bank credit and home holdings of money are even embarrassingly so. The standard errors of estimate for official reserves and the exchange rate of only 1.6 to 1.8 % are also highly satisfactory. In the OLS estimates the R^2 of the reaction function for the exchange rate is 93 %. Since this equation would be the logical one to use in predicting e based on the OLS estimates, our simultaneous-equation estimates clearly give rise to a sizeable improvement in the estimate of the exchange rate.

Looking at the individual equations, we find that CC is highly significant in the supply of commercial bank credit. Similar regressions for earlier years, covering different parts of the 1960-1975 period, used to show the same sort of restrictions as moderately significant at best (see Antoine COUTIÈRE [1975], André FOURÇANS [1978], MELITZ [1973, 1975] and MELITZ and STERDYNIAK [1979]). Econometric analysis therefore corroborates the general impression of a strengthening of the « encadrements du crédit » in the 1970's (compare also ARTUS et al., METRIC [1981], p. 396). It is also frequently assumed in France that the commercial banks basically offset movements in unborrowed reserves through changes in refinancing. In conformity, our estimate of the influence of B_u shows only a small positive effect of B_u in the current quarter. However, the estimate also shows a large effect of B_u within a year. One additional franc of unborrowed reserves eventually raises commercial bank credit by 2.80 F. Furthermore the presence of this influence in the equation does nothing to mask the effect of the other essential variables in it. The indicator Z_1 in the supply of credit implies that the commercial banks were unusually restrained in their supply around the time of the May 1978 legislative elections. We generally avoided such dummy variables in the estimates, of which there is only one other example (in the reaction function for the exchange rate). But in both cases the dummy variable substantially improved the Durbin-Watson in the OLS estimate.

The negative influence of transitory income in the demand for credit of firms appears both in the negative sign of Y_t/Y and the positive one of TENS, an indicator of tension in the labor market which occurs frequently in French econometric models. This is acceptable since Y_t/Y and TENS have markedly different time profiles and refer to distinct, though related, phenomena. The household demand for securities and mortgages has only one unsatisfactory feature: namely, the immediate effect of the foreign interest rate but the two-quarter lag in the influence of the bond rate and the cost of bank credit as adjusted for anticipated inflation. The negative influence of e_a in this equation supports the interpretation of this variable as reflecting anticipated depreciation (rather than desired diversification between home and foreign securities). With regard to the estimates as a whole, we find a lot of influences of the foreign interest rate and the anticipated value of the franc on private agents.

Outside of the two reaction functions, the only coefficient that worries us is the negative sign of transitory income in the home demand for money, for which we have no explanation except as a general-equilibrium consequence of the sharp negative effect of Y_t/Y on firms' demand for credit. Omitting Y_t/Y from the home demand for money damages the equation.

Some of the relative magnitudes of the coefficients in the two official reaction functions also seem to require a bit of explanation. [12] The RM equation would imply that the French authorities are much more sensitive to the dollar than the deutschemark in determining this rate. Yet, based on the OLS estimates, they also respond much more to the German Lombard rate than the eurodollar rate (which is why we weigh R^{ger} three times as much as R^{us} in the equation). The much lower coefficient of DM/$ than e in the RM equation therefore probably may be viewed as an artifact, possibly due to the much higher sampling variance of the franc/dollar than the franc/deutschemark.

There are also legitimate doubts about the low coefficient of the DM/$ in the exchange rate equation of only 0.43. [13] Yet the coefficient could be right since our sample period ends before the European Monetary System (EMS) began, and France was only a member of the snake for ten quarters in the sample (April 1972 to January 1974 and July 1975 to March 1976). It is not even clear that the coefficient has risen closer to one since the EMS began in 1979. Already the central rate of the franc relative to the deutschemark has been reduced by 18 1/2 % since then (by 8.5 % in October 1981 and 10 % in June 1982). Further the admissible range of variation of the FF/DM in the system is 4 1/2 %. The dummy variable in the exchange rate equation indicates unusual support of the franc in the first two quarters of 1976, when France left the snake, and seems entirely reasonable.

Figures 1 and 2 permit a comparison of the estimates with the observed values of e and R, or the two basic price variables in the system. It can be seen that the model tracks e almost perfectly, even at the turning points. The same quality of performance is true for official reserves (which is why we do not bother to show it). The errors are substantially larger for R. In regard to R, there seem to be problems both at the beginning and the end of the sample period, though the overall performance is still good.

Part C of table 3 answers a logical query about the nature of the implicit private French demand for foreign assets (which Part B has already shown us not to be highly accurate). This demand was calculated by expanding the terms in the budget constraint of firms and households [eq. (5)] on the basis of the parameter estimates in Part A (using a linear approximation

---

11. The ρ of D may be also considered excessive, but this variable has only modest import-ance in the system: its sole role is to modify ß in the supply of commercial bank credit.

12. We remind the reader that our measure of F_g is not affected by changes in e.

13. The upward adjustment of this coefficient in light of the cross-effect of DM/$ on e via RM is entirely negligible.

FIGURE 1

The exchange rate

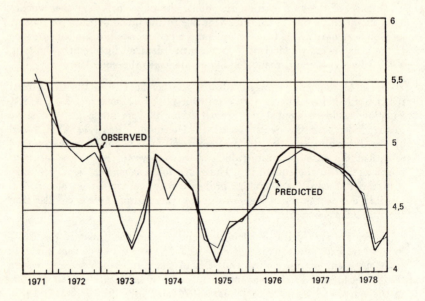

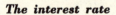

FIGURE 2

The interest rate

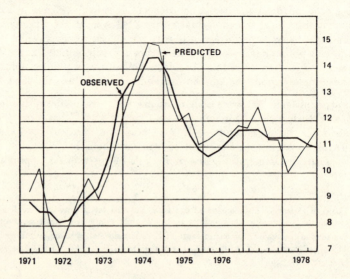

around the means). We present both the cumulative, long run, and the current-quarter values, of the coefficients. This gives an idea of the lagged influences in the equation. The only apparently incorrect sign is for R_b, the interest rate on bonds. [14] Yet contrary to impression, the sign makes sense, which is a point of some theoretical interest.

We generally expect a rise in the home interest rate to lead to a fall in the home demand for foreign assets, at least on the spot market. But the opposite can happen in our framework because ours is a porfolio model where people choose between three assets not two : M, B, and F. When R_b rises, agents wish to switch from F to B. But they also wish to switch from M to B. This last desired switch will then spark an attendant movement out of money and into foreign securities in order to maintain portfolio balance or the desired ratio of foreign to total securities. If the added demand for F from this last source is greater than the reduced demand for F stemming from the fall in the desired ratio of eF to $eF + B$, the aggregate demand for F will rise. Our estimate confirms this last possibility. In addition, since R_b does not affect the foreign demand for home assets (in our estimates), the positive effect of R_b on the private home demand for F implies a similar positive effect of R_b on e, thus a tendency for a rise in R_b to depreciate the franc.

But the matter is more complicated in our model because the private sector not only divides up its assets between M, B, and F, but also borrows. If the price of commercial bank credit, R, rises together with R_b, and the two rise as much, then our estimates also say that there will be an appreciation of the franc. That is, the restrictive effect of R on the supply of money (or more precisely, this restrictive effect on the home-asset counterpart of the stock of money) will be stronger than the restrictive effect of R_b on the demand for money. This will mean a spillover out of foreign assets into home ones. If R^{us}, R, and R_b all rise together, then our estimate further implies essentially no change in the demand for foreign assets. This is acceptable, though it is not a theoretically essential result. Nonetheless and quite significantly, the franc will depreciate in this last case. The reason is that the increase in the foreign interest rate will lower the foreign demand for franc assets. With eF_{fh}/P essentially the same, but $(M_n + S_n)/P$ lower, the franc must depreciate [see eq. (8.2)]. [15]

There is admittedly one disturbing element in our estimate of eF_{fh}/P, however : this is the higher positive sign of R_b than R^{us} in the equation. This last implication cannot really be accepted.

---

14. The positive sign of R_c, the rate of return on capital, may also look questionable at first. However, the sign is natural since investment, and therefore capital or equity in capital, are exogenous. Under these conditions, a rise in R_c, raising the demand for bank borrowing (a form of dissaving), necessitates a matching accumulation of financial assets, including foreign assets.

15. One limitation of our model which should (and we have reason to believe, can be) remedied in the future is our treatment of foreign borrowing in francs as exogenous. There may be some basis for this treatment in the fact that most bank loans to foreigners are subsidised loans to foreign importers. C_n may then be considered as an officially determined subsidised line of credit. But we are not entirely satisfied with this view.

Conclusion

In conclusion, we may return to the discussion in the introductory section where we defended the complexity of our approach. [16] The last few considerations shed a lot of light on the matter. Simple models of the exchange rate generally yield an unambiguous sign of the relationship between the home interest rate and the exchange rate. Yet the simple models also disagree about this sign of the relation. Thus the asset-market approach implies that a higher interest rate will lead to exchange rate appreciation by attracting foreign capital. But the monetary approach to the exchange rate says the opposite: that a higher interest rate will lead to depreciation by reducing the demand relative to the supply of money. Jeffrey FRANKEL [1979] has proposed an attractive compromise between the two approaches, which consists of saying that R and e will be negatively associated in the short run, in accordance with the asset market approach, but positively associated in the long run, in accordance with the monetary approach. The basis for this compromise is that a higher interest rate may reflect a higher anticipated inflation in the long run, and therefore an anticipated depreciation of the currency. Since higher inflation can stem from more rapid monetary growth, the conformity of this view with both the asset-market and the monetary approaches is apparent. [17] However, we can see from our model that FRANKEL's compromise is not the only one. The ambiguity of the sign of the relation between R and e can also be explained without any reference to long run price influences and expectations.

In any model with three or more markets, a rise in R can be associated with a rise in the demand for foreign as well as home securities. Home individuals may simply wish to move out of the third asset into both of the first two. This makes good general sense because we know that even when a rise in the home interest rate involves tight monetary policy, the result may be to discourage the demand for money more than the supply, in which case there will be a spillover into foreign assets, thus a tendency toward depreciation. This possibility, of course, admits the possible responsiveness of the money supply to the interest rate, in accordance with the type of model we have presented.

---

16. Unfortunately, we are not yet able to report on any simulation exercises. These seem to make heavier demands on our computer program than any of our other work.

17. Advocates of the monetary approach, indeed, invite this long run interpretation of their position, since they emphasize purchasing power parity, and therefore the positive relation between money and the commodity price level. See Jacob FRENKEL [1976] and John BILSON [1978, 1979].

● References cited

ARTUS J. — (1976) « Exchange rate stability and managed floating : the experience of the Federal Republic of Germany », IMF *Staff Papers*, 23, July, p. 312-333.

ARTUS P., BOURNAY J., MORIN P., PACAUD A., PEYROUX C., STERDYNIAK H., TEYSSIER R. — (1981) *METRIC : Une modélisation de l'économie française*, INSEE.

ARTUS P., MORIN P. and STERDYNIAK H. — (1979) « La flexibilité des changes : modélisation et conséquences macroéconomiques », *Statistiques et études financières*, direction de la Prévision, ministère de l'Économie, nº 37, p. 3-41.

BILSON J. — (1978) « The Monetary approach to the exchange rate: some empirical evidence », IMF *Staff Papers*, 25, March, p. 48-75.

—— (1979) « The Deutsche Mark/Dollar rate: a monetary analysis », in BRUNNER K. and MELTZER A., eds., Carnegie-Rochester Conference Series on Public Policy, Vol. 11, *Policies for Employment, Prices and Exchange rates*, p. 59-102.

BRANSON W. — (1977) « Asset markets and relative prices in exchange rate determination », *Sozialwissenchaftsliche Annalen des Instituts für Höhere Studiën*, Vienna, p. 69-89; also Princeton University reprints in *International Finance*, nº 20, June 1980).

BRANSON W., HALTTHUNEN H. and MASSON P. — (1979) « Exchange rates in the short run: the dollar-deutschemark rate «, *European Economic Review*, 10, December, p. 303-324.

CLAASSEN E. and WYPLOSZ C. — (1982) « Capital controls : some principles and the French experience », *Annales de l'INSEE*, nº 47-48 (this number).

COUTIÈRE A. — (1975) « Un modèle du système monétaire français », *Statistiques et études financières*, ministère de l'Économie et des Finances, 17, p. 33-80.

—— (1977) *Le Système monétaire français*, Economica, Paris.

FAIR R. — (1979 *a*) « A model of the balance of payments », *Journal of International Economics*, 9 (1), p. 26-46.

—— (1979 *b*) « On modelling the economic linkages among countries », *in* DORNBUSCH R. and FRENKEL J., eds., *International Economic policy: Theory and evidence*, Johns Hopkins Univ. Press, ch. 6, p. 209-239.

FOURÇANS A. — (1978) « The impact of monetary and fiscal policies on the French financial system », *Journal of Monetary Economics*, 4 (3), p. 519-541.

FRANKEL J. — (1979) « On the Mark: a theory of floating exchange rates based on real interest rate differentials », *American Economic Review*, 69, September, p. 610-622.

FRENKEL J. — (1976) « A monetary approach to the exchange rate: doctrinal aspects and empirical evidence », *Scandinavian Journal of Economics*, 78 (2), p. 200-224; also in FRENKEL J. and JOHNSON H., eds., *The Economics of exchange rates: selected studies*, Addison-Wesley Pub. Co., ch. 1, p. 1-25.

HENDERSON D. and ROGOFF K. — (1981) *Net Foreign asset positions and stability in a world portfolio balance model*, Federal Reserve International Finance Discussion Paper no 178, March.

—— (1981) « Net Foreign asset positions and Stability in a world portfolio balance model », *Federal Reserve International Finance Discussion Paper*, 178, March.

MARTIN J. and MASSON P. — (1979) « Exchange Rates and portfolio balance », *NBER Working Paper*, 377.

MATHIS J. — (1981) « L'évolution des mouvements de capitaux à court terme entre la France et l'extérieur de 1967 à 1978 », *Economie et Prévision,* n° 2, p. 27-58.

MELITZ J. — (1973) « Une tentative d'explication de l'offre de monnaie en France », *Revue économique,* 24, septembre, p. 761-800.

—— (1975) « Offre de crédit et offre de monnaie », *Revue économique,* 26, septembre, p. 705-733.

—— (1982 *a*) « The stability of the spot price of foreign exchange in the absence of speculative influences », *Journal of International Economics,* 12 (1), p. 1-24.

—— (1982 *b*) « The French financial system: mechanisms and propositions of reform », *Annales de l'INSEE,* n° 47-48 (this number).

—— (1983) « How much simplification is wise in modelling exchange rates? » *in* Paul de Grauwe and Theo Peeters, eds., *Exchange Rates in multicountry models,* Macmillan.

MELITZ J. and STERDYNIAK H. — (1979) « The monetary approach to official reserves and the foreign exchange rate in France, 1962-1974 : some structural estimates », *American Economic Review,* 69, December, p. 818-831.

PENAUD R. — (1978) *Les Institutions financières,* Paris, Banque.

WIHLBORG C. — (1978) « Currency Risk in International Financial Markets », Princeton University, *Studies in International Finance,* n° 44.

Comments

by Barry J. EICHENGREEN

Harvard University

FEROLDI and MELITZ have set for themselves a difficult, ambitious and important task: to estimate a disaggregated model of the French financial sector and to use it to analyze the determination of the exchange rate. Their approach is predicated upon a recognition that the structure of French financial markets renders assets denominated in different currencies imperfect substitutes in the portfolios of investors. To analyze the determination of the exchange rate, they develop a framework that explicitly incorporates important institutional characteristics of the French financial sector, distinguishes among different classes of assets and agents, and identifies channels through which the structure of French financial markets constrains and influences investors' behavior.

Many features of the model will be familiar to afficionados of the portfolio balance approach. The model distinguishes five categories of investors (households, nonbank firms, banks, foreigners, and the government) and five categories of assets (money, securities, short-term bank credit, long-term bank credit, and foreign assets). The authors reduce this large number of asset demand functions to eight which must be estimated econometrically. The number of demand functions is reduced in four ways : (*i*) WALRAS' Law is invoked to suppress the demand for foreign assets; (*ii*) a number of specialization assumptions are adopted, such as the assumption that households do not borrow from abroad; (*iii*) a number of aggregation assumptions are applied; (*iv*) and, finally, a number of perfect substitutability assumptions are imposed. Asset demands depend in standard fashion on expected rates of return on assets, permanent and transitory incomes, and various measures of wealth.

Along with these eight asset demand functions, the empirical model includes four additional structural equations: three reaction functions for the banking sector and the central authorities which determine supplies of bank credit and of domestic and foreign bonds to the private sector, plus an *a priori* relationship governing the formation of exchange rate expectations. The reaction functions for the authorities determine settings for the two instruments at their command: the stock of foreign assets held by central bank and the discount rate.

At least four features of this model of the financial sector are uniquely French:

1. The bond rate is set exogenously by the authorities.

2. Bond supplies are not perfectly elastic at the exogenously set bond rate; rather, the corporate sector is always rationed on the bond market, while government bonds get first place in the queue.

3. The central bank satisfies all commercial bank demands for refinancing at the rediscount rate.

4. The supply of bank credit is constrained only by considerations of profitability and by the operation of the *encadrement du crédit*.

The *encadrement du crédit* will appear familiar to English-language readers: the British need only think of their late and unlamented Corset, while Americans might wish to think of Regulation Q on its head. The *encadrement* limits the rate of expansion of bank credit by stipulating a target rate of increase in net assets for each financial institution. The penalty for exceeding the target is the imposition of a reserve requirement that rises geometrically with the extent of the violation. There is a secondary market on which entitlements to expand net assets are traded among banks. Since there is no reason to suspect that the interbank rate for credit within official ceilings fails to clear the market for entitlements, it seems reasonable to assume that the supply of bank credit is only constrained by considerations of profitability in which the *encadrement* plays a part.

In this paper, FEROLDI and MELITZ analyze how the structure of the French financial sector, and particularly the extent to which that structure permits agents in different markets to substitute between home and foreign assets, enter into the process of exchange rate determination. A related question is how the structure of the financial sector influences the evolution of the economy and whether it helps to insulate the French economy from external shocks. If we are willing to abstract for the moment from the existence of rationing in the bond market (as well as credit controls, transactions costs and other reasons why assets denominated in different currencies may be imperfect substitutes in portfolios), we can add a simple version of the French money supply process to DORNBUSCH'S [1976] overshooting model and use it to derive preliminary answers to these questions.

The model is sufficiently familiar to be concisely stated.

(1) $\qquad m - p = y - \lambda r$ $\qquad\qquad\qquad\qquad\qquad \lambda > 0$

(2) $\qquad Dp = \Phi(q/y) = \Phi[\{\delta(e + p^* - p) - \gamma r\} - y]$ $\qquad \Phi, \gamma, \delta > 0$

(3) $\qquad De = r - r^* - \tau$

(4) $\qquad m = \bar{m} + \alpha(r - r_d) - c(m - m^*)$ $\qquad\qquad\qquad \alpha, c > 0$

The notation is as follows, where all variables except for r, r^*, r_d, and τ are in logs.

m = money stock
$\bar{m}$ = exogenous component of the money stock
m^* = exogenous monetary target above which penalty for violating the *encadrement* is effective
p = domestic commodity price.
p^* = exogenous foreign commodity price
y = exogenous domestic output

r = domestic nominal interest rate on non-money assets
r_d = exogenous central bank rediscount rate
r^* = exogenous foreign interest rate on non-money assets
q = aggregate demand
e = exchange rate (domestic currency price of foreign currency)
τ = exogenous deviation from open interest parity due to capital controls

Eqs. (1) and (2) are the money demand and price adjustment relations respectively. Eq. (3) is the open interest parity condition adjusted for the impact of French capital controls, as in Frankel's article in this volume. Here, as throughout, expectations are taken as rational. Eq. (4) is the French money supply process, the only unfamiliar element of the model. The money supply is comprised of its autonomous component $\bar{m}$, a component which depends on the profitability of bank lending as measured by the differential between r and r_d, and a component which depends on the penalty for violating the *encadrement*, represented by c. This last penalty is an increasing function of the discrepancy between the actual money supply and the official target. The state-space representation of the model about its initial equilibrium is:

$$\begin{bmatrix} De \\ Dp \end{bmatrix} = \begin{bmatrix} 0 & \dfrac{1}{\lambda + \alpha/(1+c)} \\ \Phi\delta & -\Phi\left(\delta + \dfrac{\gamma}{\lambda + \alpha/(1+c)}\right) \end{bmatrix} * \begin{bmatrix} e - \hat{e} \\ p - \hat{p} \end{bmatrix}$$

The system is saddle-point stable, as is the case when the money supply is taken as exogenous ($\alpha = c = 0$). Thus, the *Banque de France's* willingness to satisfy all commercial bank demands for financing alters the slope of the stable trajectory but not the saddle-point stability of the system.

Consider the impact on this economy of foreign price and interest rate disturbances. Neither the willingness of the *Banque de France* to satisfy all commercial bank demands for refinancing, as represented by α (.), nor the penalty for violating the *encadrement*, as represented by c (.), have any effect on the response to a foreign price shock. The exchange rate appreciates instantaneously to exactly offset any rise in p^*, just as when $\alpha = c = 0$. In contrast, the elasticity of the money supply process does affect the economy's sensitivity to foreign interest rate disturbances. The change in the long run equilibrium values of p and e is given by:

$$\frac{dp}{dr^*} = \lambda + \frac{\alpha}{1+c}$$

$$\frac{de}{dr^*} = \frac{\gamma}{\delta} + \lambda + \frac{\alpha}{1+c}$$

In the long run, the domestic price and exchange rate responses to a foreign interest rate disturbance are increasing functions of α. For example, a permanent increase in foreign interest rates must raise domestic interest rates by the same amount, *ceteris paribus*. This reduces money demand, raising the price level and causing the exchange rate to depreciate. Given eq. (4), higher interest rates expand the money supply in addition to reducing money demand, increasing the magnitude of the required price and exchange rate responses. Strikingly, however, the implications for short-run dynamics are quite different. By altering the slope of the stable trajectory, a positive value of $\alpha/(1 + c)$ reduces the amount by which, for a given foreign interest rate shock, the exchange rate overshoots its long run equilibrium value, and it increases the speed with the exchange rate approaches its new steady state value. Thus, an assessment of the insulation properties of the French money supply process hinges crucially on the type of foreign shocks to which the economy is exposed, and on whether policymakers are primarily concerned with short-run volatility or the magnitude of the long-run adjustment. FEROLDI and MELITZ may feel that this simple model abstracts from the essential (namely, imperfect substitutability and the endogenously determined risk premium with which it is associated), but it remains to be seen whether added complications would fundamentally alter the results.

Turning to the estimation of the empirical model, some questions could be raised about the treatment of interest elasticities of demand for assets. For example, the authors choose not to impose symmetry across equations on the cross-interest elasticities of demand, which means that a proportional rise in all interest rates, *ceteris paribus,* can lead to far-reaching changes in portfolio composition. Multicollinearity among bond rates and inflationary expectations leads them to drop the latter from the demand for money: similarly, the appearance of incorrectly-signed interest elasticities in the equation for households' security demands moves them to treat the mortgage-security decision as a unique, two-step problem. Rather than introducing further changes in specification, the authors might consider imposing cross-equation restrictions on the parameters. One option is to adopt Bayesian methods, using the THEIL-GOLDBERGER technique as a way of incorporating prior information. This is the approach taken by FRENKEL and CLEMENTS [1981] to estimate a single-equation model of exchange rate determination and by the Yale Flow of Funds Project to estimate a disaggregated model of the US financial sector. Another option would be to impose the cross-equation restrictions suggested by theories of finance such as the capital asset pricing model.

Many readers already will have been struck by the authors' specification of exchange rate expectations, which are assumed to depend on the purchasing power parity gap, the interest rate differential, and previous values of the exchange rate. This formulation bears a resemblance to others current in the literature: DORNBUSCH'S assumption that the exchange rate is expected to adjust to eliminate deviations from purchasing power parity, and FRANKEL'S formulation which takes into account also the secular inflation differential. However, unlike the DORNBUSCH-FRANKEL specification, FEROLDI and MELITZ's model is based upon the assumption that there exists a (possibly time-varying) risk premium. Hence, their assumption about exchange rate expectations cannot be rationalized by appealing to open interest parity. In this model, exchange rate expectations may consistently be in error; the authors argue that the importance of this feature is unclear, since theins is a model with exchange risk. Yet there is an important difference between a model in which unanticipated shocks give rise to prediction errors despite the fact that rational agents make efficient use of the available information, and one in which expectations may be persistently and systematically incorrect. The fact that in their model agents are permitted to form expectations which are persistently and systematically incorrect is bound to prove problematic when FEROLDI and MELITZ attempt policy simulations. It is difficult to imagine a change in regime to which Lucas' critique would apply with greater force than to recent developments in France.

There appear to be a number of productive directions in which the model could be extended. For example, it would be instructive to see French capital controls analyzed in greater detail. Export credits have for periods been exempted from the *encadrement* and at other times been subject to specially reduced reserve requirements. The treatment of export credits is important in this context because it has implications for exports, for the current account, and hence for the foreign exchange value of the franc. It also would be instructive to see further research on the bank credit supply process. If there exists an efficient secondary market on which entitlements to increase net assets are traded, then there is no obvious reason why a rationing effect should be apparent in bank's credit supplies. The CC variable, which denotes the extent to which firms, not banks, have unsatisfied demands for credit, would belong in the asset demand functions but not in the bank credit supply function, where it also presently appears. If banks willingly depart from their notional supply curves whenever firms are rationed, perhaps to provide services to their most-favored customers, then CC might appear in the banks' supply function. In addition, the authors cite the increasing propensity of French banks to turn to the security market for funds; to the extent that this market was a source of funds *on the margin* even before 1979, this practice might help to explain CC's significance in the credit supply function.

Finally, there is the problem of segregating agents' flow allocations to the financial sector from their flow allocations to the real sector, such as their consumption and investment decisions. Obviously, rationing in the bond market spills over onto other markets in the economy. French firms' excess demands for credit should have counterparts in excess supplies in other markets—perhaps in the market for their output. Analyzing this question requires an integrated model of flow allocations to both asset and commodity markets. If I read the paper correctly, an integrated model along these lines is the authors' ultimate objective. If so, then we can look forward with relish to the appearance of future installments.

● References

DORNBUSCH R. — (1976) "Expectations and Exchange Rate Dynamics", *Journal of Political Economy*, 84, pp. 1161-1176.

FRENKEL J. and CLEMENTS K. — (1981) "Exchange Rates in the 1920's: A Monetary Approach", *in* M. J. Flanders and Assaf Razin, eds., *Development in an Inflationary World*, New York: Academic Press, pp. 283-318.

Comments

by **Richard C. MARSTON**

Wharton School, University of Pennsylvania

This paper by FEROLDI and MELITZ is in the best tradition of financial modelling. The authors have succeeded in capturing many of the institutional details unique to the French financial system, while still retaining the analytical structure of a consistently specified financial model. Table 1 of their paper sets out clearly the balance sheets constraints of the individual sectors in a matrix that summarizes the sources and uses of each asset in the economy. The reader is apprised of the salient features of the French system, but without losing the overall view of how the markets interact.

Studies of financial markets seldom report the implicit equations of the model, equations which are not directly estimated but instead obtained by using the balance sheet constraints. This study should be commended for doing so, since at the end of the paper the implicit equation for foreign assets is reported and discussed. The equation is a perfectly respectable one, although as the authors point out there are problems in interpreting the interest rate coefficients. I would doubt that the omitted equations of most financial models would bear such close scrutiny.

If there is one thing missing in this study, it is a more complete discussion of how French monetary policy works, and how that policy is reflected in the specification of the equations. I am particularly interested in the key equation for bank credit (11) and the reaction functions for the discount rate and exchange rate (equations 20 and 21). These equations raise some interesting issues about French monetary policy which need to be analyzed in greater detail.

The first issue concerns the offset effect of discount borrowing, the tendency of borrowing at the discount window to offset changes in the unborrowed reserve base. Forty years ago NURKSE emphasized the importance of this effect, but it needs reemphasis today, especially in the context of the French financial system. Discount borrowing by banks can offset direct policy initiatives affecting the unborrowed base or changes in foreign exchange reserves due to exchange market intervention. This offset effect is distinct from the conventional offset effect of capital flows, but the two effects work in a similar way. A policy-induced contraction of the unborrowed reserve base can be offset just as effectively by a rise in borrowing at the discount window or by an inflow of foreign exchange reserves. The important difference, however, is that the discount offset can take place even under flexible exchange rates.

Just how important is the offset effect in the French system? For the 1959-1971 period, André FOURÇANS [1978] found that 70% to 90% of the movements in the unborrowed base were offset by borrowing at the discount window. In his words, "(t)he central bank gives back with its left hand what it takes out with its right hand" (p. 536). The results of FEROLDI and MELITZ for the recent period are more difficult to assess since these involve the impact of unborrowed reserves on the supply of bank credit rather than on discount borrowing directly. Their equation (11) indicates that a change in unborrowed reserves by 1 franc raises bank credit by 2.80 francs. If the ratio of reserves to credit were 10% (the actual ratio varies over the period as does the reserve requirement), the 2.80 coefficient would represent a substantial offset, although it would by no means be complete. So the availability of discount borrowing is a crucial feature of the system which by itself seriously weakens monetary control.

Discount borrowing comes at a price, however, and in the French system that price is itself an important instrument of control. Policy regarding the discount rate (actually the "money market" rate, RM) has been closely attuned to foreign monetary conditions, with the rate at times in the past following the Eurodollar rate quite closely. The equation (20) which the authors estimate for RM reveals a looser link for the recent period, with the German Lombard rate a more important influence than the Eurodollar rate. But the determination of RM is still dominated by external conditions. Thus the net effect of external disturbances on the French monetary system is difficult to assess. Consider the case of a rise in foreign interest rates. On the one hand discount borrowing can offset changes in the unborrowed base due to foreign exchange outflows. But on the other hand changes in foreign interest rates can trigger changes in the discount rate which discourage such borrowing. The net effect on bank credit is not obvious from the equations.

Before leaving the equation for the discount rate, I should note the essential interdependence between the authorities' reaction function for RM and for e, the exchange rate. Discount rate policy and intervention policy should be very closely coordinated, especially when the discount rate is geared towards foreign conditions, but the coordination both in theory and practice might take a number of different forms. In the paper, this issue is not addressed in analytical terms, although the interdependence between the two policies is taken into account empirically by the presence of RM and e in both reaction functions.

French monetary policy also works through direct controls on credit, the *encadrements du crédit*, a potentially powerful instrument if used effectively by the authorities. (See the discussion of the *encadrement du crédit* in Jacques MELITZ [1982].) Estimates for earlier periods suggested that these credit controls were only moderately effective. FEROLDI and MELITZ, in contrast, show that in the recent period the controls exert a major influence on the total supply of bank credit. (See the CC variable in equation 11.) The authors do not discuss, however, the extensive controls on international transactions that are necessary if these credit controls are to be effective. In the absence of controls on international transactions, the credit controls would encourage a two-way flow of funds between France and financial markets abroad. Non-banks would resort to financing from abroad when they are denied bank loans. Banks, in turn, would invest abroad given the limits on lending at home. So in order to make credit controls effective, there is a natural progression to other controls: first come controls on banks' net foreign asset positions. Then non-banks must be denied access to the Euro-dollar market as well as other sources of financing abroad. The *encadrements du crédit* provide a powerful method for controlling national monetary conditions, but this method is ineffective if not accompanied by extensive controls on international transactions. Such controls are important in France, but just how they are reflected in the equations is not made clear in the paper.

A system of credit controls would certainly modify the impact of any discount offset effect. Indeed, if the controls were rigid enough (and accompanied by international controls), we would not need to worry about offsets *per se*. The French system, however, combines credit controls that permit many exceptions with discount borrowing that is controlled, but only indirectly through the discount rate. The net effect of this system is unclear. If any one of the instruments were used exclusively, then the analysis of its effects would be straightforward, but not when there is a mixture of policy instruments, each turned on only part way. In this paper, key questions about the relative importance of these instruments remain unanswered. The authors, however, have succeeded in providing a solid empirical basis for analyzing such a complex system.

● References

Fourçans André. — (1978) "The Impact of Monetary and Fiscal Policies on the French Financial System", *Journal of Monetary Economics,* p. 536.

Melitz Jacques. — (1982) "The French Financial System: Mechanisms and Questions of Reform", *Annales de l'INSEE,* this issue.

On the Franc

Jeffrey A. FRANKEL*

*University of California, Berkeley, U.S.A. I would like to thank Charles ENGEL for extremely efficient research assistance, Olivier BLANCHARD for helpful discussion, and Jacques MELITZ and Charles WYPLOSZ for useful suggestions. I would also like to thank the Institute of Business and Economic Research at the University of California at Berkeley, the National Bureau of Economic Research 1982 Summer Institute and the National Science Foundation under Grant No. SES-8007-162 for research support.

Six assumptions that any exchange rate theory must take into account are tested on French data : covered interest parity, rational expectations, exchange risk premium, political risk premium, money demand function and slow adjustment to purchasing power parity. The evidence is consistent with what has been found for other countries, with the important qualification that French capital controls require that interest parity be amended. There is a term analogous to a "tax" on foreign assets. The building blocks are then combined in various ways into three alternative exchange rate models : a stickyprice monetary model, portfolio-balance model and synthesis model.

Introduction

There are a number of special factors that make the case of the French franc an interesting one, and more than just another proving-ground for our asset-market models of exchange rate determination.

First, the existence of joint floating arrangements with other European currencies means that the franc/dollar exchange rate is affected by developments in other European countries. Second, following a brief spell of free capital movements, some exchange controls have been continuously in effect in France since November 24, 1968 (Annual Report on Trade Restrictions and Exchange Controls, IMF, 1981. p. 167, and ARTUS, MORIN, and STERDYNIAK [1979], p. 10). There is some question whether controls have been an effective barrier to the international movement of capital during most of the floating rate pediod. (The controls were less severe after 1971 [until 1981] than previously, according to MATHIS [1981], p. 37.) But it is very possible that the imposition of more stringent capital controls in a series of measures beginning May, 1981 has now invalidated the standard assumption of capital market efficiency for France (Le Monde, October 7, 1981, p. 8: Economist, March 27, 1982; and Le Monde, March 31, 1982). A conceptually distinct point is that even if the existing level of controls was not high enough to invalidate efficiency, say before May 1981, there has always been the risk that effective capital controls would be imposed in the future. This source of « political risk », like the standard factor of exchange risk, makes it likely that residents want to diversify their holdings and thus that they view French bonds and foreign bonds as imperfect substitutes. Finally, the transition to a Socialist government beginning May 10, 1981, led to a capital outflow and consequent large depreciation of the franc (which of course was the occasion for the tightening of capital controls).

This paper is an attempt to develop an empirical model of exchange rate determination appropriate to the franc/dollar rate. The standard « semi-reduced form » exchange rate equations turn out to yield the same mixed empirical results for the franc as they have recently been seen to yield for other currencies. Partly for this reason, this paper follows a « back to basics » approach, considering in turn five building blocks *that any exchange rate model must take into account: interest rate parity, rational expectations, the risk premium, the money demand function, and adjustment to purchasing power parity. We then combine the building blocks into alternative complete models: a monetary model, a portfolio-balance model and a synthesis model. An appendix, describing the data used throughout the paper, is available on request from the author.*

1 Covered interest parity and capital controls

One property shared by most « asset-market » models of exchange rates is the assumption that transaction costs, capital controls, and other barriers to the international movement of capital are not important enough to prevent the actual portfolios held by investors from adjusting instantaneously to desired portfolios. One testable implication of this assumption is that arbitrage insures that the domestic interest rate equals the foreign interest rate covered on the forward exchange market, i. e. that covered interest parity holds:

$$(1 + r_t^F) = \frac{F_t}{S_t}(1 + r_t^\$)$$

where r^F is the one-month franc interest rate, $r^\$$ the one-month dollar interest rate, S the spot exchange rate in francs per dollar and F the forward exchange rate. Equivalently,

$$f_t - s_t - (i_t^F - i_t^\$) = 0$$

where f, s, i^F and $i^\$$ are the logs of F, S, $1 + r^F$ and $1 + r^\$$ respectively. (For small values, $i^F \approx r^F$ and $i^\$ \approx r^\$$.) Tests of covered interest parity have shown it to hold up well between, for example, Germany and the United States (See, for example, FRENKEL and LEVICH [1977]).

In the case of France, however, the existence of capital controls requires us to view covered interest parity sceptically. As soon as we turn to the data, the point is clear. Deviations of the covered interest differential from zero are very large; the root mean squared error is 0.0043 for the one-month US deposit rate relative to the French interbank rate. This, assuming a normal distribution, implies that deviations as large as plus or minus 10.3 percent per annum occur! (All calculations reported here were performed on a one-month basis. The coefficients must be multiplied by 12 for comparisons with conventionally-quoted per annum interest rates.) Some of the variation can be explained by a significant constant term, as shown in table 1. The term is positive (0.00175), as one would expect from the existence of capital controls: the controls act as a « tax » on French residents' holdings of foreign assets, and so Frenchmen require a higher return abroad than they do on untaxed assets issued within France. And the inclusion of a dummy variable for the period since the month Mitterrand took office and controls were tightened, May 1981, suggests that the effective magnitude of this « tax » was quadrupled. However most of the variation remains unexplained by the constant terms; the remaining standard error is 0.00373.

The effect of the controls should apply equally to the differential between the offshore Eurofranc rate and the domestic French interbank rate, since what matters for capital controls is the location of the asset, not its currency of denomination. Table 1 indicates a constant term and Mitterrand dummy that are almost as large for this differential as for the covered interest differential. Indeed, on May 22, 1981, the day after controls were tightened (Le Monde, October 7, 1981, p. 8), the Eurofranc rate jumped from 20.75 to 30 percent.

There is another way, besides looking at the gap between French and foreign interest rates, that we can get an idea as to the magnitude of the effective tax on foreign assets created by capital controls. There exists a price at which French residents can obtain foreign assets : the financial franc exchange rate. From late 1973 until March 21, 1974 France had an official two-tier exchange system, consisting of a commercial franc rate for current account transactions and a financial franc rate for capital account transactions. Currently there is no such system, but there is still a market exchange rate at which Frenchmen can buy dollar assets from other Frenchmen, the « devise titre. »

The excess of the financial franc rate over the commercial franc rate represents the effective tax on foreign assets. To see this, consider the options facing a French investor. For every franc he invests in domestic bonds, he receives $1 + r^F_{dom}$ francs back in one period. His alternative is to spend the franc on a dollar bond, in which case he can buy 1/FS dollars, where FS is the financial franc spot rate. It will pay $r^\$/FS$ dollars of interest. But the Frenchman is forced to convert the interest back to francs at the less-favorable commercial spot rate CS_{+1}, because interest payments are current account transactions. So it will pay $r^\$ CS_{+1}/FS$ francs of interest. Under the two-tier system he could repatriate the principal at next period's financial franc rate FS_{+1}. Equivalently, under the current system he can resell the bond to another Frenchman at the rate of next period's « devise titre » FS_{+1}. Thus he would receive $(FS_{+1} + r^\$ CS_{+1})/FS$ francs back in one month. Arbitrage should insure that

$$1 + r^F_{dom} = (FS^e_{+1} + r^\$ CS^e_{+1}) FS,$$

where the suprascript e denotes market expectations (FLOOD and MARION [1981]) include this equation as their equation (14), and give further references on two-tier systems). Define $1 + \tau \equiv FS/CS$ and assume it constant :

$$(1) \qquad 1 + r^F_{dom} = \left(1 + r^\$ \frac{1}{1+\tau}\right) \frac{FS^e_{+1}}{FS}$$

If the financial franc rate FS never deviated from the regular franc rate CS, then τ would be zero and (1) would reduce to uncovered interest parity: the domestic interest rate would equal the foreign interest rate plus expected depreciation. But to the extent that FS > CS, τ represents a positive tax on foreign assets, which must as a consequence pay more to compete with domestic assets.

In December 1973, the financial rate was about 4 percent above the commercial rate. The gap narrowed steadily thereafter, in anticipation of the return to a uniform exchange system (FLOOD and MARION [1981]). In June 1981, the month after Mitterrand's election and the tightening of controls, the gap varied from 6 percent to 11 percent. The « devise titre » jumped up in early October in anticipation of the devaluation that did in fact take place October 10; the gap was 24 percent (*Le Monde*, courtesy of Olivier BLANCHARD). While the variability of these numbers suggests they may not be a reliable indicator of anything, they do support the idea that there is an effective tax on foreign assets that has gone up in magnitude since May 1981.

The magnitude of the tax computed from the financial franc data is not comparable with the constant terms in the interest differential that were estimated in table 1. But equation (1) contains the key to estimating properly the magnitude of the tax from the interest rate data, even when reliable financial franc data are not available. Assuming uncovered interest parity still holds for offshore interest rates, i.e.

$$S_{+1}^e/S = (1 + r_{eur}^F)/(1 + r_{eur}^\$)$$

we can substitute in for expected depreciation to get an observable measure of the tax :

(2)
$$1 + \tau = \cfrac{r_{eur}^\$}{\left[(1 + r_{dom}^F)\cfrac{1 + r_{eur}^\$}{1 + r_{eur}^F} - 1 \right]}$$

An approximation to (2) is

$$1 + \tau = \cfrac{r_{eur}^\$}{r_{dom}^F + r_{eur}^\$ - r_{eur}^F}$$

In general $r_{dom}^F < r_{eur}^F$ so the ratio is greater than one, meaning that the tax τ is positive.[1]

I computed a series for the magnitude of the tax, $1 + \tau$, from one-month interest rates as in equation (2). The series fluctuates erratically. The average value for the period January 1974 to April 1981 is 1.248, implying a 25 percent tax, which is much higher than the value estimated from the financial franc rate. The average value for the period after May 1981 goes up by 23.632. The figure seems far too high to be credible, but it reflects the very high estimated value in a single month, September 1981, which in turn reflects a one-month Eurofranc interest rate of 35.5 percent per annum at a time when the domestic French interest rate was only 18.875 percent per annum. The Eurocurrency rate rose to reflect the expectation of the imminently upcoming devaluation. The one-year Eurofranc rate rose to the more reasonable level of 0.2300 which, with a one-year Eurodollar rate of 0.1737 and a long-term French commercial bond rate of 0.1663, implies a value of $1 + \tau = 1.54$. (These numbers are for the end of September 1981, from Morgan Guaranty and Trust's *World Financial Markets*.) This value is much more credible. Perhaps the erratic nature of the values calculated from one-month Eurocurrency rates is due to the thinness of that market. The view of capital controls as creating a roughly constant tax on foreign assets may be more appropriate to assets of maturity equal to one year or longer.

In section 4 below, we will consider more carefully the possibility of a fluctuating political risk premium that separates the return on assets held in France from that on assets held abroad, even when covered on the forward exchange market. But first we examine the efficient markets hypothesis for *uncovered* exchange transactions.

---

1. One might wonder what would happen if r_{eur}^F were so large that the denominator of $1 + \tau$ were zero or even negative. But this should never happen, so long as there is a finite price at which Frenchmen can buy off-shore assets. If it did, no Frenchman would hold any domestic assets, because the domestic rate of return $(1 + r_{dom}^F)$ would be exceeded by the expected appreciation of foreign assets $\left(\dfrac{FS_{+1}^e}{FS} = \dfrac{1 + r_{eur}^F}{1 \times r_{eur}^\$} \right)$ alone, leaving aside any foreign interest earned $(r_{cur}^\$)$.

TABLE 1. — *The effect of capital controls on covered interest parity U.S.- French differential* (Sample period : Jan. 1974 to April 1982)

	MSE	Constant	Mitterrand dummy	s.e.r.	R²	D.W.
$f_t - s_t - (i_{ib}^F - i_{ib}^{\$})$	0.00430	0.00175* (0.00039)		0.00394		1.30
One-month U.S. deposit rate relative to French interbank rate, covered.		0.00126* (0.00040)	0.00408* (0.00115)	0.00373	0.11	1.44
$i_{eur}^F - i_{ib}^F$	0.00280	0.00148* (0.00024)		0.00239		1.09
One-month Eurofranc rate relative to French interbank rate.		0.00113* (0.00023)	0.00297* (0.00067)	0.00219	0.17	1.29

* Significant at the 95 % level (standard errors in parentheses).

2 Rational expectations in the forward and eurocurrency markets

The hypothesis that the forward exchange market is efficient consists of two propositions: (1) investors' expectations of the future spot exchange rate are rational, given all information available to them, and (2) their expectations are reflected in the forward rate, without effective interference from transactions costs, capital controls, or other barriers to the international movement of capital. While the preceding section called the second proposition into doubt on account of French capital controls, we will proceed under the argument that controls should not affect the forward rates or Eurocurrency rates in New York. The hypothesis that we test in practice is that the forward rate is an unbiased predictor of the future spot rate, conditional on some information' set. This hypothesis requires a third proposition in addition to those needed for forward market efficiency: (3) no risk premium exists to separate investors' expected future spot rate from the forward rate. This will hold, for example, if investors are risk-neutral.

The hypothesis to be tested, unbiasedness, would seem to be represented

$$(3) \qquad\qquad ES_{t+1} = F_t$$

where E represents the mathematical expectation contingent on a given information set. But there is the SIEGEL paradox to contend with: if equation (3) holds, then the analogous equation from the viewpoint of the foreign country,

$$(4) \qquad\qquad E\,(1/S_{t+1}) = 1/F_t$$

cannot hold. The solution to the SIEGEL paradox is that the correct arbitrage condition is written in real terms, rather than nominal terms :

$$(5) \qquad\qquad E\,(S_{t+1}/P_{t+1}) = E\,(F_t/P_{t+1})$$

where P is the price index expressed in francs for the consumption basket of the investor in question. I. e., the expected value in real terms of the future spot purchase of a dollar equals the expected value in real terms of the current forward purchase of a dollar. (See for example, FRENKEL and RAZIN [1980], FRANKEL [1980] or ENGEL [1981].) In the special case in which the investor consumes only French goods, and the prices of French goods are nonstochastic in terms of francs, equation (5) reduces to equation (3). In the special case in which the investor consumes only US goods and the prices of US goods are nonstochastic in terms of dollars, equation (5) reduces to equation (4).

192

In the more general case, we represent the price index as a weighted geometric average:

$$P = (P_{US}S)^{1-\alpha}P_F^\alpha$$

where P_{US} is the price of US goods expressed in dollars, P_F is the price of French goods expressed in francs, and α is the share of consumption expenditure falling on French goods in a COBB-DOUGLAS utility function. If P_{US} and P_F are nonstochastic and S is distributed log-normally (which will be the case if S follows a proportionate diffusion process when expressed in continuous time), equation (5) becomes

(6)
$$E(s_{t+1}) = f_t + \left(\frac{1}{2} - \alpha\right) V(s_{t+1})$$

where s is the log of S and V is the conditional variance.[2] An alternative representation of equation (6) is

$$s_{t+1} - f_t = \left(\frac{1}{2} - \alpha\right) V(\varepsilon) + \varepsilon_{t+1}$$

where ε is the random error that by hypothesis must be independent of all information available at time t :

$$E(\varepsilon_{t+1}|I_t) = 0$$

The simplest test looks for unconditional bias in ε. It seems unlikely that investors could be so irrational as to overestimate (or underestimate) the spot rate persistently. A finding of unconditional bias would more plausibly be interpreted as evidence of a risk premium. Note however that a finding that the average value of $s_{t+1} - f_t$ was significantly different from zero would not in itself constitute bias. We would have to see first if the constant could be explained by estimates of the convexity term $\left(\frac{1}{2} - \alpha\right) V(\varepsilon)$. ($\alpha$ could be estimated from consumption data and $V(\varepsilon)$ from the sample variance of $s_{t+1} - f_t$.)

As can be seen in table 2, the average value of the forward rate prediction error $s_{t+1} - f_t$ for the franc/dollar rate, using monthly observations from September 1973 to May 1981, is not statistically different from zero. There is no point comparing it to a measure of $\left(\frac{1}{2} - \alpha\right) V(\varepsilon)$. The forward rate passes this first (very easy) test.

---

2. Proof: using the arbitrage condition (5), the definition of the price index, and the assumptions of nonstochastic prices and a log-normally distributed spot rate,

$$f \equiv \log F = ES_{+1}^\alpha - \log ES_{+1}^{\alpha-1}$$

$$= \left[\alpha Es_{+1} + \frac{\alpha^2}{2} Vs_{+1}\right] - \left[(\alpha-1) Es_{+1} + \frac{(\alpha-1)^2}{2} Vs_{+1}\right]$$

$$= Es_{+1} + \left(\alpha - \frac{1}{2}\right) Vs_{+1}$$

TABLE 2. — *Tests of efficiency in the forward and eurocurrency markets.*

Dependent variable	Constant	Lagged dependent variable	Forward discount	s.e.r.	D. W.
$s_{t+1} - f_t$			$f_t - s_t$		
Sample : September 1973 to May 1981	+ 0.00120 (0.00346)			0.0334	1.97
93 observations	+ 0.00132 (0.00352)	0.0143 (0.0156)		0.0338	1.95
	+ 0.00525 (0.00334)		− 2.020* (0.487)	0.0308	2.25
$s_{t+1} - s_t - (i^F_{eur} - i^\$_{eur})$			$i^F_{eur} - i^\$_{eur}$		
Sample : January 1974 to March 1982	− 0.00017 (0.00315)			0.0314	2.01
99 observations	0.00049 (0.00313)	− 0.0346 (0.1007)		0.0310	2
	0.00570 (0.00331)		− 3.026* (0.779)	0.0293	2.34

$$S_{t+1}/P_{t+1} - F_t/P_{t+1}$$

Sample : September 1973 to May 1981

93 observations

P index measured by			
US CPI	0.018 (0.105)	0.000006 (0.000412)	− 0.000015 (0.000418)
French CPI	0.026 (0.105)	− 0.000396 (0.002960)	− 0.000547 (0.003000)
average CPI	0.005 (0.105)	− 0.000067 (0.001100)	− 0.000125 (0.001110)

* Significantly different from hypothesized value of zero at 95 % level. (Standard errors reported in parentheses.)

A somewhat harder test is to include the lagged value of the forward rate prediction error in the information set I_t, i.e., to see if ε is serially correlated. A finding of serial correlation, again, could be interpreted as evidence of a risk premium, since the variables to which the risk premium would in theory be related (asset supplies and wealth distribution, as we will see in section 3) are themselves serially correlated. Such a finding could of course also be interpreted as a failure of rational expectations. But the autocorrelation coefficient of the forward rate prediction error is again not statistically significant.

Another common test is to include the forward discount $f_t - s_t$ itself in the information set :

(7) $$s_{t+1} - f_t = \gamma + (\beta - 1)(f_t - s_t) + \varepsilon_{t+1}$$

or equivalently

$$\Delta s_{t+1} = \gamma + \beta(f_t - s_t) + \varepsilon_{t+1}$$

The null hypothesis is that $\beta = 1$. A finding of $\beta > 1$ would indicate that speculators suffer from inertia, that they underestimate trends in the exchange rate. A finding that $\beta < 1$ would indicate that speculators are overly excitable, that they over-estimate trends in the exchange rate. (The inertia/overexcitability characterization is due to BILSON [1981b].) One special case is $\beta = 0$, which would imply that the spot rate follows a random walk. The random walk case is *not* the same as market efficiency: indeed, it would imply that one could expect to make money by betting against the forward rate. (Among those finding that the lagged spot rate is often a better predictor of the future spot rate than is the forward rate are FRANKEL [1980], BILSON [1981a], and MEESE and ROGOFF [1983].)

The estimate of $\beta - 1$ is a statistically significant -2.0 We reject not only efficiency but the random walk as well. This is a surprising finding. When the forward market expects the spot rate to move in one direction, it on average moves the same distance in the opposite direction! If this implausible finding were believed, it would support in an extreme way BILSON'S [1981a] claims that one can expect to make money by betting against the forward market.

If covered interest parity holds for the Eurocurrency interest differential, then we should be able to repeat the efficiency tests using it in place of the forward discount. The second third of table 2 reveals the same results for the Eurocurrency differential as for the forward discount: no statistically significant mean or autocorrelation in the prediction errors, but a highly significant tendency for the spot rate to move in the *opposite* direction from that predicted by the interest differential.

In section 7 below, we will argue that goods prices are sticky in the short run, which would constitute a rationale for the nonstochastic-prices assumption that allowed us to pass from equation (5) to equation (6). However, some may take exception with this assumption. An alternative is to test equation (5) directly with the use of actual price index data. (See, ENGEL [1981].) The equation will be different depending on the consumption basket of the particular investor whose behavior we are examining. Table 2 repeats the constant terms and autocorrelation tests for three possible price indices: the US CPI, relevant for a US investor, the French CPI, relevant for a French investor, and a equal-weighted geometric average of the two, relevant for an international investor. Note that the joint null hypothesis (market efficiency and no risk premium) now requires a zero constant term; there is no convexity term. All results in the last third of table 2 indicate a failure to reject the null hypothesis.

3 The exchange risk premium

As we have seen, the proposition that the forward rate is an unbiased predictor of the future spot rate consists of two joint hypotheses: market efficiency and the absence of the risk premium. In this section we take market efficiency more or less for granted and concentrate on modeling the exchange risk premium.

We assume that French investors balance their portfolios between franc assets B and dollar assets D, as a function of the relative rate of return. The relative rate of return is the one-month interest differential in excess of expected depreciation, or, equivalently (given interest parity), the forward discount in excess of expected depreciation or, equivalently, the log of the forward rate in excess of the log of the expected future spot rate.

$$(8) \qquad B_{f_t}/W_{f_t} = a_f + b\left(f_t - s^e_{t+1}\right)$$

where we have defined total French wealth $W_f = B_f + SD_f$. It has been shown that if investors maximize a one-period function of the mean and variance of real wealth and exhibit constant relative risk aversion, then the linear functional form assumed in (8) will be correct, and the parameters will take on particular values. (See, for example, SOLNIK [1974], ADLER and DUMAS [1981], DORNBUSCH [1982], KRUGMAN [1981] and FRANKEL [1982b].) In the special case considered in the efficiency tests above, in which the prices of the goods produced in each country are nonstochastic when expressed in their own currencies, a_F becomes α_F, the share of expenditure by French residents that falls on French goods, and b becomes simply $1/\rho V(\varepsilon)$ where ρ is the constant of risk-aversion and $V(\varepsilon)$ is the conditional variance of the spot rate. The first term in (8), a_f, is called the minimum-variance portfolio; if risk-aversion is very high, investors will hold assets in the same proportion (α_f and $1 - \alpha_f$) as the « liabilities » represented by their consumption patterns. The second term is called the speculative portfolio; to the extent that risk-aversion is low, a higher expected return on franc assets will induce investors to hold more of their portfolio in the form of franc assets. In the extreme case of risk neutrality, b is infinite and arbitrage insures that the risk premium ($f_t - s^e_{t+1}$) is zero.

In a small-country portfolio-balance model, only the holdings of domestic residents, as specified in equation (8), would matter. But in general we must recognize that franc assets are also held by residents of the United States and the rest of the world:

$$(9) \qquad B_{us_t}/W_{us_t} = a_{us} + b\left(f_t - s^e_{t+1}\right)$$

$$(10) \qquad B_{r_t}/W_{r_t} = a_r + b\left(f_t - s^e_{t+1}\right)$$

To aggregate the three equations, we multiply (8) by $w_f \equiv W_f/W$, (9) by $w_{us} \equiv W_{us}/W$ and (10) by $w_r \equiv W_r/W$, where we have defined total world wealth $W \equiv W_f + W_{us} + W_r$. The sum of the three equations is then

$$x_t = a_f w_{f_t} + a_{us} w_{us_t} + a_r w_{r_t} + b\left(f_t - Es_{t+1}\right)$$

where we have defined the total share of world wealth allocated to franc bonds:

$$x \equiv B/W \equiv (B_f + B_{us} + B_r)/W$$

We use $w_r \equiv 1 - w_f - w_{us}$ and solve for the risk premium:

$$(11) \qquad f_t - s^e_{t+1} = \frac{1}{b}x_t + \left(\frac{a_r - a_f}{b}\right)w_{f_t} + \left(\frac{a_r - a_{us}}{b}\right)w_{us_t} - \frac{a_r}{b}$$

We see from (11) that the risk premium $(f_t - s^e_{t+1})$ or expected relative return, depends on three variables. First, an increase in the supply of franc relative to dollar assets, x_t, requires an increase in their relative return, for them to be willingly held. Second, assume that French residents have a greater relative propensity to hold franc assets than do residents of the rest of the world: $a_f > a_r$. (For this to be the case in the mean-variance maximizing model, French residents must have a greater relative propensity to consume French goods: $\alpha_f > \alpha_r$). Then a redistribution of wealth toward French residents from the rest of the world, such as would result from a French current account surplus, will raise the net world demand for Franc assets and thus require a fall in their relative return. Third, and analogously, assume that $a_{us} < a_r$. Then a redistribution of wealth toward US residents will *lower* the net world demand for Franc assets and thus require a *rise* in their relative return.

To estimate equation (11) we must add to it the assumption of rational expectations:

$$s^e_{t+1} = s_{t+1} + \varepsilon_{t+1}$$

$$(12) \qquad f_t - s_{t+1} = \frac{1}{b}x_t + \left(\frac{a_r - a_f}{b}\right)w_{f_t} + \left(\frac{a_r - a_{us}}{b}\right)w_{us_t} - \frac{a_r}{b} + \varepsilon_{t+1}$$

where ε_{t+1} is independent of all information available at time t, in particular x_t, w_{f_t} and w_{us_t}, allowing us to run a regression. Notice that the dependent variable in equation (12) is the same as the dependent variable in the efficiency tests in the last section. Under the null hypothesis of no risk premium, all coefficients should be zero, and the dependent variable should consist purely of random expectational errors. Under the alternative hypothesis we are estimating an inverted portfolio-balance function. The three coefficients should be positive, negative and positive, respectively, and the constant term should be negative. If we choose to adopt the mean-variance maximization rationale for the portfolio-balance function, then the coefficient $1/b$ of the relative asset supply x should equal $\rho V(\varepsilon)$. If we got a meaningful estimate of the coefficient, we could divide it by the estimated variance of the error term (the standard error of the regression, squared) to obtain an estimate of the constant of risk-aversion. To help get a more efficient estimate of $1/b$ we can impose the constraint that a_f, a_r and a_{us} are equal to the shares of consumption falling on French vs US goods, estimated at

$$\alpha_f = 0.988, \ \alpha_r = 0.336 \text{ and } \alpha_{us} = 0.001, \text{ respectively}$$

Table 3 reports estimates of equation (12). The coefficient $1/b$ of x is not of the correct sign: an increase in the relative supply of franc assets fails to induce an increase in the expected relative return on francs. The failure holds regardless whether we measure the relative return using the forward discount, the Eurocurrency interest differential, or the difference between the domestic French and US interest rates. The coefficients on the variables representing the distribution of wealth, w_f and w_{us}, vary in sign. But all coefficients are statistically insignificant in any case. When we impose the constraint that the a's are determined by the consumption shares, the estimate of $1/b$ is again incorrect in sign. If we include an unconstrained constant term and Mitterrand dummy to allow for the possible effect of the level of French capital controls on offshore interest rates, the estimate of $1/b$ appears statistically significant, when the constraint on the a's is imposed, but remains incorrect in sign. This absence of a positive correlation between relative returns and asset supplies constitutes a failure to reject the null hypothesis of uncovered interest parity against the alternative hypothesis that a meaningful portfolio-balance function and risk premium exist. Of course, one possible interpretation of all these results is that the tests lack power.[3]

---

3. Note however that to the extent that the variance of the regression error is high—and there is good a priori reason to believe that it is, i.e., that most of the exchange rate changes are due to the « news »—the power of our test is high, not low. This unusual fact holds because, although the denominator of the t-ratio goes up with the standard error of the regression as usual, under the maximization hypothesis the numerator of the t-ratio is proportional to the variance, and thus goes up faster.

4 The political risk premium

For the regressions in table 3, the asset supplies were calculated as the net supplies of franc-denominated assets and dollar-denominated assets, respectively, held in the world market. Each country's accumulated government debt was corrected for that part of the debt denominated in other currencies (e.g., CARTER bonds, in the case of the United States), for the amount of its currency taken out of circulation in foreign exchange intervention by its central bank (inferred from reserve data), and for the amount of its currency taken out of circulation in foreign exchange intervention by all *other* countries' central banks. The justification for distinguishing among assets by currency of denomination is the assumption that it is exchange risk that renders them imperfect substitutes in investors' portfolios.

However ALIBER [1973] and DOOLEY and ISARD [1980] have argued that political risk may be as important a determinant of investors' portfolio behavior as exchange risk. This argument seems particularly relevant to France, since a tightening of capital controls has always been a serious possibility. We discovered in section 1 that a large gap separated the French interbank rate from the offshore interest rate, regardless whether the latter was measured as the Eurofranc rate or the US interest rate covered on the forward market, and that constant terms could explain only a small part of this gap. This suggests a (fluctuating) premium paid on foreign assets due to political risk. Equations (8), (9), (10) would still describe investors' behavior, but with the assets defined by the country of issuance of an asset rather than its currency of denomination.[4] Thus when the three equations are aggregated, what matters are the net supplies of French-issued assets and US-issued assets, respectively, held in the world market. These are the accumulated governmental debts *not* corrected for foreign currency denomination or foreign exchange intervention. Table 4 repeats the unconstrained regression of the risk premium equation from table 3 with the asset supplies measured this way.

In table 4 the supply of French assets does consistently have the hypothesized positive effect on their relative return. French wealth has the hypo-

---

4. From the viewpoint of the Mitterrand period, it might seem that the only source of political risk was the possibility that restrictions would be placed on holdings by French residents of foreign assets, as they now have been, which would apply to equation (8), but not equations (9) and (10) describing the behavior of investors in the United States and the rest of the world. However restrictions on holdings by foreign residents of French assets, as in Germany, Switzerland and Japan, have been a possibility, indeed a reality, during much of the floating rate period. « Le système combinait des mesures pour faire face à la fois aux entrées et aux sorties de capitaux ». — ARTUS, MORIN and STERDYNIAK, 1979, p. 10.

TABLE 3. — *Test of exchange risk premium*

Technique : ordinary least squares

Sample	Dependent variable	Unconstrained				Mitterrand dummy	R^2	s.e.r.	D. W.
		Constant	x	w_f	w_{us}				
June 1973 to September 1981	$f - s_{+1}$	− 0.062 (0.155)	− 0.336 (0.250)	0.002 (0.080)	0.065 (0.110)		0.03	0.033	2.10
	$i^{F}_{eur} - i^{\$}_{eur} - (s_{+1} - s)$	− 0.068 (0.153)	− 0.302 (0.246)	− 0.004 (0.079)	0.067 (0.109)		0.03	0.033	2.10
January 1974 to September 1981	$i^{F}_{ib} - i^{\$}_{td} - (s_{+1} - s)$	0.055 (0.153)	− 0.312 (0.235)	0.149 (0.099)	− 0.041 (0.112)		0.05	0.031	2.24
		0.065 (0.156)	− 0.291 (0.243)	0.174 (0.120)	− 0.052 (0.117)	0.006 (0.017)	0.05	0.031	2.25
		Constrained							
		$x - (\alpha_f - \alpha_r)\, w_f + (\alpha_f - \alpha_{us})\, w_{us} - \alpha_r$							
June 1973 to September 1981	$f - s_{+1}$			− 0.013 (0.036)			0	0.033	2.07
				− 0.021 (0.033)			0	0.031	2.12
January 1974 to September 1981	$i^{F}_{tb} - i^{\$}_{td} - (s_{+1} - s)$	0.026* (0.012)		− 0.284* (0.131)		0.008 (0.015)	0.05	0.030	2.25

* Statistically significant but not of the hypothesized sign (standard errors in parentheses).

x, w_f and w_{us} are shares of the aggregate portfolio: (respectively) denominated in francs, held by French residents, and held by US residents. The asset supplies are supplies of net government debt corrected so as to reflect currency of denomination.

TABLE 4. — *Test of political risk premium*

Sample : June 1973 - September 1981

Technique	Dependent variable	Constant	x'	w_f'	w_{us}'	Mitterrand dummy	R^2	s.e.r.	D.W.	$\hat{\rho}$
OLSQ		0.003 (0.016)	0.059 (0.060)	− 0.042* (0.019)	− 0.002 (0.015)	− 0.010* (0.002)	0.33	0.003	1.60	
CORC		0.002 (0.019)	0.068 (0.071)	− 0.041 (0.023)	− 0.001 (0.018)	− 0.010* (0.002)	0.35	0.003		0.17
OLSQ		− 0.002 (0.009)	0.028 (0.033)	− 0.026* (0.011)	0.003 (0.008)	− 0.007* (0.001)	0.42	0.002	1.14	
CORC		− 0.003 (0.014)	0.036 (0.048)	− 0.021 (0.017)	0.003 (0.013)	− 0.007* (0.001)	0.51	0.002		0.42

* Statistically significant and of the hypothesized sign (standard errors in parentheses).

x', w_f' and w_{us}' are shares of the aggregate portfolio : (respectively) issued in France, held by French residents, and held by U.S. residents. The asset supplies are supplies of net government debt *not* corrected so as to reflect currency of denomination.

thesized negative effect on the relative return when the possibility of exchange risk is eliminated by using as the "foreign" interest rate the offshore Euro-franc rate, or else the dollar rate covered on the foreign exchange market, rather than using the dollar rate subject to the uncertain future exchange risk. A dummy variable for the Mitterrand period beginning May 1981, to capture the increase in the effective tax on offshore assets created by capital controls, appears highly significant and of the hypothesized negative sign. But when we use the Cochrane-Orcutt technique to correct for serial corre-lation, none of the other coefficients appears statistically significant at the 95 percent level. The results in table 4, while a lot more encouraging for the notion of political risk than the results in table 3 were for the notion of exchange risk, again technically constitute a failure to reject the null hypo-thesis of perfect substitutability. We will proceed in the following sec-tions under the assumption that we can ignore any premium for either poli-tical risk or exchange risk, and that domestic and foreign bonds are perfect substitutes. However the issue is far from closed, and we will be bringing the risk premium back in, in sections 8 and 9.

5 Money demand

One could model domestic bonds and foreign bonds as perfect substitutes, and yet apply the portfolio-balance model to the choice between money and bonds. But in practice, believers in uncovered interest parity tend to adopt the transactions model of money demand. Bond supplies do not matter and "the responsibility for determining the exchange 'rate is thrown onto the money markets".

We adopt a standard functional form for the money demand equation:

$$(13) \qquad m - p = \Phi y - \lambda i$$

where m is the log of the nominal money supply, p is the log of the price level, y is the log of real income, and i is the level of the domestic interest rate. The equation is estimated for France during the floating-rate period in table 5. When we allow for lagged adjustment of the real money stock, all coefficients are of the correct sign. The interest rate, represented by the three-month French money market rate, shows up significantly. The point estimates imply a semi-elasticity with respect to the interest rate of —0.143 in the short run and — 0.598 (that is, — 0.143/(1 — 0.761)) in the long run. The coefficient on real income is not high enough to be significant, perhaps because income had to be proxied by industrial production to get monthly observations. The point estimates imply an elasticity with respect to income of 0.033 in the short run and 0.138 in the long run. A dummy variable for the Mitterrand period shows up positive and significant, reflecting a sharp jump in French interest rates after May 1981 that did not correspond to any fall in the real money supply.

TABLE 5. — *Money demand function for France.*
Dependent variable: m − p.

Sample	Technique	Constant	Industrial production y	Money market Interest rate i	Lagged real Money supply $m_{-1} - p_{-1}$	Real wealth $w - p$	Mitterrand dummy	R^2	s.e.r.	D.W.	$\hat{\rho}$
March 1973 to October 1981	OLSQ	3.091 (0.195)	0.276* (0.042)	− 0.498* (0.079)				0.38	0.022	0.79	
	CORC	1.672 (0.296)	− 0.073 (0.063)	0.064 (0.149)				0.70	0.015		0.86
	OLSQ	0.181 (0.135)	0.033 (0.037)	− 0.143* (0.064)	0.761* (0.072)			0.71	0.015	1.91	
March 1973 to September 1981	OLSQ	0.116 (0.158)	0.052 (0.044)	− 0.146* (0.067)	0.737* (0.079)	0.004 (0.008)		0.71	0.015	1.83	
		0.278 (0.078)		− 0.114 (0.061)	0.801* (0.057)	− 0.001 (0.009)		0.71	0.015	1.85	
		0.110 (0.135)	0.054 (0.037)	− 0.249* (0.080)	0.746* (0.071)		0.019* (0.009)	0.72	0.015	1.94	

* Significant at the 95 % level (standard errors reported in parentheses).

One alternative to real income as the appropriate transactions variable in the money demand equation would be to use real wealth. This alternative has some attraction because it would imply a link between the cumulated current account surplus, which is a determinant of financial wealth, and the value of the currency, within the monetary model of exchange rate determination. (Such a model can help explain the sharp appreciation of the mark against the dollar that culminated in 1978: FRANKEL [1982a].) A French wealth term is included in table 5. The results are no better, and no worse, than those with industrial production.

6 Adjustment to purchasing power parity

We now turn from the financial markets to a brief consideration of the goods markets. The benchmark characterization of international goods markets is that purchasing power parity (PPP) holds;

$$(14) \qquad s - p + p^* = 0$$

where p^* is the log of the foreign price level; i.e., the real exchange rate is constant. An examination of the real exchange rate between France and the United States during the period March 1973-January 1982, using consumer price indices, reveals that it is very far from constant. Its standard deviation on a monthly basis is 0.0907, implying that fluctuations as large as plus or minus 18 percent are common. (There is a long history of empirical studies of deviations from PPP. A recent study is FRENKEL [1981a].)

One possibility is that the changes in the real exchange rate are due to fundamental long-run shifts or trends in the terms of trade due to factors like oil price shocks and productivity trends. But a regression of the real exchange rate against a time trend reveals a coefficient that is insignificantly different from zero, once we correct for very high autocorrelation.

It is possible that fundamental "permanent" shifts in the terms of trade do take place, but that they take place in both directions, and frequently enough that they do not show up as steady long-run trends. HOOPER and MORTON [1982] have argued, in the context of a monetary model of exchange rates like that explained below, that trade balance announcements affect the exchange rate because the market infers from them the latest information about fundamental shifts in the value of the real exchange rate that is necessary for long-run external balance. Table 6 contains a very simple test of this hypothesis: the real exchange rate is regressed against French exports and imports. To correct for the obvious difficulty that simultaneous equations exist in which exports and imports depend on the real exchange rate, domestic and foreign income (proxied by industrial production) are used as instrumental variables. There is no indication that an increase in French

TABLE 6

Purchasing power parity

Dependent variable : $s_t + p_{F_t} - p_{SU_t}$.
Sample: March 1973-January 1982

Technique	Constant	Time Trend	Exports	Imports	Lagged Real Exchange Rate	R²	s.e.r.	D.W.	$\hat{\rho}$
CORC	1.807 (0.258)	0.0016 (0.0022)				0.88	0.032		0.96
FAIR	2.028 (0.145)		0.003 (0.004)	— 0.004 (0.006)		0.86	0.034		0.95
OLSQ	0.104 (0.068)				0.947* (0.034)	0.88	0.032	2.08	

* Significant at the 95 % level (standard errors in parentheses).
Instrumental variables for FAIR: logs of US and French industrial production and lagged values of exports, imports, and the dependent variable.

206

exports causes a real appreciation or, in imports, a real depreciation. In fact, the signs of the coefficients are incorrect. The finding is the same regardless whether we use Fair's method to correct for serial correlation.

This leaves as the leading explanation for the large deviations from PPP temporary deviations due to macroeconomic disturbances in the face of sticky goods prices. The autocorrelation coefficient for the real exchange rate is a highly significant 0.947. This estimate implies that, when a disturbance such as a monetary expansion creates a deviation from purchasing power parity, 94.7 percent of the deviation remains one month later, and 52.02 percent of it (that is, 0.947^{12}) remains one year later. If price adjustment to PPP in the two countries were expressed as

$$(15) \qquad \dot{p} - \dot{p}^* = \theta\,(s - p + p^*),$$

a point estimate of δ on an annual basis could be calculated from the fact $0.947 = \exp(-\hat{\delta}/12)$:

$$\hat{\theta} = -12 \log .947 = .28$$

7 The monetary model of the exchange rate

We now begin trying to put the building blocks together into a model of the exchange rate. For the moment, we adopt for simplicity the assumption that goods prices are perfectly flexible and that purchasing power parity, equation (14), therefore holds instantaneously. We combine this equation with the other pillar of monetarism, the money demand function (13), assumed to hold for the United States as well as France. The result is the flexible-price version of the monetary equation of exchange rate determination developed by FRENKEL [1976] and BILSON [1978], and applied to the French franc in one form by MELITZ and STERDYNIAK [1979]:

$$16) \qquad s = (m - m^*) - \Phi\,(y - y^*) + \lambda) + \lambda\,(i - i^*),$$

where m^*, y^*, and i^* are the log of the money supply, the log of real income, and the interest rate, respectively, for the foreign country, in this case the United States. (Note that the originators of the strictly flexible-price form of the monetary model have recently dropped their attachment to it: FRENKEL [1981a, b].)

Here we use the assumption that there is no risk premium in international capital markets, so expected depreciation is given by the difference between the French interest rate and the US interest rate, the latter corrected for the level of the effective tax τ imposed by capital controls on French holdings of dollar assets:

$$(17) \qquad \Delta s^e = i - \frac{i}{1+\tau} i^*$$

Equation (17) is simply a logarithmic approximation to equation (1), where $\frac{1}{1+\tau} = CS/FS$. We express purchasing power parity (14) in terms of expected rates of change:

$$\Delta s^e = \pi - \pi^*$$

where π and π^* are the expected domestic and foreign inflation rates, and combine it with uncovered interest parity (17) to obtain real interest parity:

$$i = \frac{1}{1+\tau} i^* + \pi - \pi^*,$$

When we substitute this equation into (16), we obtain an alternative form of the flexible-price monetary equation:

$$(18) \qquad s = (m - m^*) - \Phi(y - y^*) + \lambda(\pi - \pi^*) - \lambda \frac{\tau}{1+\tau}(\pi^* + \bar{r}),$$

where $\bar{r}$ is the constant long-run real interest rate.

As we found in section 7, and as indicated by a large number of other studies, the evidence is strongly against the hypothesis of instantaneous purchasing power parity (14). This leads us to the "overshooting" or sticky-price version of the monetary model, due to DORNBUSCH [1976]. We assume that PPP holds only in long-run equilibrium:

$$\bar{s} = \bar{p} - \bar{p}^*.$$

Then equation (18) is a relevant description of the exchange rate only in a long-run equilibrium.

In the short run, the spot rate can deviate from its equilibrium value. But the market expects the spot rate to regress toward its equilibrium value at a rate proportional to the gap.

$$(19) \qquad \Delta s^e = -\theta (s - \bar{s}) + \bar{\pi} - \bar{\pi}^*.$$

This form of expectations turns out to be rational in a model in which goods prices adjust gradually over time in response to excess goods demand, but also move in line with the underlying inflation rate $\bar{\pi}$ (FRANKEL [1979].) We combine a long-run version of equation (18) with the expectations equation (19) and the uncovered Eurocurrency interest parity condition (17) to obtain the sticky-price monetary equation of exchange rate determination:

$$(20) \quad s = (m - m^*) - \Phi(y - y^*) + \left(\lambda + \frac{1}{\theta}\right)(\bar{\pi} - \bar{\pi}^*) - \frac{1}{\theta}(i_{\text{eur}} - i^*_{\text{eur}}) - \lambda \frac{\tau}{1+\tau} \bar{\pi}^*.$$

The flexible-price version can be viewed as the special case in which adjustment to long-run equilibrium is instantaneous, so $\theta = \infty$ and the coefficient on the interest differential is not less than zero.

There are four empirical implications for the coefficients in a regression of equation (20), extending beyond their signs to their magnitudes. The coefficient of the relative money supply should be not only positive, but equal to one. The coefficient of relative real income should be not only negative, but comparable with estimates of the elasticity of money demand with respect to income, Φ (estimated for France in table 5, though very imprecisely). The coefficient on the expected inflation differential should be not only positive, but, when added to the coefficient of the interest differential, comparable with estimates of the semi-elasticity of money demand with respect to the interest rate, λ (estimated for France in table 5). Finally, if the sticky-price version of the monetary model is correct, not only should the coefficient of the interest differential be negative, but its inverse should be related to the speed of adjustment in goods markets (estimated in section 7). Note however that if expectations are not rational, then θ, the inverse of the coefficient, could be greater or less than the speed of adjustment in goods markets. Indeed, findings like $\beta < 1$ in tests of the efficiency condition (5) imply that θ is higher than is rational. ((See BILSON [1981b] and FRANKEL [1981].) A possible fifth empirical implication is that when we include a dummy variable for the Mitterrand period multiplied by the foreign inflation rate, to represent the May 1981 tightening of capital controls, not only should it be negative, but its value divided by an estimate of $-\lambda$ should be comparable with the increase in $\tau/1+\tau$, where τ is the percentage excess of the financial franc rate over the commercial franc rate.

Table 7 presents some estimates of the monetary model, equation (20), including the flexible-price special case represented by equation (16) or (17). The signs are generally as hypothesized, at least on the real income variable (proxied by industrial production) and on expected inflation (proxied by actuel CPI inflation over the preceding year). When we use the Cochrane-Orcutt technique to correct for high autocorrelation, the signs on the relative money supply and the interest differential are also generally correct. But the standard errors are too large to permit rejection of zero values for all of the coefficients, let alone to permit meaningful comparison with the money demand elasticities or the speed of goods market adjustment. It makes little difference whether or not we impose the constraint that the money demand elasticities are equal in France and the United States. Nor does it matter whether we measure nominal interest rates by the domestic three-month money market rate or the one-month Eurocurrency rate.

When a dummy variable is included for the period beginning May 1981, it has a significant positive effect on the franc/dollar rate. Obviously the currency depreciated in response to the election of Mitterrand. The anti-franc speculation induced by the election could be represented in our model as an increase in expected inflation not measured by our proxy (the lagged inflation rate). When we add the US inflation rate separately, with and without multiplication by the Mitterrand dummy, the coefficients are not statistically insignificant.

TABLE 7

The monetary equation of exchange rate determination
Dependent variable : log of franc/dollar rate
Sample : March 1973 - October 1981
Technique : Cochrane-Orcutt

Const.	mlfr-mlus	yfr	yus	inflfr	influs	i3nfr-i3mus	ieurfr-ieurdo	Mitterand dummy	Mitterand dummy × influs	R²	s.e.r.	ρ̂
-1.058 (1.374)	0.118 (0.195)	-0.074 (1.034)	0.584* (0.271)	1.126 (0.973)	-1.055 (0.814)	0.004 (0.240)				0.73	0.046	0.90
1.138 (0.071)	1.000 (Constrained)	-0.077 (0.139) {yfr, yus}		0.659 (0.802) {inflfr, influs}		-0.169 (0.254)				0.91	0.035	0.94
1.490 (0.091)	0.062 (0.193)	-0.151 (0.128)		0.992 (0.721) {inflfr, influs}			-0.060 (0.095)			0.88	0.031	0.93
1.501 (0.077)	-0.020 (0.183)	-0.129 (0.128)		1.076 (0.699) {inflfr, influs}			-0.107 (0.097)	0.075* (0.033)		0.88	0.031	0.90
1.445 (0.089)	0.087 (0.158)	-0.127 (0.131)		1.341 (0.900)	-1.355 (0.788)		-0.100 (0.103)	-0.122 (0.261)	2.086 (2.754)	0.75	0.032	0.88

* Significant at the 95 % level and of the hypothesized sign. Standard errors in parentheses.

While one can make endogeneity arguments about each of the right-hand-side variables, the money supply and interest rate variables are particularly vulnerable to this source of inconsistency in the estimates. The reason is that the French government is known to use foreign exchange intervention (which feeds into the money supply, to the extent that it is not sterilized) and the interest rate as policy tools that react to the exchange rate. In particular, France's commitment to maintain exchange rates vis-a-vis Germany and the other members of the European Monetary System within 2 1/4 percent margins [5], while not sufficiently absolute to preclude periodic devaluations, is strong enough to bring about foreign exchange intervention and interest rate changes when the franc hits its limit against any other EMS currency.

The likely endogeneity of the money supply arising from foreign exchange intervention, or from other sources like shifts in the money demand function, is easily handled. We merely impose the constraint of a unit coefficient on the relative money supplies, which theory says should hold anyway. When this is done in table 7, the estimates of the remaining coefficients are little affected.

The endogeneity of the French interest rate is a little more difficult. But the statement of the problem (government response to the mark/franc exchange rate) contains the key to the solution: obtain instrumental variables related to the value of the mark. Neither the mark/franc rate nor the mark/dollar rate would be an appropriate instrument; if they were exogenous variables then their ratio, the franc/dollar rate would be an exogenous variable. But exogenous German determinants of the value of the mark are appropriate instruments: German real income and expected inflation.

We apply the instrumental variables technique in table 8. The results are improved, especially when we use Fair's method to correct for high autocorrelation. All coefficients are of the correct signs. The coefficient on the inflation differential is now statistically significant, as are the coefficient on relative income in the first regression and the coefficient on the Eurocurrency differential in the last. The dummy variable multiplied by the US inflation rate, as in the last table, is not of the correct sign to indicate a favorable effect of tightened capital controls on the value of the franc.

There is a way that we can use the high correlation of the value of the franc with the value of the mark to further advantage. We would expect the error terms in the franc/dollar equation to be highly correlated with the error terms in the mark/dollar equation. For example, a shift in US money demand should in theory affect both equally. Zellner's technique of Seemingly Unrelated Regressions takes advantage of the joint distribution of the error terms to get more efficient estimates of the parameters. Three-stage least squares (3SLS) in addition allows for the endogeneity of the interest rate while still taking advantage of the joint distribution of the error

---

5. The franc has been a member of the EMS since March 13, 1979, despite devaluations in October 1981 and June 1982. Before that it was in the Snake, except for two periods: January 19, 1974 to July 10, 1975, and after March 15, 1976 (ARTUS, MORIN and STERDYNIAK [1979], p. 9-10).

TABLE 8

The monetary equation with endogenous french interest rate

Dependent variable : log of franc/dollar rate

Sample : January 1974 - October 1981

Technique : Fair's method. Instrumental variables for i3mfr are German income and inflation. And, since we are correcting for serial correlation at the same time, lagged values of all included exogenous and endogenous variables are added to the list of instruments.

Const.	Mfr-mlus	Yfr-yus	Inflr	Influs	I3mfr-i3mus	Ieurfr-ieurdo	Mitterand dummy	Mitterand dummy × influs	R²	s.e.r.	ρ̂
1.341 (0.078)	0.263 (0.177)	— 0.249* (0.127)	1.756* (0.733)		— 0.300 (0.318)				0.89	0.029	0.89
1.076	1 (constrained)	— 0.196 (0.137)	1.582* (0.801)		0.221 (0.361)				0.92	0.032	0.90
1.485 (0.107)	0.169 (0.168)	— 0.196 (0.125)	1.261 (0.912)	— 2.319* (0.734)		— 0.268* (0.132)	— 0.276 (0.240)	3.867 (2.549)	0.90	0.029	0.86

* Significant at the 95 % level. Standard errors in parentheses.

TABLE 9

The monetary equation estimated by three-stage least squares with own-country interest rates (ieur) endogenous

Sample : February 1974 - October 1981

Dependent variable : first difference of log of	Coeff. of ml-mlus	Φ minus coeff. of y-yus	λ Coeff. of infl-influs	θ Minus inverse of coeff. of ieur-ieurus	s.e.r.	D. W.	$\hat{\rho}$
Franc/dollar rate	0.503* (0.200)	0.042 (0.124)	1.085 (0.830)	1.241* (0.541)	0.0378	1.86	1
Mark/dollar rate	0.171 (0.242)	− 0.099 (0.1 3)	0.577 (0.624)	1.268* (0.458)	0.0334	2.06	1

* Significant at the 95 % level.   Standard errors in parentheses.

terms.   Table 9 reports the results of 3SLS estimation of (20).   The covariance matrix of untransformed residuals showed a correlation of errors in the two equations of .718, confirming the suggestion that the technique will improve the efficiency of our estimates.   Each of the four coefficients in the franc/dollar equation is of correct sign.   Those on the relative money supply and interest differential are significant.

8 The porfolio-balance model of the exchange rate

We turn now to a brief consideration of the alternative to the monetary model, the portfolio-balance model, developed by BRANSON [1977] and KOURI [1976] and applied to the French franc by ARTUS, MORIN and STERDYNIAK [1979, 1981].   As the starting point, we repeat the risk premium equation (11), inverted so as to give the aggregated demand for franc assets relative to dollar assets as a function of their expected relative return and the world distribution of wealth :

$$(21) \qquad x_t = a_r + bz_t + (a_f - a_r)\, w_f - (a_r - a_{us})\, w_{us}$$

where z is the expected relative return on franc assets :

$$f_t - s_{t+1}^e \quad \text{or} \quad i_t^F - i_t^S - \Delta s_{t+1}^e + \tau.$$

Since x_t is defined as $B_t/(B_t + S_t D_t)$, the equilibrium spot rate S is determined by the asset supplies (francs B and dollars D) outstanding in the world market and the asset demands given by equation (21).

A complete model of exchange rate determination requires some specification of what determines the expected returns. Presumably the interest rates are determined endogenously by the composition of the asset stock variables as between money and bonds, while expected depreciation could be determined statically, adaptively, or rationally. But here we simply assume expected returns constant. Furthermore we assume a linear functional form. In these simplifications we are following BRANSON, HALTTUNEN, and MASSON [1977]. We regress the exchange rate against B, D, W_f and W_{us}. The expected signs are clear : respectively, positive and negative (an increase in the supply of dollar assets D reduces their price S; an increase in franc assets has the opposite effect), then negative and positive (a redistribution of wealth toward French residents lowers net world demand for dollar assets and thus lowers their price S; a redistribution toward US residents has the opposite effect).

How we choose to define the asset supplies B and D depends on why we think they are imperfect substitutes in investors' portfolios. If we think that exchange risk is the main reason for imperfect substitutability, as in section 3, then B and D should be the net supplies of franc-denominated and dollar-denominated assets in the market : the cumulated supplies of government debt corrected for any foreign exchange intervention or for government debt issued in foreign currency. On the other hand, if we think that political risk is the main reason for imperfect substitutability, as in section 4, then B and D should be the net supplies of French-issued and US-issued assets in the market : the cumulated supplies of government debt *not* corrected for foreign exchange intervention or for government debt issued in foreign currency.

In table 10 we find that D and W_{us} have the hypothesized sign and are highly significant, even when we correct for high autocorrelation. The coefficients on B and W_f are insignificant and incorrect in sign. A dummy variable for the Mitterrand period, surprisingly, has a significant negative effect on the franc/dollar rate. This would seem to suggest that the tighter capital controls succeeded in reducing the expected relative return on foreign assets by more than Mitterrand's election raised it, as perceived by speculators. The results are the same regardless of whether we use the exchange risk or political risk interpretation in classifying assets.

TABLE 10

The portfolio-balance equation of exchange rate determination

Dependent variable : Level of franc/dollar rate
Sample : March 1973 - September 1981
Technique : Cochrane-Orcutt

Classification of assets	Constant	B	D	W_f	W_{us}	Mitterrand dummy	R^2	s.e.r.	$\hat{\rho}$
Currency of denomination............	1.770 (0.606)	— 0.793 (0.887)	— 6.961* (0.814)	1.320 (0.939)	1.563* (0.044)	— 0.103* (0.040)	0.99	0.038	0.99
Country of issuer............	3.530 (0.582)	— 1.922 (1.771)	— 6.955* (0.514)	2.129 (1.736)	1.532* (0.043)	— 0.104* (0.040)	0.99	0.037	0.95

* Significant at the 95 % level. Standard errors in parentheses.

B : is the level of the net supply of French debt (in billions of francs), corrected for foreign-denominated debt and foreign exchange intervention in the case where assets are classified by currency of denomination. D : is the level of the net supply of US debt (in billions of dollars), defined the same way. W_f and W_{us} are the levels of wealth held by French and US resident respectively (in billions of francs), calculated as the cumulation of government debt and the current account surplus.

9 Incorporation of the risk premium into the monetary model of the exchange rate

Three components of the sticky-price monetary model — efficient capital markets (subject to the constraint of capital controls), the money demand function, and gradual adjustment to purchasing power parity — appear reliable building blocks. But it may be desirable to alter the fourth building block, the assumed absence of a risk premium, to integrate the monetary model with the portfolio-balance model. To do so, we simply replace the uncovered interest parity condition (17) with our expression for the risk premium, equation (11). The exchange rate equation (20) then becomes (setting $\tau = 0$) :

$$
\begin{aligned}
(22) \quad s = (m - m^*) - \Phi(y - y)^* + \left(\lambda + \frac{1}{\theta}\right)(\overline{\pi} - \overline{\pi}^*) - \frac{1}{\theta}(i - i^*) + \frac{1}{\theta b}x \\
- \frac{a_f - a_r}{\theta b} w_f + \frac{a_r - a_{us}}{\theta b} w_{us} - \frac{a_r}{\theta b}.
\end{aligned}
$$

In addition to the usual effects in the monetary equation, an increase in the relative supply x of franc debt (even if not monetized) raises s. A French current account surplus decreases s. And a US current account surplus raises s. The earlier monetary model is the special case of perfect substitutability : $b = \infty$ and so the new variables drop out.

The synthesis model, equation (22), is estimated in table 11. First the asset supplies are classified by currency of denomination to get at the exchange risk premium, with the coefficients on the wealth unconstrained. Then the coefficients are constrained to fit consumption shares as dictated by the portfolio optimization theory. Finally the asset supplies are classified by countries of issuance to get at the political risk premiums. The results are striking for the risk premium variables. The coefficients of all three are always of the hypothesized sign and almost always highly significant. Relative income, the inflation differential and the interest differential enter with the correct signs, but when we correct for very high serial correlation, none of the variables from the monetary model produces coefficient estimates that are statistically significant. We also allow for the endogeneity of the interest differential, arising from French government reaction to the franc/mark exchange rate, by using German income and inflation as instrumental variables. This technique markedly improved the significance levels of the monetary variables when we used it in table 8, but it makes little difference here. The Mitterrand dummy is significant throughout and is positive in sign, reflecting speculators' perceptions that the franc will continue to lose value.

TABLE 11. — *Synthesis : monetary equation with risk premium variables*
Dependent variable : log of franc/dollar rate

Classification of assets	Technique	Constant	mlfr-mlus	yfr-yus	inffr-inffus	i3mfr-i3mus	Risk premium variables x	w_f	w_{us}	Mitterrand dummy	R²	s.e.r.	$\hat{\rho}$
Currency of denomination	CORC	1.289 (0.403)	-0.042 (0.115)	-0.039 (0.070)	0.116 (0.413)	-0.202 (0.135)	3.615* (0.792)	-5.517* (0.449)	0.468 (0.261)	0.055* (0.019)	0.96	0.018	0.98
	FAIR	1.240 (0.418)	-0.006 (0.119)	-0.054 (0.075)	0.196 (0.471)	-0.342 (0.253)	3.972* (0.955)	-5.694* (0.591)	0.503* (0.281)	0.060* (0.022)	0.96	0.017	0.97
							Constrained $x - (\alpha_f - \alpha_r)\,w_f + (\alpha_r - \alpha_{us})\,w_{us} - \alpha_r$						
	CORC	0.713 (0.171)	0.095 (0.163)	-0.068 (0.101)	0.247 (0.597)	-0.200 (0.195)		6.417* (0.846)		0.056* (0.028)	0.92	0.025	0.96
	FAIR	0.857 (0.156)	0.141 (0.169)	-0.109 (0.110)	0.764 (0.677)	-0.648 (0.400)		5.046* (1.048)		0.075* (0.033)	0.92	0.025	0.96
Country of issuer	CORC	-0.040 (0.648)	-0.065 (0.096)	-0.069 (0.059)	0.052 (0.349)	-0.187 (0.114)	7.617* (0.964)	-7.059* (0.397)	1.827* (0.577)	0.046* (0.016)	0.97	0.015	0.98
	FAIR	0.306 (0.655)	-0.061 (0.093)	-0.068 (0.059)	-0.136 (0.378)	-0.206 (0.195)	8.276* (1.008)	-8.125* (0.514)	1.574* (0.591)	0.044* (0.017)	0.98	0.014	0.97

* Significant at the 95 % level. (Standard errors in parentheses).
CORC : Cochrane-Orcutt. Sample is March 1973 - September 1981.
FAIR : Fair's method when correcting for serial correlation of adding to the list of instrumental variables (which already includes German income and inflation as instruments for the endogenous French interest rate i3mfr), lagged values of all endogenous and exogenous variables.

Conclusion

There is one unavoidable modification in the standard asset-market models of exchange rates that one must make for the French franc. That is the recognition that capital controls create a gap between expected returns on French assets and expected returns on foreign assets. The gap can be illustrated by computing the differential between the French interest rate on the one hand and the Eurofranc interest rate, or alternatively the dollar interest rate covered on the foreign exchange market, on the other hand. The differential averaged .00113 on one-month deposits until May 1981, and then increased to four times that level due to the imposition of more stringent controls. A more precise way of quantifying the gap is to think of capital controls as creating an effective « tax » on the holding of foreign assets by Frenchmen. This tax is defined as the excess of the exchange rate at which Frenchmen can obtain foreign assets, equal to the financial franc rate when it exists, over the regular commercial exchange. Data on the financial rate to compute this measure directly are limited. But the measure can be computed from data on the domestic French interest rate, Eurodollar rate, and Eurofranc rate. It shows an average tax of 25 percent for the period before May 1981, and an increase for the period thereafter.

One possible approach to modeling the financial markets is to assume that US bonds and French bonds are perfect substitutes in investors' portfolios, subject to the tax. This would imply that expected returns are equalized across the two countries, again subject to the tax, i.e., that there is no premium for exchange risk or political risk. This approach leads us to the monetary model, in which exchange rates are determined by the demand and supply of money, to the exclusion of bonds and other assets. This paper found some empirical support for a conventional money demand function in France, and for a description of goods markets in which purchasing power parity holds in the long run but is subject to large deviations in the short run due to sticky prices that adjust only gradually to excess demand. Combining these assumptions leads us to the sticky-price version of the monetary equation. The franc/dollar rate depends positively on the relative French money supply, negatively on relative French income, positively on the expected inflation differential and negatively on the interest differential. In addition, a rise in the effective tax on foreign returns should appreciate the franc.

Econometric estimation of the monetary equation of exchange rate determination is complicated by the endogeneity of the money supply and interest rate. In the case of France, these two variables are varied by the government to attempt to keep the value of the franc in line with the value of the mark. When we take proper econometric account of this simultaneous relationship the results offer moderate support for the sticky-price monetary model.

The alternative approach to modeling the financial markets is to assume that US and French bonds are imperfect substitutes. This could be true either due to exchange risk, in which case we should distinguish among assets according to their currency of denomination, or to political risk, in which case we should distinguish among assets according to their country of issuance. (The political risk argument is supported by the apparent high level and variability of the effective tax on foreign assets arising from capital controls.) Attempts to relate relative bond returns to asset supplies and wealth distribution, as suggested by the theory of portfolio optimization, gave somewhat more support for the existence of a premium for political risk than for exchange risk. In either case the null hypothesis of perfect substitutability could not be rejected statistically.

If we assume expected returns constant in the risk premium equation, we get a relationship between the exchange rate, asset supplies, and wealth levels. Econometric estimation of such an equation offered some limited support for the portfolio-balance approach to exchange rate determination. Alternatively, we can append the risk premium equation to the monetary approach and obtain an equation that combines the two approaches. The risk premium variables perform very well econometrically in the synthesis equation, but the monetary variables do not.

In conclusion, we have a long way to go before arriving at a model of the franc/dollar exchange rate that is at once theoretically respectable and econometrically viable. This paper can claim no more than to have identified some of the building blocks, how one could go about testing them, and the alternative ways in which they could be combined into complete models.

● References

ADLER M. and DUMAS B. — (1981) *International Portfolio Choice and Corporation Finance: A Survey*, CESA, December.

ALIBER R. — (1973) « The Interest Rate Parity Theorem: A Reinterpretation », *Journal of Political Economy* 81, no. 6, November, p. 1451-1459.

ARTUS P., MORIN P. and STERDYNIAK H. — (1979) « La flexibilité des changes : modélisation et conséquences macroéconomiques », *Statistiques et Études financières*, série orange, 37.

—— (1981) « La détermination du taux », *METRIC Une modélisation de l'économie française*, 6e partie, p. 341-407.

BILSON J. — (1978) « The Monetary Approach to the Exchange Rate : Some Empirical Evidence », *IMF Staff Papers*, 25, March, p. 48-75.

—— (1981) *Profitability and Stability in International Currency Markets*, NBER Working Paper, no. 664, April.

—— (1981) « The "Speculative Efficiency" Hypothesis », *Journal of Business*, July.

BRANSON W. — (1977) « Asset Markets and Relative Prices in Exchange Rate Determination », *Sozialwissenschaftliche Annalen,* 1, p. 69-89.

BRANSON W., HALTTUNEN H. and MASSON P. — (1977) « Exchange Rates in the Short Run : The Dollar-deutschemark Rate », *European Economic Review,* 10, p. 303-324.

DOOLEY M. and ISARD P. — (1980) « Capital Controls, Political Risk and Deviations from Interest-Rate Parity, *Journal of Political Economy,* 88, no. 2, April, p. 370-384.

DORNBUSCH R. — (1976) « Expectations and Exchange Rate Dynamics », *Journal of Political Economy,* 84, December p. 1161-1176.

—— (1982) « Exchange Risk and the Macroeconomics of Exchange Rate Determination », in *The Internationalization of Financial Markets and National Economic Policy.* Edited by R. Hawkins, R. Levich and C. Wihlborg. Greenwich, Conn. : JAI Press.

ENGEL C. — (1981) *Testing for Risk-Neutrality and Rationality,* University of California, Berkeley, April.

FLOOD R. and MARION N. — (1974) « Exchange-Rate Regimes in Transition : Italy 1974 », *International Finance Discussion Paper,* no. 193, Federal Reserve Board, November.

FRANKEL J. — (1979) « On the Mark: A Theory of Floating Exchange Rates Based on Real Interest Differentials », *American Economic Review,* 69, no. 4, September, p. 610-622.

—— (1980) « Tests of Rational Expectations in the Forward Exchange Market », *Southern Economic Journal,* 46, no. 4, April, p. 1083-1101.

—— (1981) *The Effect of Excessively-Elastic Expectations on Exchange-Rate Volatility in the Dornbusch Overshooting Model,* University of California, Berkeley, October. Forthcoming, *Journal of International Money and Finance,* 2, 1983.

—— (1982) « The Mystery of the Multiplying Marks : A Modification of the Monetary Model », *Review of Economics and Statistics,* 64, 3,August, p. 515-519.

—— (1982) « In Search of the Exchange-Risk Premium: A Six-Currency Test Assuming Mean Variance Optimization », *Journal of International Money and Finance,* 1, 3, December, p. 255-274.

FRENKEL J. — (1976) « A Monetary Approach to the Exchange Rate: Doctrinal Aspects and Empirical Evidence », *Scandinavian Journal of Economics,* 76, no. 1, May, p. 200-224.

—— (1981) « The Collapse of Purchasing Power Parities During the 1970s. », *European Economic Review,* 16, 1, p. 145-165.

—— (1981) « Flexible Exchange Rates, Prices, and the Role of "News": Lessons from the 1970s », *Journal of Political Economy,* 89, June.

FRENKEL J. and LEVICH R. — « Transactions Costs and Interest Arbitrage : Tranquil versus Turbulent Periods », *Journal of Political Economy,* 85, no. 6, December, p. 1207-1224.

FRENKEL J. and RAZIN A. — (1980) « Stochastic Prices and Tests of Efficiency of Foreign Exchange Markets », *Economic Letters,* 6, p. 165-170.

HOOPER P. and MORTON J. — (1982) « Fluctuations in the Dollar: A Model of Nominal and Real Exchange Rate Determination », *Journal of International Money and Finance,* 1, no. 1, April, p. 39-56.

Kouri P. — (1976) « The Exchange Rate and the Balance of Payments in the Short Run and in the Long Run », *Scandinavian Journal of Economics 78*, no. 2, May, p. 280-308.

Krugman P. — (1981) *Consumption Preferences, Assets Demands and Distribution Effects in International Financial Markets*, NBER Working Paper, no. 651, March.

Mathis J. — (1981) « L'Évolution des mouvements de capitaux à court terme entre la France et l'extérieur de 1967 à 1978 », *Statistiques et Études financières*, Economie et Prévision, 47, p. 27-59.

Meese R. and Rogoff K. — (1983) « Empirical Exchange Rate Models of the Seventies : Do they fit out of Sample? », *Journal of International Economics*, forthcoming.

Melitz J. and Sterdyniak H. — (1979) « The Monetary Approach to Official Reserves and the Foreign Exchange Rate in France, 1962-1974 : Some Structural Estimates », *American Economic Review*, 69, no. 5, December, p. 818-831.

Solnik B. — (1974) « An Equilibrium Model of The International Capital Market », *Journal of Economic Theory*, 8, 4, p. 500-524.

Comments

by John F.O. BILSON *

University of Chicago and NBER

Jeffrey FRANKEL's paper contains a great deal of information on a number of topics. A full discussion of all of the issues would require a comment whose length would exceed the length of the original. For this reason, I have decided to discuss some general issues in the econometric testing of arbitrage conditions while illustrating the discussion with examples drawn from Professor FRANKEL's paper. In order to be consistent with the paper, I will order the discussion by the examples, the first of which is the model of covered interest rate parity and capital controls.

1. Covered interest rate parity and capital controls

In his discussion of capital controls, FRANKEL constructs a model through which the height of the control can be measured by the difference between the commercial and financial exchange rates. The question for the reviewer, then, is whether this particular model of capital controls is appropriate.

FRANKEL's own test of the model is primarily judgemental. After noting that the estimated tax rate for one month financial instruments is 22,632 per cent for the period after May 1981, an estimate that is "far too high to be credible", he justifies the model by mentioning a far more reasonable estimate of 54 % for assets with a maturity of one year. There is, however, a fundamental problem with this approach because the model implies a constant tax independent of the maturity of the asset. The reason for this result is that the model proposed only applies the tax to the interest income on the asset, since the stock transfers are all exchanged at the financial franc rate. In other words, one test of the model proposed by FRANKEL is that the implicit tax rate is independent of the maturity of the asset. Although this test is not undertaken in the paper, the evidence surely leads to a rejection of the model.

2. Rational expectations in the forward market

In this section, FRANKEL presents some tests of the hypothesis that the forward exchange rate is an optimal forecast of the future spot rate. I intend to discuss the empirical methodology behind the tests and the implications

---

* I would like thank Jacques MELITZ and Charles WYPLOSZ for their help in organizing my thoughts on the topic. I remain responsible for any views expressed.

drawn from the tests by FRANKEL. To focus the discussion, I reproduce a typical result from table 2 of the paper.

$$(1) \qquad s_{t+1} - f_t = 0.00525 - 2.020 \, [f_t - s_t] + u_t$$
$$\phantom{(1) \qquad s_{t+1} - f_t = } (0.00334) \; (0.487)$$

Standard errors are presented in parentheses beneath the coefficients. Under the optimal forecast hypothesis, the regression coefficient on the forward premium $(f_t - s_t)$ should not be significantly different from zero. FRANKEL interprets this regression as supporting my finding (BILSON [1981]) that speculators could profit from borrowing in low interest rate currencies and lending in high interest rate currencies.

Although I have no difficulty with the assertion, it is important to stress that the regression reported in equation (1) is not a sufficient test for the profitability of a particular speculative strategy. Apart from the normal problems with in-sample tests of speculative rules, and ignoring the fact that distributions of exchange rate innovations tend to have fat tails, the probability that the franc will break from various European monetary arrangements gives a "peso problem" flavor to the analysis. While FRANKEL is aware of these problems, his statement that the results support my conclusion that foreign exchange speculation is profitable is only correct if the same empirical methodology is employed. Apart from the fact that my empirical results were based upon a far larger sample, the most important difference is that my tests for profitability were based upon a post-sample data set that was independent of the sample upon which the estimates of the forecasting equation were based.

In order to compare the two approaches, it is useful to illustrate how a speculator would have performed if he (or she) had followed the forecasting equation estimated above in a post-sample test. For the post-sample, I use the data from March to September 1982. I shall ignore the constant term in the regression and I shall also by-pass issues of estimation risk. The speculators' problem may be stated as that of choosing a set of positions that will maximize the following indirect utility function :

$$(2) \qquad \mathrm{EU}\,(\Pi) \,=\, \mathrm{E}\,(\Pi) - \frac{a}{2} \mathrm{V}\,(\Pi)$$

where $\mathrm{E}\,(\Pi) =$ the expected profit from the position, and $\mathrm{V}\,(\Pi)$ is the expected variance. This indirect utility function may be derived from an exponential utility function in actual profits.

The solution to the maximization problem is a vector of positions, q, for each time period. The typical element of q is defined by :

$$(3) \qquad q_t = \bar{r}_t / a \sigma_t^2$$

where $\bar{r}_t$ is the expected return at t, and σ_t^2 is the expected variance. Over T trials, the expected profit and expected variance are given by :

$$(4) \qquad \mathrm{E}\,(\Pi) \,=\, \Sigma\, \bar{r}_t\, q_t$$

and

$$(5) \qquad \mathrm{V}\,(\Pi) = \left(\frac{1}{a}\right)^2 \Sigma\, (\bar{r}_t/\sigma_t)^2\, \sigma_t^2$$

224

If the model is correct, observed *ex post* profits should not be significantly different from expected profits. The test statistic $[\Pi - E(\Pi)]/[V(\Pi)^{0.5}]$ provides an appropriate test of the hypothesis.

The details of the analysis are presented in table 1. For the purposes of this example, the parameter $(1/a)$ is set equal to 100. This arbitrary constant only influences the scale of the position. The obvious lesson from table 1 is that our hypothetical speculator would have been wiped out by the devaluation of the French franc in June 1982. However, even if this event is excluded from the analysis, the total profits from the strategy were still negative. It may be, however, that the poor performance was a chance event and that the model itself is not rejected by the data. In order to examine this hypothesis, the test statistic on total profits may be calculated to be

$$(6) \qquad [\Pi - E(\Pi)] / [V(\Pi)^{0.5}] = -3.1079$$

which is significantly less than zero at standard confidence limits. The probability of achieving this result if the model is correct is less than 2 per cent. We are therefore led to reject the model of speculative trading proposed by FRANKEL. A similar approach could be taken to the testing of exchange risk and political risk premiums. However, given that the in-sample results for the risk variables are weak, it is perhaps unreasonable to expect them to withstand more rigorous tests.

3. The portfolio balance equations

One of the most promising results reported in FRANKEL's paper are the estimates of the portfolio balance model of exchange rate determination. Even after correcting for strong serial correlation in the level of the exchange rate, the estimates reported in table 10 of the paper show highly significant coefficients on both the net supply of US debt and the level of US wealth as determinants of the franc/dollar rate. If we leave aside the other regressors—whose coefficients are typically insignificant anyway—the estimated equation 1 in table 10 is

$$S(FF/\$) = \underset{(0.814)}{-6.961\,D} + \underset{(0.044)}{1.563\,W_{us}} + u$$

The first coefficient is estimated to be 8.55 standard deviations from zero and the second coefficient is estimated to be 35.52 standard deviations from zero. Given the results reported by MEESE and ROGOFF [1983] which suggest that exchange rate changes are largely unpredictable, it is surprising to see that these two variables have such a consistent and significant impact on the exchange rate.

In order to understand the results, it is useful to carefully consider the definitions of the two variables. The net supply of US debt is measured in billions of US dollars. The measure of US wealth is the dollar value of US debt plus the cumulative current account surplus translated into French francs at (presumably) the spot franc/dollar rate. Since the cumulative current account surplus is likely to be small relative to the stock of debt, this term can then be ignored without great injustice to the model.

We then have

$$S \text{ (FF/\$)} = b_1 D + b_2 S \text{ (FF/\$)} D$$

Now it is possible that the significant coefficients are purely the consequence of using the current spot rate as the translation variable in the second term.

TABLE 1 :

Post-sample performance of the speculative rule

Date	E (r)	A (r)	t (r)	q	E (Π)	A (Π)
March	0.00261	0.02602	0.08471	275	0.717	7.156
April..........	0.01291	0.00289	0.41916	1 360	17.557	3.930
May............	0.01695	− 0.10278	0.55032	1 786	30.272	− 183.565
June...........	0.00329	0.00119	0.10682	346	1.138	0.412
July...........	0.00222	− 0.02583	0.07208	234	0.519	− 6.044
August..........	0.00968	− 0.00436	0.31429	1 020	9.873	− 4.447
September.......	0.01329	− 0.01036	0.43149	1 401	18.621	− 14.514
				Total.................	78.697	− 197.072

NOTES. — *All data from International Financial Statistics, October 1982, except for the spot rate on November 1st. Three-month forward rates were used to calculate expected returns. All data is end of period.*

Definitions : E (r) = Expected return per dollar per month ;
A (r) = Actual return per dollar per month ;
t (r) = Expected return /standard déviation ;
q = Position taken in dollars' worth of French francs ;
E (Π) = Expected profit on position in dollars ;
A (Π) = Actual profit on position in dollars.

We could, for example, write the relationship as

$$(7) \qquad S - \bar{S} = b_2 (S - \bar{S}) D$$

if we impose the constraint that $b_1 = -b_2 \bar{S}$ and allow for the introduction of a constant term. If the constraint is justified, it should be the case that b_1/b_2 is equal to $\bar{S}$, the average exchange rate over the sample period. Since the actual value of the ratio of the coefficients is 4.4536, and the actual average exchange rate over the sample period was approximately 4.63, this constraint appears to be justified.

In this instance, the problems with the equation are exacerbated when the first difference transform is applied since the month to month changes in the regressor are likely to be dominated by the month to month changes in the exchange rate. The US government deficit has been, and hopefully will continue to be, substantially less volatile than the exchange rate. Given this fact, the highly significant coefficient on the US wealth variable is probably a consequence of the inclusion of the exchange rate on both sides of the equation. For this reason, the results are probably uninformative about the relationship between portfolio theory and exchange rate changes.

Conclusion

The problems discussed above are certainly not specific to FRANKEL's paper or, more generally, to the case of the French franc. They rather reflect the general problems encountered when regression methodology is applied to asset prices. It is certainly not the case that we do not know what determines the exchange rate, since long run or cross sectional studies validate both the purchasing power parity condition and the monetary approach to the exchange rate. Instead, the problem is that economists do not have the data, or the empirical tools, to accurately model the way in which market participants form their views of the future evolution of these determinants. While rational expectations provides a theoretical guide to modelling the exchange rate, it is less useful as an empirical tool because of the difficulty of modelling the flow of information. Furthermore, the rationality of the foreign exchange market, particularly during the early years of the float, cannot be taken for granted. It may well be the case that international finance should follow domestic finance in abandoning attempts to forecast asset prices. In the same way that a corporate executive does not have to be able to forecast equity prices in order to know what is best for the country, so policy makers should not base their policies on econometric models of exchange rate determination.

● References

BILSON John F. O. — (1981) "The Speculative Efficiency Hypothesis", *Journal of Business,* (July).

MEESE Richard and ROGOFF Kenneth. — (1983) "Empirical Exchange Rate Models of the Seventies : Do They Fit the Sample?", *Journal of International Economics.*

Comments

by **Bruno SOLNIK**

CESA, Jouy-en-Josas

Jeffrey FRANKEL's paper is an important piece of empirical work on French data. It attempts to test the asset-market model of exchange rates in the French case, modelling the specific feature of our exchange and credit controls. This is a most interesting attempt but the results are a little bit disappointing.

I will limit my comment on two aspects of this paper, namely the theoretical definition of the exchange control tax and the econometric methodology.

First let me stress that exchange controls create two French credit markets, one for residents (domestic money market) and one for non-residents (Euro-franc market). Differences in the interest rates are proof of the efficacy of the exchange controls. Therefore we have two different forward exchange rates depending on the geographic status of the contractor. However in these two segmented markets covered interest parity holds *exactly* for the Franc.

Let's turn now to the definition of the tax given in equation (2) of the paper. First I am not sure why this interest rate differential should be called a tax and more importantly, I fail to understand its measure :

$$(2) \qquad \tau = -1 + \frac{r^{\$}_{eur}}{r^{F}_{dom} + r^{\$}_{eur} - r^{F}_{eur}}$$

Over 1974, τ moved from -300% to $+300\%$ which is a strange result for a tax. Looking at equation (2) one should remember that for institutional reasons the eurofranc rate r^{F}_{eur} is always larger or equal to the domestic rate r^{F}_{dom}, otherwise legal arbitrage will take place. Rewriting (2) yields (2') :

$$(2') \qquad \tau = -1 + 1 \Big/ \left(1 - \frac{r^{F}_{eur} - r^{F}_{dom}}{r^{\$}_{eur}}\right) = -1 + \frac{1}{1-x}$$

When the French interest rate differential is zero, the tax is rightly zero, but if the eurodollar rate is zero (which happened for the Swiss Franc). The tax is -100% even if the French differential is very large and therefore calls for a positive tax. Strangely enough the tax becomes infinite if the French differential is equal to the eurodollar rate. There is *no* economic relation between the two numbers since the first is linked to the expected depreciation of the French Franc while the second one depends on U.S. monetary considerations, so there is no reason to expect the French differential to be smaller or larger than the U.S. interest rate. It is not an economically meaningful comparison but still gives surprising results in FRANKEL's formula. Note that the tax computed on monthly rates is close to infinity in September 1981 and would be very negative if the French differential was larger than the U.S. interest rates. Also note that if the Euroswiss Franc or DM was used as the foreign yardstick instead of the dollar, the tax, as defined by FRANKEL, would have been negative in many months since 1981 which is meaningless since they correspond to periods where the controls were really biting.

To summarize, I could not understand the logic of this tax definition and would have preferred to see the domestic eurofranc interest differential used in the empirical tests.

Most of the models developed in the second part of the paper call for a measure of expected exchange rate. As is usually the case in this field, FRANKEL has to use the ex-post exchange rate as a proxy for ex-ante expectations, which introduces a lot of noise. One has therefore to be very careful in the econometrics and must first push the theoretical analysis as far as possible to design the most powerful test.

For example, the tests are conducted on levels (with Cochrane-Orcutt adjustments) while some theories call for tests on variations rather than levels.

Another illustration is the dollar translation problem in the tests of portfolio-balance models. In table 10 for example W_{us}, the level of wealth of U.S. residents, is the dollar value of their holdings (which is fairly stable) translated at the Franc/Dollar rate which turns out to be the dependent variable. The t-statictics of the coefficient of W_{us} is more than 30 but it is a purely technical result with little economic meaning.

Finally let me point out a problem that I have with Frankel's conclusion in section 6 on PPP. He concludes from his tests that real exchange rate variations are auto-corrective. Again his tests in table 6 bears on levels with CORC adjustement. Calling X_t the real exchange rate, the regression tested is :

$$X_t = \alpha + \beta \, X_{t-1} + \Sigma_t$$

A test of auto-correction of real exchange rates is whether β is equal to one. If β is not significantly different one, then changes in the real exchange rate, i. e. $X_t - X_{t-1}$, follow a random walk. ROLL [1979], FRENKEL [1981] or DARBY [1980] have directly tested the autocorrelation of $X_t - X_{t-1}$ and cannot reject the random walk hypothesis. FRANKEL sticks with levels and finds a coefficient of 0.947 with a standard error of 0.034. Note that the autocorrelation in the residuals is small because the coefficient is close to one. Furthermore, β is not significantly different from one at the 95 % level, so even this evidence does not allow us to reject a random walk (i. e. no auto-correction).

It is always easy to criticize when there is such a density of empirical tests. FRANKEL's paper is an important contribution to the study of the French economy. These results leave us with the same frustation as the U.S. results which do not allow conclude on the appropriate model of exchange rate determination. A major difference however is the significance of the "Mitterrand Dummy"; I just regret that a "Reagan Dummy" was not introduced since we deal with the Franc/Dollar exchange rate.

● References

DARBY Michael. — (1980) "Does Purchasing Power Parity Works?", *NBER working paper*, 607, December.

FRANKEL Jeffrey. — (1982) "On the Franc", *Annales de l'INSEE*, this issue.

FRENKEL Jacob. — (1981) "Flexible Exchange Rates in the 1970's", *Journal of Political Economy*, Vol. 89, August.

ROLL Richard. — (1979) "Violations of Purchasing Power Parity and their Implications for Efficient International Commodity Markets" in Sarnat and Szego (eds), *International Finance and Trade*, Ballinger.

Comments [p 185]

by Jacob A. FRENKEL

University of Chicago and NBER

One of the various issues that are analyzed by Mathieu FEROLDI and Jacques MELITZ in their paper "The Franc and the French Financial Sector" and by Jeffrey FRANKEL in his paper "On the Franc" concerns the relation between the exchange rate of the French Franc in terms of foreign exchange and the Franc rate of interest relative to foreign rates of interest. The empirical record of the 1970's and the early 1980's reveals an apparent instability in the relation between exchange rates and interest rates. For example, an examination of the U.S. dollar-French Franc exchange rate suggests that during much of the 1970's a rise in the U.S. rate of interest (relative to the French rate of interest) was associated with a weakening of the U.S. dollar relative to the French Franc; on the other hand during the more recent period (from about mid 1979) this relation reversed itself, and a rise in the U.S. relative rate of the interest has been associated with a strengthening of the U.S. dollar and weakening of the French Franc. FEROLDI and MELITZ interpret this apparent instability in terms of a portfolio-balance model which allows for a variety of substitutability-complementarity relations among the various assets that are denominated in various currencies. FRANKEL interprets the observed behavior in terms of a sticky-price variant of the monetary model of exchange-rate determination which draws a distinction between the roles of the real rate of interest and of inflationary expectations.

In my comments I will also interpret the record in terms of the distinction between the real rate of interest and inflationary expectations. Generally, the essence of this distinction is that during inflationary periods the primary cause for variations in rates of interest are likely to be variations in inflationary expectations. In such an environment a relatively rapid rise in prices is associated with a high *nominal* rate of interest as well as with a depreciation of the currency in terms of foreign exchange. These seem to be the circumstances underlying the relation between the U.S. dollar and the interest differential during most of the 1970's. The reversal of the relation since 1979 indicates that recently the prime cause for the fluctuations in interest rate differentials have not been variations in inflationary expectations but rather variations in the *real* rates of interest (which are possibly occasioned by the large current and expected budget deficits).

The relation between the exchange rate, the real interest rate and the expected rate of inflation (relative to corresponding foreign rates) can be derived from the following basic parity conditions. Equation (1) describes the interest parity condition that is implied by uncovered interest arbitrage :

$$(1) \qquad s_t = E_t \, s_{t+1} + i_t^* - i_t$$

where s_t denotes the logarithm of the exchange rate in period t, E_t denotes the expectation operator (based on information available at period t) and thus, $E_t s_{t+1}$ denotes the expected (logarithm of) the exchange rate for period $t + 1$ based on the information available at period t; i_t and i_t^* denote the rates of interest on domestic and foreign securities that are identical in all respects except for the currency of denomination.

The second parity condition is the Irving FISHER condition which expresses the nominal rate of interest i as the sum of the real rate r and the expected inflation. Equations (2) and (3) describe this condition for the domestic and the foreign rates of interest :

(2) $$i_t = r_t + E_t\,(p_{t+1} - p_t)$$

(3) $$i_t^* = r_t^* + E_t\,(p_{t+1}^* - p_t^*)$$

where p_t denotes the (logarithm of) the price level in period t and where an asterisk denotes variables pertaining to the foreign country.

Using equation (1), the interest parity for period $t - 1$ is

(4) $$s_{t-1} = E_{t-1} s_t + i_{t-1}^* - i_{t-1}$$

Subtracting equation (4) from equation (1) and using equations (2) and (3) yields

(5) $$s_t = s_{t-1} + [(p_t - p_{t-1}) - (p_t^* - p_{t-1}^*)] + [(r_t^* - r_{t-1}^*) - (r_t - r_{t-1})]$$
$$+ (E_t s_{t+1} - E_{t-1} s_t) + (E_t p_{t+1}^* - E_{t-1} p_t^*) - (E_t p_{t+1} - E_{t-1} p_t)$$

In deriving equation (5) it was assumed that the expected value of a variable for period t, based on the information available in period t, equals to the actual value of that variable, e. g., $E_t p_t = p_t$.

Equation (5) demonstrates the relation between the exchange rate and the components of the nominal rate of interest. (The framework underlying equation (5) is based on ISARD [1983]. See also the discussion in EDWARDS [1983].) The first bracketed term in equation (5) suggests that a rise in the domestic rate of inflation relative to foreign inflation is associated with a *depreciation* of the domestic currency (a rise in s_t). The second bracketed term in equation (5) suggests that a rise in the domestic *real* rate of interest relative to the foreign rate is associated with an *appreciation* of the domestic currency (a fall in s_t). The additional terms on the right hand side of equation (5) describe changes in expectations concerning the exchange rate and prices. These changes in expectations are likely to be in response to new information and thus reflect the association between the exchange rates and "News". It is important to emphasize that equation (5) has *not* been derived from a specific structural model but rather it summarizes relationships that are implied by the fundamental parity conditions. As such, this relation is almost "model free" and it should be consistent with a variety of models as long as they incorporate the basic parity conditions.

To illustrate the empirical content of this analytical framework I turn now to a brief discussion of the empirical record. Table 1 illustrates the relation between exchange rates and interest rates by regressions of various exchange rates on a constant, lagged one-month forward exchange rates

TABLE 1

One-Month Interest Rate Differentials and Forecast Errors of Exchange Rates ; Instrumental Variables*

Monthly data : June 1973—July 1979 and August 1979—January 1982

(standard errors in parentheses)

Dependent Variable $ln\,S_t$	Constant	$ln\,F_{t-1}$	$[(i-i^*)_t - E_{t-1}(i-i^*)_t]$	s.e.	R^2	D.W.
Period : June 1973—July 1979						
Dollar/Pound	0.021 (0.017)	0.959 (0.024)	0.433 (0.182)	0.026	0.96	1.77
Dollar/Franc	−0.243 (0.077)	0.839 (0.051)	0.247 (0.167)	0.028	0.80	2.06
Dollar/DM	−0.017 (0.027)	0.978 (0.031)	0.403 (0.348)	0.031	0.93	2.03
Période : August 1979—January 1982						
Dollar/Pound	0.008 (0.047)	0.982 (0.061)	−0.825 (0.220)	0.029	0.91	2.02
Dollar/Franc	−0.033 (0.067)	0.985 (0.043)	−0.545 (0.171)	0.032	0.95	2.09
Dollar/DM	−0.035 (0.038)	0.967 (0.056)	−0.537 (0.348)	0.036	0.92	2.06

* Note. — Interest rates are the one-month (annualized) Euromarket rates. The expected interest rate differential $E_{t-1}\,(i-i^*)_t$ was computed from a regression of the interest differential on a constant, two lagged values of the differential, and the logarithm of the lagged forward exchange rate. Two-stage least squares estimation method was used. The instruments were a constant, Durbin's rank variable of the unexpected differential, and the logarithm of the lagged forward exchange rate. $(i-i^*)_t$ denotes the actual interest rate differential where i denotes the rate of interest on securities denominated in U.S. dollars and i* denotes the rate of interest on securities denominated in foreign currency. The unexpected interest differential is denoted by $[(i-i^*)_t - E_{t-1}\,(i-i^*)_t]$, s.e. is the standard error of the equation A quasi-R^2 was computed as $1 - Var\,(u_t)/Var\,(ln S_t)$.

(which are viewed as proxying the expected exchange rate) and on the *unexpected* interest differential. The unexpected interest differential is assumed to reflect the "news". As may be seen these relations illustrate the reversal that occurred since mid 1979. Until mid 1979 the exchange rates and the interest differentials (the unexpected part thereof) were related positively as was reported previously in FRENKEL [1981]. Since mid 1979, however, the relation reversed itself. These findings are consistent with the hypothesis (based on equation [5]) that during the latter period the main component of the variability in the nominal interest rate differentials has been variations in the real rates; in contrast during the first period the main component of the variability was variations in inflationary expectations. The same inference can be drawn by a comparison of the correlation coefficients of exchange-rate innovations and innovations in the one-month interest rate differentials. For example, for the Dollar/Pound, Dollar/Franc and the Dollar/DM exchange rates the correlation coefficients during the first period were 0.27, 0.30 and 0.25, respectively while the corresponding correlation coefficients during the second period were — 0.65, — 0.38 and — 0.30 respectively.

It is concluded, therefore, that in interpreting the relation between exchange rates and nominal rates of interest it is crucial to know the source of variations in the nominal rates since changes in inflationary expectations are likely to relate to exchange rates in an opposite way to changes in real rates of interest.

● References

EDWARDS Sebastian. — [1983] "Comments on 'An Accounting Framework and Some Issues for Modelling How Exchange Rates Respond to the News'", in Frenkel, Jacob A. (ed.) *Exchange Rates and International Macroeconomics*, Chicago : University of Chicago Press, forthcoming.

FEROLDI Mathieu and MELITZ, Jacques. — (1982) "The French Franc and the French Financial Sector", *Annales de l'INSEE*, July-December, this volume.

FRANKEL Jeffrey. — [1982] "On the Franc", *Annales de l'INSEE*, July-December, this volume.

FRENKEL Jacob A. — [1981] "Flexible Exchange Rates, Prices and the Role of « News » : Lessons from the 1970 's", *Journal of Political Economy*, 89, No. 4 (August), pp. 665-705.

ISARD Peter. — [1983] "An Accounting Framework and Some Issues for Modelling How Exchange Rates respond to the News", in Frenkel Jacob A. (ed.), *Exchange Rates and International Macroeconomics*, Chicago, University of Chicago Press, forthcoming.

Capital controls: some principles and the French experience

Emil-Maria CLAASSEN
and Charles WYPLOSZ*

E.M. CLAASSEN: University of Paris-Dauphine and INSEAD; C. WYPLOSZ : INSEAD. We have benefited from very useful discussions with Francesco GIAVAZZI, Herwig LANGOHR, Jacques MELITZ, and Maurice OBSTFELD, but all the errors are ours. We also thank Mehmet ODEKON for help in the empirical work, and Bruno SOLNIK for making data available to us.

The first part of this paper considers the extent of the case for capital controls in the literature. It examines the long run effects of such controls on resource allocation, and the possibility that the controls increase policy independence in the short run. The second part is empirical and attempts to assess the French experience. The results suggest that capital controls did reduce the degree of substitutability between domestic and foreign assets, but they do not rule out the possibility of perverse effects on the offset coefficient and capital movements,

237

Introduction

The instinctive reaction of the professional economist is that capital controls are not a desirable tool of economic policy because they reduce the opportunity set of economic agents. Two main classes of arguments are usually offered to support this broad assertion. The first one suggests that these controls interfere with the process of allocation of ressources at the world level. At first sight, free capital movements are Pareto optimal. To the extent that the marginal return on capital diverges between countries, world income is increased by capital movements from the low return countries to the high return ones, and there is a specialization of the former in savings, the latter in investment. But even if the marginal returns of capital were identical everywhere in the absence of capital movements, differences in time preference or differences in liquidity preference would call for international capital flows (cf. KINDLEBERGER [1967], p. 602). Of two countries, the one with a lower preference for current consumption could shift its consumption into the future through net capital exports while the other country shifted its future consumption into the present, to the mutual advantage of both (cf. KOURI [1982]). If there is no difference in the productivity of capital and in time preference, gross (though not net) capital movements would still increase total welfare in the presence of different liquidity preferences since the country with a high liquidity preference could import long-term capital in return for short-term capital exports. Consequently, whatever the hypothesis we make about world rates of return, Pareto optimality would be achieved by a laissez-faire regime for international capital movements.

A second class of arguments suggests that capital controls would not even be efficient in maintaining a fixed parity. Because a "wrong" exchange rate will ultimately need to be ajusted, controls may, at best, delay this outcome. But, in the meantime, it essentially benefits those who are in a position to speculate and who can take advantage of the usual one-sidedness of such operations. Furthermore, capital restrictions on transactions by residents are often riddled with loopholes and fail to prevent non-residents from exerting a powerful pressure on the parity.

Yet, it is a fact that, permanently or temporarily, almost all countries have used some capital controls, even those countries known for their adherence to free markets [1]. Although the widespread existence of capital controls is certainly not a proof of their usefulness, it would indicate that the question requires investigation. The literature is too thin to warrant any definitive statement, and as we will show, the few references that we have found take a cautious stand.

In this paper, a very tentative inquiry into a topic which is not amenable to simple statements, we pursue two objectives. First, we try to outline which arguments could be made in favor of capital controls, drawing on the existing literature. In section 1, we consider the long-run aspects of these controls, outlining four arguments which may sometimes justify imposing restrictions on capital movements, at least from a nationalistic point of view. In section 2, we discuss the shorter run aspects of controls, as an accompaniment of a typical policy-mix and as a way of stabilizing the real exhange rate.

The second objective of the paper is empirical. We consider the case of France, a country where free capital movements have been rather exceptional since World War II, but which is also quite integrated in the world markets and has a fairly well-developed financial structure. In section 3, we briefly review how the controls operate. Section 4 provides an assessment of their effectiveness. We attempt in the next two sections to measure the respective effects of capital controls on short-term offsetting capital flows and on long-run investments. Needless to say, since little work has been done in this area, the results are crude and very tentative.

---

1. The outstanding exception seems to be Lebanon. Although Germany, Switzerland, the UK and US are now free from such restrictions, they have enforced some of them in the recent past. Countries like France, Italy, Belgium, Japan have more or less always used some forms of controls and the LDC's (with some exceptions as Mexico until August 1982), with limited capital markets, often dominated by the monetary authorities, usually control directly all capital movements and also, sometimes, the trade flows.

1 Long-run aspects of the efficient allocation of resources

The presumption is that capital controls entail welfare losses from the point of view of resource allocation. In this section, we examine whether a case for capital restrictions could be made if the conditions of Pareto optimality are not fulfilled in a world characterized by externalities due to market failures or distortions due to government interferences. As far as externalities are concerned, a control of capital exports could be justified —but only from a national point of view— if the private return on capital invested abroad is higher than the social return. In the case where government interventions are responsible for pushing the private rate of return on domestic capital under the social rate of return, there may be grounds for further interventions reducing capital exports according to the "theory of the second best" a theory which has taught us, if anything, that "two wrongs may make a right" (FIELEKE [1971], p. 6). The issue then may be seen as whether we can empirically pinpoint some externalities and distortions which call for capital controls.

1.1. Political default argument

It is sometimes argued that countries —in particular capital-rich countries— tend to overlend because they underestimate the possibility of default (KEYNES [1924]). Of course, private investors will require a rate of return allowing for any default risk on capital invested abroad. But if the default risk is linked to the political risk that foreign governments will repudiate a loan by domestic residents or may confiscate a direct investment, then the social return on capital invested abroad may be well below the private return. The political implication would be that the home countries should control capital exports to other countries with a high political default risk, but only if the market does not take the possibility of confiscation into account. However, government may not be a better predictor of political default risks than the market, in which case the political default argument for capital controls is irrelevant.

1.2. Tax structure argument

Another divergence between the private and the social rate of return on capital may arise from differing tax structures. Suppose the same rate of private and social return on capital in the home and foreign country. A tax on interest income (and/or capital gains) would let the private rate of return fall below the social rate of return of capital at home and below the private as well as the social rate of return of capital abroad. Freedom of capital movements would then imply capital exports by the home country even though they are contrary to economic efficiency in the allocation of capital in the world economy. An interest-equalization tax by the home country consequently would be an appropriate second-best measure. However, the foreign country would be foolish not to adopt an equivalent tax on interest income in so far as there is an agreement between the two countries allowing full credit on foreign taxes. Of course, either an interest-equalization tax, or a uniform fiscal treatment of earnings in the two countries, would only be a second-best solution. The first-best solution would be a removal of the fiscal burden on interest income.

1.3. Credit control argument

Those countries who keep interest rates artificially low at home through credit controls must necessarily make use of capital controls in order to lock-in domestic savings. Here again, as with the previous argument, one intervention calls for another one.

In France credit markets are characterized by a considerable number of regulations and restrictions. As described by MELITZ [1982], corporate financial needs are satisfied primarily through borrowings from banks and only secondarily through the stock exchange and the bonds market. In both the bank credit and securities markets, there seems to be more rationing and queuing than price competition, primarily because of a complex web of regulations ensuring that the public sector borrowing requirements are satisfied at favorable rates. In addition, credit-ceilings are often enforced by the central bank as a way of controlling the money supply. Furthermore, there exists in France a whole host of financial organizations, both bank and non-bank, whose *raison d'être* is to provide cheap loans to specific industries or for local needs. Thus, the huge network of savings institutions (*caisses d'épargne*) is geared towards the support of local governments and small industries which emphasize local development. There exist similar institutions subsidizing the agricultural sector, retail stores, the tourism industry, the export sector or small businesses. Finally, mortgages have always benefited from a favorable tax treatment, thus probably channelling an excessive share of savings towards home buying and repairs, and involving several interest rate subsidies to low income and large families in a highly segmented credit market. The upshot is that hardly any domestic rate can be taken as representing the outcome of an unregulated interplay of market forces. The overall tendency is to maintain interest rates at a low level, thus resulting in a widespread system of transfers from asset holders to borrowers.

If credit controls aim to lower domestic interest rates, as they do in France, then capital controls (e.g., in the form of taxes on capital exports and subsidies to capital imports), can make a useful contribution since they reduce the degree of substitutability between domestic and foreign financial assets. In the empirical part of the paper, we will test two propositons related to the credit-control argument for capital controls. On the one hand, we will ask whether capital controls did succeed in preventing private savings from flowing abroad despite lower interest rates resulting from credit controls. On the other hand, we will ask whether capital controls have helped to disconnect the home interest rate from the foreign one, for those financial assets which are quite apart from credit controls.

1.4. Optimal tax argument

A policy of low interest rates via capital controls can be defended on the basis of the existence of positive externalities associated with capital accumulation. One relevant type of externalities concerns the gain in labor income when savings are not invested abroad but at home, thus calling for an optimal tax on capital exports, as has been shown by MacDougall [1960] and Kemp [1966]. This argument resembles the one for an optimal tariff in some essential respects. First, the argument requires the home country to be sufficiently large to be able to affect the interest rate by investing abroad. (The same is true for the optimum tariff on imports which can only apply if the importing country can alter the price of the imported goods on the world market.) Second, although the home country achieves a welfare gain, the foreign country suffers an even higher welfare loss, so that the world as whole faces a net welfare loss.

The optimal tax argument can be interpreted in the following way. A capital-exporting country obtains the interest income, but not the labor income from its investment abroad. Consequently, there are negative externalities associated with capital exports in the form of loss of labor income which goes to the foreign country (and corresponding positive externalities associated with capital imports) : the private marginal return on capital exports thus exceeds the social marginal return. As in the case of all negative externalities, there is an over-production — here it is an over-investment or an over-lending abroad. An interest equalization tax should be levied in order to eliminate the excess of the private rate over the social rate of return on capital invested abroad. The assumption that capital exports influence the foreign interest rate is essential in this argument since, in the absence of such an influence, any restriction of capital exports would not increase the yield on the domestic capital invested abroad. It should be noted that the externality in question only exists for the national economy and that this type of externality raises a pure *distributive* issue at the world level (aside from the world income loss due to the higher marginal productivity of capital in the foreign country).

When the home country imposes an "optimal" capital control, there is also a change in income distribution within the country in favor of labor income. For a given input of labor, the real wage rate rises. This outcome may explain the sympathy that the labor force and, in particular, the trade unions often express for controls of capital exports. Furthermore, by assuming constant returns of scale and a certain rate of unemployment, the restriction on capital exports would produce a favorable employment and income effect for the domestic economy. However, if the foreign country similarly faces unemployment, the enforcement of capital exports by the home country would cause an export of unemployment of the domestic to the foreign country.

The above analysis of the optimal capital control from the point of view of a single country has only limited application value for two reasons. First, it is concerned with direct investment as a particular type of capital movement. However, the capital-exporting country need not be an exporter nor even a producer of capital goods. As long as the country has a current account surplus, it will obtain control over investments abroad via lending and it is a subordinate issue whether the foreign country obtains the capital goods by trade or production. Second, the analysis is a partial equilibrium one [2].

As shown by KEMP [1966] and JONES [1967], by changing the conditions of supply and the level of income at home an abroad, international investment may modify the terms of trade, thereby affecting both the optimal tariff on trade and the optimal tax on capital movements.

In sum, the first three of our four arguments for capital controls may be ascribed to distortions created by government. The political default risk argument arises because the foreign government may be dishonest. The tax structure argument calls for a harmonization of income taxes on interest payments, if such taxes happen to be already (but erroneously) imposed. The credit control argument requires capital controls if influential credit rationing and credit selection measures are in place. The fourth argument, or the optimal tax one, is different as it relates to externalities, but it can only be defended from a stricty national point of view.

A last, technical issue concerns the best type of capital controls to adopt. It is possible to impose quantitative restrictions or taxes (or subsidies) on either capital income or capital transactions. Taxation may be more appropriate than administrative interference in so far as the latter may inhibit very profitable transactions while failing to interfere with barely profitable ones, whereas a uniform tax would eliminate all transactions which are below a certain level of profitability. As FLEMING [1974] has shown, a third type of capital controls, consisting of separate exchange rates for current account and capital transactions, could even be superior to taxation. Dual exchange rates, in case the "financial" rate of exchange is above the "commercial" rate of exchange, imply a uniform (though not a constant) tax on capital exports, combined with an equivalent subsidy on capital imports (provided that the interest payments are converted at the commercial rate of exchange).

2 Short-run aspects of macro-economic stabilization policies

From a macroeconomic point of view, the control of capital movements can be conceived as a superior alternative to interest rate policy in order to achieve the external equilibrium under fixed exchange rates, and as a superior alternative to foreign exchange intervention in order to dampen the volatility of the real exchange rate under floating exchange rates. So far as the empirical part of our paper deals with the macroeconomic issue, it is only concerned with the question of whether capital controls have increased the degree of autonomy of French monetary policy under the current system of a managed float.

---

2. This assumption simplifies the analysis. If there are differentiated products in both countries, there may be a favorable effect of the home investment abroad on the home country terms of trade by obtaining imports at a lower price.

2.1. Fixed exchange rates

HARRY JOHNSON [1967] put forward a case for capital controls as a stabilization device in a system of fixed exchange rates. We know that monetary policy has only a limited degree of autonomy in the short-run under this sort of exchange rate regime. This short-run autonomy is the more limited the more capital is internationally mobile. One prominent suggestion in the 1960's was that the authorities adopt a certain type of policy mix : an interest rate policy so as to realize external equilibrium and a fiscal policy so as to realize internal equilibrium or full employment. JOHNSON then raised the interesting question whether the use of capital controls would not be superior to a mix of monetary and fiscal policy from the standpoint of efficient resource allocation. He himself opted for capital controls.

Suppose there is full employment and a balance of payments deficit. An increase of the interest rate would improve the balance of payments via the capital account. However, the higher interest rate would lower domestic investment and increase domestic saving, thus requiring an accompanying government budget deficit in order to maintain full employment. There would then be a wastage of domestic saving because a part of it would be invested in government debt with a social yield of zero unless the government used the deficit to finance productive investment. Except in this last case then, the yield on the government debt would come entirely from additional future taxes. A better solution would be to avoid the policy mix, therefore also the fiscal deficit, but impose controls on capital outflows.

JOHNSON's efficiency argument is only valid for a "temporary" disequilibrium in the balance of payment. In the case of a permanent disequilibrium, it would constitute a second-best solution, the first best one being a devaluation in order to advoid the real transfer implied by the conjunction of a current account surplus and a capital account deficit.

2.2. Floating exchange rates

Based on the recent experience of the extreme variability of the real exchange rate, one could argue that policy action is necessary in order to smooth the heavy ups and downs of the real exchange rate, since the exchange rate is not only like other asset prices but is also a relative price linked to the goods market. In the latter role, its movements affect inflation, competitiveness and economic activity, and therefore may be excessive.

One possible way to avoid these real effects would be to have official (sterilized) intervention on the foreign exchange market. This would require, in accordance with Friedman's profit criterion (FRIEDMAN [1953]) central banks to buy foreign exchange when the price is low and sell when the price is high, thus implying profits. However, we observe that government interventions have not avoided excessive fluctuations in the real exchange rate. One possible explanation may be that central banks have not followed FRIEDMAN's profit criterion. [3] Another explanation could be the inability of central banks to reduce a massive under or overshooting of the real exchange rate because the required intervention would be too high, especially if the market believed in a temporary divergence of the real exchange rate from the equilibrium long-run one. A second possible way to avoid the extreme volatility of the real exchange rate would be to introduce capital controls in the form of an interest rate equalization tax, usually either on a permanent basis (TOBIN [1978]) or a transitory one in case of unusually large real interest rate differentials (DORNBUSCH [1982]). Whether intervention policy or capital control policy or even a mix of both is best can only be determined by a cost-benefit analysis which has yet to come.

3 An overview of capital controls in France

3.1. Principles

We first distinguish between capital controls affecting banks and controls imposed on non-bank residents. Regarding bank controls, the cornerstone is the proscription of an open position in foreign currency. This means that banks must continuously cover the net foreign assets positions that their customers acquire through their services or, in other words, that banks are prevented from acting on their own to take speculative positions. In order to strengthen controls, occasionally the *Banque de France* further regulates the position that banks can take *vis-à-vis* their non-resident customers, in Francs, or in foreign currencies, or both. As foreigners may speculate by borrowing Francs or, equivalently, by selling Francs forward, banks may be prohibited from entering into such contracts, which effectively restricts the availability of Francs to non-residents.

As far as non-bank residents are concerned, if we leave aside a series of restrictions dealing with tourism and transfers, the most important regulations concern holdings of foreign assets, and the leads and lags. Since May-June 1981, for example, French residents can only trade foreign securities among themselves. Non-residents who wish to bring foreign assets into France have to deposit them in "dossiers" kept by authorized banks, and there may be strict limitations on the sales of these assets. Concerning leads and lags, the controls set a deadline for the repatriation of the proceeds of exports, another deadline for the sale of foreign currency thus obtained to authorized banks. Similar limits apply to the forward markets : sales of francs are allowed only if they correspond to registered transactions in goods or services, and even then, such sales can only be arranged within well specified deadlines. Export credits (although with numerous exceptions) can be limited in terms of both their size and their maturity. Finally residents are not allowed to hold demand or time deposits abroad, and non-residents who hold such accounts in France are not allowed to use them to transfer, or receive, funds from residents accounts.

---

3. TAYLOR [1982] has shown that the central banks of Canada, Germany, Italy, Spain, Switzerland, England and the United States, made a loss of approximately 12 billion dollars during the 1970s.

3.2. Representative dummy variables

All these controls are frequently modified, depending upon the situation. As we wish to develop a measure of the tightness of capital controls we use the three-step scale proposed by MATHIS [1981]. He distinguishes between restrictions imposed on banks from those affecting non-bank residents. These measures are summarized on figure 1 below.

In our econometric experiments, we introduce some dummy variables which are simply a reflection of this figure. (The only departure is for DB in 1974:1 where we disagree with MATHIS.) DB relates to controls on banks, DNB to controls on non-bank residents, their values ranging, in absolute terms, from 0 to 3 (negative signs correspond to the period when controls were intended to prevent capital inflows). The overall effect is captured by the variable $D = DB + DNB$.

Figure 1 reflects the history of controls in France and is, by and large, self-explanatory. Of interest is the fact that in the earlier part of our sampling period, controls aimed at reducing pressures in favor of the franc as the dollar was under attack. From August 21, 1971 to March 20 1974, a two-tier market was in place with one market for current account transactions (where the Central Bank intervened) and another market for capital account transactions. Also, it is noteworthy that controls remained virtually unchanged between 1974 and 1981, despite a number of important events as France left [January 1974], then re-entered [July 1975] and then left again [March 1976] the "snake", before the creation of the EMS [March 1979]. In May 1981, after the election of President MITTERRAND, controls were tightened to their strongest degree.

TABLE 1

Degrees of Tightness of Capital Controls

Measures	Degree of tightness values
Controls on non-bank residents	
Forward cover cannot exceed 3 months......................	1
Forward cover cannot exceed 1 month......................	2
Forward cover cannot exceed 1 month, and less for some (or all) selected items...	3
Controls on banks	
Banks cannot increase their spot position in F.F. vis-à-vis non-resident customers.....................................	1
Banks cannot increase their spot and forward positions in F.F. vis-à-vis non-resident customers............................	2
Banks cannot increase their spot and forward positions, both in F.F. and foreign currencies vis-à-vis non-residents, *and* in foreign currencies vis-à-vis resident customers........................	3

FIGURE 1

Degree of tightness

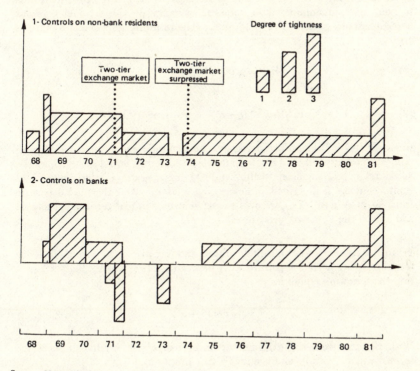

Source : MATHIS (1981).

4 The effectiveness of capital controls measures

ALIBER [1973] has shown that capital controls reduce capital movements through two different channels. First, by imposing regulatory constraints, they restrict, if not entirely eliminate, arbitrage and speculative operations which would normally be carried out. Second, by generating uncertainty about the possibility of additional restrictions, they increase the risk of international operations. DOOLEY and ISARD [1980] have developed a technique to separate out these two effects, which we use in order to assess the effectiveness of the existing measures.

The model of DOOLEY and ISARD may be briefly described as follows. Assume that domestic residents choose between government debt, with a yield of r, and assets denominated in foreign currency, which bring a yield of $(r^* + \hat{e})$, the sum of the foreign interest rate r^* and of the expected rate of depreciation $\hat{e}$. Non-residents face the same choice, but can also choose to hold assets denominated in domestic currency on the external markets, here Eurofranc assets, with a yield of $\tilde{r}$. The resulting asset demand funtions are :

(1) $$H/P = h\,(r - r^* - \hat{e},\ w;\ D)$$

(2) $$H^*/P = h^*\,(r - r^* - \hat{e},\ r - \tilde{r},\ w^*;\ D)$$

where H and H* denote, respectively, the domestic and foreign holdings of domestic government debt issued in domestic currency, w and w^* the domestic and foreign real financial wealth, and D, our measure of the tightness of capital controls, is described in the previous section. Note that, as a departure from DOOLEY and ISARD, we define asset demands in real terms, dividing H and H* by the domestic price level.

In the absence of both capital controls and risk aversion, market efficiency would translate perfect substitutability between assets of similar characteristics into the following equalities :

(3) $$r = \tilde{r} = r^* + \hat{e}$$

With risk aversion, the existence of an exchange risk would eliminate the second equality in (3), or introduce a risk premium, p :

(3′) $$r = \tilde{r} = r^* + \hat{e} + p$$

Only capital controls can lead to a breakdown of the first equality, because of both the implicit tax effect of such restrictions and the induced political risk which renders domestic currency assets held at home imperfect substitutes for domestic currency assets held abroad :

(3″) $$r \neq \tilde{r} = r^* + \hat{e} + p$$

Thus, capital controls are observed as discrepancies between the internal and external interest rates on assets denominated in domestic currency. If $\bar{H} = H + H^*$ is the total supply of government debt, we can solve for this interest differential from (1) and (2) :

(4) $$\tilde{r} - r = F\,(\bar{H}/P,\ r - r^* - \hat{e},\ w,\ w^*,\ D)$$

We note from (3″) that :

$$r - r^* - \hat{e} = r - \tilde{r} + p$$

248

and upon substitution in (4), we obtain :

(4')
$$\tilde{r} - r = G\,(\text{H}/P,\ p,\ w,\ w^*,\ D)$$

There remains the problem of specifying the behavior of the risk premium. Formal treatment of this factor has been offered in the literature. It is usually found to be related to the supply of assets and to demand factors such as wealth, risk aversion, and the covariances of returns. [4] DOOLEY and ISARD propose the following, simple, formulation : [5]

$$p = p\,(\text{H}/P,\ w,\ w^*)$$

which upon substitution in (4'), leads to the following, testable, equation:

(5)
$$\tilde{r} - r = g\,(\text{H}/P,\ w,\ w^*,\ D)$$

Discrepancies between r and $\tilde{r}$ may be due to a lack of arbitrage because of the existing controls, D, or to the imperfect substitutability between internal and external assets denominated in domestic currency, which is due to the risk of potential changes in the regulation, as measured by the other explanatory variables. Except for D, we have no prior expectations concerning the signs of the coefficients of the variables in (5).

The estimates of equation (5) are presented in table 2. Data construction and sources are described in the appendix. [6] The sample period is entirely dictated by data availability. Regression (2.1) clearly establishes that existing exchange controls, as measured by the dummy variable D, have a significant impact. For example, in late 1981, with D set at a value of six, existing controls would allow for an interest differential of 5.6 percent. [7] This is made apparent on figure 2 where we depict the evolution of $(\tilde{r} - \tilde{r})$ over the sample period and compare it with the impact of existing controls as obtained by the fitted value of regression (2.2). The difference between the two curves is meant to capture the remaining influence attributed to "political risk".

---

4. See, for example, SOLNIK [1974] for a detailed treatment. DORNBUSCH [1980] offers an appealing, simple interpretation of the risk premium, based on the difference between the share of such assets in the minimum variance portfolio and the existing supply. For an attempt to bring in a macroeconomic perspective, see also WYPLOSZ [1982].

5. In view of DORNBUSCH's derivation, the chief missing variable is the subjective variance of the real exchange rate. An ex-post measure of this variance is not interesting of course. The regression implied by (5) is likely to be consistent, unless one can show that this variance is systematically related to the other explanatory variables or to the error terms.

6. In order to keep the same data definition as in later sections, domestic wealth and assets are constructed somewhat differently from DOOLEY and ISARD. Here both H and W have a broader coverage, including all outside government debt i.e. the money base. We have experimented with the same definition as in DOOLEY and ISARD, and the results are roughly identical.

7. We have also tried to assess the role of the two-tier exchange market in use over the period 1971: 3 - 1974: 1. The corresponding dummy variable is never statistically significant.

TABLE 2

The differential between external and internal interest rate 1972:1 - 1981:3 — Ordinary least squares*

	fi/P	w	w*	D	DB	DNB	R²	SEE	DW
2.1	— 0.050 (—3.16)	0.038 (1.75)	— 0.565 (— 3.13)	0.928 (5.76)			0.57	0.81	1.76
2.2	— 0.049 (—3.16)	0.035 (1.63)	— 0.770 (— 3.56)		0.292 (0.69)	1.983 (2.98)	0.39	0.79	1.83
2.3	— 0.046 (—2.71)	0.036 (1.51)	— 0.418 (— 2.08)		1.311 (4.82)		0.50	0.88	1.65
2.4	— 0.047 (—3.10)	0.032 (1.54)	— 0.855 (— 4.84)			2.358 (6.13)	0.60	0.78	1.83
				D1 (72: 1–73: 1)	D2 (74: 1–78: 1)	D3 (78: 2–81: 3)			
2.5	— 0.060 (—3.50)	0.048 (2.09)	— 0.378 (— 1.12)	1.496 (1.49)	3.864 (3.44)	7.888 (6.28)	0.61	0.77	1.88

* t—statistics are given in brackets. The constant is not reported. The dummy variables D, DN and DNB are explained in the text above. D1, D2 and D3 are dummy variables which take zero values everywhere except during the indicated periods, where they take the value one. All other variables are described in the appendix.
Average values and standard deviations over the sample period : r — r = 1.48 (1.8), D = 1.77 (1.42). Correlation coefficient between DB and DNB = 0.753.

Figure 2

The difference between the external and the internal interest rates

(Three-months interbank on Francs in London and Paris)

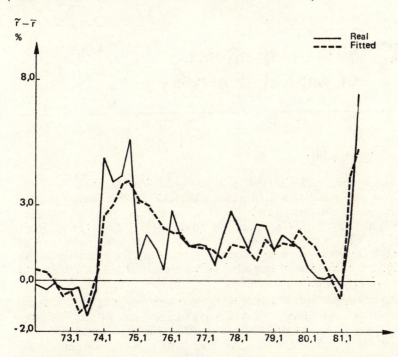

The distinction between capital controls on banks and non-banks in regressions (2.2), (2.3) and (2.4), yields a further interesting result. If we consider jointly controls on banks and on non-banks in (2.2), controls on banks seem to have no effects on the interest differential. When DB and DNB are taken separately, as in (2.3) and (2.4), both DB and DNB enter significantly, but the various statistics of (2.3) indicate a less satisfactory fit than in (2.4). The conclusion is that when controls are simultaneously imposed on banks and non-bank residents, the former add little to the latter. If they were to be used alone, each of them would achieve some success, with controls on non-banks about twice as effective as controls on banks. [8] One interpretation is that banks have ways to circumvent the controls as far as arbitrating between internal and external returns on Franc assets are concerned. Their ability to escape controls is sufficient to make them of little effectiveness when non-banks are simultaneously controlled, yet it is only partial so that, if used alone, such controls do produce the desired effect. Another interpretation is that controls on banks act largely as substitutes for direct controls on their clientele. It is then to be expected that controls on banks have little to add when controls on non-banks are already enforced.

---

8. This might, of course, simply reflect a problem of collinearity between DB and DNB. But, with a correlation coefficient of 0.753, this is unlikely.

Finally, in regression (2.5) we test the arbitrary choice of value ascribed to D, using three (0,1) dummy variables for periods where D is set at 1, 2 and 6 respectively. The estimated values are sufficiently close to justify the earlier choice.

5 Short-run effects of capital controls

5.1. The model

As discussed earlier in section 2, one possible justification for capital controls is to reconcile a fixed parity with independent monetary policies. The empirical literature is usually cast within the framework of the offset coefficient (PORTER [1972], KOURI and PORTER [1974], KOURI [1975], NEUMANN [1978]): the idea is to measure the proportion of newly created money base which leaks out abroad through central bank reserve losses. The objective of this section is to study whether capital controls have succeeded in reducing the offset coefficient.

Early estimates of the offset coefficient were obtained from reduced form equations. Recently, OBSTFELD [1980] and LASKAR [1982], following earlier work by HERRING and MARSTON [1977], have shown that such OLS estimates are significantly biased, resulting in offset coefficients much larger than those obtained through structural equation systems. OBSTFELD'S work also suggests that applying two-stage procedures to the reduced forms does not solve the problem (as had been noticed earlier by ARGY and KOURI [1974]).

The analysis is conducted by considering a three-asset portfolio, where domestic residents hold domestic money M, domestic government debt, H, and net foreign assets, the value of which, in foreign currency, we denote by F. By virtue of Walras' law, we eliminate the government bonds market. We allow for a delayed adjustment toward desired asset holdings. The resulting asset demand functions are: [9]

(6) $$m^d = M/P = a_0 + a_1 r + a_2 \bar{r}^* + a_3 y + a_4 w + a_5 m_{-1}$$

(7) $$f^d = eF/P = b_0 + b_1 r + b_2 \bar{r}^* + b_3 y + b_4 \dot{y}^* + b_5 w + b_6 w^* + b_7 f_{-1}$$

The demand for real cash balances is related to domestic real financial wealth w, to transaction needs, as measured by the real GNP, and to both the domestic interest rate r and the foreign interest rate r^*, adjusted for the forward discount $\bar{f}$, so that: $\bar{r}^* = r^* + \bar{f}$. [10] Net demand for foreign assets is translated into domestic currency through the exchange rate e. It is a function of both domestic and foreign demand and therefore of the real GNPs, y and y^*, of real domestic and foreign wealths, w and w^*, and of the relevant interest rates.

The last relation, the money supply equation, is formulated as :

(8) $$m^s = M/P = c_0 + c_1(r - \delta) + c_2 b + c_3 \psi + c_4 m_{-1}$$

with c_1, c_2, c_3 and c_4 assumed to be positive.

The money supply adjusts gradually towards its desired level, which is a function of the cost of refinancing, i.e. the difference between the interest rate r (bank credit rate) and the discount rate δ, and of the adjusted real money base. The nominal adjusted base is defined as:

$$B = F^o + T^o + D^o$$

with:

F^o the international reserves of the Central Bank;

T^o the Central Bank's credit to the Treasury;

D^o the demand deposits within the Post Office system, [11]

where T^o and D^o are the exogenous components of the adjusted money base, $\bar{B} = T^o + D^o$.

The last argument in (8) is $\psi = (1-\alpha) D/M$, where α is the required reserves ratio and D/M represents the proportion of the total money stock held in the form of deposits with commercial banks. An increase in ψ,

---

9. Equation (7) is likely to be misspecified for two reasons. First, as a *net* demand for foreign assets, f^d is the difference between net domestic demand for foreign assets and net foreign demand for domestic assets. With flexible exchange rates, capital gains or losses occur and it would be desirable to separate out the two behavioral relationships, as is done in FEROLDI and MELITZ [1982]. Second, by foreign assets, we mean a whole array of currencies, the relative prices of which cannot be assumed to be constant when PPP is known not to hold. This would call for a further disaggregation, obviously leading to a considerably heavier model. Another difficulty arises from the construction of the data : f^d is the cumulated capital account deficit, which leaves out capital gains on losses on the stock of actually held net foreign currency assets as the exchange rate fluctuates. In order to account for this effect, we would need to know, at least at one point in time, the value of these stocks, but such information is not available (so that we do not even know the *sign* of the assets position, i.e. whether we should observe gains or losses).

10. The forward discount is used here to measure the effective return on foreign covered assets. Of course, inasmuch as foreign assets are held without forward cover, we should use a measure of expectations of exchange rate change, as in LASKAR (1982). Another solution is to use an external forward premium as a measure of these expectations. But there are two problems with this approach. First, the forward premium is known to be a bad predictor of exchange rate changes. Second, if we use such a premium $\bar{f}$ in $\bar{r}^* = r^* + \bar{f}$, since $\bar{f} = \tilde{r} - r^*$ what we call $\bar{r}^*$ is actually equal to $\tilde{r}$, the external rate on *domestic* assets, which is a bad measure of the return on foreign assets unless exchange risk is assumed away.

11. This is one of several particularities of the French financial system. Post Offices offer checking account facilities, but do not engage into the granting of credits. The funds thus collected are deposited with the Treasury and belong therefore to the money base. For a more detailed analysis of the French system, see MELITZ [1982].

ceteris paribus, leads to an increase of M as banks lose fewer deposits and suffer fewer reserve losses when they expand their credits. [12]

We next derive a "reduced form" equation *à la* Kouri-Porter. We assume money market equilibrium in order to eliminate r with (6) and (8), and we make use of the balance of payments accounting identity:

$$CA + KA = CA - edf = dF^o$$

Then, overlooking the capital gains or losses due to exchange rate changes, we obtain:

$$(9) \quad -\Delta f = d_1 (\Delta \bar{b} + ca) + d_2 \Delta r^* + d_3 \Delta y + d_4 \Delta y^* + d_5 \Delta w + d_6 \Delta w^*$$
$$+ d_7 \Delta \delta + d_8 \Delta \psi + d_9 \Delta m_{-1} + d_{10} \Delta f_{-1}$$

with $d_1 = - b_1 c_2 / (b_1 c_2 + a_1 - c_1)$, $d_2 = (a_2 b_1 + b_2) / (b_1 c_2 + a_1 - c_1)$, etc., and where $\bar{b} = \bar{B}/P$ and $ca = CA/P$. The signs of the coefficients are unambiguous in the following cases:

$$d_1 < 0, \ d_2 < 0, \ d_7 > 0, \ d_8 < 0, \ d_{10} < 0.$$

The coefficient d_1 is the short-run offset coefficient corresponding to an open-market credit expansion (we can readily derive a "money rain" offset coefficient when the increase in the monetary base also increases private wealth: this leads to very similar results). The long-run offset coefficient corresponds to the case where the adjustments allowed for in (6) to (8) have taken place, so that we replace in the expression for d_1, b_5 by $b_5/(1-b_7)$, c_1 by $c_1/(1-c_4)$, etc.

Without capital controls, and with risk neutrality, we would expect d_1 to assume a unit value since b_1 is negative infinite. Both risk aversion and capital controls reduce the absolute value of b_1 and b_2, and this is precisely what we want to measure. From the adding-up constraints (see BRAINARD and TOBIN [1968]), it must also be that a_1 and a_2 are similarly affected. We therefore assume that all of these four parameters should decrease, in absolute value, when capital controls are increased:

$$a_1 = a_1(x), \ a_2 = a_2(x), \ b_1 = b_1(x), \ b_2 = b_2(x).$$

where x is a measure of the severity of capital controls.

Capital controls may also have an influence on the money supply process: domestic banks may be induced to expand more domestic credit, so that for a given cost of refinancing, money supply is larger. Also, if controls succeed in locking-in more capital, a given money base may support more money creation. Consequently we make the following, testable, assumptions:

$$c_1 = c_1(x), \ c_2 = c_2(x), \ c'_1 > 0, \ c'_2 > 0.$$

In order to give an operational content to this approach, we need to define x, the measure of capital controls. From the previous section, we know that the difference between the external and the internal interest rates does reflect capital controls, both those in place and prospective ones, so that we simply define:

$$x = |\tilde{r} - \hat{r}|$$

In taking the absolute value of the interest differential, we assume that the magnitude, not the direction, of the controls should matter as far as asset substituability is concerned. We next specify a simple linear relation of the above coefficients to x:

(10) $a_1 = \bar{a}_1(1 + \alpha_1 x)$ $a_2 = \bar{a}_2(1 + \alpha_2 x)$ $b_1 = \bar{b}_1(1 + \beta_1 x)$ $b_2 = \bar{b}_2(1 + \beta_2 x)$

$$c_1 = \bar{c}_1(1 + \gamma_1 x) \quad c_2 = \bar{c}_2(1 + \gamma_2 x)$$

where α_1, α_2, β_1 and β_2 are expected to be negative, and γ_1 and γ_2 positive. As can be shown by substituting (10) into (9), the effects of capital controls on the offset coefficients are ambiguous. To see why, consider an increase in the exogenous component of the money base, and for simplicity, let $\gamma_1 = \gamma_2 = 0$. Equations (6) and (8) imply that this will normally lead to a lower interest rate since if we assume money market equilibrium:

(11) $$dr = -\frac{c_2}{c_1 - a_1}\,d\bar{b}, \; c_1 \text{ and } c_2 > 0, \; a_1 < 0.$$

From (7), we see that this lower interest rate will prompt a capital outflow proportional to b_1. But, as b_1 is reduced by the controls, this outflow is smaller, which is the channel for the expected reduction in the offset coefficient. But there is another effect involved. If capital controls reduce the coefficient a_1, as follows from (11), a *given* increase in the money base will lead to a larger decline in the interest rate, prompting *ceteris paribus* a larger capital outflow. Thus the overall effect depends on the relative importance of these two channels: the larger β_1 and the smaller α_1, in absolute values, the better are the chances of reduced outflows. (If γ_1 is positive, reduced interest rate discourages even more the expansion of credit, leading to lower capital outflows. On the other side, a positive γ_2 means that a given increase in the money base leads to more money creation and therefore more capital outflows, thus worsening the offset coefficient.)

5.2. The structural portfolio balance equations

Recognizing that the domestic interest rate, the money base and the real GNP are endogenous, we estimate (6), (7), and (8), with (10), using a two-stage least squares procedure. The results appear in table 3.

---

12. This is an important aspect of the specific process of money supply in France, which has been emphasized e.g. by MELITZ and STERDYNIAK [1979]. Commercial banks can freely refinance themselves by borrowing from the Banque de France at a fixed discount rate, which they do as a function of their profit margin. The result is that if banks increase their share of the money stock, a given base supports a larger money supply. With the usual balance sheet identities, it can be shown that $M = (1 - \psi)^{-1}(\beta + \gamma)$ where γ is the refinancing function of the commercial banks.

TABLE 3

The portfolio balance model 1972:1 - 1981:3 - Two-stage least-squares *

1. Money Demand

$$m^d = -(3.70 - 1.35\,x)\,r + (0.12 - 1.21\,x)\,r^* + 0.15\,y + 0.69\,m_{-1}$$
$$(-2.14)\ (3.09) \qquad (0.09)\ (-2.73) \qquad (2.99) \quad (7.55)$$

$$\bar{R}^2 = 0.984 \qquad SEE = 0.011 \qquad DW = 2.08 \qquad h = -0.30$$

2. Net Foreign Assets

$$f = -(2.28 - 0.69\,x)\,(r - r^*) - 0.04\,y + 0.17\,w - 0.002\,w^* + 0.59\,f_{-1}$$
$$(-2.64)\ (2.60) \qquad (2.55) \quad (2.91) \quad (-2.03) \qquad (4.68)$$

$$\bar{R}^2 = 0.730 \qquad SEE = 1.962 \qquad DW = 2.15 \qquad h = -0.76$$

3. Money Supply

$$m^s = -0.35\,(r - \delta) + (0.60 + 0.03\,x)\,b + 226.11\,\psi + 0.81\,m_{-1}$$
$$(-0.34) \qquad (2.90)\ (3.21) \qquad (3.34) \quad (15.70)$$

$$\bar{R}^2 = 0.984 \qquad SEE = 0.011 \qquad DW = 2.14 \qquad h = -0.45$$

* t – statistics are given in brackets. The constant terms and quarterly seasonal dummies are not reported. The endogenous variables are : r, y and b. The instruments are : world real GNP (proxied by the OECD and US real GNP's), the present and lagged budget surplus, the lagged forward discount, the lagged real GNP of France, and an index from INSEE measuring the tightness of credit controls. All data are described in the appendix.

There are a few differences with the theoretical specification. In the money demand equation (6), wealth is not significant and the sign of $\bar{a}_2$ is wrong, but not significant either. In (7), foreign real income y^* does not enter, and the coefficients of r and r^* easily pass the test that they be equal with opposite sign (with an F [2,30] = 0.97). Finally, in the money supply equation (8), the sign of $\bar{c}_1$ is wrong, but again this coefficient does not differ significantly from zero. The remaining coefficients are all statistically significant and do not deviate from theoretical expectations. The speeds of adjustment in the two asset demand equations are comfortably close, while the money supply seems to be adjusting more slowly than usually expected.

For our purposes, the important coefficients are those corresponding to (10). The implied effects of capital controls are shown in table 4 below. They are derived from table 3 where the products $\bar{a}_1\, \alpha_1$, $\bar{a}_2\, \alpha_2$, etc., are all statistically significant, [13] except for $\bar{c}_1\gamma_1$ (not reported).

TABLE 4

Effects of capital controls on asset substitutability

$$\alpha_1 = -\ 0.36$$
$$\alpha_2 = -\ 10.32$$
$$\beta_1 = -\ 0.30$$
$$\beta_2 = -\ 0.30$$
$$\gamma_1 = \text{not significant}$$
$$\gamma_2 = 0.05$$

The coefficients all bear the expected sign and would indicate that, indeed, capital controls do produce sizeable portfolio effects. [14] But this does not mean, as we have seen, that controls reduce the offset coefficient. Indeed, the fact that the coefficient α_1 is larger than β_1 raises the possibility of the perverse result of larger capital outflows for a given increase in the exogenous

---

13. We have used a linear specification to estimate these coefficients. For example in regression 4 : 1, we have $\bar{a}_1 r + \bar{a}_1 \alpha_1 . rx$, where rx is a regressor.

14. There are some unsatisfactory results though. It appears that for large enough values of x the signs of a_1, a_2, etc., are reserved which is not part of the hypothesis. This is a consequence of the linear specification in (10). We have attempted a non-linear procedure with $a_1 = \bar{a}_1$. exp $(-\alpha_1 x)$ but the program failed to converge. We have also substituted $|D|$ $|DB|$, and $|DNB|$, for x without getting significantly different results.

components of the money base. [15]   Table 5 shows how the offset coefficient, as defined in (9), varies with x given the estimated equation.

TABLE 5

Implied offset coefficients [16]

$x = (\tilde{r} - \bar{r})$	Short term	Long term
0	0.271	0.597
0.25	0.277	0.604
0.50	0.284	0.611
0.75	0.291	0.620
1	0.300	0.630
1.25	0.311	0.642
1.50	0.325	0.657
1.75	0.344	0.676
2	0.373	0.703
2.25	0.423	0.745
2.50	0.534	0.820

Does this mean that capital controls have always had a perverse effect in France? Probably not, because the model assumes that the interest rate is determined by the money market equilibrium condition, whereas in France interest rates are basically set by the *Banque de France*, even in the absence of credit controls [17] which, anyway, have been in effect during most of the period under study.

If then, we consider that the interest rates are exogenously set by the monetary authorities, all that matters in order to assess the effect of capital controls is the sign and significance of the effect of x on b_1 in (7). Viewed this way, capital controls produce the desired effect. For example, assume that the domestic interest rate is reduced by one percent. In the absence of controls, this would trigger an outflow of FF 2.28 billions. If, at the same time, capital controls establish a one percent differential between the internal and external rates, the outflow is reduced by FF 0.69 billions. In section 1 we argued that capital controls may be a necessary companion to credit rationing. Now we reach the conclusion that, in view of the parameters estimated in table 3, regulated interest rates are needed if capital controls are to succeed in reducing the capital outflows triggered by an expansion of the money base.

6 Long-run effects of capital controls

As discussed earlier in section 1, while capital controls are welfare-reducing in a first-best world, in the real world they have some justification, at least from a purely national point of view: an oft-stated objective of capital controls is to lock-in private savings, in order to channel them towards investment at home rather than abroad.   As it turns out, the rate of saving is pretty much a national characteristic, essentially related to the degree of time preference, the social security and retirement benefits systems and other similar considerations.   In particular, the effect of interest rates on the rate of savings is well known to be ambiguous, involving offsetting price and income effects so that we take savings as exogenous. [18]   Consequently, the rate of investment

---

15. As a check of this result, we have estimated a standard reduced form equation à la KOURI-PORTER, simply adding as a regressor the variable representing capital controls (as well as the rate of exchange rate change to possibly account for capital gains or losses).   The result for the short-term capital account, using two-stage least squares is :

$$STKA = 0.750 + 0.336 \, \Delta \, \bar{B} - 1.221 \, (CA + LTKA) + 0.065 \, \Delta \, r^* + 0.027 \, \Delta Y$$
$$\quad (0.21) \quad (1.89) \quad (-5.55) \quad\quad (0.10) \quad\quad (0.41)$$

$$\quad - 0.126 \, \Delta W - 12.65 \, \Delta W^* - 0.157 \, (\Delta \, e/e) - 3.82 \, (\tilde{r} - \bar{r})$$
$$\quad (-1.43) \quad\quad (-0.89) \quad\quad (-2.17) \quad\quad -(2.71)$$

$$\bar{R}_2 = 0.35 \quad\quad\quad\quad SEE = 1.62 \quad\quad\quad\quad DW = 1.88$$

with t − statistics in parentheses. $\bar{B}$ (the domestic component of the money base), CA + LTKA (the sum of the current account and the long-term capital account) and $\tilde{r} - \bar{r}$ are taken as endogenous.   The instruments are: foreign GNP (proxied by the US and OECD GNPs), ψ, a variable measuring credit controls, $\bar{H}$ and seasonal dummies.
   The offset coefficient (the coefficient of $\Delta \bar{B}$) is of the wrong sign but not statistically significant, a result not uncommon with two-stage least squares reduced equations as discussed by OBSTFELD [1982].
   Interestingly, the capital control variable, $\tilde{r} - \bar{r}$, enters with a negative and significant coefficient, lending some indirect support to the possibility of a perverse effect.

16. The values in this table are computed from (9), using the estimates of table 3, except for c_1 that we set equal to zero.   We can compare these values with other estimates.   MELITZ and STERDYNIAK [1979], with a FIML technique, obtain a long-run coefficient of 0.70.   LASKAR [1982], also with a FIML technique, and including exchange rate expectations, gets values between 0.45 and 0.67 for the short-run coefficient.

17. We have attempted to introduce an explanatory variable measuring the tightness of credit ceilings in the money supply equation, but it turned out not to be statistically significant.   Consequently, we have used it as an instrument.

18. We have used a Granger-Sims causality test of the dependence of the rate of saving on the long term real interest rate.   The proposition that interest rates cause the rate of saving can be rejected at the 95 percent confidence level.

is likely to be, on average, essentially determined by the rate of saving and we study here whether capital controls have succeeded in increasing the rate of investment, *given* the rate of saving. It must be emphasized, again, that we do not deal with the more important question whether increasing the rate of investment through capital controls improves or not, the national welfare.

We note that investment at home is the sum of investment by residents, I^d financed by domestic savings, and investment by non-residents I^f :

$$I = I^d + I^f$$

We also break up domestic savings into four categories: the acquisition of domestic "private" assets A, government debt H, foreign assets F and cash balances M :

$$S = \Delta A + \Delta H + e\Delta F + \Delta M$$

What we want to test is the influence of capital controls on the difference between total investments and total savings. As by definition, $I^d = \Delta A$, we have:

(12) $$I - S = (I^f - e\Delta F) - (\Delta H + \Delta M)$$

The second bracket in (12), representing the accumulation of overall government debt by residents, can be safely considered as independent of capital controls. Thus we may concentrate on the first bracket. The capital account is:

$$KA = I^f - e\Delta F + \Delta H^*$$

where H^* represents foreign holdings of government debt. Hence we are interested in:

(13) $$\frac{I^f - e\Delta F}{Y} = \frac{KA - \Delta H^*}{Y}$$

Of course, we will consider only the long term capital account.

In order to formulate the behavior of (13), we develop a portfolio model. We note that $I^f = \Delta A^*$, where A^* represents foreign holdings of productive assets at home, and we assume:

(14) $$A^*/Y = f(R, R^*, w^*, x)$$

(15) $$eF/Y = g(R, R^*, w, x)$$

where R and R^*, respectively, are the real long term interest rates at home and abroad, w and w^* domestic and foreign real wealths, and $x = |\bar{r} - \bar{r}|$ our measure of capital controls. We assume:

$$\delta f/\delta R > 0, \quad \delta f/\delta R^* < 0, \quad \delta f/\delta w^* > 0, \quad \delta f/\delta x < 0.$$

$$\delta g/\delta R < 0, \quad \delta g/\delta R^* > 0, \quad \delta g/\delta w > 0, \quad \delta g/\delta x < 0.$$

Taking first differences of (14) and (15), and overlooking the valuation effects of exchange rate changes, we obtain:

(16) $$\frac{I^f - e\Delta F}{Y} = F\,(\Delta R,\ \Delta R^*,\ \Delta w,\ \Delta w^*,\ R\ R^*,\ w,\ w^*,\ X)$$

where the only unambiguous sign restrictions are:

$$\delta F/\delta\,(\Delta R) > 0, \quad \delta F/\delta\,(\Delta R^*) < 0, \quad \delta F/\delta\,(\Delta w^*) > 0, \quad \delta F/\delta\,(\Delta w) < 0.$$

We expect capital controls, x, to reduce the outflow of domestic savings, i.e., to lead to a reduction in ΔF. However, as they also restrict the repatriation of earned incomes, or threaten to do so, they may well discourage foreign investors, and *ceteris paribus*, reduce I^f. The total effect of capital control is therefore ambiguous. The regression analysis appears in table 6, where we have eliminated the variables that were not significant (w, w^*, Δw^*, R, R^*) and where Δw is proxied by y, the real French GNP. The variables Δw, ΔR and ΔR^* enter with the expected sign and are significant, thus supporting the underlying portfolio model.

Regressions (6.1) and (6.2) might give the impression that capital controls have no effects, since both x and the representative dummy D enter with a negative, but statistically insignificant coefficient. (A dummy representing the two-tier exchange market was also tested but produced no significant result.) A quite different picture emerges from regression (6.3): while controls on banks seem to enhance investment, those imposed on non-banks appear to have an undesirable effect. The tentative interpretation is that the controls on banks do prevent outgoing transfers of domestic savings while those on non-banks work as a deterrent on foreign investors.

TABLE 6

Long term effects of capital controls dependent variable: $(If-e\Delta F)/Y$ 1972:1 - 1981:3 - Two-stage least-squares *

	y	ΔR	ΔR^*	x	D	DB	DBN	$\bar{R}^2$	SEE	DW
6.1...........	— 0.007 (— 3.03)	1.87 (2.32)	— 1.25 (— 3.38)	— 0.11 (— 0.61)				0.30	1.041	2.14
6.2...........	— 0.006 (— 2.49)	1.75 (2.41)	— 1.19 (— 3.48)		— 0.13 (— 0.47)			0.32	1.024	2.13
6.3...........	— 0.007 (— 3.48)	1.04 (2.04)	— 0.89 (— 3.29)			0.92 (2.23)	— 1.69 (— 2.56)	0.49	0.889	2.38

* t – statistics in brackets. Data are described in the appendix. The constant is not reported. The endogenous variables are y and ΔR. The instruments are listed in table 1.

Conclusion

We have argued that there may exist, in the real world, various deviations from the efficient market paradigm which could justify the use of capital controls, at least from a national point of view. This does not mean that controls are welfare-increasing for the world as a whole. However, even that cannot be ruled out without further investigation. It seems that controls may be a useful companion tool for macroeconomic stabilization policies, especially when other controls, e.g. credit ceilings, are already implemented in place.

The empirical study yields a certain number of interesting results about the French experience over the last ten years. What stands out is the distinction between restrictions applied to banks and non-bank residents. Controls on banks appear to be less effective as far as the objective is to regain control of the internal short-term interest rate or to prevent short-term outflows, but produce a significant effect in locking-in long-term domestic savings. Non-bank restrictions, on the other side, are efficient in reducing short-term capital outflows and allowing for a better control of the short-term interest rate, but they produce undesirable long-run effects as they discourage foreign investment. These results are intuitive and leave us with the impression that the blessings of capital controls are mixed: the short-run effectiveness of controls on non-bank residents carries a cost in terms of capital accumulation, while controls on banks, however much they may succeed in preventing the exit of domestic savings, fail to increase the freedom of short-term policy making. Finally we have seen that capital controls would possibly increase the offset coefficient if the domestic interest rate responded freely to market forces, which is not the case in France.

DATA APPENDIX

1. Variables

Money Base: B includes postal checking accounts. *Source: IFS* (line 11 + line 12a — line 16c — line 17r + line 24i). $\check{B} = B - \Delta RR$ where $\Delta RR = (\alpha - \alpha_{-1}) D$ is an adjustment for changes in required ratios. B is from *IFS*, line 24 and 25. α is from *Banque de France, Bulletin trimestriel*, and separates out time and demand deposits. $\psi = (1 - \alpha) D/M$.

Government Debt: $\check{H} = \Sigma BD + \Sigma BOP$, with the budget deficit BD = line 80 of *IFS*, and the balance of payments BOP = the sum of lines 77 in *IFS* (converted in billions of francs).

Net Foreign Assets: $F = - \Sigma KA$, with KA = Capital Account. *Source: IFS* (converted in billions of francs).

Money Supply: M includes postal checking deposits. *Source: IFS*, line 34 + 35.

Wealth: Domestic Wealth = $W = \Sigma BD + \Sigma CA$, with BD defined above and the current account CA from *IFS*, lines 77aad to 77agd (converted in billions of francs).
Foreign Wealth: $W^* =$ World stock market wealth. *Source: Capital international perspective.*
$w^* = e W^*/P$ is converted in francs.

GNP: Y and y are, repectively, nominal and real GDPs for France (*Source: IFS*). y^* is the US real GNP (*Source: IFS*) or the industrial production index for all OECD (*Source: OECD, Main Economic indicators*).

Interest Rates: r is the interest charged on demand deposits overdrafts. *Source: INSEE*; $\tilde{r}$ is the London Interbank 3-months rate on francs, and $\bar{r}$ is the Paris interbank 3-months rate. *Source: Harris Bank, Weekly Review.*

$\bar{r}^* = r^* + \bar{f}$, with r^* the 3 months euro-dollar rate and $\bar{f}$ the 3-months discount on the franc. *Source: IFS*, (lines 60d, b and ae).

R and R^* are long-run real rates, i.e. government bonds yields less " expected " inflation, i.e. next year's inflation. *Source: IFS* (line 61 and 64x).

δ is the discount rate. *Source: IFS* (line 60).

Net long-term
private investment: $I' - \Delta F = LTKA - \Delta H^*$, with LTKA = long term capital account (*Source : IFS,* lines 77*b*) and H* is foreign currency government debt (*Source: IFS,* line 89*b*),

Price Index: P, *Source : IFS* (line 64).

Exchange Rate: *e, Source : IFS* (line *rf*).

2. Instruments (in addition to other variables listed above)

FACOC, survey measure of Credit Controls (*Source :* INSEE). Budget Surplus (*Source : IFS*; line 80).

3. Dummy variables

D : Capital control variables D = DB + DNB .

DB : Capital controls on banks (*Source:* MATHIS [1981]) DB = 0 (72: 1 — 72: 4); — 2 (73: 1 — 73: 3); 0 (73: 4); 1 (74: 1 — 81: 1); 3 (81: 2 — 81: 3)

DNB : Capital controls on non-bank residents (*Source :* MATHIS [1981]). DNB = 1 (72: 1 — 73: 1); 0 (73: 2 — 73: 4); 1 (74: 1 — 81: 1); 3 (81: 2 — 81: 3).

● References

ALIBER R. Z. — (1973) " The Interest Rate Parity Theorem: A Reinterpretation ", *Journal of Political Economy*, November-December, pp. 1451-1459.

ARGY V. and KOURI P. J. K. — (1974) " Sterilization Policies and Volatility in International Reserves ", in R. Z. Aliber (ed.), *National Monetary Policies and the International Fianacial System*, Chicago.

BRAINARD W. C. and TOBIN J. — (1968) " Pitfalls in Financial Model Building ", *American Economic Review*, May, pp. 99-122.

CUMBY R. E. and OBSTFELD M. — (1981) " Capital Mobility and the Scope for Sterilization; Mexico in the 1970s ", *NBER Working Paper*, no. 770, September.

DOOLEY M. P. and ISARD P. — (1980) " Capital Controls, Political Risk, and Deviations from Interest Rate Parity ", *Journal of Political Economy*, April, pp. 370-384.

DORNBUSCH R. — (1982) *Equilibrium and Disequilibrium Exchange Rates*, unpublished majuscript, MIT, April.

FEROLDI M. and MELITZ J. — (1982) "The Franc and the French Financial Sector", *Annales de l'INSEE,* this issue.

FIELEKE N. S. — (1971) *The Welfare Effects of Controls over Capital Exports from the United States*, Essays in International Finance, no. 82, January, Princeton University.

FLEMING J. M. — (1974) " Dual Exchange Markets and Other Remedies for Disruptive Capital Flows ", *International Monetary Fund Staff Papers*, pp. 1-27.

FRIEDMAN M. — (1953) " The Case for Flexible Exchange Rates ", in M. Friedman, *Essays in Positive Economics*, University Chicago Press, Chicago.

GRISSA A. — (1982) " The French Monetary and Exchange Rate Experienced in the 1920s ", in E. Claassen and P. Salin (ed.), *Recent Issues in the Theory of Flexible Exchange Rates*, North-Holland, Amsterdam.

GROSSMAN S. and SHILLER R. — (1981) " The Determinants of the Variability of Stock Prices ", *American Economic Review*, May.

HERRING R. J. and MARSTON R. C. — (1977) *National Monetary Policies and International Financial Markets*, North Holland, Amsterdam.

JOHNSON H. G. — (1967) " Theoretical Problems of the International Monetary System ", *Pakistan Development Review*, pp. 1-28; reprinted in R. N. Cooper, *International Finance*, Harmondsworth, 1969, pp. 304-334.

JONES R. W. — (1967) " International Capital Movements and the Theory of Tariffs and Trade ", *Quarterly Journal of Economics*, February, pp. 1-38.

KEMP M. C. — (1964) *The Pure Theroy of International Trade*, Prentice-Hall, Englewood Cliffs.

KEMP M. C. — (1966) " The Gain from International Trade and Investment: A New-Heckscher-Ohlin Approach ", *American Economic Review*, pp. 788-809.

KEYNES J. M. — (1924) " Foreign Investment and the National Advantage ", *Thel Nation and Athenaeum*, August 9, pp. 584-587.

KINDLEBERGER C. P. — (1967) " The Pros and Cons of an International Capita Market ", *Zeitschrift für die Gesamte Staatswissenschaft*, pp. 600-617.

Kouri P. J. K. — (1975) " The Hypothesis of Offsetting Capital Flows ", *Journal of Monetary Economics,* pp. 21-39.

Kouri P. J. K. — (1982) " Macroeconomics Adjustment to Interest Rate Disturbances: Real and Monetary Aspects ", in E. Claassen and P. Salin (ed.), *Recent Issues in the Theory of Flexible Exchange Rates,* North-Holland.

Kouri P. J. K. and Porter M. G. — (1974) " International Capital Flows and Portfolio Equilibrium ", *Journal of Political Economy,* June, pp. 443-467.

Laskar D. M. — (1982) " Short Run Independence of Monetary Policy Under a Pegged Exchange Rates System: an Econometric Approach ", *Journal of International Money and Finance,* April, pp. 57-60.

MacDougall G. D. A. — (1960) " The Benefits and Costs of Private Investment from Abroad: A Theoretical Approach ", *Economic Record,* March.

Mathis J. — (1981) « L'évolution des mouvements de capitaux à court terme entre la France et l'extérieur de 1967 à 1978 », *Économie et prévision,* no 2.

Melitz J. and Sterdyniak H. — (1980) « Masse monétaire, réserves officielles et taux de change en France (1962-1974) », *Cahiers du séminaire d'économétrie,* no. 21.

Melitz J. — (1982) " The French Financial System: Mechanisms and Propositions of Reform ", *Annales de l'INSEE,* this volume.

Neumann M. J. M. — (1978) " Offsetting Capital Flows: A Re-examination of the German Case ", *Journal of Monetary Economics,* January, pp. 131-142.

Nurkse R. — (1944) *International Currency Experience: Lessons from the Inter-War Period,* League of Nations, Princeton University Press, Princeton.

Obstfeld M. — (1980) " Sterilization and the Offsetting Capital Movement: Evidence from West Germany, 1960-1970 ", *NBER Working Paper,* no. 494, June.

Porter M. G. — (1972) " Capital Flows as an Offset to Monetary Policy: The German Case ", *IMF Staff Papers,* July, pp. 395-424.

Taylor D. — (1982) " Official Intervention in the Foreign Exchange Market, or, Bet against the Central Bank ", *Journal of Political Economy,* April, pp. 356-368.

Tobin J. — (1978) " A Proposal for International Monetary Reform ", Cowles Foundation Discussion Paper 506, Yale University.

Wyplosz C. — (1982) " The Interest and Exchange Rate Term Structure under Rational Expectations and Risk Aversion ", *Journal of International Economics,* November, forthcoming.

Comments [p237] 269 - 73

4312
3112
France

by Paul DE GRAUWE

University of Louvain

The paper of Emil CLAASSEN and Charles WYPLOSZ (CW) contains an original attempt at modelling the French capital controls system in the framework of a portfolio balance model. My comments concentrate on the way CW do this. Some criticism will be formulated and alternative methods will be outlined.

1. The model used and tested by CW can be represented graphically as follows. On the vertical axis

FIGURE 1

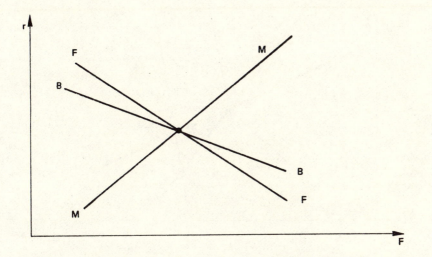

the domestic interest rate(r) is set out; on the horizontal axis the holdings of foreign assets (F) by residents. The MM-line is the equilibrium relation between *r* and F in the money market: an increase in F raises private wealth, and induces an increased demand for money. Thus, the domestic interest rate must increase to maintain money market equilibrium. The FF-line represents the demand curve for foreign assets by residents. Note that in this small country model the supply of foreign assets to residents is perfectly elastic. Finally, there is the BB-line which represents the combinations of r and F which equilibrate the bond market: an increase in F raises the demand for domestic bonds (through the wealth effect) and necessitates a decline in the interest rate on domestic bonds.

Capital controls now tend to make the interest sensitivity of the demand for foreign assets (b_1 in CW's paper) lower. Graphically the FF-line becomes streeper. In a portfolio balance model the wealth contraint ensures that the decline in b_1 will be matched by a decline (in absolute value) of the *sum* of the interest elasticities of the demand for bonds and money. Algebraically we have:

$$a_1 + b_1 + h_1 = 0$$

where h_1 is the interest elasticity of the demand for domestic bonds, a_1 is the interest elasticity of the demand for money.

One of the main results of CW, i.e. that in a system of capital controls the offset coefficient may increase, instead of decline, can now be understood as follows. In figure 2 the FF-line has become steeper due to capital controls.

FIGURE 2

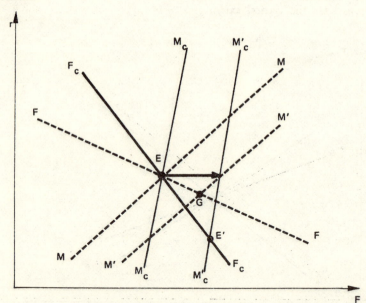

It is represented by the $F_c F_c$ line. Suppose now that as a result of capital controls the interest sensitivity of the demand for money (a_1) declines more than the interest sensitivity of the demand for foreign bonds (b_1) [Note that given the adding-up restriction, this implies that the interest sensitivity of the domestic bond demand (h_1) also decreases more than the interest sensitivity of the demand for foreign bonds]. In that case, the MM-line tends to increase its slope more than the FF-line. In figure 2, the MM-line rotates to $M_c M_c$. A monetary expansion now shifts the $M_c M_c$-line to the right (to $M'_c M'_c$). The new equilibrium point is E'. There will be an accumulation of foreign

270

assets. Thus, the monetary expansion is " offset " by a capital outflow. This accumulation of foreign assets following a domestic monetary expansion will be higher with capital controls than without. This is shown in figure 2 by comparing the effect of a monetary expansion in the absence of capital controls as represented by the shift of the MM-line to M' M'. The new equilibrium point is G, which in this case is to the left of E'. As a result, the offset coefficient is smaller in the absence of capital controls.

Theoretically this is an unlikely situation. To the extent that domestic bonds and foreign bonds are closer substitutes than domestic money and foreign bonds, one expects that the interest elasticity of the demand for domestic bonds will be more affected by capital controls than the interest elasticity of the demand for money. If this is true, the FF-line and the BB-line will become steeper, following capital controls, with a smaller effect on the slope of the MM-line. In figure 3, the (extreme) assumption is made that as a result of capital controls, the interest elasticities of the demand for domestic and foreign bonds decline in the same proportion, so that the MM-line maintains the same slope. It can then easily be shown that a monetary expansion in a system of capital controls will always reduce the offset coefficient. In the capital controls regime we move from E to E'. In a system without capital controls we move to G.

FIGURE 3

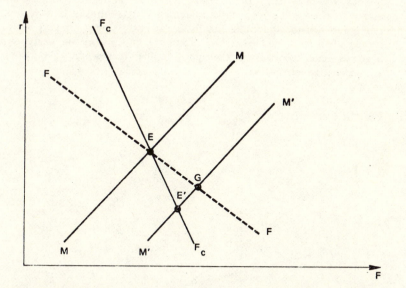

In their empirical investigation, CW observe a situation as depicted in figure 2, i.e. capital controls in France tend to increase the offset coefficient. Thus, the empirical evidence obtained by CW contradicts our theoretical priors about the degree of substitution between the different assets in the model. It should be pointed out here that CW obtain these results by an unconstrained estimation of the demand for money and the demand for foreign assets. As a suggestion for further research, a full information estimation procedure which takes into account the bond market equation might be used.

Also, it should be pointed out that the estimations for France obtained by CW imply that with increasing capital controls (as represented by the variable x) the interest elasticity of the demand for money becomes positive, and the interest elasticity of the demand for domestic bonds becomes negative. CW are aware of this (see footnote 21). However, the practical implication of this result is that in most periods of intense capital controls (as measured by the variable x) this case occurs. For example CW's results imply that with $x \geqslant 2.74$ the interest elasticity of the demand for money becomes positive. This situation occured in many periods during 1973 – 1981 as can be seen from figure 5.

2. An important feature of the French system of capital controls is that there is a permanent control system in place, which sometimes is *binding* and sometimes is not. In my opinion this feature of the French system is not modelled satisfactorily by CW.

In order to model this aspect of the French system one might start from the model represented in figure 4. Capital controls here take the form of an absolute limit on the holdings of foreign assets by residents. This is represented by the vertical line $\bar{F}$. In figure 4 it is assumed that the ceiling is binding. (The ceiling will be non-binding if the equilibrium point is to the left of the $\bar{F}$-line.) There will now be disequilibrium in the financial markets. The economy will move to a point on the line segment $\bar{F}$ between H and K. Suppose this is G. In G the interest rate is too high to equilibrate the money market. There will be excess supply of money. At the same time the interest rate is too low to equilibrate the bond market. There will also be excess supply of domestic bonds. Put differently, in G domestic wealth-owners have more domestic assets in their portfolio than they would willingly hold in an unconstrained system. [1]

FIGURE 4

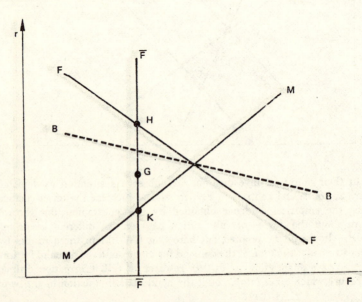

This situation will most likely lead to spill-over effects in other markets, in particular in goods markets. It may also lead to black market phenomena. It may be useful to extend the analysis into this direction.

To conclude, I want to stress that Emil CLAASSEN and Charles WYPLOSZ have done a fine job in modelling the French capital controls, and in analyzing the implications of capital controls in portfolio balance models.

---

1. Note that in the terminology of disequilibrium models, we have *a demand constrained regime* in the money and bond markets.

Comments [p 237]

by Maurice OBSTFELD*

Columbia University

Control over capital movements has emerged as a central policy issue in the 1980s. Doubt regarding the merits of free capital mobility is not a new phenomenon, of course, but it is being expressed in more urgent tones after a decade of unprecedented expansion in international financial intermediation. The CLAASSEN-WYPLOSZ paper reflects this renewed concern, as well as the multidimensional nature of the capital mobility problem.

The two questions that seem central to the paper are: What policy toward capital movements achieves the best allocation of national resources in the long run? How do capital controls affect the efficacy of short-run domestic stabilization policies? I will concentrate on these questions in this comment; but it should be kept in mind that the discussion ignores important aspects of the capital mobility problem (such as international "lender of last resort" issues) which are at the forefront of current research.

1. Long-run resource allocation

The economist's presumption is that smoothly-working markets produce Pareto-optimal outcomes; and this presumption applies to economies engaging in *intertemporal* (as well as international) trade with other economies. In assessing the need for capital account restrictions, therefore, a natural first step is identification of the market failure or distortion that endows official intervention with the potential to raise domestic welfare. The second step is to ask whether interference with international capital movement is the best way to attack the distortion in question.

Some guidance concerning the relevant considerations can be drawn from the theory of optimal policy intervention in open economies (BHAGWATI and RAMASWAMI (1963) and JOHNSON (1965) are the classics). Pareto optimality in resource allocation requires the coincidence of the domestic rate of transformation between present and future consumption, of the domestic rate of substitution between these two goods, and of the foreign rate of transformation, the rate at which present consumption can be traded for future

* Financial support from the National Science Foundation is acknowledged with thanks.

consumption on the world capital market. A divergence between the domestic rates of transformation and substitution—as could arise, for example, if domestic investment activities generated external economies, or if the product of domestic investment activity were taxed—is optimally eliminated through a countervailing subsidy to investment. If such subsidies are for some reason infeasible, there is no "second-best" presumption that a tax on international lending or borrowing will improve domestic welfare.

Capital market interventions do lead to first-best optima when the domestic rates of intertemporal substitution and transformation coincide but differ from society's foreign rate of intertemporal transformation. A divergence of this type occurs, as CLAASSEN and WYPLOSZ note, when a country's behavior influences the world rate of return, so that the economy has monopoly power in the world capital market. As in the "optimal tariff" argument, the welfare of the home country can be raised (at the foreigners' expense) through an appropriately-chosen tax on international borrowing or lending. It is clearly suboptimal, in the case of monopoly power, to eliminate intertemporal trade with the rest of the world; and both countries suffer if competitive retaliation chokes off international capital movement entirely.

Recent research on "immiserizing" capital inflows illustrates how difficult it is to design second-best policies in the presence of irreversible domestic distortions. BRECHER and DIAZ ALEJANDRO (1977), for example, demonstrate that a tariff-ridden economy can be made worse off by an inflow of foreign capital, even when that economy is small in the markets for its imports and exports. The optimal policy is the removal of the tariff, but if that is impossible, it is not at all clear that the prohibition of capital inflow is advisable. To achieve a second-best equilibrium, the gains from eliminating capital inflow must be balanced against the harm done to consumers by denying them access to the world capital market.

2. Short-run stabilization policy

The decade of booming international lending has coincided with the postwar period of generalized floating exchange rates. The abandonment of the Bretton Woods system of fixed but adjustable parities was forced in part by unmanageable speculative capital movements that undermined domestic monetary goals. While the early years of exchange-rate flexibility saw a marked loosening of capital controls, the policy autonomy predicted by JOHNSON (1969) never really materialized. Instead, the inflationary effect of exchange rate depreciation emerged as the new external constraint on the conduct of monetary policy. The recognition of this constraint gave rise to proposals by TOBIN (1978) and others recommending that short-term capital movements be impeded in order to enhance the efficacy of monetary policy. Daunting as the task may be, an evaluation of these proposals requires identification of the distortions that make stabilization policies necessary. It may well be that feasible policies other than restrictions on capital movements attack the problems at their sources.

CLAASSEN and WYPLOSZ mention sterilized foreign exchange intervention as a possible means through which a central bank can simultaneously attain independent exchange rate and monetary targets. As their empirical analysis shows, however, the issue of sterilized intervention cannot really be divorced from that of capital controls, as the degree of substitutability between domestic and foreign bonds is bound to depend on uncertainty regarding capital controls that might be imposed in the future. Unfortunately for the monetary authority, the likely instability of asset demand functions makes the use of any but the most stringent capital controls very risky, particularly when speculators are offered a one-way bet. The empirical results indicating that capital controls aggravate the capital-account offset to domestic credit policy are not surprising when viewed in this light.

● References

BHAGWATI J. N. and RAMASWAMI V. K. — (1963) "Domestic Distortions, Tariffs and the Theory of Optimal Subsidy", *Journal of Political Economy*, 71, pp. 44-50.

BRECHER R. A. and DIAZ ALEJANDRO C. F. — (1977) "Tariffs, Foreign Capital and Immiserizing Growth", *Journal of International Economics*, 7, pp. 317-322.

JOHNSON H. G. — (1965) "Optimal Trade Intervention in the Presence of Domestic Distortions" in R. E. Baldwin *et al.*, *Trade, Growth and the Balance of Payments: Essays in Honor of Gottfried Haberler*, Rand-McNally, Chicago, pp. 3-34.

JOHNSON H. G. — (1969) "The Case for Flexible Exchange Rates, 1969", *Review*, 51, pp. 12-24, Federal Reserve Bank of St. Louis.

TOBIN J. — (1978) "A Proposal for International Monetary Reform", Cowles Foundation Discussion Paper no. 506, Yale University.

The effects of economic structure and policy choices on macroeconomic outcomes in ten industrial countries

Stanley W. BLACK*

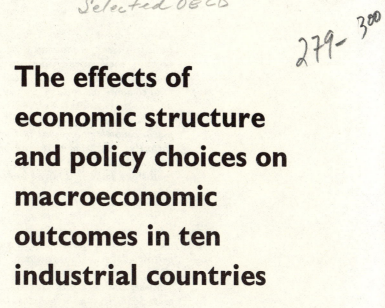

This paper seeks to explain why macroeconomic *outcomes*, such as the level and variability of inflation and unemployment, have differed widely across a group of ten industrialized countries during the 1970's. Cross-section regressions on average data for 1971-80 relate differences in outcomes to differences in economic *structure* (open-ness, dependence on oil imports), *institutions* (in the labor market and the capital market), and *policies* (as measured by monetary policy reaction functions). The results show that each of these factors matters, supporting a " political game " hypothesis that the degree of cooperation in bargaining and political control affect policy choices and the trade-off between inflation and unemployment.

W. BLACK, Vanderbilt University, USA Financial support of the Ford Foundation gratefully acknowledged.

Introduction

The techniques of macroeconomic policy-making in industrialized economies are today under attack because they have failed to perform satisfactorily during the difficult decade of the 1970's. One response is to compose an epitaph for the subject of macroeconomic theory. Another is to demonstrate the existence of a possible set of conditions under which systematic macroeconomic policy will in fact fail to perform satisfactorily. Subsequently, one may show that it is impossible to reject the hypothesis that the stated conditions hold in today's world.

The approach preferred by this writer should appeal to lovers of the detective novel. We know that, despite the general deterioration of macroeconomic conditions in most industrialized countries, some countries performed better than average while others were distinctly worse than average. Consider Arthur Okun's « misery index », the sum of the rates of consumer price inflation and unemployment, on the internationally comparable calculations of the OECD. [1] During 1965-1970, the misery index for ten industrial countries (unweighted) averaged 6.5 percent, with a range across countries from 3.5 percent to 9.1 percent and a standard deviation of 1.5 percent. During 1971-1980, the misery index averaged 13.6 percent, with a range across countries from 7.6 percent to 20.5 percent and a standard deviation of 3.8 percent. Thus not only the level of « misery » but also its dispersion increased during the 1970's.

The objective of this paper is to attempt to explain why macroeconomic performance has differed so widely across countries. If a solution to that mystery can be found, even if perhaps not beyond a reasonable doubt, it should provide at least the beginnings of an answer to what is wrong with the techniques of macroeconomic policy-making.

The methodology to be used in solving the mystery is based on cross-country comparisons. Two basic issues must be faced in applying such a methodology. First, what are the factors to be compared? And second, what is the framework or technique of the comparison? The choice of factors to be compared must inevitably depend on the underlying hypothesis about the divergence of macroeconomic performance. Several hypotheses have recently been put forth.

The « *political business cycle* » *literature* (NORDHAUS, LINDBECK) *views the politicians as Machiavellian vote-maximizers, exploiting the lag between the output effects and the price effects of expansionary macroeconomic policies to fool a myopic public into acceptance of short-run gains in output at the expense of long-run inflationary costs. The major empirical implication of this theory is a correlation between elections and the timing of expansionary macroeconomic policies, independent of the political coloration of the government.*

At the opposite extreme, the « *new classical macroeconomics* » (LUCAS, SARGENT and WALLACE) *argues that the public is so clever at anticipating policy and markets so responsive to changes in policy tools that the output effects of any systematic macroeconomic policy will be fully offset by market reactions. The* « *invisible hand* » *of the market will keep the economy in macroeconomic equilibrium if stable policies are followed. The major empirical implications are that systematic macroeconomic policies mainly affect prices rather than output, that unsystematic policies can have (deleterious) real effects, and that differences in economic structure may not be independent of differences in policies.*

---

1. *OECD Economic Outlook,* 30 (December 1981), tables R 10, R 12.

1 The problem and general approach

This paper examines the evidence for a conflict or "political game" model (BLACK [1982 *a*]) which views macroeconomic policy choices as taking place under conditions described by game theory. According to this rather Kaleckian view, income redistribution in favor of some socio-economic or political group is a "hidden agenda" item in the macroeconomic policy debates among the social partners as represented by business, labor, and other groups such as the retired or the poor. Macroeconomic outcomes for prices, wages, profits, and employment are assumed to be determined in the context of a centralized model of bargaining over nominal wages and prices.

The objectives of business and labor, in a simple case explored by BLACK [1982 *a*] depend only on the rates of increase of wages $(\hat{w})$ and prices $(\hat{p})$, which determine between them the rate of inflation, the real wage (w/p) and the shares of national output going to each group. Let us assume that the preferences of business depend positively on real after-tax profits and negatively on the variability of inflation, which represents uncertainty about the future inflation rate. Furthermore, one can expect the average tax rate on business profits to increase with the rate of inflation, if depreciation is based on historical cost data and the real value of the deduction shrinks with inflation (TIDEMAN and TUCKER [1976]). Because the variability of inflation is likely to increase with the level of inflation, these two factors (taxation and risk) will imply that after some point the benefits to business of increasing prices are outweighed by increasing tax costs and uncertainty. Similarly, business management seeking to exercise monopsony power in the labor market would be interested in reducing the real wage to a point, but not beyond it, because of diminishing returns to the increasing use of labor with a given capital stock. It is therefore assumed that the preferences of business can be represented in Figure 1 by concentric ellipses centered on the point B, denoting the "optimal" inflation and real wage from the point of view of business. Moving northeast along the lower edge of an indifference curve above the line BL, the gain from a lower real wage is offset by the cost of higher inflation. As the curve bends back beyond a 45-degree line through B (not drawn, parallel to the one shown), the real wage has been reduced too much and must be compensated by lower inflation.

The preferences of labor are assumed to depend positively on real after-tax income and negatively on the variability of inflation, again measuring uncertainty about future inflation. Both the variability of inflation and the average personal tax rate can be expected to rise with the actual inflation rate, in the absence of full indexation. In addition, there is a maximum increase in the real wage that would benefit labor unions attempting to exercise monopoly power in the labor market, if they are interested in both employment and wages. Thus, labor's preferences are assumed to be represented by concentric

282

ellipses centered around an "optimal" inflation rate and real wage represented as point L in Figure 1. Moving northeast along the top edge of an ellipse above BL, improvement in the real wage is offset by the costs of higher inflation.

The conflicting objectives of business and labor in this model can be resolved in several ways. If labor and management can bargain cooperatively, they will choose some point along the *contract curve* BL, with the actual point achieved depending on the relative bargaining power of the two parties, their ability to enforce an agreement, and their influence over the macroeconomic policies affecting inflation and employment. On the other hand, non-cooperative equilibrium could be found at the intersection N of the dashed *reaction curves* passing through points B and L of Figure 1. The curve BN represents passive price responses by business to various wage offers by labor, while the curve LN represents labor reactions to price proposals made by business. Further discussion of this model in the context of game-theoretical solutions is provided in BLACK [1982 a]. The conclusion is that the state of bargaining relationships may have a large influence on the way the macroeconomic game is played.

In an open economy, internally-generated fluctuations in real wages are usually associated with fluctuations in the balance of payments and the level of employment. For example, a rise in real wages tends to lead to unemployment and a current-account deficit, as output is reduced relative to demand. Macroeconomic policies can either support or undermine such an outcome, which requires borrowing abroad to finance the deficit and paying benefits to unemployed workers or finding them alternative employment. Political control of the macroeconomic policy tools of the government is then a tactical objective in this struggle, enhancing as it does the power of enforcing a particular outcome of the macroeconomic game.

The institutional structure of labor markets and capital markets also influences the relative bargaining power of business and labor, and thus the likelihood of conflict, cooperation, or dominance by one party or other in the macroeconomic game. Incomes policies, according to this theory, may succeed in reducing the redistributional possibilities open to the players and thus defuse the confrontational aspects of the game.

Given this basic hypothesis, the explanatory factors to be compared across countries can be grouped into differences in economic *structure,* such as open-ness, size, degree of dependence on petroleum imports; differences in economic *institutions,* such as bargaining arrangements in labor markets, indexation, and the extent and depth of securities markets; and differences in economic *policies,* such as monetary, fiscal, exchange rate, and wage/price policies. The effects of these explanatory factors on macroeconomic *outcomes,* such as inflation and unemployment, will be studied in a effort to explain the differences in outcomes. [2]

---

2. This schema is very similar to that proposed by KOOPMANS and MONTIAS [1971] relating outcomes *o* to environment *e* (here called « structure »), system *s* (here called « institutions ») and policies *p,* as

$$0 = f(e, s, p).$$

FIGURE 1.

The Political Game Model

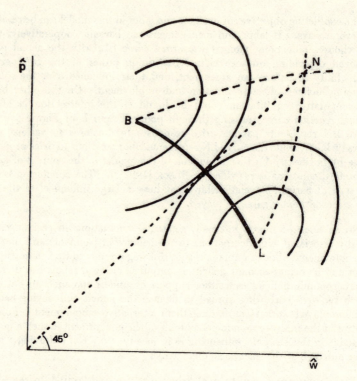

It remains to describe the technique of comparison. One possibility is to estimate a complete model of each economy, which ideally should capture in its coefficients the differences in structure and institutions. Such an approach has been advocated by AOKI [1981, ch. 5,13]. Suppose the economy is described by the system

$$(1) \qquad \dot{Z} = f(Z, X, t, \theta),$$

where Z is the state vector, X an instrument vector including exogenous variables, and θ a vector of parameters. Relative to a "reference" time path $\bar{Z}$ satisfying (1) with $X = \bar{X}$, any other time path in the neighborhood of $(\bar{Z}, \bar{X})$ will approximately satisfy

$$(2) \qquad \dot{z} = A(\theta, t) z + B(\theta, t) x,$$

where $z = (Z - \bar{Z})/\bar{Z}$ and $x = (X - \bar{X})/\bar{X}$ are relative deviations and A and B are time-varying Jacobian matrices with respect to Z and X, respectively.

With this notation, parametric differences in economic structure and institutions would be described by differences in the coefficients θ. Differences in policies, if treated as exogenous, would be incorporated into the instrument vector. The solution paths for two different countries denoted 0 and 1 could then be computed in the neighborhood of a common reference path from

$$(3) \qquad \dot{z}_1 = A(\theta_1) \, z_1 + B(\theta_1) \, x_1$$

$$(4) \qquad \dot{z}_0 = A(\theta_0) \, z_0 + B(\theta_0) \, x_0.$$

Defining

$$\delta z = z_1 - z_0, \, \delta x = x_1 - x_0, \, \delta A = A(\theta_1) - A(\theta_0), \, \delta B = B(\theta_1) - B(\theta_0),$$

we have the variational equation after subtracting (4) from (3)

$$(5) \qquad \dot{\delta z} = A(\theta_1) \, \delta z + \delta A \cdot z_0 + B(\theta_1) \, \delta x + \delta B \cdot x_0.$$

Thus one could decompose the variation in outcomes δz into that part due to parametric differences in structure and institutions (δA, δB) and that part due to differences in policies and other exogenous factors (δx). Of course, the question whether there may be some correlation between differences in structure and differences in policies would be an interesting one to study. According to the conventional, pre-rational expectations point of view, causation would run from structure to policies. But according to the newer rational expectations view, causation may run both ways. That is, the behavior of economic agents may change with different policies.

An alternative way to use the AOKI approach would rely on the concept of policy reaction functions, whereby the policy variables endogenously react to movements in target variables, other state variables, and exogenous variables. In this case, the differences in policy behavior in different countries would also be incorporated in the matrices A and B of (2), since the policy variables are included in z.

Given a decision on the treatment of policy variables, the technique of comparison would involve estimation of comparable models for all of the relevant countries, solution of those models in variational form over some time period, and evaluation of the differences in the time paths of selected target variables such as inflation and unemployment. If the models represented their respective economies adequately, the results should explain the differences in observed inflation and unemployment, at least to a reasonable degree of approximation.

This approach has actually been carried out by TAYLOR [1982], using a simple prototype model for seven large industrial economies during the 1970's. Unfortunately, the model has to be kept very simple, proxying employment by output, omitting capital flows and reserve movements as well as interest rates and fiscal policies. Interesting institutional differences relating to labor markets and capital markets cannot be dealt with. Nevertheless, the results obtained are at least suggestive and interesting.

The AOKI-TAYLOR approach attains rigor at the cost of over-simplification. In this paper an alternative approach will be followed which, it is argued, will allow the consideration of a larger and richer menu of parametric differences across countries while avoiding the necessity of constructing complete macroeconomic models, however simple, for each country. The technique is to identify on theoretical grounds certain parameters θ representing economic structure, institutions, and policy behavior. These parameters may then be estimated for each country. In AOKI's notation, we expect the differences in macroeconomic performance $z_1 - z_0$ to depend on the differences in parameters $\theta_1 - \theta_0$. Rather than estimating a complete model and *simulating* the effect of differences in parameters on macroeconomic outcomes, we can directly *test* for the effects of differences in parameters by running a cross-section regression. The dependent variable will be a measure of differences in macroeconomic outcomes, such as the average inflation rate or the standard deviation of inflation and average unemployment or the standard deviation of unemployment.

The advantage of this technique is its ability to allow the consideration of a much wider range of differences in country characteristics than the AOKI-TAYLOR approach. Thus it is particularly well-adapted to an intensive study of several different countries. There is, however, a necessary trade-off between the number of countries and the intensity with which each country is studied. In the project reported on here, the choice has been made to concentrate on the analysis of differences in macroeconomic policy behavior in seven large and three smaller industrial countries. Considerable effort has gone into estimation of the relevant country-specific parameters. The shortcoming of the technique is the limited sample size, which may leave the results rather sensitive to individual observations. Various sensitivity tests on the regressions reported below suggest that this is not a serious problem here. Another problem is the choice of independent variables. Since the focus of this study is differences in monetary policy, these variables were entered first, followed by the most obvious structural and institutional variables (petroleum dependence and labor relations). Other variables were then tested one at a time.

2 Measuring the differences among countries

2.1. Macroeconomic performance

The "misery" index contains two important measures of macroeconomic performance that should be used in any comparison, inflation and unemployment. For the sake of international comparability, annual data on consumer price indexes and the OECD-adjusted unemployment rates will be used in this paper, as specified precisely in Appendix A, with symbols. Both the mean (p) and standard deviation (sdp) of annual inflation rates over the period 1971-1980 are considered as indicators of national inflation performance, on the argument that both the level and variability of inflation have effects on economic welfare (FISCHER and MODIGLIANI [1978]). Mean and standard deviation are appropriate if the welfare function is approximated by a quadratic. As is generally understood and demonstrated in section 3 below the variability of inflation tends to increase with the level of inflation.

The extensive literature on the Phillips curve makes it clear that the relevant trade-off between inflation and unemployment is primarily a short-run phenomenon, albeit one of great significance to policy-makers. Differences between decade average unemployment rates in different countries will then mainly reflect differences in labor market structure and size of country rather than the effect of macroeconomic management. On the other hand, the standard deviation of the unemployment rate (sdu), using annual data over the period 1971-1980, should primarily reflect cyclical fluctuations associated with macroeconomic performance.

The rate of growth of output as measured by real GDP (y) and its variability (sdy) over the period 1971-1980 will also be considered as indicators of macroeconomic performance related directly to a country's ability to support consumption, the primary end of economic activity. The balance of payments can be regarded as an intertemporal constraint on foreign borrowing or lending. If this constraint was binding at some time over the decade, its effect should appear in the level and variability of inflation, output, and unemployment through the process of adjusting the payments imbalance, whether the adjustment takes the form of exchange rate movements, monetary policy, or fiscal policy. Thus, the balance of payments will be treated indirectly in the analysis of macroeconomic performance below.

2.2. Economic structure

Theory suggests several structural factors that may be of importance in explaining differences in macroeconomic performance. Two of them, openness and dependence on petroleum imports, are primarily measures of vulnerability to external inflationary shocks, although open-ness also indicates the extent to which domestic policy actions tend to spill over into the balance of payments. Dependence on petroleum imports is measured by the share of net petroleum imports in total primary energy consumption in 1973 (PETRO), according to OECD figures. Open-ness is measured by the 1973-1978 average share of imports in GDP (OPEN).

Theory also suggests that the "effectiveness" of macroeconomic policy should influence its use. Two useful measures of policy effectiveness are tne traditional Keynesian multiplier for the effect of fiscal policy on aggregate demand and the slope of the short-run Phillips curve, for the effect of a change in aggregate demand on the rate of inflation. The OECD has assembled comparable estimates of the multiplier for its cross-country studies of fiscal policy (MULT). BRUNO and SACHS, among others, have estimated Phillips curves for seven of the industrialized countries studied here (PHIL).

2.3. Institutions

The "political game" model of macroeconomic policy discussed earlier suggests that the nature of bargaining relationships in labor markets and the degree of reliance on market forces in capital markets will influence the type of macroeocnomic policies adopted. The measures of labor market relation-ships considered here include the degree of indexation in wage contracts, the degree of centralization of bargaining, the length of labor contracts, the incidence of strikes, and the overall degree of cooperation in labor-management relationships (See BLACK [1982b] for data and further discussion). Based upon investigation of these factors, the degree of strike incidence was chosen by the IDE International Research Group as a measure of the overall degree of cooperation in labor relations, and it will be used as the relevant measure here (LABREL).

Similarly, studies of the institutional structure of capital markets have considered the breadth of the market for government securities, the use of a broad or narrow monetary target, the use of open market operations versus credit controls as a monetary instrument, the use of exchange controls and the use of a pegged or floating exchange rate. Typically, countries which do not rely heavily on market forces in capital markets tend to use credit controls as an important instrument of monetary policy. Therefore, the use of credit controls (CC) will be taken as a measure of the institutional structure of capital markets.

2.4. Macroeconomic policies

Differences in the use of macroeconomic policies are rather more difficult to measure than economic structure and institutions. A recent study by the author (BLACK, [1983]) has estimated monetary policy reaction functions from monthly data over the period 1964-1979 for the ten countries examined in this paper. These reaction functions estimate the relationship of monetary policy *instruments,* such as discount rates, open market operations, credit controls, and discount quotas, to the *targets* of monetary policy, including inflation, unemployment, and the balance of payments. Their coefficients measure the relative weight given to each target in the conduct of monetary policy in each country. Cross-country comparisons are most easily based on coefficients in the discount rate reaction functions, since that instrument is used in all countries in this study.

The discount rate reaction functions are assumed to depend upon currently observed values of the inflation rate (p), unemployment (u), the ratio of reserves to imports (p/m), the ratio of exports to imports (x/m) as a proxy for the current account, competitiveness as measured by relative unit labor costs (p/ep^*) and the Euro-dollar interest rate (r^*).

$$(6) \qquad Rd = F\,(\overset{+}{p}, \overset{-}{u}, \overset{-}{f/m}, \overset{-}{x/m}, \overset{+}{p/ep^*}, \overset{+}{r^*})$$

Higher inflation, lower unemployment, or a worsened balance of payment position would be expected to lead the authorities to tighten monetary policy, as shown by the signs above the coefficients. The results of estimating these equations are reported in BLACK [1983] and summarized in Appendix B. The most important coefficients for current purposes are those giving the response of the discount rate to inflation (βp) and unemployment (βu). These coefficients thus measure the relative response of the monetary authorities in each country to a one percentage point increase in the inflation rate or the unemployment rate, *ceteris paribus.* The relative importance of external targets in the reaction functions is also of interest. This is measured by ranking across countries the size of the coefficient of each external variable in the reaction function (reserves/imports, exports/imports, relative price competitiveness, and the Euro-dollar/interest rate). Then for each country, the average rank (EXT) of its external coefficients is computed. These results are given in Table 1.

Additional variables measuring the use of fiscal policy and exchange rate policy were calculated but did not add significantly to the regression.

TABLE 1

Consistent coefficients for discount rate equations

Coefficient and Rank	BG	CN	FR	GR	IT[a]	JP	NL	SW	UK	US
Internal Variables										
p	1.21	− 0.08	0.87	1.14	0.95	0.41	0.02	0.42	− 0.22	0.79
	1	9	4	2	3	7	8	6	10	5
u	− 0.43	− 0.39	− 0.38 [b]	− 0.38	− 1.17	− 1.18 [b, c]	− 0.41 [b]	− 1.32	− 0.05	0.76
	5	5	5?	5	2	2?	5?	1	10	4
Average Rank	3	7	4.5	3.5	2.5	4.5	6.5	3.5	10	4.5
External Variables										
f/m	− 0.81	− 1.69	− 0.79	0.06	− 0.31	− 0.68	0.59	− 1.92	− 4.92	0.34
	4	3	5	9	8	6	10	2	1	7
x/m	− 1.85	1.52	− 6.77	− 0.14 [d]	− 0.85	− 7.04	− 1.63	0.08	− 10.06	0.86
	4	10	3	7	6	2	5	8	1	9
p/ep*	0.01	0.01	− 1.74	0.05	− 0.45	− 7.32	0.11	0.03	0.08	− 0.06
	5	5	9	3	8	10	1	4	2	7
r*	0.36	–	0.28	0.67	− 0.25	0.16	0.42	0.06	0.31	–
	3	8	5	1	10	6	2	7	4	9
Average Rank	4	6.5	5.5	5	7.75	6	4.5	5.25	2	8

a. Estimated Coefficient times 0.65 = 124/190 to allow for non-use in 1963-1969.
b. Not comparable as u = # unemployed/#vacancies.
c. Estimated coefficient times 0.1 based on regression of # unemployed/#vacancies on unemployment rate.
d. Independent variable is change in net foreign assets.

Source : Appendix A Table, coefficients divided by bias factor.

3 Explaining the differences in macroeconomic performance

Five measures of macroeconomic performance have now been introduced: inflation and its variability, output growth and its variability, and the variability of unemployment. A variety of parametric differences between countries have been suggested that might help to explain differences in these measures of macroeconomic performance. There are four structural factors: dependence on petroleum imports, open-ness, the size of the Keynesian multiplier, and the slope of the short-run Phillips curve; two institutional factors: labor relations and the degree of reliance on market forces in capital markets; and three policy factors: inflation and unemployment coefficients and the relative ranking of external variables in monetary policy reaction functions. The impact of discretionary and automatic fiscal policies, and the variability of the exchange rate and exchange market intervention were also considered.

Given the small number of observations available in a ten-country sample, it is obvious that only a few explanatory variables will enter any given regression. The largest number in any case below is four, including a constant term, or three economic variables. With six degrees of freedom, a t-statistic must exceed 2.447 to be significantly different from zero on a two-tailed test at the five percent level, or 1.943 on a one-tailed test at the five percent level. The F-statistic to test the overall significance of such a regression should exceed 4.76 at the five percent level or 9.78 at the one percent level. In the subsequent regressions, the actual significance level will be given in parentheses following the F-statistic.

According to equation (7), inflation differences among the ten countries can be well explained by just three variables: the responsiveness of the monetary instrument to inflation (βp), dependence on petroleum imports (PETRO), and the degree of cooperation in labor relations (LABREL).

$$p = 11.17 - 2.77\ \beta p + 5.38\ \text{PETRO} - 4.98\ \text{LABREL}$$
$$(14.3)\quad (4.0)\qquad (4.6)\qquad\qquad (6.1)$$

(7)

$$\bar{R}^2 = 0.89 \qquad\qquad F_{3,6} = 24.1\ (0.1\ \%)$$

Each of the three types of factors discussed earlier—structural, institutional, and policy—appears to play an important role in explaining differences in this aspect of macroeconomic performance. The petroleum factor helps Canada, the Netherlands, and the United States, while hurting France, Italy, Japan, and Sweden. On the other hand, labor relations help Germany, Japan, the Netherlands, and Sweden, while hurting Italy and the United Kingdom.

Figure 2 shows the partial relationship between observed inflation and the relative weight given to inflation in monetary policy. The residuals

290

FIGURE 2

Relationship between observed inflation and the relative weight given to inflation in monetary policy.

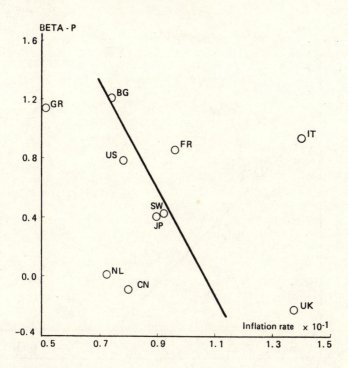

around the regression line are explained by the oil factor and labor relations, according to equation (7). Thus the high policy weight given to inflation in Belgium, Germany, and the United States helps explain their relatively good performance, while the low weight for the United Kingdom helps explain its poor performance over the period.

As suggested by the "new classical macroeconomics" literature, differences in economic structure may not be independent of differences in economic policy behavior. This hypothesis may be tested by adding an interaction term to equation (7).

$$p = 10.47 - 1.29\,\beta p + 5.62\,\text{PETRO} - 3.56\,\text{LABREL} - 3.19\,\beta p * \text{LABREL}$$
$$\quad\;\;(17.9)\;\;(1.8)\qquad(7.1)\qquad\quad(4.8)\qquad\qquad(2.9)$$

(7')

$$\bar{R}^2 = 0.95, \qquad F_{4,5} = 41.6\ (0.1\ \%)$$

This result can be interpreted in either of two ways. Either the efficacy of monetary policy is dependent on the state of labor relations (the coefficient of βp is —1.29 — 3.19 LABREL), or the beneficial effect of cooperative labor relations is strengthened by a non-accomodative monetary policy (the coefficient of LABREL is —3.56 — 3.19 βp).

FIGURE 3

Relationship between the variability of unemployment and the unemployment coefficient in the reaction function

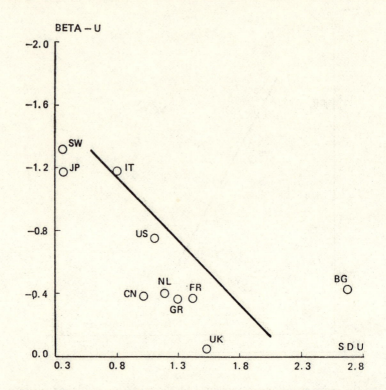

Unemployment is the second component of the "misery" index, here measured by its variability. Equation (8) shows that the variability of unemployment can be rather well explained by the policy weights given to unemployment and inflation in the monetary policy reaction function.

$$sdu = 1.61 - 1.20 \,|\,\beta u\,| + 0.64\,\beta p$$

(8)   (6.2)   (3.8)   (2.4)

$$\bar{R}^2 = 0.62 \qquad F_{2.7} = 8.38\,(1.4\,\%)$$

Thus a high weight given to unemployment in the reaction function is associated with a lower variability in unemployment, while a higher weight given to inflation is associated with a higher variability in unemployment. Figure 3 shows the partial relationship between the variability of unemployment and the unemployment coefficient in the reaction function. It seems evident that policy choices have played a significant role in explaining these differences.

The role of differences in monetary policy behavior in explaining inflation and the variability of unemployment suggests a Phillips-curve type of trade-off, in this case between inflation and the variability of unemployment.

FIGURE 4

Relationship between the variability of unemployment and inflation

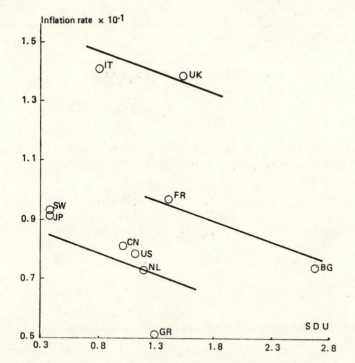

It is already clear from equation (7) that other factors will enter this relationship. Equation (9) shows that there is a very strong relationship and that these other factors are the institutional properties of labor markets and capital markets.[3] Figure 4 indicates that there are virtually three separate trade-offs, depending on the state of cooperation in labor market relationships. Given a high degree of cooperation in labor markets, Sweden and Japan have chosen to avoid variability in unemployment at the cost of somewhat higher inflation, while the Netherlands and Germany have made the opposite choice. Among countries with more difficult labor relations, Belgium has accepted the heaviest unemployment cost to control inflation, while the United States, Canada, and France placed less weight on fighting inflation and/or more weight on unemployment during the 1970s. Finally, Italy and the United Kingdom are in a class by themselves, with poor labor relations generating an extremely unfavorable trade-off.

$$p = 13.33 - 1.94\,sdu - 6.14\,\text{LABREL} + 2.60\,\text{CC}$$

(9)   (22.0)   (6.6)   (14.2)   (7.8)

$$\bar{R}^2 = 0.97 \qquad F_{3,6} = 102.9\,(0.01\%)$$

---

3. Equation (9) was estimated via two-stage least-squares, using βp and βu as instrumental variables for *sdu*.

The level and variability of the growth of output cannot be as well explained by the factors considered in this paper as the components of the "misery" index. The average rate of growth of output is perhaps naturally more a matter of supply-side factors such as the growth of capital and labor inputs and productivity. On the other hand, equation (10) indicates a weak relationship between the variability of output growth and labor relations, along with the level of growth.

$$sdy = 2.14 + 0.19y - 0.58 \text{ LABREL}$$
(10)
$$(5.5) \quad (1.6) \quad (2.2)$$
$$\bar{R}^2 = 0.32 \qquad F_{2,7} = 3.15 \ (10.5\%)$$

The variability of inflation is as noted earlier positively related to the average rate of inflation, and also to the variability of output growth.

$$sdp = -5.01 + 0.28p + 2.46 sdy$$
(11)
$$(3.1) \quad (2.7) \quad (3.2)$$
$$\bar{R}^2 = 0.78 \qquad F_{2,7} = 16.9 \ (0.2\%)$$

Conclusion

It is time for recapitulation of the evidence and analysis of the solution of the puzzle—why macroeconomic performance has differed so much among industrialized countries. The slowdown in growth, the increase in unemployment, and higher inflation have been endemic in the 1970's. Major differences in macroeconomic performance—the levels of the trade-offs in figure 4—appear to be due to differences in the institutional conditions in capital markets and labor markets that affect the bargaining environment in which wage and price decisions are taken. This finding is consistent with the "political game" model discussed in section 1 of the paper. Countries with cooperative labor-management relationships and emphasis on market forces in capital markets appear to reach better macroeconomic solutions to their internal problems.

Secondly, given these institutional conditions, the orientation of monetary policy towards fighting inflation or unemployment appears to have a significant effect on the resulting mix of inflation and variability of unemployment. This finding is also consistent with the "political game" model, which suggests that political factors influence the choice of macroeconomic policy.

Data Appendix

Country Codes:

BG Belgium;   JP Japan;
CN Canada;   NL Netherlands;
FR France;   SW Sweden;
GR Germany;   UK United Kingdom;
IT Italy;   US United States.

Measures of Performance:

p Annual average inflation rate, 1971-1980, OECD, *Economic Outlook*, 30 (December 1981), Table R 10, Consumer prices;

sdp Standard deviation of annual inflation rate, 1971-1980, same source;

sdu Standard deviation of unemployment rate, 1971-1980, same source, Table R 12, Standardized unemployment rates;

y Annual average growth rate of real GDP, 1971-1980, same source Table R 1;

sdy Standard deviation of output growth, 1971-1980, same source.

Structural Variables:

PETRO   1973 ratio of net oil imports to total primary energy consumption, OECD, *Energy Balances of OECD Countries.*

OPEN   1973-1978 average import/GDP ratio, OECD, *National Account of OECD Countries*, vol. I, 1980.

MULT   First year unlinked multiplier for effect of government non-wage expenditure on real GNP, OECD, *Economic Outlook Occasional Studies* (July 1980), "Fiscal Policy Simulations with the OECD International Linkage Model", Table 2 A.

PHIL   Estimated effect of manhours on wages, Bruno and Sachs (1979), Table 2.

Institutional Variables:

LABREL   Degree of cooperation of unions and employers, High (1), Medium (0.5), or Low (0), according to Table 14.3 of *European Industrial Relations* (Oxford, 1981), p. 266. Values interpolated by the author: Japan (1), US (0.5), Canada (0.5);

CC   Reliance on credit controls as a primary instrument of monetary policy, Black (1983), Appendix on Institutions.

Policy Variables:

βp Response of central bank discount rate to inflation, based on
OLS regression from monthly data 1964-1979, correcting for
estimated bias due to "threshold" effect, text, table 1;

βu Response of central bank discount rate to unemployment, same
source as above;

EXT   Average rank by size of coefficient of response of central bank
discount rate to four external variables — reserves/imports,
exports/imports, relative price competitiveness, Eurodollar
interest rate, same source as above.

Appendix B

Sources: IFS International Financial Statistics (IMF, Washington).
     MEI Main Economic Indicators (OECD, Paris).

Country Codes:

BG Belgium;	JP Japan;
CN Canada;	NL Netherlands;
FR France;	SW Sweden;
GR Germany;	UK United Kingdom;
IT Italy;	US United States.

SA indicates seasonal dummies used.

Dependent Variable:

RD   Central bank discount rate, percent, end of month. IFS *l.*60.

Independent Variables (lagged one period, where indicated):

$\hat{p}_{-1}$ Rate of change of consumer price index. IFS *l.*64;

u_{-1} Unemployment rate, except for FR, JP, NL—number of unem-
ployed/number of vacancies. MEI;

gap_{-1} Manufacturing output, deviation from exponential trend up
to 197401. IFS *l.*66c;

$(f/m)_{-1}$ Foreign exchange reserves/imports. IFS *l.*1*d.d./l.*71*d*;

$(x/m)_{-1}$ Exports/imports. IFS *l.* 70*d/l.* 71*d*, except GR, change in
net foreign assets of central bank. IFS *l.*11;

$(p/ep^*)_{-1}$ Relative normalized unit labor costs, corrected for exchange
rates. IFS *l.*65 umc;

r*   Three-month Eurodollar rate of interest, in percent, end of
      period. IFS *l.*60*d* (UK);

t   Time trend.

Dummy Variables:

BG   D 1 Use of required reserves;

CN   D 1 Since Quebec Separatist election victory; D 2 During
      agreement with US on reserve ceiling;

FR   D 1 After Giscard's election before re-entry into Snake; D 2
      Strikes;

GR   D 1 Availability of dollar swaps with central bank;

IT   D 1 Period of communist strength in elections;

JP   D 1 Period of policy to aid "Yen shift": repayment of foreign
      borrowings; D 2 Commencement of open market opera-
      tions at market prices.

NL   D 1 Periods of interregnum; D 2 Use of required reserve sys-
      tem;

SW   D 1 "Bourgeois" parties in power; D 2 Floating exchange rate;

UK   D 1 From August to December 1971; D 2 Increases in January
      1974, and January 1979; D 3 Heath goverment; D 4
      Thatcher government;

US   D 1 Increases in January 1974 and January 1979; D 2 Price
      and wage controls; D 3 New policy of exchange market
      intervention; D 4 Adoption of monetary target with more
      flexible interest rates; D 5 Capital account controls.

Bias Factor for OLS Regression:

As explained in Black (1983, Appendix on Threshold Regression), when
the dependent variable is only adjusted infrequently, the appropriate statistical model is *threshold* regression, in which the dependent variable adjusts
to equal the value of the regression function only if the implied change
exceeds an estimated threshold value. Under certain assumptions, it is
possible to calculate consistent estimates of the regression coefficients by
means of a simple correction to the ordinary least squares estimates.

The intuition behind the correction can be explained if one considers
the *desired* change in the dependent variable, from (6), say $z^* = rd^* - rd_{-1}$,
as a normally distributed random variable with mean μ and variance σ^2.

POLICY CHOICES 297

APPENDIX B
Monthly discount rate reaction functions, 1963-1979

	BG	CN	FR	GR	IT	JP_SA	NL	SW	UK	US
$\hat{p}_{-1}$	0.87 (4.2)	—0.06 (0.3)	0.46 (2.0)	0.72 (3.4)	0.82 (4.0)	0.23 (2.6)	0.01 (0.1)	0.22 (3.3)	—0.21 (1.6)	0.55 (3.5)
u_{-1}	—0.31 (4.6)	—0.28 (2.8)	—0.20 (6.6)	—0.24 (3.2)	—1.01 (4.6)	—6.60 (3.7)	—0.26 (2.8)	—0.70 (9.3)	—0.05 (0.2)	—0.53 (10.0)
$(f/m)_{-1}$	—0.58 (1.5)	—1.20 (7.2)	—0.42 (3.2)	0.04 (0.5)	0.27 (1.5)	—0.38 (6.3)	0.38 (1.4)	—1.02 (12.9)	—4.72 (5)	—0.24 (1.2)
$(x/m)_{-1}$	1.33 (1.3)	1.08 (1.1)	—3.59 (3.2)	—0.09 (1)	0.73 (0.6)	3.94 (6.3)	1.04 (1.0)	0.04 (0.1)	—9.66 (3.2)	0.60 (1.3)
$(p/ep^*)_{-1}$	0.01 (0.5)	0.01 (0.8)	—0.92 (0.2)	0.03 (2.0)	—0.25 (9.4)	—4.10 (3.5)	0.07 (3.2)	0.013 (2.5)	0.074 (2.5)	—0.04 (6.1)
r^*	0.26 (6.9)		0.15 (4.4)	0.42 (11.1)	0.14 (2.8)	0.09 (1.9)	0.27 (7.8)	0.03 (1.4)	0.30 (2.7)	
time	0.024 (6.7)	0.018 (4.8)	0.046 (14.4)	—0.015 (3.2)	0.032 (5.4)	0.01 (2.7)	—0.002 (0.8)	0.007 (6.3)	0.135 (3.9)	—0.005 (1.4)
gap_{-1}	—1.36 (5.3)	—2.59 (6.3)	—2.08 (7.9)	—1.25 (7.6)	2.26 (6.4)	8.21 (4.6)				
D1		—1.02 (4)	—1.10 (1.2)			1.71 (8.7)	1.56 (7.8)	1.09 (5.7)	—1.46 (1.5)	2.14 (6.9)
D2						—0.50 (1.9)	0.62 (2.7)	0.37 (1.7)	1.25 (1.9)	0.79 (4.8)
D3									1.69 (2.9)	2.49 (12.2)
D4									1.29 (1.5)	2.24 (7.2)
D5										1.56 (9)
R^2	0.64	0.82	0.90	0.64	0.92	0.63	0.68	0.82	0.85	0.93
P	0.25	0.24	0.14	0.19	0.15	0.15	0.19	0.14	0.60	0.23
B	0.72	0.71	0.53	0.63	0.56	0.56	0.64	0.53	0.96	0.70
Se	0.98	0.94	0.88	0.84	0.99	0.80	0.70	0.47	1.15	0.48

Note : *t* ratios in parentheses; P is percent of observations with change in Rd, B is bias factor for OLS regression, Se is standard error of regression.

Then the *observed* change z will be equal to zero unless $z^* \geqslant k$ or $z^* \leqslant -k$, where k is the threshold, in which cases it is equal to z^*. If we standardize to $(z^* - \mu)/\sigma$, there is a central region of the standard normal distribution whose area corresponds to the percentage of "no change" cases, an upper tail whose area corresponds to the percentage P_1 of "increases", and a lower tail corresponding to the percentage P_2 of "decreases". The abscissas of the boundaries of these areas are easily shown to be $-(k + \mu)/\sigma$ and $(k - \mu)/\sigma$ which can be estimated from the sample proportions P_1 and P_2.

It can be shown that the variance of the observed changes z is a downward-based estimate of the variance of the desired changes, with a bias factor approximately equal to $B = P_1 + P_2 + \dfrac{k}{\sigma}(f_1 + f_2)$, where f_1 and f_2 are the ordinates of the standard normal corresponding to the abscissas of the boundary points noted above. Similarly, it can be shown that the ordinary least squares regression coefficients are biased downward by a factor exactly equal to B.

● References

AOKI M. — (1981) *Dynamic Analysis of Open Economies,* New York, Academic Press.

BLACK S., W. — (1980) *Central bank intervention and the stability of exchange rates,* Seminar Paper No. 136, Institute for International Economic Studies, University of Stockholm.

—— (1982 *a*) "Strategic aspects of the political assignment problem in open economies", *in* Lombra, Raymond E. and Witte, Willard E., eds., *The political economy of domestic and international monetary relations.* Ames, Iowa State University Press.

—— (1982 *b*) *Politics versus markets : international differences in macroeconomic policies,* Washington : American Enterprise Institute for Public Policy.

—— (1983) « The use of monetary policy for internal and external balance in ten industrial countries », In Frenkel, Jacob, ed., *Exchange rates and international macroeconomics.* Chicago, University of Chicago Press forthcoming. Also Working Paper No. 81, W13 Revised, Department of Economics and Business Administration, Vanderbilt University.

BRUNO M. and SACHS J. — (1982) "Supply versus demand approaches to the problem of stagflation", *Weltwirtschaftliches Archiv* 118.

FISCHER S. and MODIGLIANI F. — (1978) "Towards an understanding of the real effects and costs of inflation", *Weltwirtschaftliches Archiv* 114, 810-833.

IDE International Research Group. — (1981) *European industrial relations.* Oxford, Clarendon Press.

KOOPMANS T. C. and MONTIAS J. M. — (1971) "On the description and comparison of economic systems", *in* Eckstein, Alexander, ed., *Comparison of economic systems,* Berkeley, University of California Press.

LINDBECK A. — (1976) "Stabilization Policies in Open Economies with Endogenous Politicians", *American Economic Review Papers and Proceedings*, 66, 1-19.

LUCAS R. E., Jr. — (1976) "Econometric Policy Evaluation : A Critique", *in* Brunner, Karl and Meltzer, Allan H., eds., *The Phillips Curve and Labor Markets*, Amsterdam, North-Holland.

NORDHAUS W. — (1975) « The Political Business Cycle », *Review of Economic Studies*, 42, 169-190.

SARGENT T. J. and WALLACE N. — (1975) « "Rational" Expectations, the Optimal Monetary Instrument, and the Optimal Money Supply Rule », *Journal of Political Economy* 83, 241-257.

TAYLOR J. B. — (1982) "Macroeconomic tradeoffs in an international economy with rational expectations", *in* Hildenbrand, Werner, ed., *Advances in Econometrics*, Cambridge, Cambridge University Press, forthcoming.

TIDEMAN T. N. and TUCKER D. P. — (1976) "The Tax Treatment of Profits Under Inflationary Conditions", *in* Aaron, Henry J., ed., *Inflation and the Income Tax*, Washington, The Brookings Institution.

Comments

by **Giorgio BASEVI**
University of Bologna

Let me say frankly, if bluntly, that I find this latest one in a long series of papers produced by BLACK on the subject of comparing industrial countries' economic policy a disappointing product. And the reason lies less with the poverty of results than with the height of expectations which the author somewhat imprudently generates on the part of the reader in his introductory remarks. Thus the stated objective of the paper is to attempt to explain why macroeconomic performance has differed so widely across countries, and also, possibly, what is wrong with the techniques of macroeconomic policy making.

For this purpose differences in measures of economic performance should be attributed to differences in variables that might be usefully classified in three categories:

(*a*) economic structure, (*b*) economic institutions, (*c*) economic policies.

The well-known criticism of the rational expectation theorists whereby category (*a*) is not independent of category (*c*) is immediately evoked by BLACK, thus generating in the apprehensive reader the comfortable feeling that something will be done about it. The tiring perspective of having to build complete models for each economy, capable of capturing international differences in structure and institutions and thus allowing allocation of differences in performance to the three categories of variables stated above, is dismissed by BLACK, with relief to the reader, as unnecessary. Moreover, such an approach, although more rigorous, is indicated as dangerous because of the cost of oversimplification that econometric model-builders usually have to pay at the expense of realism when dealing with multicountry models.

The reader is thus induced to expect a strategy for research that should be full-proof to the rational expectations criticism and at least as rich in design than the alternative strategy dismissed by the author: "the advantage of this technique is its ability to allow the consideration of a much wider range of differences in country characteristics than the AOKI-TAYLOR approach" (BLACK, p. 286).

However, the use of the proposed technique is from the beginning limited by the smallness of the cross-country sample size. Yet, while the ten sample observations available to the author allow little room for testing the connection between measures of economic performance and measures of structural, institutional and policy control variables, BLACK seemingly avoids the problem by limiting the number of explanatory variables and thereby obtaining statistically significant results. But the cost of this procedure is that we are confronted again with the oversimplification of reality which the proposed technique was supposed to avoid relative to the alternative of building multicountry econometric models. Moreover, not only we are limited to explaining differences in economic performance with a maximum of three economic variables and a constant; what is more, we are not told whether and how the numerous combinations of variables which could have been chosen for analysis have been confronted and discarded. Thus it appears (from an earlier version of the paper) that the author had a choice of four structural, two institutional, and seven policy variables, plus some number of dummy variables and the constant. Even leaving aside this latter group, the possible combinations of three explanatory variables out of a total of thirteen are 286. Considering that there are five measures of economic performance as candidates for dependent variables, we obtain a total of 1430 possible regressions. This number could indeed be greatly reduced by imposing, as the author seems to suggest, that the explanatory variables belong each to a different class (structural, institutional, policy); in this case the theoretical number of regressions is reduced to a minimum of 56 (to a total of 280 considering the alternative of five dependent variables).

Out of so large a choice, only two basic regressions are presented [equations (7) and (8)], and we are not told what happened to the remaining lot. Moreover, this lot is greatly enlarged by the procedure followed in equations (9)-(11), where among the explanatory variables some of the economic performance variables themselves are introduced. While this detour is taken for the purpose of briefly discussing the trade-offs between economic objectives, it does not clearly fit in with the general purpose and proposed technique of the paper.

The claim to richness of detail as opposed to oversimplification is thus not respected in the author's application of the proposed technique. As to the rational expectations criticism to which the alternative technique would be exposed, it is not clear how the present one avoids it. True enough, equation (7') is an attempt to allow for the fact that differences in economic structure may not be independent of differences in economic policy behaviour. However, rather than giving a systematic treatment to this problem with appropriate estimation techniques, the author in equation (7') simply allows the coefficient of an institutional variable to depend upon the state of a policy variable. The constraint thus implied in equation (7') could have been tested as against equation (7); this is not done, leaving the reader with the impression of hurried *ad hoc* work. Moreover, and what seems to me most damaging, the partition itself of variables into policy variables on one side, and the other variables on the other side, is incorrect in so far as the policy variables used by BLACK (i.e.: the estimates of coefficients in each country's reaction functions) do not simply measure "the relative weight given to each target in the conduct of monetary policy in each country" (BLACK, p. 288). As is well known, coefficients of reaction functions are a combination of parameters that are structural, institutional and weights in the authorities' objective functions. They cannot therefore be separated from the other two classes of variables used by BLACK in explaining economic performance.

Leaving aside a few other problems—such as testing for a positive relation between mean and standard deviation of inflation (a relation which is inherent in the definition of standard deviation); including a measure of openness together with the size of the multiplier without considering that the latter depends on the former—it seems possible to conclude that by distilling so much out of his previous careful studies of industrial countries' economic policies BLACK has wasted the richness and flavor of reality that were contained in those studies, and thus proved against his stated assertion that there is no short-cut to a deep and detailed study of specific countries' historical experiences, when the purpose is to throw light on the question of why macroeconomic performance differs so widely across countries.

Comments

by John P. MARTIN
OECD*

This paper is very ambitious since Stan BLACK's aim is nothing less than to explain the mystery of why some countries recorded a much more satisfactory macroeconomic performance than others over the last decade. Since I work for an organisation which has this issue under continuous review, I naturally read the paper with great interest.

My comments on the paper are organised around four main themes: (*i*) the underlying "political game" model; (*ii*) the measurement of institutional differences between countries; (*iii*) "heroic econometrics"; and (*iv*) lack of social consensus as the villain of the piece.

1. The "Political Game" model

Right at the outset we are told that the underlying hypothesis rests on political game-theoretic considerations. Unfortunately, only a sketchy outline of the model is given here and the reader is referred to another paper by BLACK for further details. In essence, it appears to rest on the simple hypothesis that arguments over appropriate factor income shares are a key agenda item in discussions between the social partners and government. Thus, BLACK argues that macroeconomic performance is determined " in the context of a centralized model of bargaining over nominal wages and prices ".

While a centralised bargaining structure may be an important ingredient in resolving " competing claims " in a non-inflationary way, it does not function in a political vacuum. Here the model ignores an important strand of research in the recent literature on political economy which assumes that consumer-voters evaluate governments on the basis of their revealed economic performance. Politicans in turn attempt to manage the economy in order to maximise their votes, and, thereby, ensure their own survival in office. Thus, liberal-democratic societies have a clear potential for electorally-motivated business cycles. Such cycles arise not so much from a lack of social consensus but rather from vote-loss-minimizing behavior by the government confronted by a myopic electorate and a dynamic trade-off between inflation and unemployment.

I would argue it is a mistake to neglect such factors in any model that claims to be founded on political game-theoretic considerations. The government's ability to negotiate with the social partners and deliver effectively its side of the bargain is also highly constrained by given institutional arrangements and voters' perceptions of its actions.

---

* The opinions expressed are my own and they cannot be held to represent the views of the OECD.

2. Measuring the institutional differences across countries

BLACK argues that the difference in macroeconomic outcomes between countries can be traced to differences in economic structure, institutions and policies. The reader is faced with a long and bewildering list of possible explanatory variables. BLACK identifies four possible proxies for economic structure, two for institutional factors and no less than seven for economic policies. This is an *embarras de richesse*, the more so since one is given few details on the proxy measures.

For example, consider the proxy variable for the state of bargaining relationships in the labour market. BLACK lists a wide range of factors influencing the structure of collective bargaining and then baldly states that, as the IDE International Research Group selected " the degree of strike incidence... as a measure of cooperation in labor relations ", he will do the same. I am, however, unhappy with a measure of the degree of co-operation in the industrial relations system which just relies on strike incidence alone and ignores other important institutional elements. There is also no recognition that measures of industrial conflict are not exogenous variables but are themselves influenced by economic, political and sociological factors.

The same sleight-of-hand appears with the proxy for the degree of reliance on market forces in capital markets. We are given a tantalising reference to "studies of the institutional structure of capital markets" which have apparently examined all the relevant features. Then he bravely plumps for the use of credit controls as a proxy measure. When one looks up the Data Appendix to find out more information about this variable, one is referred to the Appendix of another unpublished paper by BLACK !

3. "Heroic econometrics"

BLACK uses cross-section regressions in order to estimate the separate effects of differences in economic structure, institutions and policies on macroeconomic outcomes. However, as he freely admits, there is one overriding problem with this approach. He has identified no less than thirteen possible explanatory variables but his sample consists of only ten observations.

I would argue that applying classical regression methods to such a small sample is not appropriate. Some of the equations reported have only five degrees of freedom. With so few degrees of freedom you only need one outlier with a bad inflation or unemployment record and a high incidence of strikes (e.g. Italy or the United Kingdom) to produce highly significant t-statistics and apparently well-determined relationships.

If BLACK wants to use regression methods for a comparative study of this kind, then he would be better advised to generate a much larger sample using mixed cross-section and time-series data. Assuming it is possible to collect sufficient time-series data, he could then apply classical regression methods to the pooled sample. If this is not possible I think it would be more fruitful to apply covariance analysis to his data set rather than regression methods.

4. Is lack of "Social Consensus" the villain of the story ?

Figure 4 appears to sum up the main message of the paper since it displays three separate trade-offs, depending on the state of co-operation in the industrial relations system. The villain of the piece, as unmasked by BLACK, appears to be none other than our old friend, lack of social consensus. Nor is he alone in this choice of the villain. McCALLUM [1981] comes to a similar conclusion based on a comparative analysis of differences in inflation performance among eighteen OECD countries in the 1970s. Social consensus is proxied by a measure of long-run strike activity and his econometric results show that a simple social consensus model fits the data much better than a simple monetary model.

What can we conclude from these results? Clearly the analyses of BLACK and McCALLUM suggest that the fostering of social consensus is a major factor in improving macroeconomic performance. The trouble is we have no real idea on how to set about this task nor is it clear that economists have any comparative advantage in this field.

One could argue that the institutional framework of collective bargaining is very important and that the poor macroeconomic performers should try to import features from the more successful countries. The problem is that there are several alternative models on offer. Take Austria and Switzerland which are two countries with a relatively good record in the 1970s. Austria has one of the most centralised systems of collective bargaining and there is continuous involvement of government in wage and price negotiations. Wage bargaining procedures in Switzerland, on the other hand, are extremely decentralised and the government adopts a hands-off approach. Social consensus is then not an easy dish to prepare even if it is such a vital factor.

Finally, I would conclude by drawing attention to the total divergence between the approach adopted here and the views of the equilibrium business cycle theorists as represented by Robert LUCAS. In his recent book LUCAS [1981] goes so far as to deny the influence of factors such as social consensus. He points out that business cycles display major regularities in all decentralized market economies. From this he concludes that " *business cycles are all alike* " and argues that this " suggests the possibility of a unified explanation of business cycles, grounded in the *general* laws governing market economies, rather than in political or institutional characteristics " (LUCAS [1981], p. 218, emphasis in original). I would like to be convinced of this but somehow I feel that Messrs. BLACK and McCALLUM have put their fingers on something important that economists find it all too easy to overlook.

● References

LUCAS R. E. — (1981) *Studies in Business Cycle Theory*, Oxford: Basil Blackwell.

Mc CALLUM J. — (1981) "Inflation and Social Consensus: Eighteen OECD Countries in the Seventies", Mimeo, Simon Fraser University, August.

(p. 279

[279] [307]

307

1331
0259
Selected
OECD

Reply to Basevi

by Stanley BLACK

Vanderbilt University

BASEVI's remarks raise the question of over-simplification of reality, because my sample size limits me to three or four economic variables to explain cross-country differences in inflation. And he believes I have wasted the richness of detail that my earlier studies contained. He also suggests I may have been data-mining, presenting only the significant regressions out of a large number of possible combinations.

Perhaps my introduction misled BASEVI as to the place of this paper in my series of studies. Having devoted heavy labor to the estimation of reaction functions and to the study of differences between countries' economic structure and institutions in earlier papers, I sought some means of effectively summarizing the results of my studies. A natural approach was to consider scatter diagrams, which were first presented in my paper in Cambridge at the NBER in November 1981.

In response to criticism of that approach by LEIDERMANN and STOCKMAN, I was led to quantify the scatter diagrams by means of simple regression equations, which then turned out to have far better statistical properties than I had any right to expect. Very few of the hypothetical regressions that BASEVI suggests were carried out, because the first few structural and policy variables worked so well. I have a total of 20 regressions in my working tabulations, compared to the 6 reported in the paper. These regressions are rather robust to the deletion of individual observations, as noted at the end of section 1 of the paper.

I believe that if the paper is read in the context of the earlier ones, it simply draws together and summarizes their findings, albeit in a very succinct manner. I had thought that the simplicity of the results would be a major appeal.

But people can disagree on such questions, as we clearly seem to. Concerning the minor points BASEVI raises, I never tried to use both open-ness and the multiplier in the same regression, although it is clear they are related as he notes. And I see no reason to be sure that populations should automatically be heteroscedastic simply because the standard deviation is measured about the mean.

Fiscal and monetary policies under a flexible exchange-rate system

Jean-Pierre LAFFARGUE *

*REMAP and University
ille II. I am grateful to
Direction de la Previ-
which financed this
arch, and to the partici-
ts at a seminar at the
ction de la Prévision,
at the ROY-MALINVAUD
inar at CNRS, for their
ful comments and sug-
ions on preliminary ver-
s of this paper. Special
ks are due to Jacques
ITZ and Charles WYPLOSZ
gave me a lot of help in
roving this paper, to my
commentators and to the
ticipants at the conference
Fontainebleau. All errors
imperfections are my
onsibility.

The main purpose of this paper is to investigate the consequences over time of monetary
and fiscal decisions taken by the government
of a small country under a flexible exchange
rate system. A numerically specified model
of 20 equations is used for that purpose This
model has been inspired by large French Keynesian econometric models, but important simplifications have been made and rational
expectations of the exchange rate have been
assumed. The next purpose of the paper is to
present internal evaluation methods of macroeconomic models, which permit a clear economic interpretation of their consequences.
The results clearly show that the effects of
economic policy are extremely sensitive to the
degree of substitutability between national and
foreign assets in the investors' portfolios.

Introduction

This paper considers a small country (SC) in an international environment unified under the denomination of the rest of the world (RW), and under a flexible exchange rate system. The first purpose of the paper is to investigate the consequences over time of monetary and fiscal decisions taken by the SC Government. The analysis proceeds on a model of SC. The structure of the model is very much in conformity with the standard Keynesian structure of large econometric models of the French economy, but some important simplifications have been made. The size of the model is 20 equations. In order to get precise results on the dynamic path followed by the economy, the equations of the model have been entirely specified. The values of the parameters have been fixed to the values usually given by econometric studies of the French economy. The initial state of the model has been taken as similar to the state of the French economy in 1976 [1].

The second purpose of the paper is to present internal evaluation methods of the model, which allows an economic interpretation of its complicated dynamic interactions. These methods decompose these interactions into simple mechanisms generated by small reference models. The size of the model has been scaled down to limit the number of elementary mechanisms into which its dynamics is decomposed. But the same method could have been applied to a larger and more satisfactory model of the French economy: the paper would not have been essentially more complicated, only longer and more cumbersome.

The structure of the model follows the traditional IS-LM line, completed by a PHILLIPS equation, a price equation, and a production function with technical progress. SC and RW each produces one commodity. These commodities can be exchanged internationally, and are imperfect substitues. The degree of substituability depends on the terms of trade. The perfect mobility of international capital flows and uncovered interest parity are assumed. The future values of the spot exchange rate are rationally expected.

The consequences of two economic policy decisions are investigated. The first, which is called fiscal policy, is defined as a permanent increase of SC government consumption by 10 % above its reference path (*the supply of SC money is kept unchanged*). The second, which is called monetary policy, consists of a permanent increase of SC money supply by 10 % above its reference path (*SC government budget is kept unchanged*). SC government budget and trade balance deficits are financed by borrowing.

The positive effect of fiscal policy on SC production is limited by a deterioration of the competitivity of SC (*measured by the terms of trade*) and a increase in its interest rate. The fact that fiscal policy is not accomodated by monetary policy causes this last result and a decrease of SC commodity price. Consequently SC currency appreciates for approximately the same reasons as in the seminal papers by FLEMING [8] and MUNDEL [12].

Monetary policy implies a sudden depreciation of SC currency, a transitory but sharp decrease of SC interest rate and a progressive increase of SC commodity price. This induces a decrease of SC user cost of capital which has a positive effect on SC investment and production.

The model is presented in Section 1. Balanced-growth paths and long-run multipliers are investigated in Section 2. Dynamic multipliers are defined, computed and given an economic interpretation in Section 3.

---

1. The same method as the one in this paper had already been used to investigate the effects of fiscal policy in a closed economy by LAFFARGUE [10].

1 The model (table 1)

Time is divided into periods. The model represents a small country (SC) in an international environment presented under the general title of the rest of the world (RW). There are two financial assets, each of a duration of one period. The first is denominated in SC currency and earns an interest rate i. The second is denominated in RW currency and earns an interest rate $\bar{i}$. If e represents the spot exchange rate and e^f the forward-exchange rate one period hence (the price of RW currency in terms of SC currency), we have the arbitrage equation :

$$(1 + i)\, e = (1 + \bar{i})\, e^f \qquad (1)$$

Speculators are assumed to expect with certainty that the spot exchange rate in the next period will take the value ${}_0 e^a_{+1}$. We have the equilibrium relation :

$$e^f = {}_0 e^a_{+1} \qquad (2)$$

The expectations of speculators are rational : speculators are assumed to know the model, the values taken by exogenous variables, and the present and past values of the economic policy variables; they hold forecasts of the future values of the economic policy variables. (1) and (2) give equation (4) of table 1.

The rest of the model assumes an IS-LM framework completed by a price and a PHILLIPS equation. Large French econometric models have the same structure, but strong simplifications are made here. I will briefly present the main features of the model.

SC and RW each produce a separate and unique good. These goods are imperfect substitutes. In order to simplify the model I have assumed that SC imports of RW commodity can only be consumed by SC households. The SC commodity can be consumed by SC households and government, can be invested, and can be exported. At a given date SC firms foresee that the demand for their product for the current and the following periods, will fluctuate around a permanent component. This component is denoted Q^* for the current period and grows at rate g, which is the natural growth rate of SC. Growth only results from technical progress and capital accumulation, as labor is assumed to be fixed. In the same way these firms foresee a permanent user cost of capital q^* (constant over time) and a permanent real rate of wages. The current value of this last variable is ω^*, and it grows at rate g. At this date SC firms determine their desired capital and labor for the current and future periods. They make their choice by minimizing their expected production cost under the constraint that the production function imposes on expected and desired values, for each of the present and future periods. I use N* to denote the desired employment of labor which is constant over time, and K* for the present value of the desired capital stock. This capital stock grows at rate g over time. Equations (5) and (6) of table 1 formalise this behavior.

Firms determine their investment I of the period in such a way that the ratio between effective and desired capital stocks at the end of the period is a geometric mean between the value of this ratio at the beginning of the period and 1 [eqs. (7) and (8)]. The permanent user cost of capital q^* is related to the permanent interest and inflation rates expected by firms : i^* and τ^* [eq. (22)]. The expectations of i^* and τ^* are adaptive [eqs. (20) and (21)]. To simplify, I have assumed that the expected permanent data Q^* and ω^* are equal to their current effective values Q and ω. I have also assumed that the effective employment of labor N instantaneously adjusts to the desired value N*. There would not be any difficulty in avoiding these simplifications by assuming adaptive expectations for Q^* and ω^*, and a progressive adjustment for N. But the interpretation of the results would become more complicated without much benefit. On the production side I only have to add that SC firms' production at each date is determined by the demand for their commodity (eq. 13.) There is no production function constraint in the short run, firms being able to adjust the intensity of the utilization of their production factors to the demand for their product. But, as we will see, the production function constraint is satisfied in the long run (on the balanced-growth path).

Equation (9) determines SC consumers' spending. It depends neither on their wealth nor the income on their wealth, which is an important simplifying assumption. The share of this spending allocated to the purchase of RW commodity is given by equation (10). γ is the exchange-rate elasticity of imports. In these equations I have substituted a permanent rate e^* to the current exchange rate e [eq. (11)]. Importers do not want to adjust their orders to short-run fluctuations of the exchange rate, because frequent and important changes of these orders are costly. Equation (12) determines SC exports, the exchange-rate elasticity of which is β.

SC budget and balance-of-payment deficits are financed by borrowing. Of course this borrowing has implications for the wealth and income on wealth of agents. But I have assumed that these variables have no influence on the demand for goods. The supply of SC currency, M, is determined by SC's central bank and is independent of SC government's budget deficits. Equation (14) gives the equilibrium between M and SC demand for money (SC agents do not hold RW currency and no SC currency is held in RW). Several formulations of the demand for money were a priori plausible; the simplest has been retained.

Equation (15) determines the SC cost-of-living index P. Equation (17) represents a PHILLIPS curve without monetary illusion. (19) is a price equation : the price level in SC is equal to the average labor cost of production increased by a mark-up. This mark-up depends on the intensity of competition with RW. To simplify I have not taken into account any direct influence of demand pressures on prices. Neither have I introduced adjustment lags in (17) and (19). Equation (23) defines the terms of trade t.

Table 1

The model

The equations

(4) $(1 + i) e = (1 + t)_0 e_{+1}^a$

(5) $Q = AK^{*\alpha} [(1 + g)^t N]^{1-\alpha}$

(6) $\dfrac{K^*}{N} = \dfrac{\alpha}{1 + \alpha} \dfrac{\omega}{q}$

(7) $K_{+1}/[(1 + g) K^*] = (K/K^*)_1$

(8) $I = K_{+1} - (1 - \delta) K$

(9) $p C + p e^* Im = c_1 p (Q - T)$

(10) $p e^* Im = c_2 [pC + pe^* I]m (pe^*/p)^{1-\gamma}$

(11) $e^* = \lambda_2 \dfrac{1+\mu}{(1 + g)(1 + \rho)} e_{-1}^* + (1 - \lambda_2) e$

(12) $Ex = E (1 + g)^t [p/(p\ e^*)]^{-\beta}$

(13) $Q = C + I + G + Ex$

(14) $M = c_3 p\ Q\ i^{-\varphi}$

(15) $P = p^\sigma (p\ e^*)^{1-\sigma}$ $0 < \sigma < 1$

(16) $\omega = w/p$

(17) $w/w_{-1} = (1 + g) (P/P_{-1}) (1 + \bar{U}n - Un)^a$

(18) $Un = 1 - N/\bar{N}$

(19) $p = (1 + m) (p\ e^*/p)^\psi\ w\ N/Q$ $\psi \geqslant 0$

(20) $i^* = \lambda_3 i_{-1}^* + (1 - \lambda_3) i$

(21) $\tau^* = \lambda_4 \tau_{-1}^* + (1 - \lambda_4) (p/p_{-1} - 1)$

(22) $q = i^* - \tau^* + \delta$

(23) $t = p\ e^*/p$

A variable followed by index 1 − (+ 1) is considered as being at the value this variable took at the previous date or period (will take at the next date or period).

Table 1 (*suite*)

The variables

EN = endogenous, EX = exogenous, EP = economic policy instrument

GROWTH RATES

    EX g = Natural growth rate of SC; constant over time;

    EP μ = Growth rate of the trend of the money supply in SC; constant over time;

    EX ρ = RW rate of inflation; constant over time;

    EN τ^* = Permanent inflation rate in SC.

STOCKS (measured at date t)

    EN e = Current exchange rate (price of RW currency in terms of SC currency);

    EN e^* = Permanent exchange rate;

    EN i = Interest rate on SC financial asset;

    EX $\bar{\imath}$ = Interest rate on RW financial asset; constant over time;

    EN i^* = Permanent interest rate on SC financial asset;

    EN K = Productive capital stock in SC;

    EN K* = Desired productive capital stock in SC;

    EP M = SC supply of money;

    EN N = Employed labor in SC;

    EX $\bar{\text{N}}$ = Available labor in SC; constant over time;

    EN p = Price index of SC commodity (in terms of SC currency);

    EX $\bar{p}$ = Price index of RW commodity; $\bar{p}_t = \bar{p}_0 (1 + \rho)^t$ (in terms of RW currency);

    EN P = SC cost-of-living index (in terms of SC currency);

    EN q = User cost of capital in SC;

    EN t = terms of trade of SC;

    EN Un = Unemployment rate in SC;

    EN w = Nominal wage rate in SC (in terms of SC currency);

    EN ω = Real wage rate in SC (deflated by p).

FLOWS [measured over period $(t, t + 1)$]

    EN C = SC households' consumption of SC commodity;

    EN Ex = SC exports;

    EP G = SC government's consumption of SC commodity;

    EN I = Gross productive investment in SC;

    EN Im = SC households' consumption of RW commodity = SC imports;

    EN Q = Production of SC commodity;

    EP T = Tax in SC (in terms of SC commodity).

2 Balanced-growth paths (table 2)

If all economic policy and endogenous variables are geometrical functions of time, and if their set satisfies the equations of the model, the economy is said to follow a balanced-growth path [2]. Thus such a path is determined by as many growth rates and a many initial values as there are economic policy and endogenous variables.

Balanced-growth paths play two roles in this paper :

— One of them will be the control or reference path in the neighborhood of which the consequences of economic policy decisions will be investigated;

— They represent the long-run states of the economy. Long-run multipliers of economic policy decisions can be deduced from the variation of these paths with changes in these decisions.

2.1. Growth rates.

SC economic policy variables are G (government consumption), T (taxes), both measured in units of SC commodity, and M (supply of money). On a balanced-growth path G and T must grow at the natural growth rate g. Now SC economic authorities can choose the growth rate of their money supply μ, and the initial values G_0, T_0 and M_0, freely.

μ contributes to the determination of the SC inflation rate (computed on the cost-of-living index P or on the SC commodity price p, and approximately equal to : $\mu - g$), of the growth of the nominal wage rate w in SC (equal to μ), and of the current and permanent exchange rates e and e^* (approximately equal to : $\mu - g - \rho$, where ρ is the RW rate of inflation). μ has no influence on the growth rates of variables measured in volume.

Numerical values of the reference path

Parameters : A = 7.66744, α = 0.2, = 1, c_1 β = 0.74746, c_2 = 0.29379, c_3 = 0.91842, δ = 1.2 %, E = 80, γ = 0.5, m = 0.25, $\bar{U}n$ = 4%, φ = 0.26, Ψ = 0.1, σ = 0.8.

Exogenous variables : g = 1.1%, i = 2.98%, $\bar{N}$ = 20.5, $\bar{p}_0$ = 1, ρ = 2 %.

Economic policy variables : G_0 = 72.5, M_0 = 1 000, μ = 3.122%, T_0 = 72.5.

Endogenous variables : C_0 = 192.55, e_0 = 0.9963, Ex_0 = 79.75, i_0 = 2.98%, I_0 = 92.25, Im_0 = 80.18, K_0 = 4 010.74, N_0 = 19.68, p_0 = 0.9994, P_0 = 0.9988, q_0 = 2.18%, Q_0 = 437.03, τ_0^* = 2%, Un_0 = 4%, w_0 = 17.76, ω_0 = 17.77.

Initial values are usually given in billions of francs. However $\tilde{N}$ and N_0 are expressed in millions of people, w_0 and ω_0 in thousands of francs, and $\bar{p}$ and $\bar{p}_0$ are indices. The period of time over which flows, growth rates and some parameters are defined, has been taken as equal to a quarter.

A few other parameters have an influence on the dynamics of the model out of its balanced growth path, but not on this path itself. They are : $a = 0.025$, $\lambda_1 = 0.96$, $\lambda_2 = 0.8$, $\lambda_3 = 0.95$, $\lambda_4 = 0.99$.

Long-run multipliers associated to an increase of SC government consumption by 10 % (given in percentage points)

$C_0 = 6.48$, $e_0 = -25.55$, $Ex_0 = -25.02$, $i_0 = 0$, $I_0 = 3.66$, $Im_0 = 16.48$, $K_0 = 3.66$, $N_0 = 0.$, $p_0 = -0.71$, $P_0 = -6.28$, $q_0 = 0$, $Q_0 = 0.71$, $\tau_0^* = 0$, $Un_0 = 0$, $w_0 = 2.92$, $\omega_0 = 2.92$.

2.2. Initial values

We have just seen that the rate of appreciation of the exchange rate e is μ - g - ρ. This appreciation rate is equal to the difference between SC and RW interest rates $i_0 - \bar{\imath}$ (24), which determines i_0. SC inflation rate being equal to $\mu - g$, SC user cost of capital is equal to $q_0 = i_0 - (\mu - g) + \delta = \bar{\imath} - \rho + \delta$ (36). The absence of monetary illusion implies that the rate of unemployment Un_0 is equal to the natural value Un, which determines employment N_0 (33,34).

If we make the simplifying assumption $\psi = 0$, SC firms' mark-up will no longer depend on competition with foreign firms, thus on the terms of trade. The production function (25), together with the equation of the minimization of the production cost (26) and the price equation (35), then yield the factor-price frontier :

$$(38) \qquad [\omega_0/(1-\alpha)]^{1-\alpha} (q_0/\alpha)^\alpha = A/[(1+m)(1-\alpha)]$$

Since q_0 is independently determined, this equation gives SC real wage rate ω_0. Then, based on q_0, ω_0 and the employment N_0, equations (25) and (26) determine the production Q_0 and the capital stock K_0. (27) further determines the amount of investment I_0 necessary to sustain SC economic growth. The monetary equilibrium (32) determines the price of SC good p_0. All these initial values of endogenous variables are independent of fiscal policy.

Then we come to the last block of equations : (28) (SC consumer gspendin), (29) (SC imports), (30) (SC exports), and (31) (equilibrium of the SC commodity market). This block determines : C_0 (consumption of SC commodity by SC households), Im_0 (SC imports), Ex_0 (SC exports), and t_0 (terms of trade). There are the only variables, together with the exchange rate e_0,

---

2. Remember that exogenous variables have been taken as constant or geometrical functions of time. On a balanced-growth path speculators know the future economic policy perfectly, so we have $_0e^a_{0+1} = e_{+1}$.

which depend on fiscal policy. We can analyse this dependance by writing (31) differently, taking (28) into account :

$$(39) \qquad Q_0 = C_0 + I_0 + G_0 + Ex_0 = c_1 (Q_0 - T_0) + I_0 + G_0 + Ex_0 - t_0 Im_0$$

This equation shows that the terms of trade t_0 are determined by the equilibrium between the predetermined production (supply) of SC commodity Q_0 and the demand for this commodity. Let us make the natural assumption that this demand is an increasing function of t_0 (i. e. of $\bar{p}_0 \, e_0/p_0$ which is the inverse of the relative price of the SC commodity in terms of RW commodity). This assumption is equivalent to the usual one that the SC balance of trade surplus is an increasing function of the exchange rate (the price of RW currency in terms of SC currency). Then there exists a unique solution t_0 to equation (39), and a unique balanced-growth path. (37) then gives the exchange rate e_0. If the SC government consumption G_0 increases, the demand for SC commodity increases and the supply of this commodity stays unchanged. The equilibrium of the market for this commodity requires a decrease in the terms of trade [i. e. an increase of the ratio between SC and RW commodity prices], which implies a decrease in SC commodity exports, and a substitution of RW commodity imports for SC commodity consumption by SC households. With the price of RW commodity $\bar{p}_0$ given and the price of SC commodity predetermined, the exchange rate e_0 decreases, i. e. the SC currency appreciates. The increase in the deficit of the SC balance of trade is financed by capital inflows from RW. [3]

These last results are about the same as those in the seminal papers by FLEMING [8] and MUNDELL [12]. They are based on two important assumptions : that SC money supply is kept unchanged when G_0 increases, and that international capital flows are infinitely elastic with respect to interest differentials and have no influence on the decisions made by SC agents.

2.3. Numerical results

Numerical values have been given to the parameters and to the initial values and growth rates of the exogenous and economic policy variables. These values have been chosen in accordance with the usual results of econometric estimates for France, and in such a way that the initial values of the balanced-growth path are near to the state of the French economy in 1976. The thus-defined path will be called *reference balanced-growth path* (table 2).

If G_0 is increased by 10%, SC goverment's consumption of each period becomes 10% higher than on the reference growth path. This change defines a new balanced-growth path. The percentages of variations of the initial values of the endogenous variables will be called *long-run multipliers*. These multipliers are given in table 2. G_0 increase is of course financed by SC government borrowings.

Table 2 shows that the increase of G_0 implies an increase of the imports Im_0 and a decrease of the exports Ex_0 and of the exchange rate e_0, in conformity with the theoretical analysis of paragraph 2.2. Now we no longer have $\psi = 0$. The decrease of e_0 implies an increase in RW competitivity which forces SC firms to decrease their mark-up on their labor cost. This implies an increase of SC real wage rate. SC firms react to that by using a more capitalistic production process. As employment stays at its natural

TABLE 2

Balanced-growth paths

Growth rates

0 for $: i, i^*, \mu, N, q, t, \tau^*, Un$;

g for $: C, Ex, G, I, Ig, K, K^*, Q, T, \omega$;

μ for $: M, w$;

$\dfrac{1+\mu}{1+g} - 1$ for $: p, P$;

$\dfrac{1+\mu}{(1+g)(1+\rho)} - 1$ for $: e, e^*$;

Initial values

(24) $(1-g)(1+\rho)(1+i_0) = (1+\mu)(1+t)$

(25) $Q_0 = A K_0^\alpha N_0^{1-\alpha}$

(26) $\dfrac{K_0}{N_0} = \dfrac{\alpha}{1-\alpha} \dfrac{\omega_0}{q^0}$

(27) $I_0 = (g+\delta) K_0$

(28) $C_0 + t_0 Im_0 = c_1 (Q_0 - T_0)$

(29) $Im_0 = c_1 c_2 (Q_0 - T_0) t_0^{-\gamma}$

(30) $Ex_0 = E \, t_0^\beta$

(31) $Q_0 = C_0 + I_0 + G_0 + Ex_0$

(32) $M_0 = c_3 p_0 Q_0 \, i_0^{-\rho}$

(33) $Un_0 = \bar{Un}$

(34) $Un_0 = 1 - N_0/\bar{N}$

(35) $Q_0/N_0 = (1+m) \, t_0^\psi \, \omega_0$

(36) $q_0 = i_0 - (1+\mu)/(1+g) + 1 + \delta$

(37) $e_0 = t_0 p_0/\bar{p}_0$

and : $e_0^* = e_0,\ i_0^* = i_0,\ K_0^* = K_0,\ P_0 = p_0^\sigma (\bar{p}_0 e_0)^{1-\sigma},\ \tau_0^* = (1+\mu)/(1+g) - 1,\ w_0^* = \omega_0 p_0$

---

3. The previous reasoning is simple but not rigorous. The rigorous reasoning is as follows. Let us define SC absorption by: $A_0 = C_0 + t_0 Im_0 + I_0 + G_0 = c_1 (Q_0 - T_0) + I_0 + G_0$. A_0 does not depend on t_0. (39) can be rewritten:

$$E t_0^\beta - c_1 c_2 (Q_0 - T_0) t_0^{1-\gamma} = Q_0 - A_0.$$

Assume MARSHALL-LERNER condition, $\beta + \gamma > 1$, and $Q_0 > T_0$. Then:

    a. If $\gamma < 1$, $Q_0 > A_0$, there exists a unique balanced-growth path with $\partial t_0/\partial G_0 < 0$;

    b. If $\gamma < 1$, $Q_0 < A_0$, there either exists two balanced-growth paths, the first with $\partial t_0/\partial G_0 < 0$, the second with $\partial t_0/\partial G_0 > 0$, only the first of which is economically reasonable; or there is no balanced-growth path;

    c. If $\gamma > 1$, there exists a unique balanced-growth path with $\partial t_0/\partial G_0 < 0$.

level, this implies that capital stock K_0, gross investment I_0, and production Q_0 increase in SC. Finally the monetary equilibrium implies that the price of the SC commodity P_0 decreases.

Long run multipliers associated with an increase of the initial value of the money supply M_0 by 10%, can be easily deduced from the neutrality of money which is verified by the model : all the real variables stay unchanged, and all the nominal variables e_0, e_0^*, p_0, P_0, w_0, increase by 10%. To keep the length of the paper reasonable I have not computed multipliers associated with a change of the money growth rate μ.

3 Dynamics of the model out of the balanced-growth paths

3.1. Methodology

We will now investigate the properties of the model in the neigborhood of its reference balanced-growth path. This path is defined by the 4 constants $\bar{G}_0$, $\bar{M}_0$, μ, $\bar{T}_0$. So at date τ the economic policy followed by SC, which is defined by : G,M,T, will not differ by much from $\bar{G}_0 (1+g)^\tau$, $\bar{M}_0 (1+\bar{\mu})^\tau$ $\bar{T}_0 (1+g)^\tau$.

A good procedure for doing that is first to make a change of variables, such that the model written in these new variables is autonomous in time and describes a dynamic evolution in the neighborhood of a steady states. Let $X(\tau)$ be an original variable of the model, and x be its growth rate on the reference balanced-growth path. I define the reduced variable $X'(\tau)$ by $X'(\tau) = X(\tau)/(1+x)^\tau$. The steady state of the model written in these new variables is the initial value of the balanced-growth path of the model written in the original variables.

Then we compute a linear approximation of the model written in these reduced variables in the neighborhood of the reference steady state (as this computation in trivial this linearized version of the model is not reproduced in the paper). This linear approximation belongs to a class of dynamic linear models with rational expectations which was investigated by BLANCHARD and KAHN [1]. The state of the economy at time τ is determined by the state of the predetermined endogenous variables at time $\tau - 1$, by the state rationally expected at time τ for time $\tau+1$ of the so-called nonpredetermined endogenous variable (the spot exchange rate), and of course by the current and past states of exogenous and economic-policy variables. BLANCHARD and KAHN assume that at each date the agents hold expectations of the exogenous and economic policy variables for all the future dates, compute the expected values of the endogenous variables for these dates by using the model, and hold bounded expectations. These authors then show that if the number of eigenvalues of the model of which modulus is larger than 1, is equal to the number of nonpredetermined variables (one here), the model determines a unique path for the endogenous variables. Our model satisfies this condition, its nonzero eigenvalues being (1) 0.867, (2) 0.980, (3) 0.516, (4) 1.013, (5) 0.939, (6) 0.989.

A good numerical evaluation of the dynamics of the model in the neighborhood of its reference balanced-growth path, is given by the dynamic multipliers of the linear approximation in the neighborhood of the reference steady state. To compute these multipliers I will assume that the predetermined variables are at their reference steady state at date 0. When expectations are rational it is possible to define two kinds of multipliers (which can easily be computed by formulae given by BLANCHARD and KAHN) :

1. The first gives the consequences of a given unforeseen change of the economic policy variables at time 0, which is subsequently sustained forever and expected to be so.

2. The second gives the consequences of a given expected change in the economic policy variables at time 0, which is correctly supposed to take place at $T > 0$ and then to continue forever.

The changes in the economic policy variables that are involved will be :

1. An increase of SC government consumption G by 10% (relative to its reference steady state, and financed by government's borrowings), which will be called fiscal policy; and

2. An increase in SC money supply M by 10% (relative to its steady state), which will be called monetary policy.

Dynamic multipliers, as shown in graphs 1, 3 and 4, represent percentage increases relative to reference balanced-growth path values. These multipliers converge to their long-run values of table 2 when time increases indefinitely, i.e. the economy is asymptotically stable. [4]

The linearized approximation of the model (and the model itself) is almost block recursive. Three blocks can identified. The first block by determines the dynamics of all the real variables in function of the evolution of the SC user cost of capital q. The second block determines the dynamics of all the nominal variables in function of the evolution of the real variables. The third block determines the dynamics of q in function of the evolution of the nominal variables. This suggests the following two-step procedure in order to provide an economic interpretation of the dynamics of the linearized model. [5]

---

4. In fact this proposition is not quite right for fiscal policy : dynamic multipliers are computed on the basis of a linear approximation of the model, and converge toward values which differ slightly from the long-run multipliers which were based on the model itself. The proposition is true for monetary policy, money being neutral both with respect to the model and its linear approximation.

5. DELEAU and MALGRANGE [5], p. 111-6, have developed this evaluation method and have made extensive applications of it on large econometric models of the French economy.

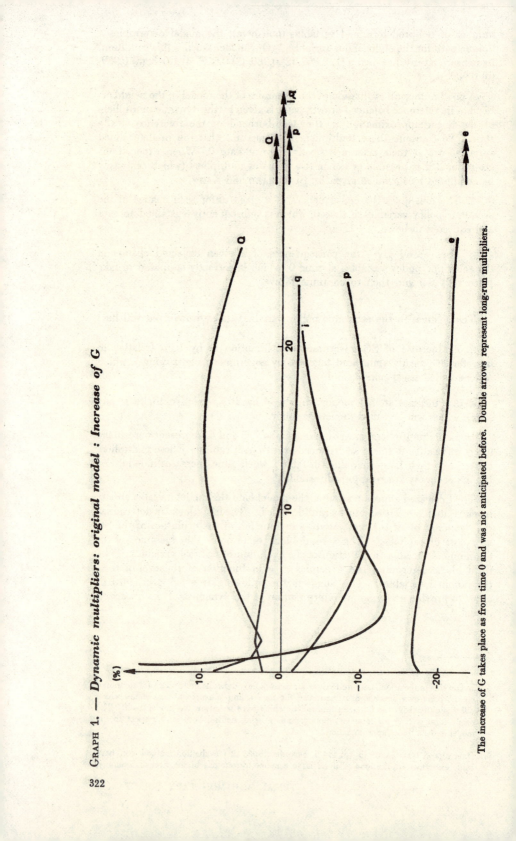

GRAPH 1. — *Dynamic multipliers: original model : Increase of G*

The increase of G takes place as from time 0 and was not anticipated before. Double arrows represent long-run multipliers.

322

1. First, give an economic interpretation of the simplified linear model obtained by removing the third block and by assuming q constant.

2. Second, study the dynamics of q determined by the third block, and see how the fact that q is not constant changes the results of the simplified model.

This procedure will be fruitful if the properties of the simplified model are reasonably near to those of the original model, so that the corrections resulting from the second step stay limited. This seems to be case here : graphs 1 and 3 exhibit limited variations of q around zero; the eigenvalues of the simplified model (given in the following paragraphs) are very near to those of the original model.

3.2. Simplified model : a first real block (SC user cost of capital q is constant)

This block may be summed up into 5 (semi-reduced) equations each having an economic interpretation.

1. *A multiplier equation.* Let us define $s_1 = 1 - c_1 \, C_0/(C_0 + t_0 \mathrm{Im}_0)$, and $s_2 = (1 - \gamma) \, \mathrm{Im}_0 - \beta \, \mathrm{Ex}_0/t_0$. Then the linear approximations of SC consumer spending equation (9), SC imports equation (10), SC exports equation (12) and the equilibrium of the market for SC commodity (13), can be summed up in a single equation :

$$(40) \qquad [(G - (1 - s_1) \, T + I]/s_1 - s_2 \, t/s_1 = Q$$

The lefthand expression represents the total demand for SC commodity which determines the production of this commodity. This demand may be interpreted as the sum of two terms : (1) the product of the autonomous demand and the Keynesian multiplier; and (2) the product of the part of the demand which is sensitive to international competition (measured by the terms of trade) and the Keynesian multiplier.

2. *An accelerator equation.* It is possible to sum up in a single investment equation the linear approximations of the investment equation (8), the equation for the adjustment of effective to desired SC capital stocks (7), the production function (5), and the equation for the minimization of the production cost in SC (6). Then we get :

$$(41) \qquad I - \lambda_1 I_{-1} = (1 - \lambda_1) \, (K_0/Q_0) \, [(1 + g) \, Q - (1 - \delta) \, Q_{-1}]$$

$$+ (1 + \lambda_1) \, (1 - \alpha) \, K_0 \, [(1 + g) \, \omega/\omega_0 - (1 - \delta) \, \omega_{-1}/\omega_0]$$

3. *A factor-price frontier.* From SC production function (5), the equation for the minimization of the production cost in SC (6), and SC price equation (19) we get the SC factor-price frontier relating the real wage rate to the terms of trade :

$$(42) \qquad (1 - \alpha) \, \omega/\omega_0 + \psi \, t/t_0 = 0$$

This equation can be written equivalently as a sort of price equation showing how variations of the SC nominal wage rate and the RW commodity price are transmitted to the SC commodity price :

(43)
$$(1 - \alpha + \psi)\, p/p_0 = (1 - \alpha)\, w/w_0 + \psi\, (\bar{p}e^*)/(\bar{p}e_0)$$

4. *A demand-for-labor equation.* It is possible to relate SC employment to SC production and the real wage rate on the basis of the linear approximations of equations (5) and (6) as follows :

(44)
$$N/N_0 = Q/Q_0 - \alpha\, \omega/\omega_0$$

5. *A Phillips relation.* The last equation is the linear approximation of the PHILLIPS equation (17) which relates the increase of the real wage rate to employment and the terms of trade :

(45)
$$(\omega - \omega_{-1})\, \omega_0 = (1 - \sigma)\,(t - t_{-1})/t_0 - a\, N/\bar{N}$$

The role of the terms of trade in this equation deserves an explanation. If RW commodity price increases and if SC commodity price p stays unchanged, the terms of trade increase. The nominal wage rate w increases in order to keep its purchasing power (w/P) unchanged. The real wage rate which is paid by SC firms $(\omega = w/p)$ increases. The PHILLIPS equation can be written in an equivalent way which shows variations in the prices of both commodities are in employment in SC are transmitted to SC nominal wage rate :

(46) $(w - w_{-1})/w_0 = \sigma\,(p - p_{-1})\, p_0 + (1 - \sigma)\,(\bar{p}e^* - \bar{p}e^*_{-1})/(\bar{p}e_0) + a\, N/\bar{N}$

Equations (40), (41), (42), (44) and (45) constitute a real model which determines the dynamics of I, N, ω, Q and t. This model has two nonzero eigenvalues 0.877, 0.983, which are close to the first two eigenvalues of the original model. This block should look familiar to a Keynesian economist. If such an economist was asked about the effects of the increase of government consumption in a small-open economy, he would probably answer : first an increase in demand for home-produced commodities; then an increase in the production of these commodities and in their relative prices in terms of foreign goods, i.e. a decrease in the terms of trade. We will see that this answer is correct for the model of this paragraph. In order to do so, I will now give an economic interpretation of two simpler versions of this block, which are obtained for particular values of some parameters.

Case a, a multiplier-accelerator model with $a = 0$.

In this case, there is no effect of a change in the employment of labor on the wage rate in the Phillips equation (46). This equation then shows that an increase of the same percentage in the prices of both commodities implies an equiproportional increase in SC nominal wage rate. The price equation (43) similarly shows that an equiproportional increase in the price of the RW commodity and the SC nominal wage rate implies an increase of the same percentage in the SC commodity price. Consequently, the ratios between these prices and the wage rate, i.e. the SC real wage rate ω and the terms of trade t, are independent of SC economic policy : $\omega = t = 0$.

Thus ω and t disappear from equations (40) and (41) which now constitute a multiplier-accelerator model giving the dynamics of SC production and investment, Q and I. We deduce from (40) and (41) the equation giving the dynamics of Q :

$$(47) \quad [s_1 - (1 - \lambda_1)(1 + g) K_0/Q_0] Q - [\lambda_1 s_1 - (1 - \lambda_1)(1 - \delta) K_0/Q_0] Q_{-1}$$

$$= G - \lambda_1 G_{-1} - (1 - s_1)(T - \lambda_1 T_{-1})$$

When λ_1, increase from 0 to $\bar{\lambda}_1 = 1 - s_1 Q_0/[(1+g)K_0] = 0.949$, the characteristic root of this equation $h(\lambda_1)$ increases from $(1-\delta)/(1+g - s_1 Q_0/K_0) = 1.03$, to $+ \infty$. When λ_1 increases from $\bar{\lambda}_1$ to 1, $h(\lambda_1)$ increases from $- \infty$ to 1. If $\lambda_1 = 0.96$, then $h(\lambda_1) = 0.897$, which is approximately equal to the first eigenvalue of the real block investigated in this paragraph. It is easy to prove that $\lambda_1 > \bar{\lambda}_1$, is equivalent to an instantaneous propensity to spend on SC commodity less than 1 : $\partial C/\partial Q + \partial I/\partial Q + \partial Ex/\partial Q < 1$. We must notice that $\lambda_1/(1 - \lambda_1)$ is the average lag in the adjustment of SC effective capital stock to the demand for SC commodity : when λ_1 increases from 0 to 1, this lag increases from 1 period to infinity. Thus, this lag must be long enough to assure an instantaneous propensity to spend less than 1, and the stability of the real block. These results are still approximately valid for the original model, as the variations of its eigenvalues with λ_1 (which are not reported here) show.

If $\lambda_1 > \bar{\lambda}_1$, and if SC government consumption is increased by a given amount ΔG at time 0, then Q increases by $\Delta G/[s_1 - (1 - \lambda_1)(1 + g)K_0/Q_0]$ at time 0, and then progressively decreases toward $\Delta G/[s_1 - (g + \delta) K_0/Q_0]$, as time increases indefinitely.

Case b, a terms-of-trade model with $\psi = 0$.

In this next case, the mark-up of SC firms is independent of the competition by RW firms, or independent of the terms of trade. Then the price equation (43) shows that all variations in SC nominal wage rate are entirely transmitted to SC commodity price. Consequently the SC real wage rate ω is independent of SC economic policy : $\omega = 0$. Let us make the second simplifying assumption $\sigma = 1$. There is then no effect of the changes of RW commodity price on SC nominal wage rate in the Phillips equation (46). Now this equation only relates SC real wage to employment in SC. Thus, as SC real wage is independent of economic policy, SC employment is also independent of SC economic policy : $N = 0$. Then equation (44) shows that we have the same result for SC production : $Q = 0$. The multiplier equation (40) comes down to the simple equation $s_2 t = G - (1 - s_2) t$. s_1 is negative under usual assumptions (those ensuring that on the balanced-growth path the SC balance of trade improves when SC currency depreciates; see paragraph 2.2). Thus an increase in SC government consumption of the SC commodity has no effect on the production of this commodity, but increases its relative price in terms of the RW commodity, i.e. decreases the terms of trade t. SC commodity exports decrease, and households substitute commodity imports from RW for SC commodity consumption. The increase in the deficit of the SC balance of trade is financed by borrowing from RW.

The analysis of these two extreme cases allows an economic interpretation of the multipliers for the simplified model, which are represented on graph 2. The positivity and the decrease of SC production Q is in conformity with the results for case a. The decrease of Q, i.e. SC commodity supply, implies an increase of the relative price of this commodity in terms of RW commodity, i.e. a decrease in the terms of trade t. This feature of the t dynamics and the negativity of t which is obtained in case b, appears on graph 2. SC imports Im follow a dynamics similar to that of SC production Q. But the trajectory of Im is higher and presents a less pronounced decrease over time than the trajectory of Q, because of the fact that the terms of trade t are negative and decrease. These features of t put a brake on the demand for SC commodity, and hence its production. Thus this production increases less at time 0 and decreases faster afterwards than in case a.

3.3. Simplified model : a second money-price block

The first block has determined the dynamics of the real variables. These dynamics, and the second block, which is made up of the linear approximations of equations (4), (11), (14) and (23), determine the dynamics of the nominal variables : e and e^* (current and permanent exchange rates), i (SC financial asset interest rate), and p (SC commodity price). Monetary policy only has an effect on these nominal variables. [6] This block has two nonzero eigenvalues 0.738, 1.085.

After the elimination of e^* the block can be summed up into 3 (semi-reduced) equations:

1. One stating the equality of the current-exchange rate to the exchange rate expected for the next period, as corrected by the interest differential :

$$(48) \qquad {}_0e_{+1}^a/e_0 - e/e_0 - i/(i+i_0) = 0$$

2. Another stating the equilibrium between the money supply M and the money demand (which depends on SC interest rate i, SC commodity price p, and the predetermined SC GNP Q):

$$(49) \qquad M/\bar{M} = -\varphi\, i/i_0 + p/p_0 + Q/Q_0$$

3. An adjustment-price equation. The terms of trade $t = \bar{p}\, e^*/p$ are predetermined. So p immediately adjusts to the permanent exchange rate e^*. But e^* progressively adjusts to the current exchange rate e : agents base their decisions (e.g. about the volume of SC imports) on the permanent and not the current exchange rate :

$$(50) \qquad p/p_0 - \lambda_2 p_{-1}/p_0 - (1-\lambda_2)\, e/e_0 = -t/t_0 + \lambda_2\, t_{-1}/t_0$$

This block is almost identical to the overshooting models which were investigated by DORNBUSCH [6], and GRAY and TURNOVSKY [9]. Its steady-state solution is:

$$(51) \qquad i = 0, \qquad p/p_0 = M/\bar{M} - Q/Q_0, \qquad e/e_0 = M/\bar{M} - Q/Q_0 + t/t_0$$

The properties of this solution are in conformity with the analysis of section 2. SC interest rate i is independent of monetary and fiscal policies. Money is neutral. An increase in SC government consumption (fiscal policy) implies an increase in SC production Q and a decrease in the terms of trade t. Thus, SC commodity price decreases and SC currency appreciates.

Let us define $k = i_0/[\varphi (1 + i_0)]$. The eigenvalues of the money-price block are the solutions of the characteristic equation:

(52)
$$X^2 - [1 + \lambda_2 + (1 - \lambda_2) k] X + \lambda_2 = 0$$

This equation has two real solutions. The first increases from 0 to 1 with λ_2 (it is slightly less than λ_2). The second decreases from $1 + k$, to 1 with λ_2. These properties are close to those of the eigenvalues 3 and 4 of the original model (the variations of these eigenvalues with λ_2 have been computed but are not reproduced here). The following interpretation of the dynamic multipliers of the simplified model as regards its nominal endogenous variables may be given.

If M increases by 10% at time 0, the long-run value (steady-state value) of the exchange rate increases by 10%. If SC interest rate i did not move, now and later, speculators would anticipate for the future dates, and would determine for time 0, an exchange rate increase of 10%. SC commodity price p does not increase by much in the short run because its adjustment to the new value of the exchange rate is progressive. Thus, the equilibrium of the SC money market requires that the increase of the money supply be balanced by a decrease in SC interest rate i. This causes the exchange rate at time 0 to overshoot its new long-run value. In the following periods p increases towards its new long-run value of 10%, i increases towards its unchanged steady-state value, and the exchange rate e decreases towards its new long-run value of 10% .[7]

If G increases by 10% at time 0, the long-run value of the exchange rate decreases. If SC interest rate i did not move, the current exchange rate e would immediately adjust to its new long-run value. This decrease of e would induce a progressive decrease of SC commodity price p. But this effect on p is counteracted by the negative effect of the increase in G on the terms of trade t (see paragraph 3.2 and graph 2). So in the short run the first effect dominates and SC commodity price p decreases; in the medium run the second effect dominates and p increases (graph 2). SC production Q increases considerably at time 0, then progressively decreases towards (approximately) its former level. The equilibrium of the money market requires the dynamics of the SC interest rate i balancing these evolutions of p and Q (the supply of money stays unchanged). Graph 2 shows that i increases a lot at time 0, then decreases, becomes negative (inferior to its

---

6. This conclusion results partly from the suppression of the feedback of the SC user cost of capital on the real block, but also from the absence of monetary illusion in the PHILLIPS equation. Many recent theoretical developments have investigated the consequences of not making this assumption. See for instance BRUNO and SACHS [2]; MARSTON [11]; SACHS [13]. The substitution of an expected rate of change of the cost-of-living index for the current one in the Phillips equation, together with adaptative expectations, would also invalidate this conclusion. See BUITER and MILLER [3] who identify a new channel of transmission of the effects of monetary policy on the real blocks through the terms of trade.

7. BLANCHARD and KAHN formulae allow establishing the intuitively appealing result that the faster the adjustment of SC commodity price p to the exchange rate e (the smaller λ_2), the smaller the extent of the overshooting, and the faster the adjustment of the nominal variables of the second block to their new steady-state levels.

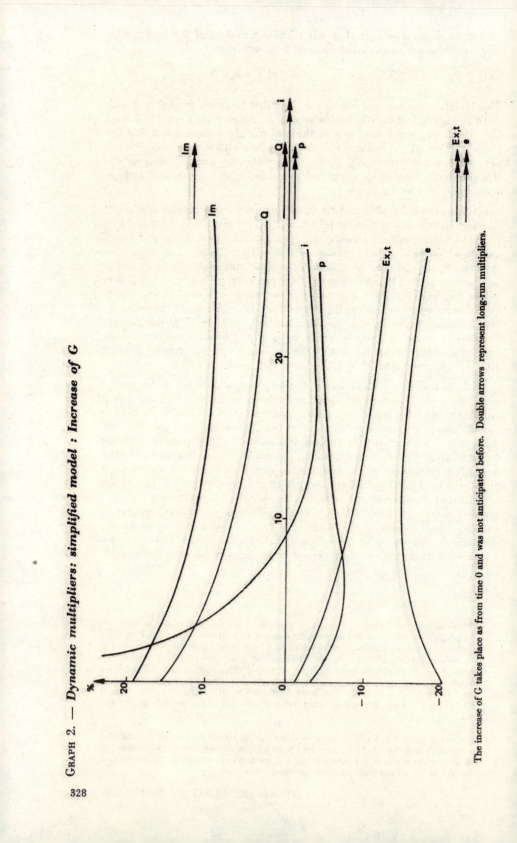

328

GRAPH 2. — *Dynamic multipliers: simplified model : Increase of G*

The increase of G takes place as from time 0 and was not anticipated before. Double arrows represent long-run multipliers.

long-run value), then increases toward 0 (its long-run value). The evolution of the exchange rate e towards its new long-run value, drawn on graph 2, can be understood by noticing that the appreciation of SC currency during a period $e - e_{+1}$, is proportional to the excess of SC interest rate over its long-run value (i.e. RW interest rate).

3.4. From the simplified to the complete model: the endogenization of SC user cost of capital

Having determined the dynamics of the endogenous variables of the two previous blocks, the simplified model determines the dynamics of the permanent SC interest and inflation rates i^* and τ^*, then the dynamics of the SC user cost of capital q, by means of equations (20), (21), (22). [8] The difference with the original model — thus the difference between graphs 1 and 2 — is that the simplified model does not take into account the feedback of q on the real block.

Let us first compare graphs 1 and 2 i.e. the effects of fiscal policy for the two models. In the simplified model, the large and sudden increase in the SC interest rate i, followed by its sharp decrease, and the consequent fall of the SC commodity price p below its reference steady state, imply an increase followed by a decrease of the SC user cost of capital q (which is not represented in graph 2 but is shown in graph 1). This evolution of q is transmitted in an inverse way to SC investment, then to SC production Q. It explains the difference of the dynamic multipliers for Q between the complete and the simplified models. The moderation of the increase of Q during the ten first periods explains why the monetary equilibrium requires a weaker SC interest rate for the complete than for the simplified model.

Let us now comment on graph 3, i.e. the effects of monetary policy for the complete model. The dynamics of SC interest rate and commodity price, i and p, for the simplified model, explain the negativity and the decrease followed by an increase of SC user cost of capital q for the complete model. This evolution is transmitted in an inverse way to SC investment, then to SC production Q. The increases of SC production and SC commodity price, imply and increase in SC demand for money, and an increase in the SC interest rate i which becomes larger than its reference long-run value (i.e. the RW interest rate). This last result explains why, in the complete model, the exchange rate tends towards its new long-run value from below and no longer from above.

---

8. The eigenvalues of this last block are equal to λ_3 and λ_4, i.e. .95 and .99. They are near to eigenvalues 5 and 6 of the original model.

GRAPH 3

Dynamic multipliers: original model : Increase of M

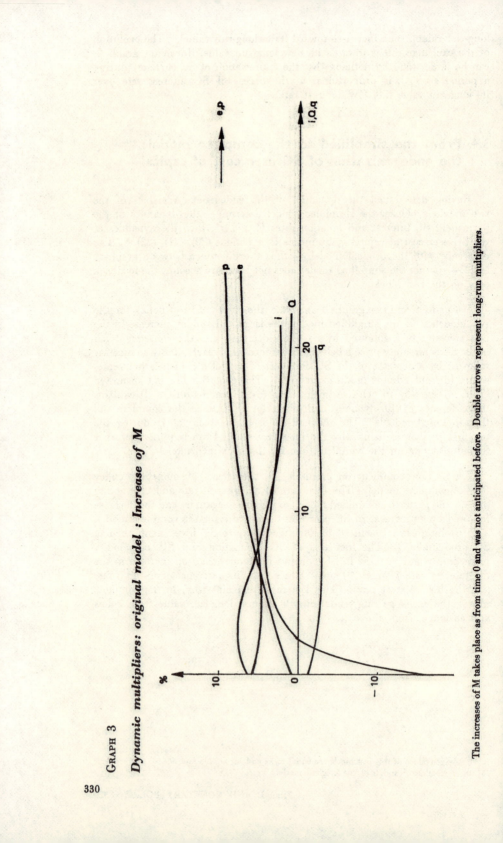

The increases of M takes place as from time 0 and was not anticipated before. Double arrows represent long-run multipliers.

3.5. Consequences of a monetary policy decision taking place at time 10, but anticipated as from time 0 (graph 4)

I will first give an economic interpretation without taking into account the feedback of the SC user cost of capital (simplified model), and then I will investigate the effects of this feedback.

For the simplified model the effects of monetary policy appear only at the level of the money-price block. From time 0 onward speculators know that the long-run value of the exchange rate is 10% higher. If SC interest rate i did not move, speculators would anticipate, and therefore would bring about at once, an exchange rate e increase of 10%. SC commodity price p, which progressively adjusts to e, would then increase over time towards a level 10% higher than its reference value. But in fact SC interest rate i must increase at time 0 to equilibrate the money market since the supply of SC money stays the same for the first 10 periods, while the increase in P puts positive pressure on the demand for money. At time 10 the supply of SC money increases by 10%. Thus, P not yet having increased by 10%, the equilibrium of the money market requires a sudden decrease of SC interest rate, which then becomes inferior to its reference value ($i < 0$). In the following periods p continues to increase towards its new steady-state value ($+ 10\%$), and i increases towards its own long-run value (0). This evolution of SC interest rate explains why the current exchange rate e increases faster and faster until time 10, then decreases more and more slowly after time 10, towards its new steady-state value.

The dynamics of i and p explain why SC user cost of capital q is positive and increases from the present up to time 9, then decreases, becomes negative, and finally increases towards its steady-state value 0. The complete model has the same dynamics for q. This evolution of q is transmitted in an inverse way to SC investment, then to SC production Q. The decrease of Q which takes place over period 0.9 limits SC demand for money and explains why the SC interest rate decreases after date 3. After time 10, Q is much higher than its steady-state value and p is not too far from it. Thus the equilibrium of the SC money market progessively drives i to positive levels. This excess of the SC interest rate over the RW interest rate explains why in the complete model, the exchange rate tends to its new steady-state value from below and no longer from above.

CRAPH 4

Dynamic multipliers : original model : Increase of M

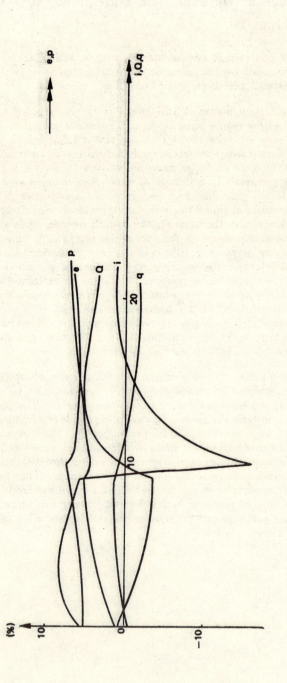

The increase of M takes place as from time 10 and was anticipated as from time 0. Double arrows represent long-run multipliers.

Conclusion

In this paper I have investigated the consequences over time of two well contrasted economic policy decisions when exchange rates are flexible, and I have tried to give an economic interpretation of these consequences.

One of my basic simplifications relates to the dynamics of adjustments and expectations. A more realistic specification would allow faster speeds of convergence of the dynamic multipliers, but a cyclical evolution of these multipliers would follow too (see DELEAU, MALGRANGE, MUET [5]). An improvement of the model in this direction would not introduce any fundamental difficulty in the computations or in the economic interpretation, but would have made the paper clumsier.

Another notable simplification in the model is the assumption that the financing of the SC deficit of the balance of trade does not alter the effects of economic-policy measures for two reasons. This deficit, and the way it is financed, have consequences on the wealth of the various SC agents (government, households), and on the incomes of this wealth. But the effects of these variables on the decisions of SC agents (consumption decisions for instance) were not taken into account in the model. Econometric studies for France, in fact, tend to validate this simplification. Further, if this deficit is financed by the issue of financial assets denominated in SC currency, the quantity of these assets detained by RW increases. In the model this is assumed not to raise any difficulty. But it would be more realistic to assume that any incrase in the quantity of SC assets held by RW would contribute to a gap between the interest rates in SC and RW. If either of these two channels of influence of the deficit of the SC balance of trade on the rest of the economy were powerful enough, some of the main conclusions of this paper might be reversed (see for instance DORNBUSCH and FISCHER [7]). In particular an increase of SC government consumption might induce a depreciation of SC currency, at least in the long run. But the results of empirical studies are still too imprecise to permit any conclusion on this question.

● References

[1] BLANCHARD O. J., KAHN C. M. — " The solution of linear difference models under rational expectations ", *Econometrica*, vol. 48, July 1980, pp. 1305-1311.

[2] BRUNO M., SACHS J. — " Macro-economic adjustment with import price shocks: real and monetary aspects ", *NBER Working Paper*, no. 340, April 1979.

[3] BUITER W. H., MILLER M. — " Real exchange rate overshooting and the output cost of bringing down inflation ", *European Economic Review*, vol. 18, May/June 1982, pp. 85-123.

[4] DELEAU M., MALGRANGE P. — " L'analyse des modèles macroéconomiques quantatifs ", *Economica*, Paris 1978.

[5] DELEAU M., MALGRANGE P., MUET P. A. — " Une maquette représentative des modèles macroéconomiques", *Annales de l'INSEE*, no. 42, April/June 1981, pp. 53-92.

[6] DORNBUSCH R. — " Expectations and exchange rate dynamics ", *Journal of Political Economy*, vol. 84, December 1976, pp. 1161-1176.

[7] DORNBUSCH R., FISCHER S. — " Exchange rates and the current account ", *American Economic Review*, vol. 70, December 1980, pp. 960-971.

[8] FLEMING J. M. — " Domestic financial policies under fixed and under floating exchange rates ", *International Monetary Fund Staff Papers*, vol. 9, 1962, pp. 369-379.

[9] GRAY M. R., TURNOVSKY S. J. — " The stability of exchange rate dynamics under perfect myopic foresight ", *International Economic Review*, vol. 20, October 1979, pp. 643-660.

[10] LAFFARGUE J. P. — "Les modèles macrodynamiques de politique économique: dialogue entre le théoricien et l'économètre ", *Annales de l'INSEE*, no. 40, October 1980, pp. 33-65.

[11] MARSTON R. C. — *Real and monetary disturbances in an exchange-rate union*, mimeographed, ESSEC, Paris, May 1981.

[12] MUNDELL R. A. — " Capital mobility and stabilization policy under fixed and flexible exchange rates ", *Canadian Journal of Economics and Political Science*, vol. 29, November 1963, pp. 475-485.

[13] SACHS J. — " Wages, flexible exchange rates, and macroeconomic policy ", *Quarterly Journal of Economics*, vol. 94, June 1980, pp. 731-747.

Comments

by **Patrick ARTUS**

INSEE, Paris

This paper is stimulating for several reasons: it gives a very careful description of the long-term equilibrium and the long-term results of budgetary and monetary policies. The initial maquette can be simplified and made almost recursive, which permits a very clear analysis of the different mechanisms. Finally, the results of the evaluation of economic policies are very different from the ones obtained with the econometric models usually run in France, which is of course striking and requires thorough analysis.

At first look, the most surprising result in this paper is certainly the public expenditure multiplier and in particular the fact that an increase in public spending permanently leads to a reduction in the price level and an appreciation of the franc. To understand those results, which differ markedly from those obtained with the typical econometric models used in France and which seem surprising in the light of the recent record of periods of expansionary fiscal policy, it is useful to cite the similarities and the differences between LAFFAR-GUE's maquette and the typical macroeconomic model of France. We shall do so both from a structural point a view and from the standpoint of dynamic adjustment. This will then also give us an opportunity to present some of the results about the functioning of the French economy based on the usual econometric models.

Structure

The similarities are:
— The effect of relative prices on factor demand with an elasticity of substitution between capital and labor of about one;
— The effect of competitivity on the mark-up rate and price formation;
— The effect of unemployment on wage formation;
— The perfect indexation of wages on prices, which is confirmed by most of the studies in France, at least up to 1981, and which implies that employment is independent of the inflation rate in the long run.

Differences :
— The choice of rational expectations for exchange rates, whereas we typically find semi-rational expectations involving a small number of key variables;
— Perfect substitutability between French and foreign assets;

— The official control of the money supply in the maquette, whereas most people in France think that money is demand determined (though influenced of course by the fact that the authorities change interest rates mostly in the light of their external targets like stabilization of exchange rates, and not internal ones, like inflation and unemployment);

— The absence of wealth effects, including interest payments on domestic and foreign debt, which is certainly a limitation of the model.

Adjustment processes

The « maquette » is here much simpler that the usual macroeconomic schema for France because of the absence of the usual adjustment lags; namely :

— The productivity cycle, coming from the lag in the adjustment of employment toward optimal employment, which is generally found to be quite long in France;

— The stickiness of price and wage formation, since cost elements except exchange rates have an immediate effect on prices (mean lag for price formation : 1 1/2 year, for wage formation : 1/2 a year);

— The rigidity of the production technique, with the use of a putty-putty production function instead of the putty-clay function, whereas the latter is the popular choice in France;

— The stickiness of consumption (mean lag on real disposable income : 1 year);

— Lags in the effects of competitivity on foreign trade (exports more than 2 years, imports 1 year).

The absence of those adjustment lags of course does not change the long-term properties of the maquette, but makes the results very difficult to compare with those of existing models, of which the dynamic properties of a simulation are dominated by the adjustment processes lasting several years after a shock. For instance, the fact that in French models an increase in prices causes a decrease in real wages and an increase in wages causes a decrease in real profits is very important for the short-medium term analysis. Also, the initial downward pressure on prices on account of the productivity cycle if production increases can have important permanent effects, especially when the exchange rate is flexible. It is interesting to see that in J.-P. LAFFARGUE's maquette the only adjustment lags concern the components of the user cost of capital and the exchange rate which is taken into account by importers, and the latter in particular has very important consequences. If those adjustment lags did not appear, thus if importers had the same rational expectation of the exchange rate as speculators, there would not be any short-run dynamics in the model and long-term equilibrium would be immediately reached. The domestic price would instantly adjust to the variations of the long-term exchange rate, and no movement of the interest rate would be necessary to bring the money market back into equilibrium after an increase, for example, in money supply. It is curious that no adjustment lags are present in the maquette in places where one generally finds long lags in macroeconomic models, which may imply that the short-run dynamics of the maquette are rather arbitrary.

I would like to return again to the two main features of the public expenditure multiplier : the decrease in prices and the appreciation of the franc. As J.-P. LAFFARGUE admits in his paper, these depend crucially on the two basic assumptions of the exogeneity of money supply and the perfect substitutability of domestic and foreign assets. If money supply was in some way linked to public expenditures in the model, the result would be quite different. Foreign indebtedness and interest payments to the rest of the world would also change the results in a notable way especially if the interest payments reduced domestic wealth and therefore domestic absorption.

Before closing, I would like to comment also on J.-P. LAFFARGUE's explanation of the recent devaluation of the French franc : he traces it to the expectation of budget deficits and consequent increases in money supply. Suppose, however, one uses the multipliers in the paper to evaluate the effects of the present economic policy. If the stimulating measures implemented represent an increase in public expenditures of 1 % of GDP, 1/3 of it financed through public debt (in accordance with the record of the last two years) and 2/3 through money creation, the money supply should increase by about 1% too. If I apply the two corresponding multipliers in LAFFARGUE's paper, I get an appreciation of the franc of 1.4% after one year, therefore it is doubtful that with rational expectations the announcement of such a policy would have led to a depreciation of the franc. The resulting question is whether the maquette itself gives misleading results or if exchange rate expectations in France are far from rational.

Comments [309]

339-42

by Marcus H. MILLER*

University of Warwick

Introduction

To investigate the impact of fiscal and monetary policy actions in a small open economy the author specifies a 20-equation macroeconomic model, which is designed to represent—in simplified form—the structure of existing, Keynesian econometric models of the French economy. Using parameter values consistent with such econometric models he computes a "steady state" solution for the model; then, by linearising the equations around this solution, he is able to investigate the behavior of the economy as it responds to policy initiatives, using only linear algebra.

By assuming that the flexible exchange rate is determined by speculators who correctly anticipate future interest rate movements, the investigation allows for the separate treatment of unanticipated and anticipated policy actions (the latter being preceded by "announcement" whose effects are also analysed), using methods proposed by BLANCHARD and KAHN.

Such a study, combining "realistic" parameter estimates with recent developments in theory and technique for analysing the behavior of floating exchange rates, is most welcome and timely. The performance of the franc on the foreign exchanges is apparently an important consideration in the conduct of macroeconomic policy in France at present, so research which shows how policy may be expected to affect the exchange rate is of considerable topical importance.

Monetary policy

In what follows, we focus on the treatment of monetary policy. As the exchange rate is freely floating and wages are fully indexed, one might expect monetary policy to affect only nominal magnitudes; this is true in the long run, but not in the interim. Considering a "stylised" version of the author's model we find that it is the distinction between the permanent and the current exchange rate which accounts for this lack of neutrality, given that the permanent exchange rate is determined in an adaptive fashion. Were it to be determined in a forward-looking fashion, as is the spot rate, then money would be neutral even in the short run. One is led, in conclusion, to query whether the French economy is in fact as close to exhibiting neutrality as the model supposes it is.

---

* On study leave as Houblon-Norman Fellow at the Bank of England 1981-1982.

For present purposes we simplify the author's equations drastically to yield a linear third-order differential equation system as follows:

Real sector

(1) $\qquad\qquad y = \delta c - \gamma r$ $\qquad\qquad$ IS curve

(2) $\qquad\qquad Dc = -\varphi y$ $\qquad\qquad$ Wage/price equations

Monetary sector

(3) $\qquad\qquad m - p = ky - \lambda r$ $\qquad\qquad$ LM curve

(4) $\qquad\qquad De = r - r_f$ $\qquad\qquad$ International arbitrage

(5) $\qquad\qquad De^* = \zeta(e - e^*)$ $\qquad\qquad$ Permanent exchange rate

Definition of competitiveness

(6) $\qquad\qquad c = e^* - p$ $\qquad\qquad$ Competitiveness

Notation

D	denotes the differential operator ($De \equiv de/dt$)	
y	output	in logs
c	competitiveness (the terms of trade)	*Idem*
e	spot exchange rate (price of foreign currency)	*Idem*
e^*	"permanent" exchange rate	*Idem*
p	price level	*Idem*
m	money stock	*Idem*
r	domestic short term, nominal interest rate	
r_f	foreign short term, nominal interest rate	

Putting these equations into "state space" form yields

$$\begin{bmatrix} Dc \\ De^* \\ De \end{bmatrix} = \frac{1}{\Delta} \begin{bmatrix} -\varphi(\lambda\delta+\gamma) & \varphi\gamma & 0 \\ 0 & -\zeta\Delta & \zeta\Delta \\ k\delta-1 & 1 & 0 \end{bmatrix} \begin{bmatrix} c \\ e^* \\ e \end{bmatrix} + \frac{1}{\Delta} \begin{bmatrix} -\varphi\gamma m \\ 0 \\ -m-\Delta r_f \end{bmatrix}$$

where $\Delta = \lambda + k\gamma$.

To consider the dynamics in more detail it is convenient to use illustrative values for the parameters (suggested by the author) as follows

$$\lambda = 4, \quad k = \gamma = \delta = \varphi = 1, \quad \zeta = \frac{1}{2} \quad \text{so} \quad \Delta = 5.$$

We find the characteristic equation then becomes

$$(\rho + 1)\,(\rho^2 + 0.5\,\rho - 0.1) = 0$$

with real roots of -1, -0.65 and $+0.15$.

The positive root is associated with the nominal exchange rate, e, which must "jump" to put the system on the stable manifold. The dynamics of adjustment on that manifold are described by the two negative roots associated with c and e^*, both sluggish variables which do not "jump".

With the parameter values assumed here the system is in fact recursive, with e^* and e being jointly determined without reference to c. The dynamic behavior of these two variables in response to an expansion in the money stock is shown by the saddlepoint phase diagram in figure 1, where the spot exchange rate is found to overshoot while the permenent rate moves gradually from e_0^* to e_1^*.

FIGURE 1

The dynamic behavior of the spot and "permanent" exchange rate in response to unanticipated monetary expansion

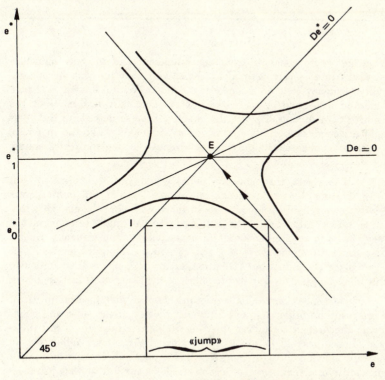

Once the spot price of foreign currency overshoots its final equilibrium (shown at point E), it declines gradually over time; but this lowers the level of interest rates domestically, which increases output in the domestic economy. (Strictly it should be the real interest rate which appears in equation (1), but in the absence of growth of the money stock, the nominal rate is used for simplicity.) It is the divergence between the spot and permanent value of foreign currency which is the source of the non-neutrality in this case.

Consider, however, what would happen if the permanent exchange rate were to be determined in a forward-looking fashion, as is the spot rate. This can most easily be analysed by simply changing the sign of the coefficient ζ in equation (5) to reflect the assumption that the exponential weighting is to extend over *future* values of e rather than past values as heretofore.

The system now has two positive roots (and figure 1 would show a completely unstable system). Assuming that e^* is a "jump" variable as well as e, however, means that this extra positive root can be excluded. But it now transpires that the effect of a monetary expansion will be neutral *in the short run*. Both e and e^* jump from I to E in figure 1; the price level being indexed will also jump, leaving real output, competitiveness and the interest rate unchanged.

Conclusions

What are we to conclude from our examination of the way monetary policy works in this sort of model? Essentially that the short-term non-neutrality of money rests on a fragile foundation. With a floating exchange rate, indexed wages and prices marked up on (nominally-flexible) costs, the only source of non-neutrality was the adaptive process describing the "permanent" exchange rate. If this is made forward-looking, like the spot rate, then monetary policy affects only prices without affecting the real economy in any way.

Views of this sort, that monetary policy would control inflation without seriously affecting the real exchange rate or the level of real output, were aired by various schools of Monetarists in the U.K. before the current administration under Mrs. THATCHER launched its "Medium Term Financial Strategy" to stop inflation without incomes policy. Subsequently British industry became uncompetitive at a rate and to a cumulative level without precedent since the Industrial Revolution, as the exchange rate strengthened but the price and wage levels failed to adjust as the Monetarists had predicted.

I conclude that it would be well worth further investigation to see if there are really no other sources of nominal rigidity in the labor and goods market in the French economy; otherwise Rational Expectations and International Monetarists will be quick to recommend that France follow Britain in checking inflation by tight monetary policy, and will be able to cite the current study, modified as we have described, in support of their case!

Roundtable discussion

[309]   343 — 358
343-46

Contribution

N A

by **William H. BRANSON**
Princeton University

---

1. Introduction

In the spring of 1981 a socialist government took power in France. With the unemployment rate above 7 percent, the new government introduced an expansionary demand policy and raised the minimum wage. Even with the demand expansion, the unemployment rate continued to rise. By the spring of 1982, the continuation of a substantial current account deficit (estimated in September 1982 to be $10 billion for the year) and an expected rise in inflation brought enough pressure on the franc that the government had to reverse policy, devaluing and tightening the budget. Why is unemployment so high and so hard to reduce? Why did the expansionary policy hit the external constraint so quickly? What are the characteristics of a policy program that could reduce unemployment and ease the external constraint in the current French situation? These seem to me to be the important macroeconomic questions now. In this short paper I will not answer these questions. But I will tell what I have learned about aspects of the answers from the three days of discussion of " International Aspects of Macroeconomics in France " in Fontainebleau.

The causes of the high and rising unemployment rate are discussed in section 2 of the paper, and the external constraint is briefly discussed in section 3. In section 4 we turn to lessons for policy, beginning with a brief analysis of what has happened, and ending with some modest suggestions for the policy program.

2. Characterization of unemployment

In 1970 the unemployment rate in France was 1.8 percent. Over the decade of the 1970's it rose nearly continuously, falling only in 1973, and by 1982 it was about 8 percent. An analysis of the causes of this rise in unemployment is required before policy can be prescribed.

We can distinguish three types of unemployment, each with a different implication for policy. *Classical* unemployment results from accumulation of real wage growth in excess of productivity growth. *Keynesian* unemployment results from a slump in aggregate demand combined with stickiness in money wages. *Structural* unemployment would come from a slow response of labor (and other factors of production) to rapid change in the structure of demand or the technological requirements for skills. All three kinds of unemployment can exist at the same time, and probably do in France in 1982.

The data presented in the paper by OUDIZ and STERDYNIAK show that classical unemployment is at least part of the problem in France. In 1973 productivity growth slowed significantly, but real wage growth continued along its previous path until around 1976. The result, using the data in table 10 of OUDIZ and STERDYNIAK, is a cumulative excess of real wage growth over productivity growth of about 9.8 percent since 1973. The gap is mainly due to real wages continuing to grow when productivity actually fell in 1974 and 1980, following the discontinuous jumps in oil prices. These two years alone account for a gap of 8.2 percent.

The rise of the real wage rate relative to productivity since the early 1970's can, with any reasonable estimate of the elasticity of demand for labor, explain all the rise in unemployment. Thus there seems to be no doubt that *some* of the unemployment in 1982 is classical. To reduce this, a policy program should include some moderation of real wage growth plus an investment and technology package that is designed to stimulate productivity growth.

What about Keynesian unemployment? In 1973 the unemployment rate was 2.1 percent. Is it possible that the inflation since 1973 has reduced real balances, or that fiscal policy has been sufficiently tight, that aggregate demand has fallen enough to generate Keynesian unemployment? Until 1981, I think the answer is no. Since 1973 the inflation rate has been about 10 or 11 percent, while the money stock grew at an annual rate of 13 to 14 percent. So real balances increased, at least until 1981. OUDIZ and STERDYNIAK argue that government spending as a fraction of GDP rose in 1970's due to an expansion of transfer payments, and the data in their table 5 do not indicate a tightening of fiscal policy overall. Finally the French current balance has not reacted to the oil price shocks so sharply as in most other Europan countries. So I find it hard to see how inflation or exogenous reductions in aggregate demand could have generated substantial Keynesian unemployment until 1981.

In 1981 and 1982, however, the situation may have changed. As the paper by BLANCHARD and SACHS shows, the widespread (and clearly excessive) fear of nationalization or other implicit increases in taxation of capital income may have generated a temporary investment slump. This could explain much of the jump of the unemployment rate from 6.3 percent in 1980 to around 8 percent in mid-1982. Thus starting from a base of around 2 percent unemployment in the early 1970's, we might attribute 4 percentage points of the increase to 1982 to classical unemployment, and 2 percentage points to Keynesian.

If only a small part of unemployment is Keynesian, why do firms perceive themselves to be demand-constrained? One reason would be that most firms are monopolistic, not perfect, competitors. They would like to sell more output at the existing price, but they cannot without reducing the price.

Another reason might be an increase in the pace of *structural change* in the economy in the 1970's. From a US perspective, it seems clear that the world composition of excess demands has been changing. The supply of consumer manufactures from the advanced developing countries has been growing rapidly, as has their demand for capital goods. This has changed the composition of US trade significantly in the 1970's, and it is changing the composition of demand facing European firms. The total may be stable, and consistent with no increase in unemployment if all relative prices were flexible and there are no adjustment costs. But with sticky prices and with adjustment costs, firms which have lost demand feel demand-constrained. I have no idea how much of the rise in unemployment should be attributed to this kind of " resistance " to structural change, but it must be significant. This is an important item on the macroeconomic research agenda, especially in Europe.

3. The external constraint

The industrial world has been in a protracted slump since the early 1970's. This has imposed an external constraint in the form of slow export growth for most European countries. Until their economies are re-structured to meet the changing composition of world demands, this external constraint will be difficult to ease.

Devaluation of the nominal exchange rate does not seem to be an effective policy for easing the constraint. OUDIZ and STERDYNIAK show that it is hard to obtain a lasting change in the real exchange rate by changing the nominal rate. Domestic prices and wages react sufficiently quickly that the real rate is restored after a nominal devaluation. Thus changes in exchange rates may destabilize the domestic price level rather than stabilize the current account balance in France.

The French economy is sufficiently open to trade that it may be best to adopt a program of gradual adjustments of the nominal exchange rate to prevent appreciation of the real rate. This is obviously politically difficult within the EMS, but it might be an appropriate objective for French policy. Gradual adjustment would be preferable to a policy of sudden devaluations after a period of protracted resistance. This maximizes uncertainty, and directs attention and resources to speculation on the timing of devaluations.

If the exchange rate is not effective in easing the external constraint, what can be done? I think a principal objective of an investment program should be precisely a re-structuring of the economy to meet shifting world demands. Short-run fluctuations will have to be buffered by reserve changes and gradual adjustment of exchange rates. But the longer-run problems are bringing productivity growth and real wage growth closer together, and orienting the economy toward the international environment. Understanding changes in the structural pattern of world trade and investment is another important item in the macroeconomic research agenda.

4. Lessons for macroeconomic policy

Two aspects of the new program in 1981 were important from the macro point of view. These were, obviously, the demand expansion and, less obviously, the nationalization of some major companies and banks. Let us discuss the latter first.

During the period before the election in spring 1981, and after, there was extensive discussion and speculation about the prospects of nationalization. This discussion was frequently excessively simple, in that it occasionally sounded as if a completely free capitalist economy was about to be socialized. In fact, the government has always been deeply involved in French commerce and industry.

The CLAASSEN-WYPLOSZ paper, for example, shows the extensive involvement through the financial system. The nationalizations were an adjustment in the nature of that involvement and a marginal extension of its scope. Only Americans and economists would picture it as socialization of a completely free-enterprise economy.

The uncertain prospect of nationalization probably contributed to the investment slump in 1981-1982. The paper by BLANCHARD and SACHS shows this nicely. The fall in expected net returns leads immediately to a drop in investment. As I noted earlier, this might have added one or two percentage points of Keynesian unemployment to the unemployment rate.

The demand expansion tended to raise internal prices, and the protraction of the world recession tightened the external constraint. The increase in domestic prices required some nominal devaluation to hold the real exchange rate constant. The consequence was the sudden devaluation in the spring of 1982, along with imposition of temporary wage and price controls and a re-tightening of the budget. How could this program be improved?

The first point to emphasize is the fundamental role of investment. In the short-run, a revival of investment may be needed to stimulate aggregate demand. In the longer run, building and modernizing the capital stock can increase labor productivity, bringing it into line with the real wage rate and reducing classical unemployment. Moderation of real wage growth will help, but it is not the only way to deal with this problem. Also, in the longer run, investment is required to re-structure the manufacturing sector to meet world demands and relax the external constraint on real income growth. Thus any successful program has to include an expansion of investment to raise productivity growth and re-structure the economy. The macroeconomic policy package has to support a program of structural and sectoral change.

A second point of emphasis is the role of expectations and uncertainty. I have already suggested that a policy of gradual adjustment of the nominal exchange rate to keep the real rate from appreciating is preferable to periodic crises and jump depreciations. The same point applies to use of wage and price controls. These may be a necessary part of a program of re-structuring and expansion. But imposing them temporarily and unpredictably increases uncertainty and speculation about their timing and effects. It might be better to have a more permanent program with clear objectives and conditions for its gradual elimination.

Macroeconomic research could be shifted at the margin to work on problems that the policy program faces. For example, more emphasis might be placed on sectoral and labor-market adjustment, with some de-emphasis of one-sector models that assume these problems away. For a time, European research in macroeconomics has tended to ignore Anglo-American research. It would be a mistake now to begin importing these models without carefully adopting them to the European situation.

Contribution

by Jacob A. FRENKEL

University of Chicago and NBER

Participants in this roundtable discussion were invited to present general comments on the French economy, and to outline an agenda for research on exchange rates and on open-economy macroeconomics with a special application to the French economy. Since other participants have already made numerous specific remarks on the performance of the French economy, I will devote my comments to research issues.

Research issues

One of the major advances of the past decade's research in open-economy macroeconomics has been the modelling of the foreign sector. By now it is well understood that a proper modelling of the open economy should *not* attach a foreign sector as an appendix to the otherwise closed-economy model. Rather, it is now clear that the entire economic system operates in a different way once allowance is made for the openness of the economy, and, therefore, open-economy considerations should be incorporated in a consistent manner through the various layers of the open-economy macro model. With this central question of modelling strategy out of the way, there are numerous conceptual and technical issues that have to be dealt with in empirical research. The following are several examples of such issues.

1. The Peso Problem

The first issue relevant for empirical research in the area of exchange rate determination may be referred to as the " Peso Problem ". The original " Peso Problem " characterized the situation with the Mexican Peso which was eventually devalued during the third quarter of 1976. Since this devaluation was expected for several years, the Peso was traded at a forward discount in the market for foreign exchange. Obviously, as long as the devaluation did not take place, the forward exchange rate proved (ex post) to have been a biased forecast of the realized future spot exchange rate. But, once the devaluation took place it exceeded the prediction that was implied by the forward discount on the Peso.

Generally, the " Peso Problem " may be viewed as a situation in which there are many observations but much fewer events. For example, in Mexico's case, there were many days (observations) during which the forward discount prevailed, and yet there was only one event: the devaluation itself. These circumstances affect the properties of the statistical distribution of rates of return and raise conceptual and practical difficulties for studies which attempt to examine the efficiency of foreign exchange markets and the biasness of forecasts of future spot rates based on lagged forward rates. Likewise in such circumstances it is not clear whether a rise in the number of observations in any sample, which is being brought about by a larger frequency of measurements, should be treated as a corresponding increase in the number of effective degrees of freedom. In a way the "Peso Problem" could be cast in terms of a small-samples problem and as such it has much wider application. However, since the foreign exchange market is strongly influenced by expectations of future events and of future policies, and since current expectations of future change in policies (like a devaluation or a specific change in intervention policies) are based on probabilistic evaluations, it is evident that the "Peso Problem" is especially relevant in the foreign exchange market. In the French context the "Peso Problem" is likely to be of special relevance in view of the widely held expectations of the imposition of various controls in the markets for goods, assets and foreign exchange.

Another example that falls under the heading of the "Peso Problem" relates to the current price of gold. Studies of optimal portfolios (e.g., HSIEH and HUIZINGA [1982]) have found little role for gold in the optimal portfolio of assets. One of the possible rationales for the observed holdings of gold can be provided by noting that current holdings and pricing of gold reflect the probability of a sharp rise in its price in the event of a fundamental change in the role of gold in the international monetary system. Again we have here a situation where there are many observations but only one (or even no) event.

2. The role of innovations

The second issue relates to the role of innovations. One of the central implications of the rational-expectations hypothesis is that unanticipated events, "news", play a predominant role in affecting real variables and asset yields. This implication has been embodied in the modern theory of exchange rate determination. Accordingly, exchange rates are presumed to reflect current as well as expected future values of the relevant economic variables. The anticipatory role of exchange rates suggests that empirical research of exchange-rate determination should relate changes in exchange rates to the *innovations* in the relevant regressors. While this methodology has a strong theoretical justification, its empirical application is extremely complicated. Since the innovations are intrinsically unobservable, any empirical analysis involves the *joint* examination of the model as well as the measurement of the innovation (i.e., the measurement of the expected values which are used in the construction of the innovations). Since there is no practical way to avoid completely the joint-hypotheses problem, it seems that inference from empirical estimates should be made with great care.

A related difficulty also relates to the anticipatory nature of exchange rates and the prompt response of asset prices to new information. It concerns the implications of different frequencies of data collections for various time series. For example data on exchange rates and interest rates are available in a much greater frequency than data on national income or on the current account. These different frequencies of data availability are reflected in different patterns of revisions of expectations and may affect systematically the time series characteristics of the innovations of the various data.

3. Structural models

Recent examinations of the various structural models of exchange rate determination, including the monetary models, the portfolio-balance models, the current-account models and others have shown that these models have not performed well in explaining movements in nominal exchange rates (e.g., MEESE and ROGOFF [1983]). With the benefit of hindsight it seems that the key reason for the poor performance of the various models is the intrinsic characteristics of exchange rates as asset prices. As indicated above, exchange rates are very sensitive to expectations concerning future events and policies. Periods that are dominated by rumors, announcements and "news" which alter expectations, are likely to induce a relatively large degree of exchange rate volatility. Since by definition "news" cannot be predicted on the basis of past information, it follows that by and large the resulting fluctuations of exchange rates are unpredictable. In a way, this asset-market perspective suggests that we should *not* expect to be able to forecast accurately exchange rate changes with the aid of the simple structural models. The role of the simple structural models is to account for the *systematic* component of the evolution of exchange rates. In cases where the systematic predictable component is relatively small, we may expect to account for only a small fraction of the variability of exchange rates. A potentially productive line of research would examine the implications of the structural models for the relation among the variance of exchange rates and the variance of the various « fundamentals. »

4. Lucas' critique

One of the central insights which has affected economic research during the past decade has been the "LUCAS Critique" (LUCAS [1976]). The key point of that critique is the observation that the behavior of economic agents reflects prevailing pattern of policies as well as agents' expectations concerning the future path of policies. As a result, policy actions which attempt to exploit a correlation between two endogenous variables, e.g., the correlation between inflation and unemployment or the correlation between exchange rates and interest rates may fail since the policy actions themselves might alter the structure of the relation between the two variables in a way that could not have been predicted from the historical correlations. Such an outcome is likely to occur when policies are based on reduced-form relations rather than structural relations.

This critique is of course fundamental for the evaluation of the results of simulations based on parameter estimates that are obtained from historical data. It is pertinent to note, however, that as a practical matter the quantitative importance of LUCAS' critique depends on the circumstances: it may be significant for some experiments while negligible for others. It certainly should not discourage further empirical research. Rather, it should encourage the use of an improved research methodology that takes into account the endogeneity of the "structural parameters." These considerations are of special importance in the context of the French economy in view of the large changes in current and prospective policy measures. Indeed several papers in the present conference have attempted to allow for the endogeneity of some key relationships. For example, the paper by BLANCHARD and SACHS [1982] allows for the endogeneity of investment, the paper by CLAASSEN and WYPLOSZ [1982] allows for the endogeneity of the offset coefficient, and the paper by KOURI, de MACEDO and VISCIO [1982] allows for the endogeneity of the technological coefficients. Further applications of the rational-expectations macroeconometrics are still desirable.

5. Additional issues

The foregoing examples illustrate the type of issues relevant for empirical research. There are of course many more issues that should be fruitfully addressed as part of a research agenda in the area of exchange rate analysis. These additional issues include the treatment and identification of risk premia, the proper definition of money, the specification of the demand for money in an open economy, the relative degree of substitution among various assets, and the role of portfolio balance in affecting exchange rates.

● References

BLANCHARD Olivier and SACHS Jeffrey. — [1982] *Anticipations, Recessions and Policy: An Intertemporal Disequilibrium Model,* this volume.

CLAASSEN Emil and WYPLOSZ Charles. — [1982] *Exchange Controls: Some Principles and the French Experience,* this volume.

FRENKEL Jacob A. — [1981] "Flexible Exchange Rates, Prices and the Role of New Lessons from the 1970's", *Journal of Political Economy,* 81, no. 4 (August), pp. 665-705.

HSIEH David and HUIZINGA John. — [1982] *An Analysis of the Management of the Currency Composition of Reserve Assets and External Liabilities of the Developing Countries,* presented at the Wingspread Conference on "The Evolving International Monetary Arrangements".

KOURI Pentti, de MACEDO Jorge and VISCIO Albert. — [1982] *Profitability, Employment and Structural Adjustment in France: The Last Ten Years,* this volume.

LUCAS Robert E. Jr. — [1976] "Econometric Policy Evaluation: A Critique", in *The Phillips Curve and Labor Markets,* edited by K. Brunner and A. Meltzer, vol. 1 of the Carnegie-Rochester Conference Series on Public Policy, a supplementary series to the *Journal of Monetary Economics,* 1976.

MEESE Richard and ROGOFF Kenneth. — [1983] "Empirical Exchange Rate Models of the Seventies: Are Any Fit to Survive ?", in *Exchange Rates and International Macroeconomics,* edited by Jacob A. Frenkel, Chicago, University of Chicago Press, forthcoming.

Contribution [309]

by Edmond MALINVAUD

INSEE, Paris

In this contribution I should like to draw attention to competitiveness. The importance and difficulty of a serious discussion of competitiveness must be considered when we deal with macroeconomics in France. Let me first speak about its importance, then about the difficulties raised by a serious analysis of the phenomenon.

1. In the whole the performance of the French economy during the postwar period has been good, whether one compares it to its own past or to other European economies. Two periods were particularly favorable : the early sixties and the early seventies.

These two periods were characterized by significant increases of French export market shares, by fast growth, and by high profit rates. Analysts of French economic growth have often refered to these two periods as having been generated by the two so-called " successful devaluations " of 1958 and 1969. By contrast one can look at the period from 1964 to 1968 and at the recent years.

During the years 1964 to the beginning of 1968 the main issue was said to be the foreign balance constraint. In order to restore French competitiveness a policy of moderate deflation was followed. It is difficult to know what would have been the eventual result of this policy, which had stopped the deterioration of French competitiveness. Indeed, the policy was reversed in the summer 1968: a stimulation of expansion was then thought to be required for social peace.

Similarly during the recent years the balance of payments constraint was the real obstacle against demand management policies that would have slowed down the rise in unemployment. It was often stated that promotion of competitiveness was the only route to a better employment situation. Indeed, any success of French firms in increasing their market shares on the domestic or foreign markets improves the balance of payments, hence gives some extra margin for autonomous demand expansion, whose unfavorable effects on this balance are well-known.

I do not need to dwell more on this issue, which is very clear and quite consonant with the discussions we had Monday. I can just mention that making the 1982 devaluation successfull is today a major challenge for the French government. We have discussed some of the reasons that make such an outcome particularly difficult for this government. But the views expressed here were probably too one-sided. One should not overlook that some unpopular but economically favorable actions will more easily be implemented by the present government than they would have been by the former one.

2. A first difficulty faced in any discussion about competitiveness concerns its measurement. In the initial paper by G. OUDIZ and H. STERDINIAK a table presents three measures of competitiveness for the years 1970 to 1981 (their table 17). All three measures show a deterioration, which is not surprising considering the fact that in 1970 French competitiveness was exceptionally good, as I said. But the extent and timing of the deterioration vary from one measure to another one.

This may be partly a statistical problem: any complete assessment about variations in competitiveness must face the two dimensions that make comparative assessments always delicate, the time dimension and the space dimension, which requires to confront data coming from different national statistical systems. But most probably the fact that various measures give different results also reveals that competitiveness has many dimensions and that indeed these measures have to give different results. Variations of unit labor cost converted in a given money at the prevailing exchange rate are not exactly reflected in proportional price variations on the various markets where the products are being sold.

Competitiveness is then a multidimensional disequilibrium concept. A comparative cost advantage of one country usually permits to have both lower prices, which help for the promotion of sales, and better profit margins, which stimulate the building of new and often more efficient productive capacities. Hence, the initial cost advantage may be reinforced. Analyzing precisely this process should be on the research agenda of macroeconomists.

3. This analysis is bound to be difficult. Indeed disequilibrium analysis is always difficult. A particularly challenging question is always to know whether and how disequilibria can be sustained for some time. In the case of competitiveness answering the question requires a good understanding of the process of exchange rates determination. But we have seen here yesterday that our knowledge of this process is still much more crude than for instance our knowledge of the process of nominal wages determination.

Another way of stating the research program consists in saying that it should clarify the degree of autonomy of an open economy such as France and how this economy can best take advantage of its autonomy.

On Monday the supermarket model of the world economy was proposed. Each country would face exogenously given import prices but would have some market power on its export prices. I agree that studying this model, which is a form of monopolistic competition model, is relevant here. But I should also like to point out that, when we look at the situation in Western Europe, a different picture seems to emerge: at least in the short run, exporters confronted with changes in the exchange rates seem to compensate for them so as to maintain rather stable prices on each one of the markets on which they sell; this means that a devaluation is far from being fully transmitted to the prices of imports. In any case, such phenomena point to the need to take imperfect competition into account, which is of course a serious source of complication.

Another source of complication comes from the fact that some macroeconomic adjustment processes significantly vary from one country to another one, as we have seen with STANLEY BLACK'S paper. National specificities exist, although they are often difficult to characterize. Explaining how these specificities interact with competitiveness and its sustainability is again a challenging problem.

4. Finally, a comment of a different kind must be made. Speaking of the international aspects of French macroeconomic problems, one must recall that, even though this country has some degree of autonomy for its economic policy, even though it can promote or deteriorate its competitiveness by more or less wise economic policies, it remains mainly dependent on the world economy. In other words, France may do a little better or a little worse than other countries, depending on how clever it will be in the promotion of its competitiveness. But essentially its fate is tied to the fate of other Western countries. A concerted world economic policy that would succeed in overcoming the present depression would by far be the best cure of French economic difficulties.

Contribution

by **Ronald I. McKINNON**

Stanford University

Before focussing critically on current French macroeconomic policies influencing the labor market, I should like to applaud the remarkably good performance of the French economy over the past 20 years. Despite concern for the uncompetitiveness of French industry at the birth of the EEC, France subsequently became internationally competitive in a variety of industries — many of them in high technology. Together with the modernization of French agriculture, this led to sustained growth in per capita real income that was remarkably good by any European or North American standard.

However, beginning in the early 1970s, a disturbing trend towards increasing disequilibrium in the labor market emerged; this is the principal theme of most contributors to this conference. Wage costs began to rise relative to growth in labor productivity. Consequently, employment remained virtually stationary, while the labor force and unemployment grew in a fairly steady fashion — unlike the cyclical variations in unemployment occurring in North America.

The French government's contributions to the continued increase in the hourly cost of employing labor are clear :

1. Mandated increases in take-home pay aggravated by officially encouraged wage indexing, officially reduced hours worked over the year, minimum wage increases, and so on.
2. Large increases in the social security tax levied on employers.

In these important respects, unemployment in France seems to be "classical" in nature with real wages faced by employers set above market-clearing levels.

Reasons for the worldwide slowdown in labor productivity growth are less clear — although many would associate it with rising energy costs and increasing financial instability in the world economy. Nevertheless, in common with other European governments, the French authorities seem to have aggravated the situation. Not only have they impeded downward adjustments in real wages, but Draconian restrictions against firing workers prevent enterprises from reshuffling their labor forces towards greater efficiency and force them to operate with redundant (older) labor. The labor market has become increasingly closed to new entrants.

As emphasized by Paul KRUGMAN, the immediate effect of carrying redundant labor is to increase labor's share in the industrial product, and to aggravate firms' cash flow squeeze from the higher hourly labor costs. With quantitative limits on bank lending to firms — *"encadrements du crédit"* —

either new investments in French enterprises will diminish or the government must pay operating subsidies over a wide range of industry, or both, if enterprises are to be kept going.

From this highly stylized statement of the French macroeconomic problem, let us analyze possible first-, second- and third-best policy responses. As we shall see, a third-best response seems most likely.

First best : reduce labor costs directly

The most direct approach is for the government to actively reduce hourly wage costs seen by enterprises, the most important component of which is the take home (before tax) pay of workers. This would require a reversal of many of the Socialist government's new policies.

A related approach would sharply reduce payroll taxes levied on employers and cut public expenditures, such as transfer payments, by an equivalent amount. Contrary to Keynesian doctrine, this "balanced-budget" decrease in government expenditures and payroll taxes would stimulate output in the open French economy for any given real exchange rate precisely because unemployment is largely classical in nature.

The immediate effect of either method of reducing firms' real wage costs would be to improve their cash flow positions. This would free financial resources for new investment that, with lower real wages, would no longer be unduly capital intensive. But from KRUGMAN's analysis, we should be very cautious in predicting any immediate increases in employment by those firms directly affected by wage reductions. Because much of French industry already carries redundant labor which could not be shed in the face of past real-wage increases, these firms will not immediately hire new workers even if real wages were suddenly cut today. However, the date at which redundant labor would be fully absorbed —and employment would begin to rise— would arrive much sooner.

Second best : operating subsidies financed by general taxation

Another approach is to compensate for firms' high labor costs by using general taxation or expenditure cuts to finance operating subsidies. The widespread nationalization of French industrial enterprises, which may then run with current operating deficits covered by the government, makes this solution simpler to administer than if all French industry were privately owned. Direct subsidies from the Treasury would cover current losses, while allowing firms to borrow from the banking system to finance new investment. Of course, the taxes levied to finance the operating subsidies must be general income or consumption taxes, not payroll taxes. Otherwise, the level of classical unemployment could actually be worsened.

In circumstances where their real wages before taxes cannot be reduced directly, workers would have to accept a lower level of disposable income *after tax*. In effect, workers must have some *tax illusion* for this policy to succeed in increasing employment.

However, tax-financed operating subsidies are only a second-best solution because real wages seen by employers would remain too high: new investment would remain too capital intensive and incentives to employ new entrants into the labor market would be inadequate. Moreover, widespread subsidies could lead to serious accounting problems: the government can no longer distinguish between efficient and inefficient enterprises, resulting in a general decline in the administrative efficiency of French industry.

Third best: cheap credits from the banking system and the inflation tax

Suppose that the unduly high real hourly wage costs seen by employers are left in place, creating a cash-flow squeeze for French industry. Instead of financing operating subsidies with general tax increases or expenditure cuts, now suppose firms are allowed to borrow freely from the banking system at low disequilibrium and officially controlled rates of interest. The Bank of France is instructed to loosen its *encadrements du crédit* — lending restraints on individual banks— to facilitate this general expansion of bank credit. Nationalized banks are simply instructed to lend more freely to nationalized industries, and perhaps also to the remaining private firms. (As noted by OUDIZ and STERDYNIAK, the Bank of France does not try to control the monetary base or any monetary aggregate directly.)

In addition to the social costs of giving firms operating subsidies associated with the second-best solution noted above, the use of cheap credits introduces two additional distortions. First, operating subsidies and the cheapening of the cost of fixed capital accumulation are mixed up. Firms with preferred access to low-cost credits have a double incentive to become more capital intensive. Not only are their wage costs high, but their cost of capital financing is low.

Secondly, because these cheap credits are not financed from general tax revenue, in effect the inflation tax must be continually levied on the holders of financial claims on the French banking system and on any other franc-denominated assets — say government bonds— where the rate of interest is artificially depressed. This method of financing industrial subsidies will cause growth in nominal money to persistently outrun the growth in the demand for real money at a constant price level. Instead of price inflation being the accidental onetime outcome of unforeseen political — economic events such as "les événements" of May 1968 or the two great shocks in world oil prices, the use of the inflation tax will become endemic: a structural part of the French public finances. And because unemployment is classical, the continual and predictable inflation itself will not lead to reduced unemployment in the Keynesian mode. Instead, financial and foreign exchange instability will be aggravated.

How best to tax the financial system in an open economy is a complex problem involving the joint manipulation of reserve requirements, controls on international capital flows, the exchange rate, as well as the rate of emission of base money. Many of the issues involved are covered in McKINNON and MATHIESON [1981]. It suffices to note here that preserving the domestic tax base — the real size of the domestic financial system as measured, say, by the ratio of M_2/GNP— must be a central objective of the financial authorities. And tighter exchange controls as described in the paper by CLAASSEN and WYPLOSZ are essential to prevent French residents from getting out for the inflation tax by discarding their franc assets in favor of dollars or deutsche marks. If the domestic financial tax base is to be preserved, the Bank of France might have to restrict French residents from borrowing —as well as depositing— in foreign currencies.

But even with the successful imposition of the inflation tax, people must be prepared to accept an after tax reduction in their real disposable incomes, although they won't accept a reduction in their before-tax real wages. If this tax illusion doesn't exist, using the inflation tax to pay operating subsidies to French enterprises will fail to maintain or increase employment. Workers without tax illusion will simply demand higher before-tax wages from enterprises to compensate for the reduction in their disposable incomes associated with the tax on their monetary assets.

The imposition of tight exchange controls on international capital movements, coupled with the continuous need to use the inflation tax, implies that the preferred foreign exchange policy might be a crawling peg that moves on a smoothly downward path preannounced by the authorities (McKINNON and MATHIESON [1981]. As long as foreign trade on current account remained fairly free, preannouncing the rate of crawl (in line with the necessary rate of inflation to finance the operating subsidies) would minimize undue exchange risk in foreign trade. Traders would no longer have to anticipate the occasional traumatic discrete devaluation, and the Bank of France would no longer need to suffer large foreign exchange losses to speculators who anticipate discrete devaluations.

In summary, there is no fully satisfactory financial solution to the problem of real product wages that are specified at too high a level. Economically, although perhaps not politically, any scheme to subsidize output and employment is much inferior to the preferred strategy of directly reducing real wages.

● References

McKINNON Ronald I. and MATHIESON Donald J. — [1981] "How to Manage a Repressed Economy", in Princeton, *Essays in International Finance*, no. 145 (December).

Appendix

This next article has been included in this volume, even though it was not presented at the conference, in order to fill a void that was expressed at various times from the conference floor and to the organisers in private. The article is a formerly unpublished text which was prepared in 1980 for a conference on " The Political Economy of France " organised by the American Enterprise Institute (Washington, DC, May 29-31, 1980). In order to preserve the essential unity of the original text, which has been circulated widely, yet somehow to bring it up to date, the author has decided to make a minimum of changes. There are only two important ones. The first is the omission of the bulk of a section dealing with issues of reform from the standpoint of the liberal philosophy of the preceding Barre-Monory administration. (A consequence of this change is the substitution of " questions " for " propositions " in the title of the article). The omitted passage is now indicated by a short summary in brackets (section 4.1). The second important change is the addition of a postscript concerning 1980-82. In other respects, the only changes are editorial except in sub-section 4.2, which was affected by the radical contraction of the preceding sub-section.

The French
financial system :
mechanisms and
questions of reform

Jacques MELITZ*

Jacques MELITZ, INSEE,
Paris, France.

The French financial system is an original
mixture of central bank refinancing, credit
ceilings and selective credit controls, which
this paper attempts to describe and to analyse.
A lot of attention is given to the merits of
various monetary reforms in France.

The government is an unusually large participant in finance in France. It not only issues currency and bonds, as other governments do, but acting through various agencies, also issues savings deposits and checking accounts. Similarly, it distributes loans to individual firms and households. Further, the French monetary authorities exercise regulatory powers over all financial intermediaries : the stock brokerage firm, the insurance company, and the sales finance company, in addition to the commercial bank. Exactly who the monetary authorities are is somewhat of a question, since there is no tradition of central bank independence in the country, and the ministers of the Economy and Finance, who used to be one and the same prior to 1978, clearly have a large hand in monetary policy. Yet the weight of the Bank of France and the general power and prestige of the civil service is such that the ministers certainly do not rule monetary policy alone. Monetary power may be said to be essentially divided between the Bank of France, these ministers, and to some extent also, the Treasury and some of the high officials in several of the satellite credit agencies in the sphere of the government.

Notwithstanding the large place of the government in finance, about twenty years ago, the state began deliberately to diminish its role as a financial intermediator and regulator of financial activity. It encouraged a reduction in its share in the issue of money. It lowered its part in the selection of loans. It sought to bring its own budget into balance, and to make the state enterprises more independent of the National Treasury. Major reforms in 1966 and 1967 gave financial firms a large degree of freedom over their interest rates on assets and liabilities. Controls over foreign capital movements lessened as well. This process of decentralisation continues to this very day. It has recently received new life under the current Barre-Monory administration. The result is an original system which combines a large and growing role of markets with far-reaching legal powers of the state over finance and an enormous volume of privileged credit. How performing can such a system be ? How much further can it go in enlarging the influence of markets without transforming itself or encountering contradiction ? What sorts of market factors can fit in readily within the system? These kinds of questions will inspire this account of the French system, in which for reasons of space, international aspects will not receive the attention that they deserve.

1 The financial panorama

The fundamental financial legislation in France goes back to two acts of 1941 and 1945, which have been subsequently amended. The institutions listed as banks in 1945 under this legislation include the four that were nationalized at the time, now three (subsequent to a merger) : la *Banque nationale de Paris*, le *Crédit lyonnais*, and la *Société générale*. In addition to the listed banks, currently numbering around 380, state institutions offering deposit facilities can be divided into five groups : (1) the postal checking system; (2) the savings banks (*caisses d'épargnes*); (3) the cooperative banks (*caisses mutuelles*), which consist predominantly of the agricultural banks affiliated with the National Agricultural Bank or CNCA (Caisse nationale de crédit agricole); (4) the system of Popular Banks (Banques populaires); and (5) the French Bank for Foreign Commerce or BFCE (*Banque française du commerce extérieur*).[1]

The postal checking system provides strictly checking accounts; the savings banks offer only the facilities of savings deposits; the other three classes of state banks offer both kinds of deposits. Historically the Popular Banks arose in order to serve the small businessman and the artisan; the cooperative banks arose in a similar way, to provide banking facilities for the rural population. Both types of banks still reflect their original avocation, but they have both branched out into other fields of banking, and can be found everywhere, in the suburbs as well as the business districts, the large metropolitan areas as well as the countryside.

Table 1 indicates the relative importance of the listed banks and the other five groupings as issuers of deposits.[2] The three nationalized banks alone account for about one-half of the deposits of the listed banks. But the CNCA is as large as anyone of the three nationalized ones. By usual counts, all four of these banks belong to the world's largest 20. This is, of course, an enormous representation at the top for a country of 53 million people, and evidently reflects the fact, which is independently verifiable, that France has a larger concentration in banking than any other large Western country.

The postal checking system does not allocate the funds it collects. This is done by the Treasury through a set of specialised intermediaries, of which the most notable are the *Fonds de développement économique et social* (FDES), the *Crédit national*, and the *Crédit foncier*. Similarly, the savings banks essentially do not allocate the funds they collect (despite a significant

---

1. Two good general descriptions of the French financial system are available : Antoine Cou-tière [1977]; and Raymond Penaud, [1978]. Jean Marchal (with Huguette Durand) [1979], containing a lot of detail, is a useful companion volume to these two.
2. This table and the next one were compiled on the basis of various issues of the *Rapports annuels* of the Conseil National du Crédit.

TABLE 1

Money and market shares

MONEY

(billions of francs)

	Currency	Commercial bank demand deposits	Postal checking accounts*	Commercial bank term deposits	Deposits with the savings banks	Non-transferable Treasury bonds	Money (sum of previous columns)
1963	57.55	72.15	20.06	19.60	43.38	28.90	241.64
1970	75.88	124.64	33.62	110.90	112.02	32.19	489.25
1978	131.94	362.02	82.59	545.99	432.92	46.39**	1,601.85

* Inclusive of minor deposit accounts with the Treasury and the Bank of France.
** Inclusive of a minor value (1,38) of term deposits with the Treasury.

TABLE 1 (*suite et fin*)

MARKET SHARES

	Demand deposits			Term deposits			Total deposits		
	1963	1970	1978	1963	1970	1978	1963	1970	1978
Listed banks..........	80	74	67.1	68	64.7	57.9	77.4	69.6	61.6
Cooperative banks..........	14.4	19.2	25.4	28.1	29.5	36.2	17.4	24.1	31.9
Popular banks..........	4.9	6.2	6.8	3.6	5.4	5.5	4.6	5.8	6
French bank for foreign commerce	0.7	0.6	0.7	0.3	0.4	0.4	0.6	0.5	0.5
TOTAL COMMERCIAL BANKS.....	100	100	100	100	100	100	100	100	100

	Demand deposits			Term deposits			Total money		
	1963	1970	1978	1963	1970	1978	1963	1970	1978
Commercial banks......	78.2	78.8	81.4	31.1	49.7	55.8	38	48.1	56.7
Public sector*..........	21.8	21.2	18.6	68.9	50.3	44.2	62	51.9	43.3
TOTAL..........	100	100	100	100	100	100	100	100	100

* Public sector demand deposit liabilities equal postal checking accounts and public sector term deposit liabilities equal deposits with the savings banks.

provision for some local allocation of the deposits received by the individual savings bank). This is done by the Bank of Deposits and Consignations or CDC (la *Caisse des dépôts et consignations*), which in part shuffles around the collection of the savings banks among the other specialised intermediaries. The CDC is also closely related to the Treasury.

Similarly the National Agricultural Bank (CNCA) and the French Bank for Foreign Commerce (BFCE) cannot dispose freely of all of their assets. They have some large assignments to fulfill: those of the CNCA prominently concern agriculture and housing, those of the BFCE export trade. This is true to a limited extent for the Popular Banks, who have some special responsibilities in the sphere of the artisan and small tradesman. These institutions therefore partly belong in the government sector with respect to issues of credit allocation. Yet their status is complicated by the fact that at least the CNCA and the Popular Banks possess large assets which they can dispose as they please. As a result, they tend to respond to any relevant shock much like any of the ordinary listed banks do. The three nationalized banks also unquestionably behave very much like the other listed banks do as a rule, even though they may occasionally be subject to more governmental pressure. It is commonly agreed therefore that so far as questions of macroeconomic analysis are concerned—issues of credit and money aggregates and interest rates— the banking sector outside of the immediate control of the authorities should be seen as including the CNCA, the Popular Banks, the BFCE, and the three nationalized banks, together with the other listed banks. This leaves the governmental part of the monetary, sector as consisting only of the postal cheking system, the savings banks, the Bank of France and the Treasury.

According to this conception of the public sector, the government's total monetary liabilities are limited to currency, postal checking accounts, deposits at the savings banks, and non-transferable Treasury bonds or "bons sur formules" (that is, government bonds with fixed nominal prices, thus akin to term deposits with the Treasury). It may be seen from table 1 that since 1963 these monetary liabilities shrank from 62 % to 43.3 % of total money. On this same view of the public sector, there was also a drop in the government's share in the distribution of loans or bank credit to the private sector from 48.1 % to 36.7 % (see table 2). "Bank credit" here refers to all loans of financial intermediaries. Such credit then includes some loans by a set of nonbank financial establishments which are generally subsidiaries of listed banks. These establishments obtain funds predominantly through the money market, of which more later. They tend to specialise in a particular form of credit: sometimes the mortgage (*hypothèque*), sometimes consumer sales credit (*ventes de crédit à tempérament*), sometimes the lend-lease contract (*crédit-bail*), etc. These institutions' share of the market for bank credit grew in the 1970's, as shown in table 2, but it has been stable in the last few years.

Total bank credit makes up more than double the combined value of quoted bonds and quoted equities in France. In fact, according to most estimates, outstanding bonds was only a quarter of bank credit on the average in the 1970's. The value of bonds, in turn, substantially exceeds that of equities, perhaps by 50 % for the 1970's on the average. In recent years, net bond financing (after retirements) has tended to be even more of the order of three times the size of equity financing. The basic key to this dispro-

TABLE 2

Bank credit to the private sector and market shares in the distribution (not the financing) of bank credit

(billions of francs)

	Listed banks	Nonbank fiinancial establishments	Cooperative banks	Popular banks	French bank for foreign commerce	Treasury plus specialised intermediaries	Total bank credit
BANK CREDIT							
1963	71.60	4.61	11.45	3.53	0.69	85.04	176.92
1970	204.70	11.34	43.32	11.70	3.38	189.76	464.20
1978	639.07	88.06	240.61	38.02	21.02	594.4	1,621.17
MARKET SHARES							
1963	40.5	2.6	6.5	2	0.3	48.1	100
1970	44.1	2.4	9.3	2.5	0.8	40.9	100
1978	39.4	5.4	14.8	2.3	1.4	36.7	100

portionate volume of bonds relative to equities is the extent of public ownership in France. Such ownership covers all utilities, all train and air transportation, most of the maritime, energy, and petrocheminal industries, all of
tobacco, and a major part of the automobile industry. Public firms have
a small quoted value on the stock market, if any, and do little equity financing.
As a corrolary, in the private non-financial sector as such, equity financing
far exceeds bond financing, and has done so for decades.

The composition of the outstanding bond issue is also important. Public
bonds made up about 70 % to 80 % of total bonds in the 1970's. Of the
public bonds themselves, Treasury bonds as such are only a minor proportion,
between 5 % to 10 % in recent years. (Of course, since we include the
Treasury "bons sur formules", or fixed-nominal-price bonds, as money, we
exclude them from Treasury bond liabilities). Much more important than
the Treasury in the issue of public bonds are the national firms (like railways, *Électricité de France*, etc.) and the specialised intermediaries in the
sphere of the Treasury. Indeed the national enterprises in the field of energy
alone account for a much larger value of the public bond debt than the Treasury does. The bond debt of either the *Crédit foncier* or the *Crédit national*
was also of the same general order of importance as the Treasury's in the
1970's. There are two basic reasons for the modest bond debt of the Treasury: first the small fiscal deficits since 1964; and second, the former habit
of financing fiscal deficits predominantly through the banking system in
the 1945-1963 period. It is true that fiscal deficits have become a regular
feature since 1975, after ten years of balanced budgets (except for 1968).
But these deficits are mild, only exceeding 2 % of GDP in the first year of
the recent rupture since the period of balanced budgets, 1975. The issue
of bonds by the specialised intermediaries like the *Crédit Foncier* and the
Crédit national shows that these institutions' lending is not always confined
to the funds assigned to them out of the collection from the postal checking
system and the savings banks. Note also that local governments are minor
borrowers on the bond market in France. These authorities obtain their
deficit financing essentially through the Bank of Deposits and Consignations
(CDC), that is, through the savings banks.

Any general sketch of the French financial system would also be incom-
plete without some reference to insurance and retirement policies outside
of the social security system. Yet life insurance is extremely underdeveloped
in France. The total assets of the insurance companies, within which it is
difficult to distinguish between life and general property insiurance, are around
12 % of those of the commercial banks. For 1974, these assets represented
about 2100 francs per person, a piddling sum by Western standards. There
are also notably over 110 mutual funds in France (SIVAC), most of which
are recent. They remain as yet a small element of the financial environment.[3]

---

3. On the issues in the last two paragraphs, COUTIÈRE [1977], ch. 6, is particularly helpful.

2 The mechanisms

2.1. The system of credit allocation

The best starting-point in order to understand the system of credit allocation in France is the capital market. The Treasury decides the level and the basic structure of interest rates on bonds in this market. Given this level and structure of interest rates, the private sector chooses how large a value of bonds to acquire. Since bond rates are kept low (in real terms), this value of desired acquisitions is perennially below the desired new issues of bonds by the corporate and government sectors combined. Hence there is always a queue on the borrowing side of the bond market. Of course, the length of this queue may be partly reduced by the decisions of corporations to substitute equity issues for bonds, but only partly since equities and bonds are highly imperfect substitutes.

First in line in the queue are the Treasury and the set of financial institutions and national enterprises under the Treasury's wing (the post office, electricity, railways, etc...). Next in line come the national firms that belong, according to generally accepted convention, in the competitive sector (Renault, aerospace, etc...) and all of the private financial institutions. Then finally come the private non-financial firms. It stands to reason that the private non-financial sector is always rationed in this arrangement. Certain reforms of the early 1970's would imply that any corporation willing to wait its turn in line will eventually be served, at least partly. But even if so, this affects the distribution, not the volume, of the rationing.

As a part of the system, the Bank of Deposits and Consignations (CDC) bears the responsibility for keeping the level and the structure of interest rates on target from day to day. Thus, this organism is supposed to iron out technical and random differences between excess demands and excess supplies of bonds on the spot market. There is obviously no similar effort to keep a leash on equity values either on the spot market or in the long run. Nonetheless, if we analyse the situation over a sequence of months or quarters, we can see that the CDC really has little to do with keeping equilibrium at the desired interest rates. Rather the equilibrium is maintained, as indicated, by allowing only as many new issues to enter the field as the market will absorb. (The cost of organising tap issues is obviously essential in explaining why it is necessary for the CDC to intervene at all in the bond market, even on a spot basis).

The dissatisfied corporate firm then must turn to the market for bank credit or else look abroad (to say nothing of possibly searching for trade credit). [4] Of course, since the situation is a permanent one, the corporate management may not sense this recursiveness in its decision-making, but may act on the basis of the ration of bond credit that it expects to get, and never ask itself how much larger an issue of new bonds it would have preferred, even at a higher interest rate. These facts clearly help in explaining why bank credit is extraordinarily large relative to bond credit in France — easily four times the size, as indicated.

Priorities affect the allocation of bank credit as well, but the system of priorities is different. There is simply a privileged circuit where the terms are more advantageous than in the rest. But outside of this circuit, supply and demand determine price. The bank credit market then is precisely where, despite oligopolistic behavior on the supply side, the borrowing behavior of non-financial firms and households has a powerful influence on price. Any qualifications to this view are not peculiar to France, but result from problems that are common everywhere else : namely, the positive impact of the size of the individual loan on the lender's evaluation of risk and usury legislation chopping off the upper range of interest rates. In particular, the French credit controls known as « encadrements du crédit » or credit ceilings — about which we shall have much to say — do not constitute an additional qualification to this idea of basic price rationing in the bank credit market. So far as these controls are effective, in principle, they reduce the supply of bank credit, thus raise the interest rate.

The privileged circuit of bank credit works through three different channels : first, through loans that are distributed by the specialised intermediaries in the sphere of the Treasury ; second through preferential terms of refinancing of the loans distributed by the commercial banks with the Bank of France (or in the case of mortages, the Crédit Foncier) ; and third, through exemptions from the credit ceilings or the "encadrements du crédit". This last channel is the basic one explaining why even the listed banks may finance some privileged — and therefore low-yielding — credit. It is important to notice that the advantages to a borrower of entry into the privileged circuit are extremely variable. They may be enormous, for example, for a milk producer, or an African government buying a large engineering contract from a French firm. But they may be quite small, as for example in the case of an exporter financing stocks. Depending on the individual agent, his cause for access to the privileged circuit, and the state of his information, he may find a different point of entry, and also a different subsidy level.

Generally speaking, the large state enterprises, the national firms in the market economy, and the big corporations who have succeeded in getting a governmental signature on a high-priority project, will be able to come right into the circuit and (depending nevertheless on their identity) deal directly with the Caisse des Marchés de l'État, the Crédit National, or another of the specialised intermediaries. Local governments similarly will be able to address themselves directly to the CDC or the appropriate affiliate of the CDC. Farmers with good cause, on the other hand, may do well to apply to a local branch of the CNCA ; the artisan or small businessman in a similar position may be well advised to apply to a Popular Bank. Those whose demands for access to the privileged circuit rest on construction or export projects may go in particularly diverse directions. Firms regularly engaged

---

4. There is no commercial paper market, as such, in France.

in constructing moderate-cost apartments (*Habitations à loyer modéré*) have a specialised intermediary at their disposal; households with a claim to a subsidised mortgage because they have fulfilled the terms of a saving-accumulation plan may simply address themselves to their local bank, whichever one it may be (though their promissory note will then often go into the coffers of the Crédit Foncier). In the case of exporters, the hotel-keeper who requests special terms of credit on grounds of wishing to furnish improved services to foreign tourists may find a Popular Bank to be particularly well suited; the exporter intending to finance a long-term investment may be able to obtain satisfaction from the BFCE. In fact virtually any other bank will do in his case, though his promissory note will likely wind up in the portfolio of the Bank of France or the BFCE. [5]

The clearing of the ordinary circuit of non-privileged credit may receive our attention next, particularly in connection with the associated money market. The latter is where banks with more deposit facilities than they have loan clients can meet others with a larger loan clientele than they are able to finance themselves, and the two groups can trade. Buyers (lenders) on this market must pay with claims on the central bank; sellers can surrender clients' paper, outright or with a repurchase agreement, or may issue their own promise to pay. In addition to every major type of private financial institution, the participants in this market include the Bank of France, the CDC, and the other specialised intermediaries in the sphere of the Treasury, most notably the Crédit Foncier (which is responsible for maintaining the official price of refinancing mortgage paper). It is the Bank of France that sets the level and for the most part, the entire structure of interest rates in this market. The central bank buys or sells the necessary volume to clear the market at its chosen prices. Needless to say, the Bank generally buys since this is an essential part of the whole arrangement : the system assures the commercial banks all the financing of reserve losses that they need. Indeed so sure are the commercial banks of getting satisfaction on the money market that they do not bother holding any earning assets for protection besides the ones that they can sell there. Thus, they do not hold any marketable securities for safety. Similarly, their excess legal reserves depend entirely on economies in transaction costs rather than any precautionary motive (which does not imply, of course, that the banks' excess legal reserves are independent of interest rates, as is sometimes falsely inferred).

But the Bank of France is not the only structural lender on the money market, even with respect to the commercial banks as a group. In recent years, often the biggest lender of all, in fact, has been the CDC, which simply collects much more from the savings banks than it requires to meet its lending assignments. The CDC automatically invests the excess collection on the money market. Among the commercial banks who participate on the market, other perennial lenders are the CNCA, one of the three large nationalised banks, and the ensemble of the small deposit banks. The major borrowers are the nonbank financial establishments, the investment banks, and most of the medium-size to large deposit banks. [6]

5. A lot may be learned about the privileged circuit by sifting through the annual reports of the *Fonds de Développement Économique et Social*, an oft-neglected source. See also Jean DONY, Alain GIOVANETTI, and Bernard TIBI [1969]; and Anicet LE PORS and Jacques PRUNET [1975].

6. One unusually rich source of detail about the French banking structure, as such, is Jean-François BELHOSTE and Pierre METGE [1977]. See also the annual reports of the *Commission de contrôle des banques*.

In this system there are evidently three major interest rates : one in the money market, one on bank credit, and one on bonds. Two of these rates are controlled, one is free, and the relation of the free one to the other two is the key to the entire structure of interest rates in France. (The unregulated interest rates on bank deposits tends to follow the rate on bank credit). If the Bank of France raises its rate of intervention on the money market (as best measured by the "taux de l'argent au jour le jour", and not the very sluggish official discount rate), the banks will raise their lending rate (as best measured by the rate on overdrafts, "le taux des découverts"). One result then will be to lengthen the queue on the bond market — that is, this result would follow unless the authorities avoided it by similarly increasing the interest rate on bonds. They typically will indeed take this complementary action since their usual reason for increasing the official rate of intervention on the money market is to protect the franc.

Suppose, as a special case, that the authorities decide to raise bond rate without similarly increasing the rate of intervention on the money market. Then we get a peculiar, but revealing result in France : ordinarily we would expect a rise in bond rate to lead to an increase in the rate on commercial bank loans, as corporations switched from issuing bonds to applying for bank loans, and commercial banks reduced their loan offers in favor of bond investments. However in France corporations are permanently starved for credit on the capital market. Hence a rise in the interest rate on bonds would induce them to exploit the ensuing opportunity to raise more funds on this market. Thus they would reduce their demand for bank credit, which would tend toward a fall in the interest rate on commercial bank loans. In addition, commercial banks do not hold any bonds in France, as already explained. (The nonbank financial intermediaries do, but to a minor extent). Therefore the banks would not restrict their loan supply in favor of bond investments. It follows that there would be a fall in the interest rate on bank credit. The only thing that would cushion this fall is the consequent inducement to the ordinary firm and household to borrow from the banks in order to invest in bonds.

Evidently then the structure of interest rates in France cannot significantly reflect anticipated changes in future interest rates, as is often supposed to be the case elsewhere. The structure of interest rates on bonds cannot be any such reflection at all since it is controlled by the authorities. Indeed nothing has ever perturbed the calm of the interest rate structure on bonds since the second world war in France apart from some isolated cases of indexed bonds — and for good caus esince the CDC owns about 15 % of the total bonds outstanding. Any impact of interest rate expectations on the interest rate structure then must concern the relation of the interest rate on bank credit to the one on bonds. But as indicated, such an impact would need to come from people who are willing to borrow from the banks in order to buy bonds (and to use the proceeds of bond sales to reduce bank borrowing). Yet the risk implications of such behavior are major : to buy (sell) a bond and to borrow to do so (to retire bank debt with the sales receipts) are two actions that both separately raise (lower) risk. On this ground, a lot of movement in the structure of interest rates would seem possible in France without any changes in expectations about future interest rates.

2.2. The system of money-stock determination

The quantity of money in France raises a separate set of issues. Let us continue to define money as all financial assets of fixed nominal price, hence currency plus total bank deposits (as in table 1). The following simplified accounting identity then holds :

$$M = L_1 + L_2 + B_{cdc} + T + F$$

where :

M   : money;

L_1 : loans to the private sector distributed by the commercial banks (including the loans that the banks refinance with the Bank of France, the CDC and the Crédit Foncier);

L_2 : loans to the economy distributed by the specialised lenders in the sphere of the Treasury;

B_{cdc} : bond assets of the CDC;

T   : net claims of the Bank of France on the Treasury;

F   : net foreign reserves.

The authorities essentially set L_2 and T. They also set B_{cdc}, at least on a quarterly basis, though not on a daily one as we have implied (given the role of the CDC in stabilizing interest rates on bonds on the spot market). This then leaves L_1 and F as the two asset-counterparts of money requiring particular attention in determining the stock of money. In order to cope with the simultaneous determination of L_1, F, and M, we must take into consideration the demand for bank credit ($L_1 + L_2$), the supply of credit by the commercial banks (L_1), and the demand for money. The system then can be described as one of four equations in four unknowns. The four equations are the previous accounting identity plus the previous three behavioral equations. The four unknowns are the stock of money, the interest rate on bank credit, the quantity of bank credit, and a fourth one which depends on the system of exchange rates. If the system is one of fixed exchange rates, this fourth variable is official reserves (F); if it is freely floating exchange rates, this variable is the foreign exchange rate; it is managed exchange rates, official reserves and the foreign exchange rate are both simultaneously determined, and there is a fifth equation in the system, which involves the authorities' willingness to sacrifice reserves in order to support the franc.

The supply of bank credit is particularly important in this monetary mechanism. Since the commercial banks can refinance themselves abundantly at a set price, the most important factor underlying their supply of credit is their rate of expected profits on loans. The supply of bank credit therefore is highly sensitive to the interest rate on loans. This elasticity of supply, in turn, means that demand is a powerful influence on volume. If the demand for bank credit rises, the result is primarily to raise the quantity of bank credit rather than the price. The cost of refinancing is the basic brake on the supply side. Further, a rise in F + T — or the narrowly defined unborrowed reserve base in the American sense — may have only a mild effect on supply. That depends on how much of the banks' response will be to reduce refinancing. There is a tradition in France, which is not universally accepted, of supposing perfect substitution between borrowed and unborrowed reserves. This is the thesis of the « interdependence of the money counterparts » ("la thèse de l'interdépendance des contreparties"). On this view, a rise in F + T would not yield any growth in bank credit. Of course, the thesis is possibly correct in the very short run since the usual bank treasurer may simply balance his books at the end of each day by modifying his position on the money market. But in the long run (which can be of a short duration in financial markets), the thesis makes no sense : the full allocation of a rise in unborrowed reserves to diminished refinancing would lower the ratio of refinancing to total credit distribution, and thereby raise bank profits. This would then provide an ordinary incentive to supply more credit on the same footing as a profit incentive from any other source. All empirical estimates of the long run substitution between unborrowed and borrowed reserves agree that this substitution (which is complete within a year) in imperfect in France. Nevertheless, it is high, probably of the order of 60 to 80 %. [7]

Another important consideration is the share of the commercial banks in the issue of monetary liabilities. Algebraically, this share is the so-called "money multiplier" of the literature. But most French authors (including this writer) would regard references to a multiplier to describe this ratio in France as an abuse of language since the reserve base is at the mercy of the commercial banks. [8] The idea of a market share really captures the heart of the matter. If the commercial banks' share of the money issue goes up, they will partly lower their refinancing, partly increase their supply of credit. During some recent episodes of high commercial bank profits, particularly in the early 1970's, efforts of the commercial banks to increase their share of the market for money issues (relative to currency, postal checking accounts, and deposits with the savings banks) became quite apparent. Econometric analysis also confirmed this sort of behavior by the banks. Close attention to the commercial banks' share of the money issue then is important in the study of the monetary mechanism in France. [9]

The preceding paragraphs only recognize one instrument of monetary control : the central bank's rate of intervention on the money market. But no central bank would feel adequately armed with this weapon alone, the effect of which depends strictly on discretionary responses by the commercial banks. Such responses, even if they come, tend to be distributed over time, and may be small and unreliable within a short policy interval. For such reasons, the Bank of France has always kept some other, more quantitative tools of control in its arsenal. These tools used to be ceilings on the non-penalized use of the traditional discount desk (which has now fallen into disfavor). Currently the foremost quantitative tool is the aforementioned "encadrement du crédit". Though once an emergency weapon, to be used

---

7. For estimates in this range, see André FOURÇANS [1978]; Jacques MÉLITZ and Henri STERDYNIAK [1979]; and by the same authors [1980].

8. Two works dealing with this point that have received wide attention in France are Jacques LE BOURVA [1962]; and Louis and Vivien LÉVY-GARBOUA [1977].

9. In addition to the previous references in n. 7, see Antoine COUTIÈRE [1978]; and Patrick ARTUS, Jacques BOURNAY, Alain PACAUD, Claude PEYROUX, Henri STERDYNIAK et Robert TEYSSIER (1981], 7e partie (« secteur financier »).

sparingly and for limited intervals, the Bank of France has been keeping the tool in permanent use since 1972 while continuously trying to perfect it. Indeed, the instrument has assumed a fairly mature form.

As currently operated, the "encadrement" combines ceilings (norms) on credit growth over the next (calendar) semester with penalties for transgressions consisting of legal reserve requirements. The legal reserve requirements are a percentage of the total credit distribution. Further, this percentage rises exponentially with the level of the transgressions. The reserve requirements become quite prohibitive for as little as a one to two percentage-point excess of credit growth, as the exact formula shows :

$$T = (0.30 + 0.15X)\,X$$

where T is the ratio of the legal reserve requirement to the credit distribution, and X is the number of percentage points of excess growth of credit. A single percentage point of excessive credit growth then requires a non-interest-bearing deposit of 45 % of the excessive credit; a two-percentage-point excess growth already requires deposits of 120 % of the excess credit. Because of this prohibitive character of the penalties, legally required reserves have been minor under the scheme.

There is a major escape valve, though. Up until 1978, virtually all subsidized credit — essentially relating to exports, housing, agriculture, and various special projects like energy-saving — were exempt from the ceilings. These types of credit then grew much faster than the rest: namely, by 38 %, 35 %, 22 %, and 24 % in 1976, 1977, 1978 and 1979 respectively, as opposed to corresponding growth rates of 11 %, 9.5 %, 9 % and 10 % for the bank credit subject to the ceilings during those years. Beginning in 1978, however, the authorities narrowed this escape valve. They began to require banks to restore a fraction of exempt credits to those to which the credit norms applied. In a recent acceleration of this process, they have raised the fraction of the reintegration to 50 percent for the second half of 1980. But the reintegration itself applies only to about one-half of the exempted credits and the rest remain fully exonerated. Hence the escape valve is only shut by about one-fourth. The fully exonerated bank credits consist of loans in foreign currencies, and for the rest, largely loans that are financed by the CNCA and the BFCE.

It should be observed that all of the exonerations from the "encadrements" could be removed without jeopardizing the system of priorities in the least. Doing so would only pose a technical problem at best. The reason is simply that the total volume of deposits collected by the organisms who specialise in subsidized credit still is much larger than the total volume of subsidized credit. In other words, the deposits of the savings banks, the postal checking system, the CNCA, and the Popular Banks, combined, still exceed considerably the total credits distributed by the Treasury, the specialised institutions in the Treasury sphere, and the exonerated credits distributed by the commercial banks. The implications are clear : if the organisms who specialise in subsidized credits would only specialise sufficiently more in these credits, and finance less non-subsidized ones, the percentage of subsidized credit could even grow further without any exemptions from the "encadrements". Managing this would simply require, for example, providing more attractive terms of refinancing of the appropriate paper with the Bank of France and (as would constitute an innovation) with the CDC, and quite significantly, simply no longer using exemptions from the ceilings to compensate the CNCA and the BFCE for the burden they bear of investing heavily in subsidized credit. (If it was deemed necessary, this burden of the CNCA and the BFCE could be divided up with the three nationalized banks). In fact, as long as the Bank of France, and more especially the CDC, continue to finance a large volume of non-subsidized credit through the money market, as they do, any exemptions from the credit ceilings for ordinary commercial banks would seem unreasonable. If in the future it ever became necessary to offer special inducements to the listed banks to hold subsidized credit, this could be done without exemptions from the "encadrements", for example, through fiscal incentives. The basic general point is that the current exonerations to the "encadrement" are not an intrinsic element of the system, therefore must not be treated as an intrinsic limitation of the "encadrement" as a tool of monetary control. In a system where, like the French, government agencies finance a lot of credit to the economy, the state is able to do a lot of credit allocation without implicating the rest of the credit system. [10]

3 Performance

For a time right after the second world war the authorities relied heavily on the financial system in order to promote capital formation. This took place during a period of reconstruction when the social productivity of many public investments — in transportation, communications, energy, and the like — was very high. Admittedly, the unusually low interest rates which were used at the time to stimulate investment did not promote household saving. But except for hoarding in land and precious metals, the controls on foreign capital movements left the household little choice but to save in the form of paper assets yielding low returns. In addition, the saving in the form of land and precious metals was not an important social loss since it absorbed few real resources. Thus it is difficult to question that the authorities succeeded in stimulating capital formation at this time.

In more recent years, sacrificing consumption for investment has not clearly remained an official objective. It has certainly not clearly been so since the growth of rates of unemployment in the 1970's has made raising productivity and aggregate demand a fundamental concern. The basic question for recent years then is whether the authorities have succeeded in reallocating resources in accordance with their designs. Once again, I see no reason for major skepticism. The French system is well conceived to

---

10. Hence the credit priorities of the state also need not promote more bank credit in the aggregate. This emphasis of course, goes contrary to the basic theme of Donald HODGMAN's chapter on France [1974], namely, that the allocative objectives of the state tend to fuel excessive growth of money and inflation.

help in launching an airbus or to restructure an ailing industry in accordance with a clearly laid plan. The funds are always there and they can be made available quickly. The subsidized loan is also a frequent form of assistance. When newspaper headlines blare forth a government agreement to undertake some multibillion-franc project in a sector of French industry (public or private), this may sound like an embrace of Keynesian principles of pump-priming; but the typical connotation is a decision to accord a public loan for the said amount. The additional cost to the Treasury then is, at the most, the interest rate subsidy on the loan, or a small fraction of the sum in the headline.

In many ways the interesting issue in France regards the unintended, and possibly undetected, effects of the financial system. Any governmental interference in credit allocation on the scale in this country is bound to have major side-effects. The clearest example is the continuous shortage of long term corporate finance capital, which is not part of anyone's intentions. But it is certainly implicit in the financial system that the corporation will hold a shorter term structure of liabilities than it would like. Consequently, the corporation seeks a higher ratio of internal to external financing, as the evidence would indicate. Another likely, more unfortunate result is a lower degree of corporate risk-taking.

This shortage of long term corporate capital has an interesting offshoot in French discussion : namely, a major preoccupation with the so-called "problème de la transformation". [11] This problem, which does not unduly seem to worry officials or economists elsewhere, regards the financing of long-term investment based on short-term or commercial bank debt. There is an understandable concern with this problem in France since, as observed, such financing is higher than the corporate sector would like. But the expression of the problem in the discussion takes a peculiar turn in which the household sector is to blame. The reasoning is that this sector simply refuses to hold debts of a long enough maturity. This behavior then tends to inhibit investment or to generate inflation or both. In response, the authorities regularly promote fairly illiquid types of bank deposits with maturity dates of up to five years. In the last decade there have also been deposits with a contractual clause binding the holder to accumulate over a period of years, in return for which the state pays him a bonus at maturity and offers him a subsidized loan at this time as well. Of course, encouraging households to hold assets of relatively low liquidity answers to the fears of inflation. But the same encouragement does not clearly promote a longer term structure of debts for firms, thus need not answer to the fears about investment. It would only do so if the commercial banks lengthened the term of their loans correspondingly as the term of their deposit liabilities rose. There is little concern in the literature on the "transformation" problem, however, with the translation of longer term deposits into longer term loans.

My only other example of an area of unintended effects of the financial system is the very complicated issue of construction. Based on all accounts, the French population is not particularly better housed than its neighbors, nor does it have a particularly worse demographic structure for housing

---

11. As an index of this preoccupation, see, for example, the published collected papers of a 1975 conference organised by the Bank of France [1976].

demand than its neighbors do. Yet the phenomenon of the housing boom is something which is much less important in the country than in either Great Britain or West Germany, for example. The construction industry now has been in the doldrums for years. One is tempted to think that this is intimately related to the financial system.

Construction is the one sector of the economy where the division between subsidized and non-subsidized credit produces a clear cleavage right within the industry. There is construction which is financed with subsidized credit and construction which is not (more generally, construction which is aided and construction which is not, for an entire system of welfare payments is involved). The general lines of the division between the two go back to the early postwar period, when the nation faced a major shortage of housing. It was then decided to give high priority to housing for low- and moderate-income groups, which meant a lot of subsidized credit for the construction of apartment buildings. But meanwhile, the individual-home buyer and the construction firm building the individual home were left out in the lurch. Such were the demands upon the financial system stemming from the subsidized sector that these parties found credit to be very difficult to obtain. Thus the buyer of a house or an apartment could only get a 5-year loan that was renewable once. When this situation was at last remedied in 1966 with the creation of the mortgage market, it seemed reasonable to limit mortgages to 20 years in order not to move too far in the opposite direction. Furthermore the 20-year mortgage became available only to the applicant with the highest priority. To the ordinary home buyer the new regime meant a maximum-term mortgage of 16 to 17 years. There the matter stands today, except for the fact that a fair amount of privileged credit now has become available for the purchase of an apartment or an individual house as well, on the basis of a widening set of criteria having increasingly less to do with redistributive welfare considerations as such. Nevertheless, the early-postwar lines of the division between privileged and non-privileged credit remain very visible in the construction industry today.

International comparisons then clearly suggest two reasons for the relatively worse performance of the construction industry in France. First, whereas in the US, Great Britain, West Germany, and many other countries, the legislation heavily tends to favor the decision to own an individual home, in France the system favors renting or owning an apartment. Fifty families in a single apartment building obviously means much less activity for the construction industry than fifty of them in individual homes. It is notable, in this connection, that the primary support in other countries for individual-home ownership, coming from the exemptions of interest on mortgages from income taxes, also exists in France, but to a modest degree : there is a maximum income-tax deduction of 7 000 francs, plus 1 000 francs per child, for interest on mortgages each year. The second factor is the ordinary ceiling on mortgages of 16 to 17 years. In countries where the terms to maturity are free, mortgages generally run up to 30 years. The effect of this difference on the individual monthly mortgage payment is considerable. At any given level of individual income, therefore, the Frenchman has access only to a smaller home, with obviously damaging consequences for the construction industry. How far these inhibiting influences, affecting a major sector of economic activity, conform to official intentions is not clear.

4 The issue of reform

4.1. General setting and problems

The authorities in France are supposed to keep watch over the public interest in the field of finance. No major section of political opinion ever questions their responsibility to censor and repress novelties in finance that they consider contrary to the general interest. Unfortunately, this produces a very timid financial sector. The private financial firm consequently has a tendency to view innovation in finance basically as the responsibility of the state. The results are far-reaching. Why, one may ask, is there no secondary market in certain types of perfectly negotiable interest-bearing bank debts known as "bons de caisse"? Why is this true even at times of falling interest rates, that is, when market expectations are likely to be contrary to the typically rising term structure of the interest rates on these debts? The response of the financier is likely to be that if the Bank of France had wanted a secondary market in these debts, it would have said so. To take another example : for years prior to 1966, the Bank of France routinely granted applications to open up new bank branches. Yet only when it ceased to require such applications that year did the number of bank branches suddenly begin to explode. In fact, the number continued to do so for the next eight years.

It is only when we recognize that the government exercises the entrepreneurial function in finance that we can properly understand the issue of reform in France. Reform is simply the ordinary way of achieving change; it acts as a substitute for market adaptation. Whenever a deficiency in finance that requires structural reorganisation becomes clear, the community knows that the problem will not be resolved without formal government inquiry and reform. Indeed the high civil servants and officials deserve credit for the fact that commissions of inquiry into particular aspects of the financial environment have become almost a regular feature of the environment in the last two decades. This does not imply any general dissatisfaction with the financial system : it is just simply how change gets done.

Quite significantly, the tone of the reports of the commissions has often been critical. This was certainly true of the two most important documents thus far: the report of the Rueff Commission of 1958 and the Marjolin-Sadrin-Wormser report of 1969. It is also true of the recent Mayoux report of 1979. [12] The basic tendency of the reform proposals has also been toward decentralisation. The current Barre government now has taken a series of steps in a liberal direction, especially since René Monory became Minister of the Economy in 1978.

---

12. Jacques Rueff [1958]; Robert Marjolin, Jean Sardin, and Olivier Wormser [1969]; and the report presided by Jacques Mayoux [1979]. For a very useful discussion of the monetary reforms of the late 1960's see also Henri Fournier [1976].

Probably the most popular of Monory's recent actions in the field of finance was to introduce an income tax deduction of up to 5 000 francs for new investments in French equities (with an additional 500 franc deduction for each of the first two children and 1 000 francs for each of the subsequent ones). As a trial balloon, the government also recently acted upon a heretofore unused provision of the Banking Act of 1945 permitting as much as 25 % private ownership of the capital of the nationalized banks, and issued some equities in the *Société générale*. A notable reform last year was to remove all margin requirements and ceilings on maturities on consumer sales credit. In addition, whereas the commercial banks had only been free to determine their interest rates on term deposits of over two years or over 200 000 francs before, they became free to do so for deposits of over one year or over 100 000 francs.

[There follows in the original paper a discussion of the question how much further a program of liberal reform in finance can go without upsetting the existing mix between private and public ownership or infringing on the privileged circuit of bank credit. The section argues that three major reforms are possible along these lines: (1) the freeing of interest rates on bonds; (2) the freeing of terms to maturity on mortgages; and (3) the freeing of all interest rates on term deposits. The ramifications of these reforms are then examined.]

4.2. The problem of monetary control

With the advent of target rates of monetary growth under the Barre administration the issue of monetary control has acquired an added dimension. For the moment this issue revolves around the "encadrement du crédit". The "encadrement", as now operated, has a major flaw as an instrument of monetary control because of the exemptions. As I have argued, though, the flaw is not clearly intrinsic. Though the point may be evident, it will be shown next that if the exonerations were removed, the "encadrement" would become a very precise and powerful instrument — in fact, a superior one to open market operations in both respects.

The "encadrement" induces the individual bank to expand credit up to the growth norm, since its stock of credit at the end of the current accounting period will be the basis for calculating its permissible amount of credit for all subsequent periods. Any shortfall below the norm then means a permanent loss at a compounded semi-annual rate. (This is a slight exaggeration since a bank may carry over a shortfall from one semester to the next within the same calendar year.) Furthermore, as long as the "encadrement" puts any pressure on aggregate credit, the individual bank need never have any difficulty in expanding its credit up to the growth limit since it has at its disposal a market where it can sell unused lines of credit growth below the norms to other banks (a clear counterpart to the federal funds market in the United States). Since the penalties for exceeding the norms are quite prohibitive, we can then conclude that, in the absence of the exonerations, the growth rate of bank credit would approximately equal the maximum.

The money measure that will concern us is M2, since the current target rates of monetary growth apply to this measure, or the sum of commercial bank deposits, postal checking accounts and currency (*i.e.* the previous money measure in table 2 exclusive of deposits with the savings banks and Treasury « bons sur formules »). Let M2 equal $F + T + L_1$ in the previous notation (where we simplify a bit by assuming that L_1 is financed entirely by M2 and L_2 by $M - M2$). If there were no exonerations and the "encadrement" therefore determined the total credit distribution of the commercial banks or L_1, then the only basis for a deviation between the actual and the target growth of M2 would be a difference between the actual and predicted values of $F + T$. A one-franc error in $F + T$, however, would mean only a one-franc error in M2. Thus with $F + T$ currently around 16 % of M2, the authorities could err by as much as 6,25 % about $F + T$ but still only be around 1 % off of their target for M2. This then is the reason for the potential accuracy and power of the tool.

Unfortunately the "encadrement" has one important drawback: by defining a common growth norm for all of the commercial banks, it freezes their relative positions. The Bank of France avoids this to some extent by making allowances for nascent banks and banks with low assets. But this is secondary on the whole. The only important source of changes in the relative positions of banks since the start of the "encadrement" of recent years has been the exemptions. The exemptions, however, are more accessible to some banks than others. Their effect on relative positions, therefore, only worsens the problem of equity without spurring competition. Under present arrangements, little could prevent an individual bank from simply coasting along, taking no pains with loan selection and customer service, and relying on others to buy its unused lines of credit growth below the norms.

The most interesting alternative to the present system, of course, is open market operations. Yet this happens to be the alternative which is least compatible with French conditions, and which would require the most extensive financial reorganisation. To explain, let us assume a wholesale abandonment of the "encadrement" in favor of a control over the Bank of France's total balance sheet through purchases and sales of assets. The assets bought and sold might be net foreign reserves, money-market instruments, bonds, or a combination of the three. Let us assume, accordingly, that the Bank of France adopted a quantitative rule of accumulation of such instruments with the usual allowances for movements in F, T, seasonal currency demands, etc. Interest rate(s) on the money market would float. What would happen ?

First of all, it would be necessary to stop the access of the commercial banks to the Bank of France's discount desk with privileged forms of paper. Otherwise the banks would be able to offset open market operations to a large and variable extent. This simply points to a general incongruity between open market operations and traditional discount desk activities. On the other hand, closing bank access to the discount desk at privileged rates would have no major implications for the administered system of credit allocation because of the breadth of other avenues for subsidizing credit in France (which might include a decision to concentrate the open market operations themselves in preferred forms of paper).

If the commercial banks then could no longer view the money market as a sure source of funds on profitable terms, they would acquire securities for their protection. Hence, the capital market would become a complementary source of liquidity for them. In this way, the system would itself generate a more active capital market, and therefore progressively provide more opportunity for the Bank of France to use bonds as well as money-market instruments in open market operations. However, any progressive increase in bonds in commercial bank portfolios must mean, for any given quantity of M2, a corresponding fall in loans. If we momentarily assume that some loans to noncorporate firms and households would be crowded out in the process, we can see a problem. Since these decision units cannot issue bonds, they could then only obtain the full satisfaction of their demand for credit within France through the emergence of new financial firms. Moreover, these new firms obviously would be unable to issue monetary liabilities or to finance their clients' paper on the money market. They would thus need to rely on internal financing and the capital market for funds. As a corrolary, interest rates on commercial bank loans would rise relative to those on bonds. Nothing short of a general transformation of the financial system therefore would be involved.

There is an intermediary solution, which deserves attention. Instead of a maximum rate of growth of bank credit, the authorities could impose a maximum ratio of refinancing to deposits. In this way, though they would still submit the individual bank to a rigorous quantitative constraint on credit expansion, they would not interfere with changes in the relative positions of individual banks.

Let us assume that the individual bank must keep its refinancing below a certain ratio of its deposits. Though individual-bank deposits then would limit credit distribution by the individual bank, the bank could grow indefinitely by drawing away deposit customers from other banks and could fail by losing deposit customers to them.

The proposal raises one technical problem, however, which must be discussed at once: namely, a common maximum ratio of refinancing to deposits for all of the commercial banks is not feasible, since some banks are heavy borrowers on the money market while others are lenders. The way to handle this problem would be to define the following common ratio for every individual commercial bank :

$$\frac{REF - NBMS}{D}$$

where REF is the net refinancing with the public monetary sector (the Bank of France, the CDC and the Crédit Foncier), NBMS is the net borrowing from the rest of the monetary sector, and D is bank deposits. NBMS cancels out over all of the commercial banks; hence the common ratio would apply to REF/D in the aggregate. (I neglect nonbank financial institutions, for which the right rule would be to limit REF to NBMS.) According to this scheme every commercial bank who lends a franc to another on the money market also cedes to it the right to a franc of borrowing from the central bank. One result would be that credit from another commercial bank will be more expensive than credit from the Bank of France. But this is not objectionable : it already costs something extra now for a bank to buy ¡an unused line of credit growth below the norms from another bank (*désencadrement*).

However there would then be a problem of monetary control, requiring the auxiliary use of open market operations. In order to see, let us simplify by assuming that all refinancing takes place with the Bank of France rather than the CDC or the Crédit Foncier. Then we have :

$$F + T + REF = B$$

where B is the Bank of France's total assets, or the reserve base in the narrow sense. We may also assume that the penalty for exceeding the ratio $(REF - NBMS)/D$ — or let us say REF/D since we know now that it comes same thing in the aggregate — is very prohibitive, so much so that required reserves are negligible. Then if we abstract further from excess legal reserves, B is simply equal to currency, C, or $M2 - D$. Hence we have

(1)
$$M2 = (F + T) \cdot \frac{M2}{F + T} = (F + T) \frac{1 + C/D}{\dfrac{C}{D} - \dfrac{REF}{D}}$$

Equation (1) shows that the ratio of currency to deposits, the ratio REF/D, and the unborrowed reserve base, $F + T$, together, determine M2. Under the proposed arrangement, the authorities could easily keep REF/D approximately equal to the maximum. This would only require holding the price of refinancing sufficiently low (within a broad range). If only then they could accurately foresee C/M and $F + T$; they could set REF/D so as to achieve their target level of M2. Nonetheless, every percentage change in $F + T$ would mean an equipercentage change in M2. Thus, no mere vague accuracy about $F + T$ — for example, the ability to predict within 5 to 10 percent — would suffice, that is, not unless REF/D could be continuously adjusted, which we assume not to be the case. Yet within a policy horizon of 6 to 12 months, there is only a vague hope, in practice, of predicting $F + T$ within 5 percent of total accuracy. Managed exchange rates makes F a creature of multiple causes. The hazards of government receipts and expenditures also make an accurate forecast of T very difficult for the next two quarters. This defines the problem in a nutshell.

It follows that the resort to a maximum ratio of REF/D would not dispense with the need for open market operations as an auxiliary in order to adhere to a monetary target. Since such operations then obviously would need to be in other assets than those included in REF (bank loans), the suitable candidate would be bonds. We thus find ourselves back again, in the case of this last reform, in a situation where open market operations are an essential element of monetary control. The basic difference, as opposed to the previous case, is that the commercial banks would continue to have major and sure access to refinancing at the central bank at a fixed and attractive price. But because this access would be limited, it would represent a pure rent which does not interfere with monetary control. Thus the solution may be properly seen as a compromise between the present system and a move toward open market operations.

There is a third and last alternative to the current system of the "encadrement" implying much less reform than either of the preceding two. This less ambitious approach would be to continue defining money-growth norms, but substantially to reduce the progressivity of the schedule of the penalties for transgressions (possibly compensating the expansionary effect of this easing by increasing the severity of the norms). In this way, the individual bank could be expected to transgress the norms to a degree, and the banks with the highest profit opportunities would transgress them more than the others. But some levels of transgression could still be made prohibitively costly. This system then obviously would not avoid the mischiefs of the existing one since it would retain the norms. But it would alleviate the harm, though at the cost of some loss of monetary control. So light would the reforms be, in this case, that the single most important change would come from the earlier suggestion of doing away with all of the exemptions to the "encadrements" and finding alternative ways to assure the same volume and distribution of subsidies.

Perhaps the most fundamental conclusion of this discussion is that there is no way to circumvent the inhibiting effect of the "encadrement" on bank competition without some surrender of monetary control. However I would not wish to leave the impression that this defect of the "encadrement" is necessarily the most serious handicap of the French financial system. That has certainly not been the basic message.

Postscript concerning 1980-1982

The election of a Socialist government in May 1981 has led to a number of policy changes and, beyond that, has altered the topical issues of reform in the field of money and finance. The most conspicuous change has been the nationalization of all home-owned commercial banks with more than one billion francs in deposits. This nationalization measure, dating to February 11, 1982, covers only 36 of the 374 formerly private commercial banks. But the 36 account for around 70 % of the deposits of the 374 banks as a group. Subsequently, for ideological reasons, one can no longer expect reforms of the "encadrement du crédit" that are inspired by ideas of increased competitivity in banking. Nevertheless, the extent to which commercial banks will alter their behavior is not clear.

The reasons for this uncertainty are implicit in the previous treatment of the French system. First, there is a tradition of decentralised management of publicly owned banks in France and a considerable experience with such management. The three large commercial banks that were nationalized en 1945 never ceased to operate essentially like private banks. The National Agricultural Bank and the system of Popular banks, which have been in the public sphere since their inception in the nineteenth century, also have always behaved partly like private banks, and increasingly so over the last 20 years. In addition, there is nothing that the government can do in the light of the recent nationalization measure that it could not have done just as easily without it. The government's potential hand in credit management was already heavy beforehand. The three banks nationalized in 1945, the National Agricultural Bank and the Popular banks, alone, supply at least three times as much ordinary non-subsidized credit as the newly nationalized banks do. In addition the government receives funds through the savings banks and the postal checking system, to say nothing of the currency issue. So large was the government's collection of funds through these sources in the seventies that, as we saw, the Caisse des Dépôts et Consignations found nothing better to do with a large part of its resources than to funnel them back to the commercial banks though the money market. As regards money and finance, therefore, the nationalization measure is much less important than the changes in policy that may go along with it.

Three other recent changes deserve notice, two of which concern the administration of the "encadrement du crédit". The first, dating back to 1979 (though with precedents that go back to 1973), is the exoneration of all bank credit financed through the issue of securities from the "encadrement du crédit". This exoneration was probably intended largely to enable the banks better to protect themselves against the losses implied by some of the other Barre-Monory measures in favor of the securities market. These other measures were expected to cost the banks some of their corporate business. But also important, it was probably felt that there was no harm in exonerating bank credit financed through issues of securities from the "encadrement" because the credit involved no monetary expansion, thus implied no threat to the monetary targets.

There was no immediate response to this last measure, but the reaction was enormous in the following year. After rising only moderately in real terms throughout the 1970's, the banks' supply of securities rose by 44 % in 1980. This was followed by an important 23 % rise in 1981.

The second change in the "encadrement", dating only to this year, or 1982, is the introduction of a growth norm for all formerly exonerated forms of credit except loans of foreign exchange. (By regulation, the latter loans are entirely matched by foreign exchange liabilities, therefore, in principle, do not affect M2). This next reform grew out of the tendency progressively to reintegrate exonerated credits within the growth norms (described in the text). When the proportion of the reintegration attained 50 %, it was found that some of the commercial banks with special access to privileged credit were under strong pressure to cut back the growth of their non-privileged credit. This next reform repairs the problem. The reform also means that any future reference to exonerated credits *in francs* is an anachronism: instead there are now simply credits that are subject to higher growth norms than the rest. (There are, howewer, exonerated credits in foreign exchange).

The third and last change deserving mention is the about-face of the current government on the decision of the preceding administration to free interest rates on term deposits of over 100 000 F but less than one year maturity. In September 1981, the minimum required deposit in order to earn an unregulated interest rate on a deposit of less than one year to maturity was raised to 500 000 F and the minimum required term to maturity on such a deposit was lengthened (from one) to six months. This next government action followed the first important disturbance in the entire structure of interest rates in the post-World War II history of France.

After the franc weakened in the European Monetary System in the first quarter of 1981, the authorities raised their rate of intervention to historic levels above 20 % as early as May. (The EMS began in March 1979.) But the authorities did not allow bond rates to go up as much. (On this one occasion they did, however, allow the premium on corporate bonds to rise sizeably relative to government bonds.) As a result, interest rates on term deposits of over 100 000 F climbed up above the rates on government bonds.

This caused the securities market nearly to dry up and provoked an upward surge in the growth of the money supply, additionally fueled by Treasury borrowing from the banks. Bank profits underwent a squeeze. The September 1981 measure remedied the situation at once. Funds switched out of deposits and into securities. The growth of M2, which had been a hefty 16.5 % at an annual rate from end-December to August, came to a virtual standstill. It was 11.4 % for the year as a whole, or only 1.4 % over the target level. The commercial banks simply turned to the securities market for finance for much of their credit expansion, as did the Treasury in order to finance its deficit.

Admittedly, the operation of the bond market during this episode does not fit well with the description in the text. Nevertheless, at no point in this period was the private corporation able to assure its desired bond sales simply by raising its interest rate. Thus, the non-price-rationing mechanism described in the text, though temporarily suspended remained in the background.

It is interesting to observe that the Socialist government has not fully reversed the Barre-Monory actions in favor of the securities market, but on the contrary has accepted a good part of them : particularly with regard to tax concessions and a more competitive level of interest rates. Similarly, the new government has retained the idea of a target for the growth rate of M2 but simply raised the target from 10 % in 1981 to a range of 12.5 to 13.5 % in 1982. On the other hand, the new government has substantially increased international capital controls, reinforced the privileged circuit of bank credit, and taken a generally much more favorable attitude toward non-price rationing.

● **References cited**

ARTUS P., BOURNAY J., PACAUD A., PEYROUX C., STERDYNIAK H. and TEYSSIER R. — (1981) *METRIC une modélisation de l'économie française,* INSEE.

Bank of France. — (1976) *Monnaie Epargne Investissements,* Paris, Fondation nationale des sciences politiques.

BELHOSTE J.-F. and METGE P. — (1977) *L'adaptation du système bancaire et le contrôle de l'accumulation dans l'industrie,* rapport CORDES (20, rue Las Casas, Paris), n° de contrat 4575.

COUTIÈRE A. — (1975) « Un modèle du système monétaire français », *Statistiques et études financières,* ministère de l'Économie et des Finances, n° 17, p. 33-80.

COUTIÈRE A. — (1977) « Le système monétaire français », *Economica,* Paris.

DONY J., GIOVANETTI A. and TIBI B. — (1969) *L'État et le financement des investissements privés,* Paris, Berger-Levrault.

FOURÇANS A. — (1978) « The impact of monetary and fiscal policies on the French financial system », *Journal of Monetary Economics,* n° 3, p. 519-541.